SURPRISE!

You may be reading the wrong way!

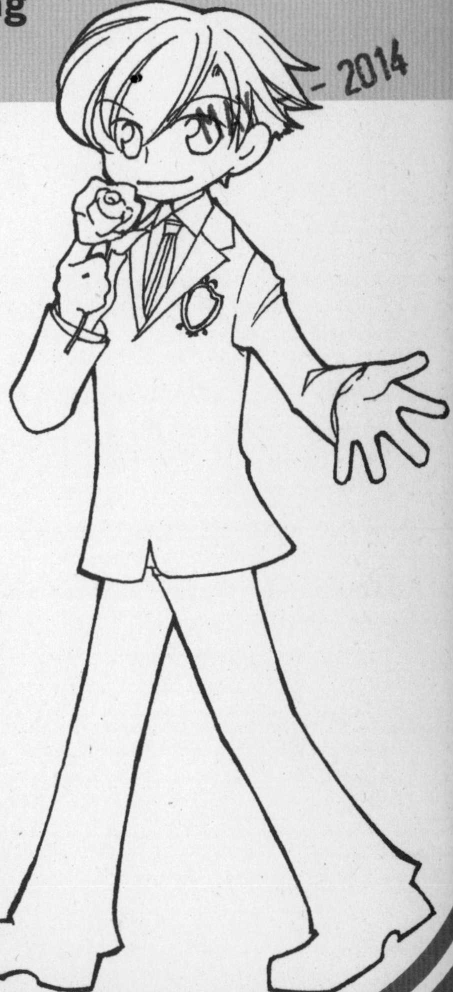

It's true: In keeping with the original Japanese comic format, this book reads from right to left—so action, sound effects, and word balloons are completely reversed. This preserves the orientation of the original artwork—plus, it's fun! Check out the diagram shown here to get the hang of things, and then turn to the other side of the book to get started!

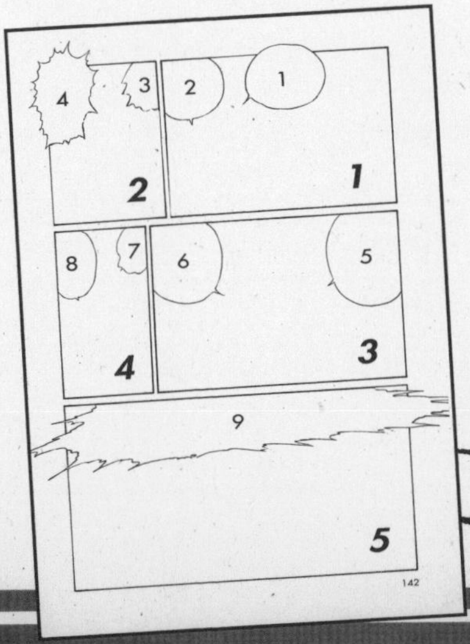
1
2
3
4
1
2
5
6
7
8
3
4
9
5
142

UIZMANGA

Read manga anytime, anywhere!

From our newest hit series to the classics you know and love, the best manga in the world is now available digitally. Buy a volume* of digital manga for your:

- iOS device (**iPad®**, **iPhone®**, **iPod® touch**) through the **VIZ Manga app**

- Android-powered device (**phone or tablet**) with a browser by visiting VIZManga.com

- **Mac or PC computer** by visiting VIZManga.com

VIZ Digital has loads to offer:

- 500+ ready-to-read volumes
- New volumes each week
- FREE previews
- Access on multiple devices! Create a log-in through the app so you buy a book once, and read it on your device of choice!*

To learn more, visit www.viz.com/apps

* Some series may not be available for multiple devices. Check the app on your device to find out what's available.

DEATH NOTE © 2003 by Tsugumi Ohba, Takeshi Obata/SHUEISHA Inc.
NURARIHYON NO MAGO © 2008 by Hiroshi Shiibashi/SHUEISHA Inc.
ONE PIECE © 1997 by Eiichiro Oda/SHUEISHA Inc.

RATED
T
FOR OLDER TEEN
ratings.viz.com

uiz media
viz.com/apps

Ouran High School
Host Club

Vol. 13
Bisco Hatori

Ouran High School

Host Club

Vol. 13

CONTENTS

OURAN HIGH SCHOOL
THE SECOND-YEAR STUDENTS
HAVE RETURNED FROM THEIR
FIELD TRIP TO FRANCE.

ON THE TOP
FLOOR OF THE
SOUTH WING...

...AT THE END OF
THE NORTHERN
HALLWAY...

Music Room 3

W O W... ♡

SUPPORTING CHARACTERS INTRODUCTION ✿

AGE 39. THE LEADER OF THE THREE
MEN. HE'S BEEN AROUND LONGEST
IN THE OHTORI FAMILY GUARD.
HE IS EXTREMELY SERIOUS AND
A LITTLE NEUROTIC SOMETIMES.
HE IS BLESSED WITH HAVING AN
UNDERSTANDING WIFE AND A
GOOD DAUGHTER, BUT ONE OF
HIS WORRIES IS THAT THE GIFTS
KYOYA RECEIVES FROM TAMAKI
(THAT KYOYA THROWS AWAY)
ARE PILING UP AT HIS HOUSE.

Tachibana

※ IT SEEMS HE IS
SYMPATHETIC TO
HARUHI, WHO IS A
FELLOW COMMONER.

3

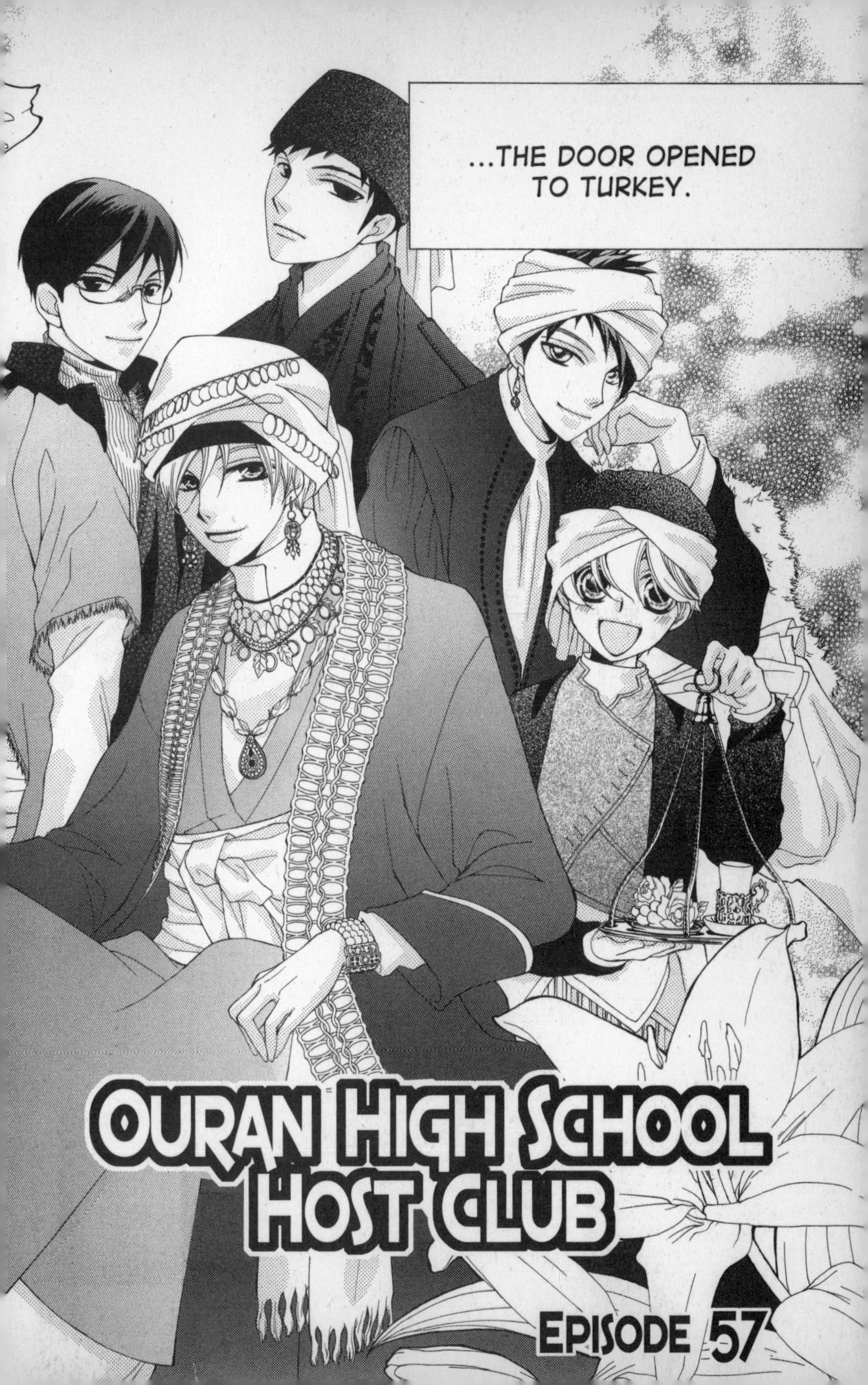
...THE DOOR OPENED TO TURKEY.
OURAN HIGH SCHOOL HOST CLUB
EPISODE 57

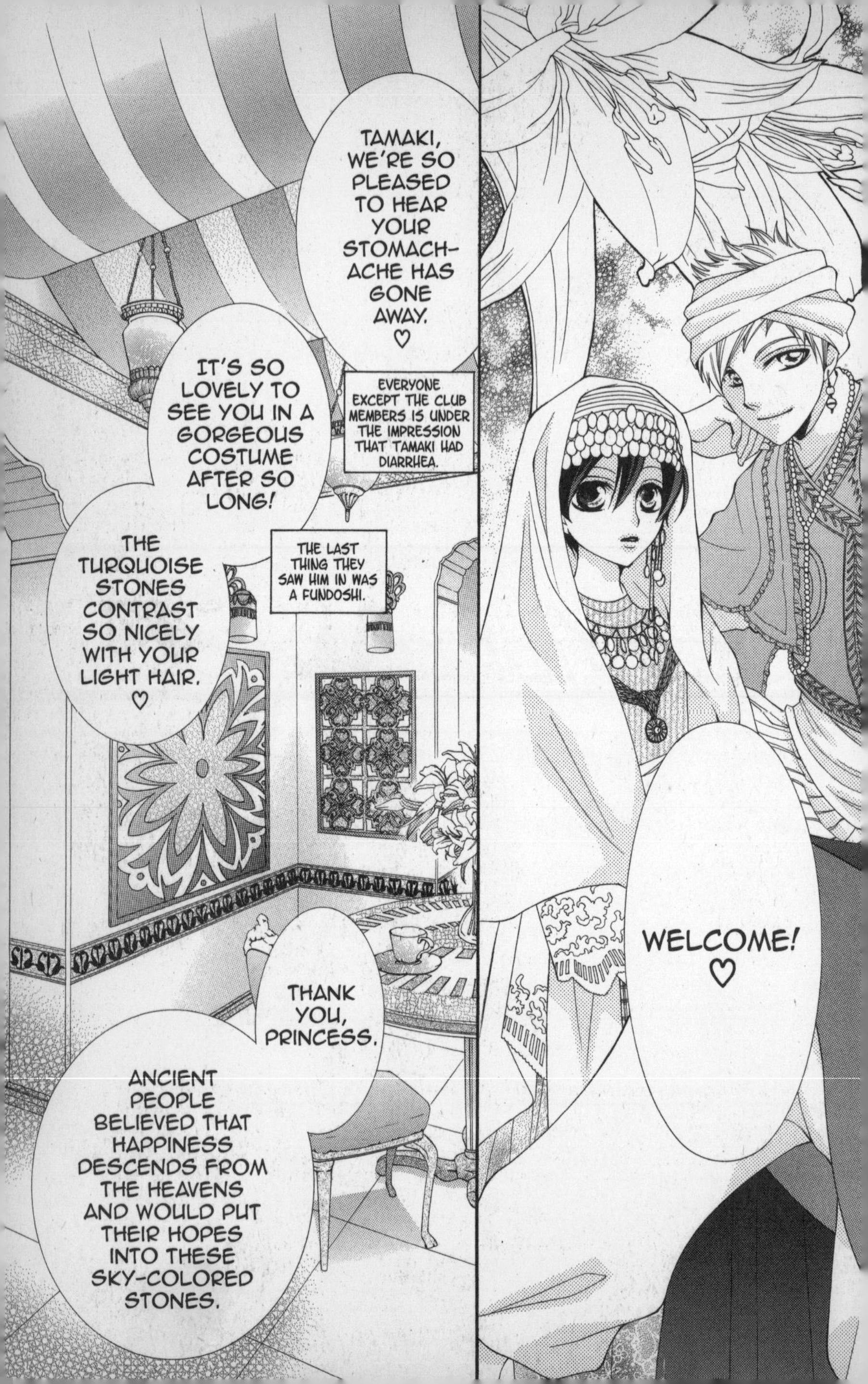
WELCOME! ♡
TAMAKI, WE'RE SO PLEASED TO HEAR YOUR STOMACH-ACHE HAS GONE AWAY. ♡
EVERYONE EXCEPT THE CLUB MEMBERS IS UNDER THE IMPRESSION THAT TAMAKI HAD DIARRHEA.
IT'S SO LOVELY TO SEE YOU IN A GORGEOUS COSTUME AFTER SO LONG!
THE LAST THING THEY SAW HIM IN WAS A FUNDOSHI.
THE TURQUOISE STONES CONTRAST SO NICELY WITH YOUR LIGHT HAIR. ♡
THANK YOU, PRINCESS.
ANCIENT PEOPLE BELIEVED THAT HAPPINESS DESCENDS FROM THE HEAVENS AND WOULD PUT THEIR HOPES INTO THESE SKY-COLORED STONES.

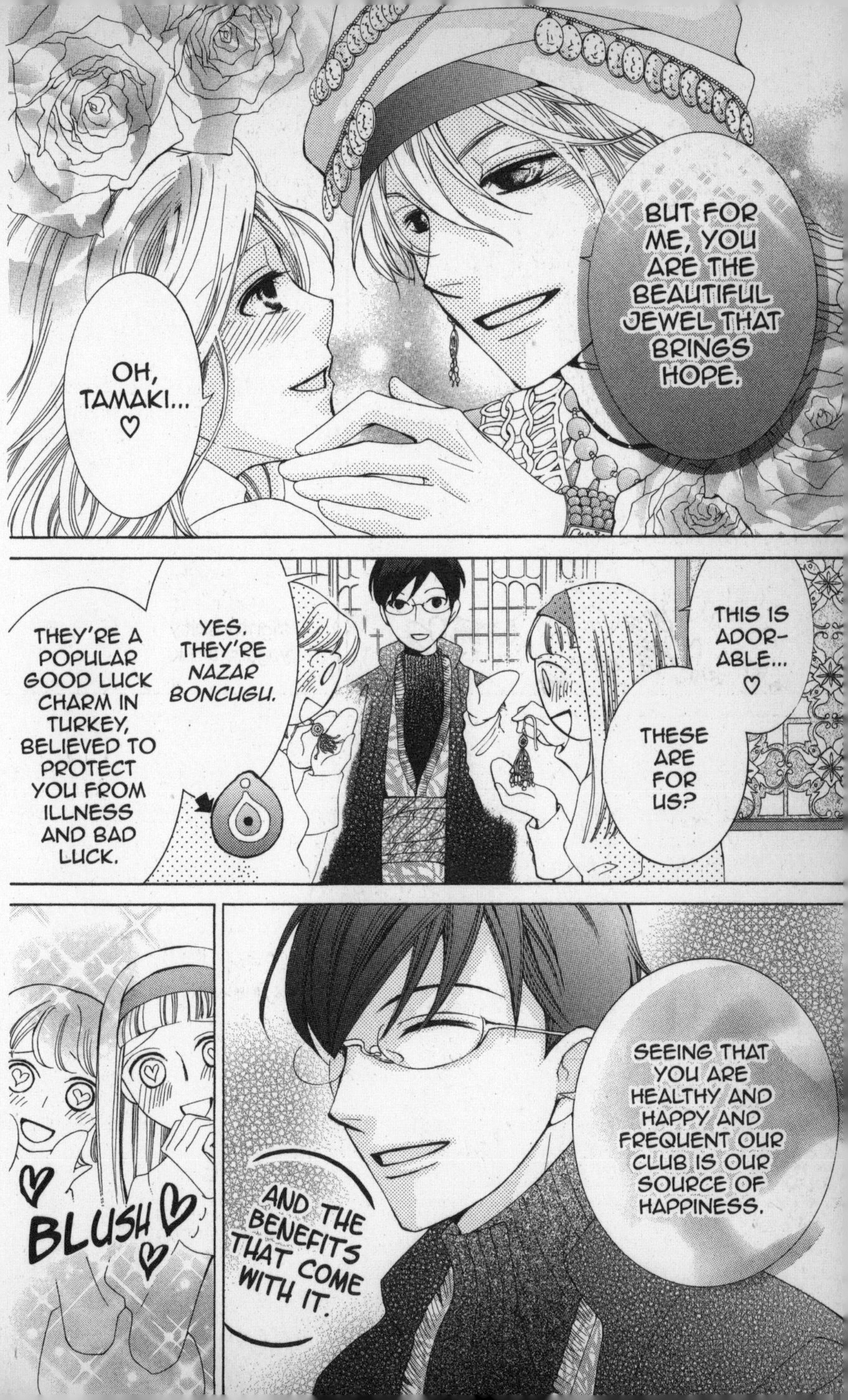
BUT FOR ME, YOU ARE THE BEAUTIFUL JEWEL THAT BRINGS HOPE.
OH, TAMAKI... ♡
THIS IS ADORABLE... ♡
THESE ARE FOR US?
YES. THEY'RE NAZAR BONCUGU.
THEY'RE A POPULAR GOOD LUCK CHARM IN TURKEY, BELIEVED TO PROTECT YOU FROM ILLNESS AND BAD LUCK.
SEEING THAT YOU ARE HEALTHY AND HAPPY AND FREQUENT OUR CLUB IS OUR SOURCE OF HAPPINESS.
AND THE BENEFITS THAT COME WITH IT.
BLUSH

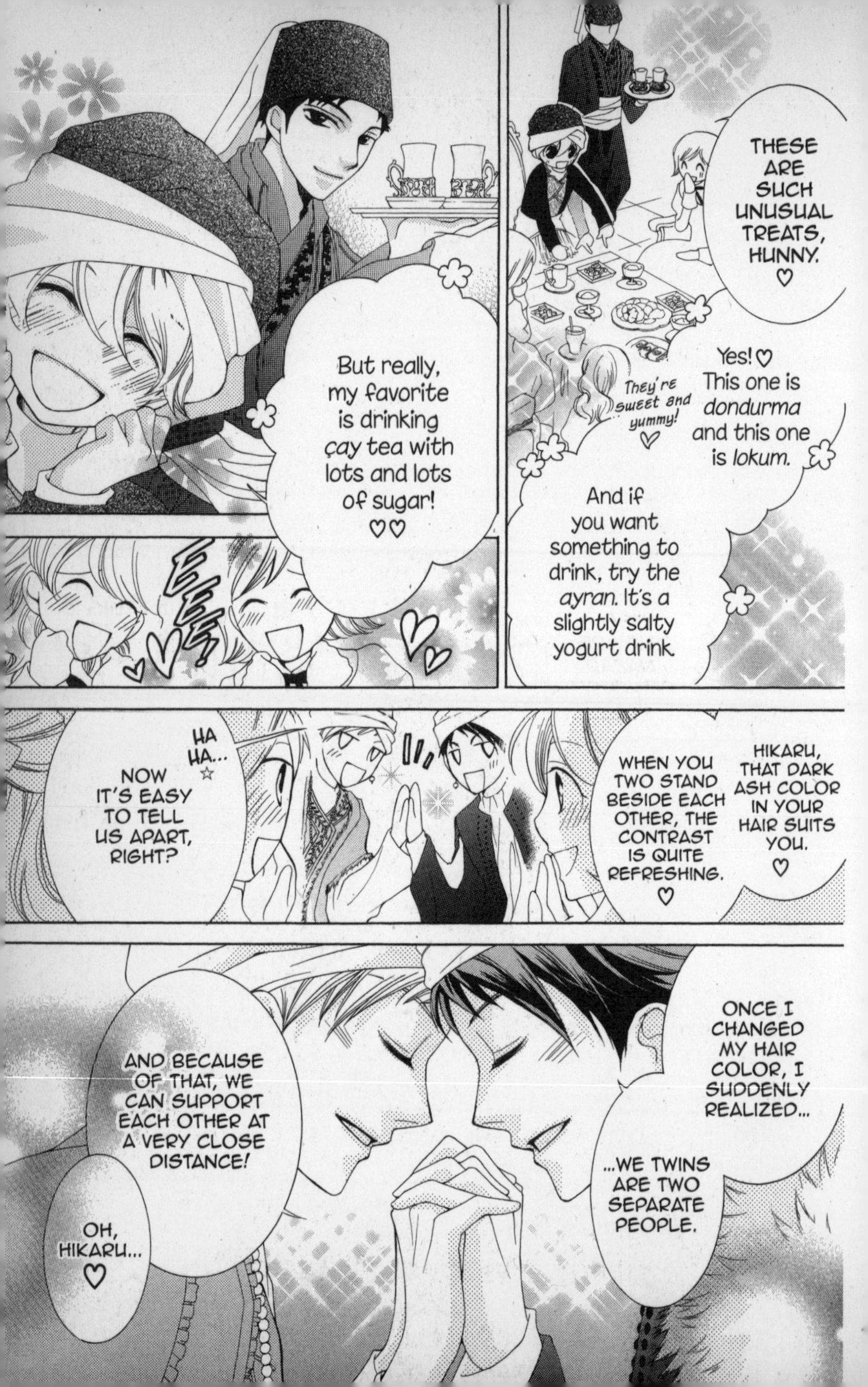
THESE ARE SUCH UNUSUAL TREATS, HUNNY. ♡
Yes! ♡ This one is dondurma and this one is lokum.
They're sweet and yummy! ♡
And if you want something to drink, try the ayran. It's a slightly salty yogurt drink.
But really, my favorite is drinking çay tea with lots and lots of sugar! ♡♡
EEE!
HIKARU, THAT DARK ASH COLOR IN YOUR HAIR SUITS YOU. ♡
WHEN YOU TWO STAND BESIDE EACH OTHER, THE CONTRAST IS QUITE REFRESHING. ♡
HA HA... ☆
NOW IT'S EASY TO TELL US APART, RIGHT?
ONCE I CHANGED MY HAIR COLOR, I SUDDENLY REALIZED...
...WE TWINS ARE TWO SEPARATE PEOPLE.
AND BECAUSE OF THAT, WE CAN SUPPORT EACH OTHER AT A VERY CLOSE DISTANCE!
OH, HIKARU... ♡

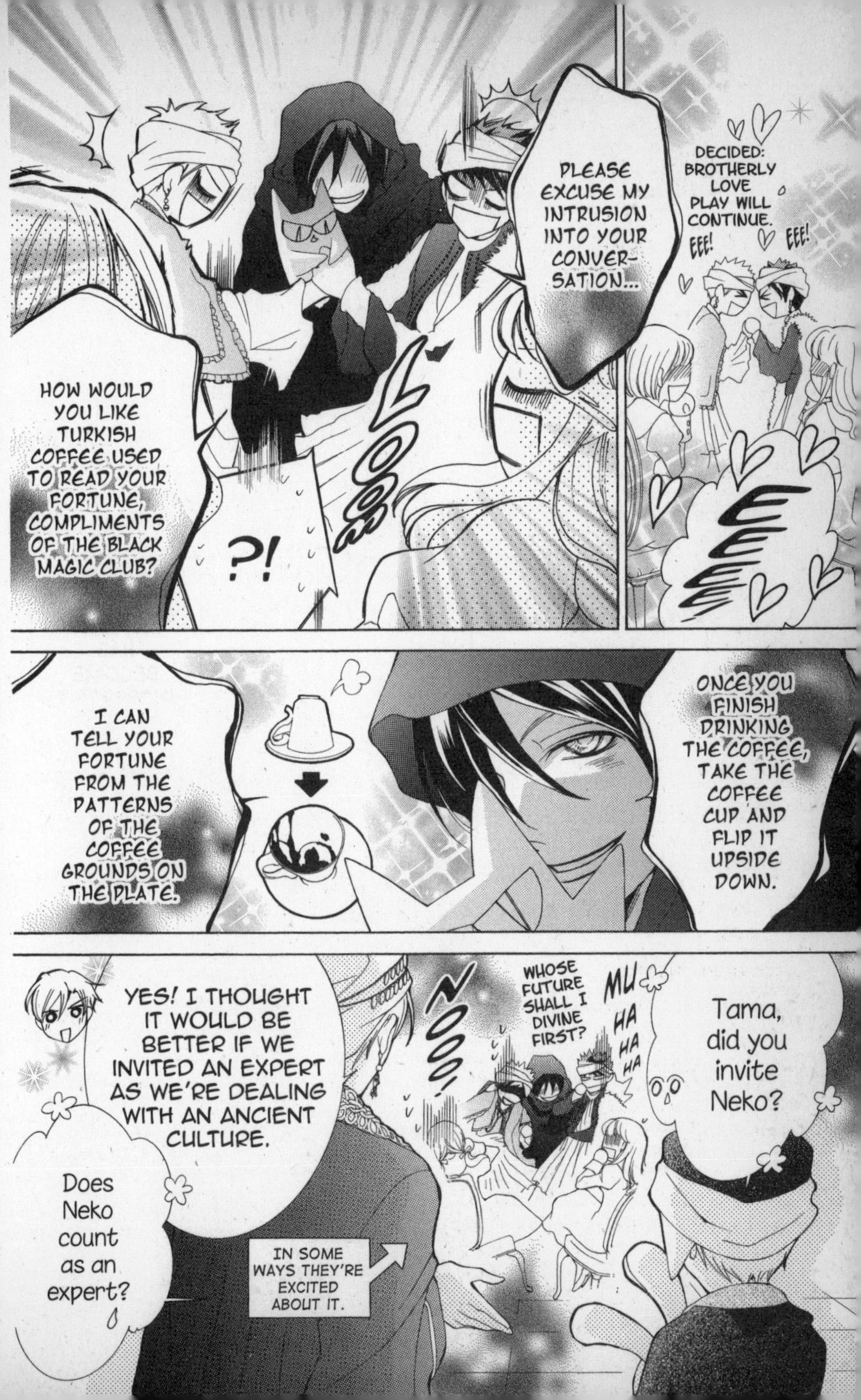
DECIDED: BROTHERLY LOVE PLAY WILL CONTINUE.
EEE!
EEE!
PLEASE EXCUSE MY INTRUSION INTO YOUR CONVERSATION...
?!
HOW WOULD YOU LIKE TURKISH COFFEE USED TO READ YOUR FORTUNE, COMPLIMENTS OF THE BLACK MAGIC CLUB?
ONCE YOU FINISH DRINKING THE COFFEE, TAKE THE COFFEE CUP AND FLIP IT UPSIDE DOWN.
I CAN TELL YOUR FORTUNE FROM THE PATTERNS OF THE COFFEE GROUNDS ON THE PLATE.
Tama, did you invite Neko?
MU HA HA HA
WHOSE FUTURE SHALL I DIVINE FIRST?
YES! I THOUGHT IT WOULD BE BETTER IF WE INVITED AN EXPERT AS WE'RE DEALING WITH AN ANCIENT CULTURE.
Does Neko count as an expert?
IN SOME WAYS THEY'RE EXCITED ABOUT IT.

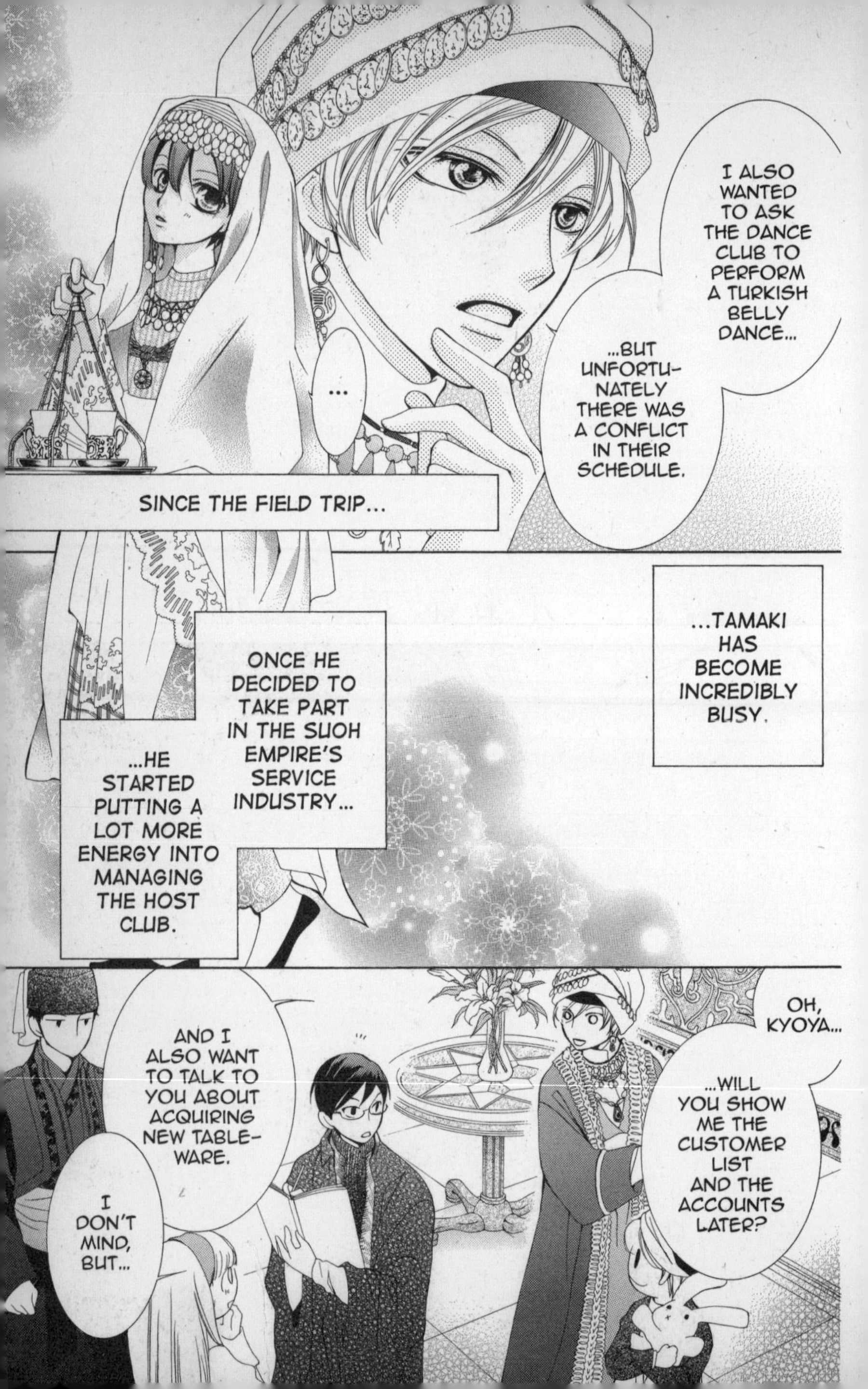
I ALSO WANTED TO ASK THE DANCE CLUB TO PERFORM A TURKISH BELLY DANCE...
...BUT UNFORTU-NATELY THERE WAS A CONFLICT IN THEIR SCHEDULE.
...
SINCE THE FIELD TRIP...
...TAMAKI HAS BECOME INCREDIBLY BUSY.
ONCE HE DECIDED TO TAKE PART IN THE SUOH EMPIRE'S SERVICE INDUSTRY...
...HE STARTED PUTTING A LOT MORE ENERGY INTO MANAGING THE HOST CLUB.
OH, KYOYA...
...WILL YOU SHOW ME THE CUSTOMER LIST AND THE ACCOUNTS LATER?
AND I ALSO WANT TO TALK TO YOU ABOUT ACQUIRING NEW TABLE-WARE.
I DON'T MIND, BUT...

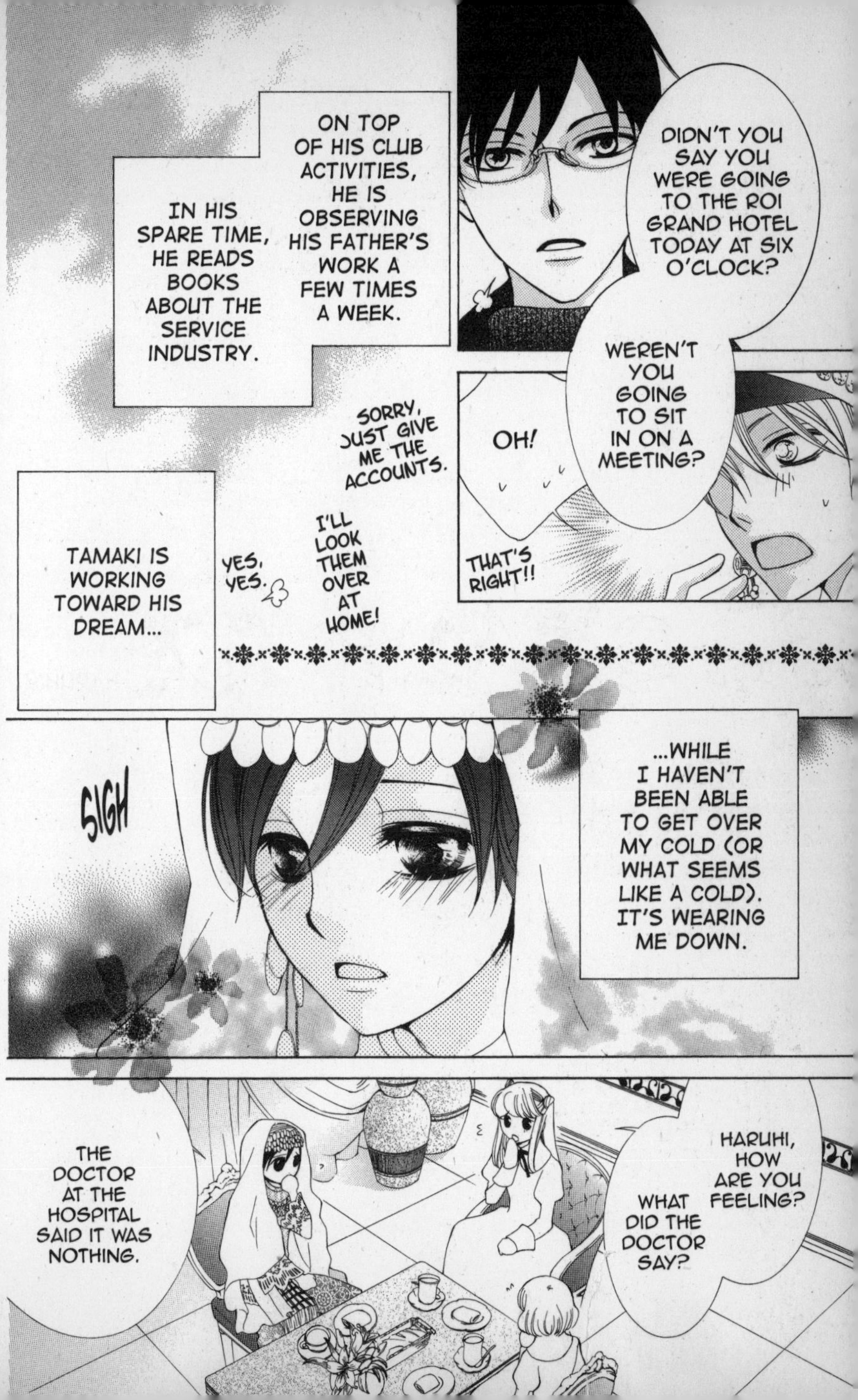
DIDN'T YOU SAY YOU WERE GOING TO THE ROI GRAND HOTEL TODAY AT SIX O'CLOCK?
ON TOP OF HIS CLUB ACTIVITIES, HE IS OBSERVING HIS FATHER'S WORK A FEW TIMES A WEEK.
IN HIS SPARE TIME, HE READS BOOKS ABOUT THE SERVICE INDUSTRY.
WEREN'T YOU GOING TO SIT IN ON A MEETING?
OH!
THAT'S RIGHT!!
SORRY, JUST GIVE ME THE ACCOUNTS.
I'LL LOOK THEM OVER AT HOME!
YES, YES.
TAMAKI IS WORKING TOWARD HIS DREAM...
...WHILE I HAVEN'T BEEN ABLE TO GET OVER MY COLD (OR WHAT SEEMS LIKE A COLD). IT'S WEARING ME DOWN.
SIGH
HARUHI, HOW ARE YOU FEELING?
WHAT DID THE DOCTOR SAY?
THE DOCTOR AT THE HOSPITAL SAID IT WAS NOTHING.

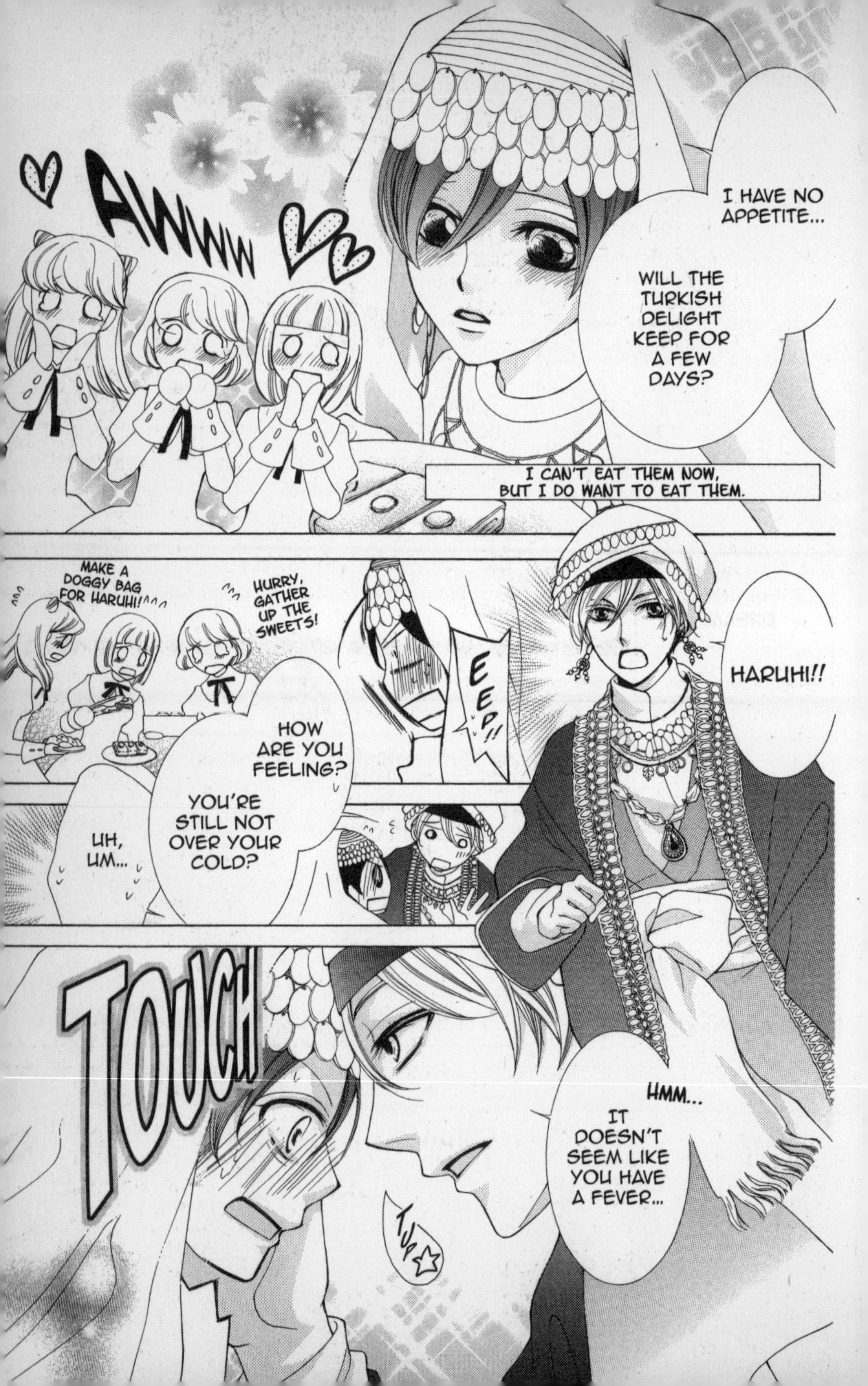
I HAVE NO APPETITE...
WILL THE TURKISH DELIGHT KEEP FOR A FEW DAYS?
I CAN'T EAT THEM NOW, BUT I DO WANT TO EAT THEM.
AWWW
HARUHI!!
EEP!!
HURRY, GATHER UP THE SWEETS!
MAKE A DOGGY BAG FOR HARUHI!
HOW ARE YOU FEELING?
YOU'RE STILL NOT OVER YOUR COLD?
UH, UM...
HMM...
IT DOESN'T SEEM LIKE YOU HAVE A FEVER...
TOUCH

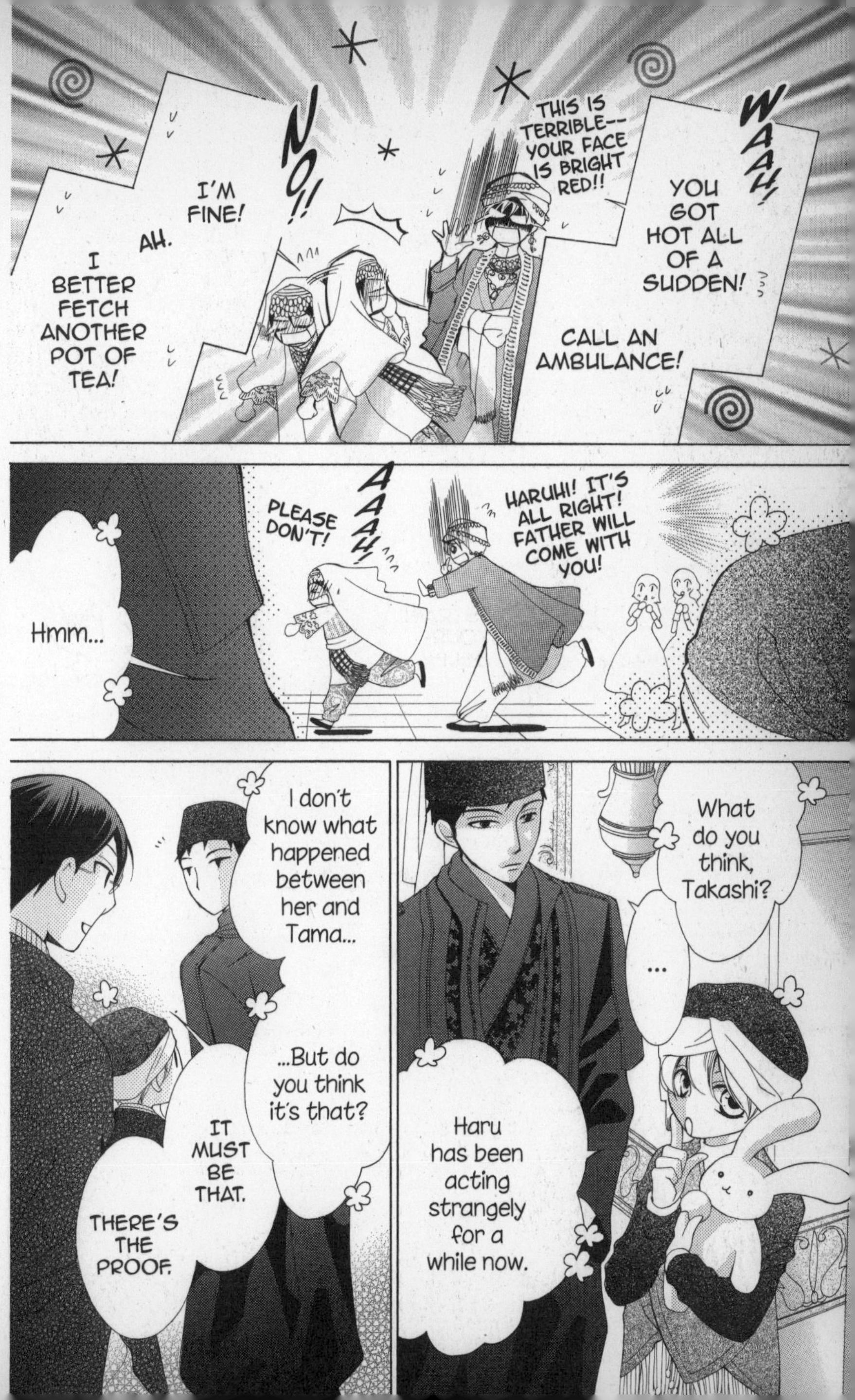
WAAAH!
YOU GOT HOT ALL OF A SUDDEN!
THIS IS TERRIBLE-- YOUR FACE IS BRIGHT RED!!
CALL AN AMBULANCE!
NO!!
I'M FINE!
AH.
I BETTER FETCH ANOTHER POT OF TEA!
HARUHI! IT'S ALL RIGHT! FATHER WILL COME WITH YOU!
AAAAH!
PLEASE DON'T!
Hmm...
What do you think, Takashi?
...
Haru has been acting strangely for a while now.
I don't know what happened between her and Tama...
...But do you think it's that?
IT MUST BE THAT.
THERE'S THE PROOF.

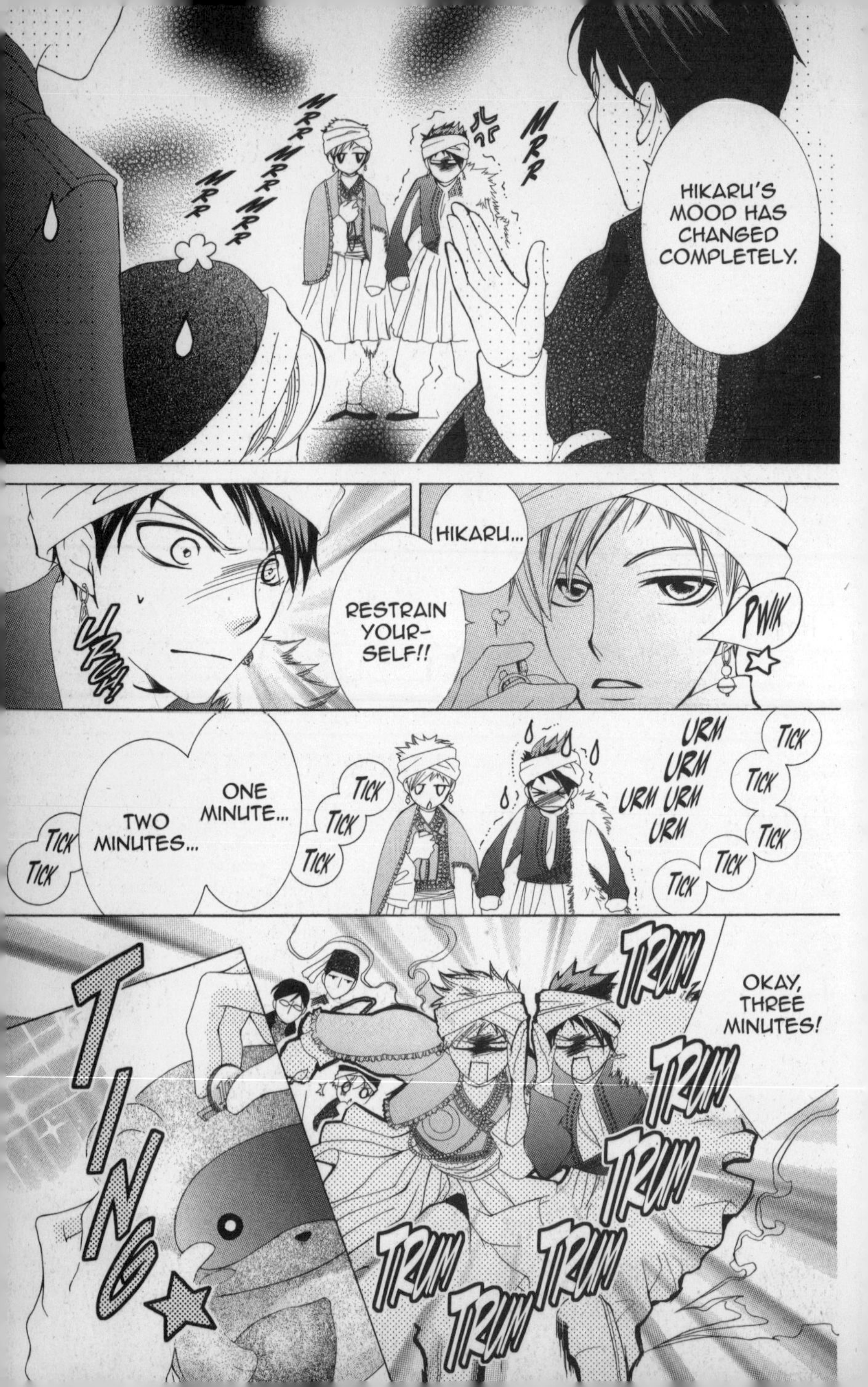
HIKARU'S MOOD HAS CHANGED COMPLETELY.
MRR
MRR MRR MRR
MRR
HIKARU...
RESTRAIN YOUR-SELF!!
PWIK
TICK TICK TICK TICK TICK
URM URM URM URM URM
TICK TICK TICK
ONE MINUTE...
TWO MINUTES...
TICK TICK
OKAY, THREE MINUTES!
TRUM TRUM TRUM TRUM TRUM TRUM
TING

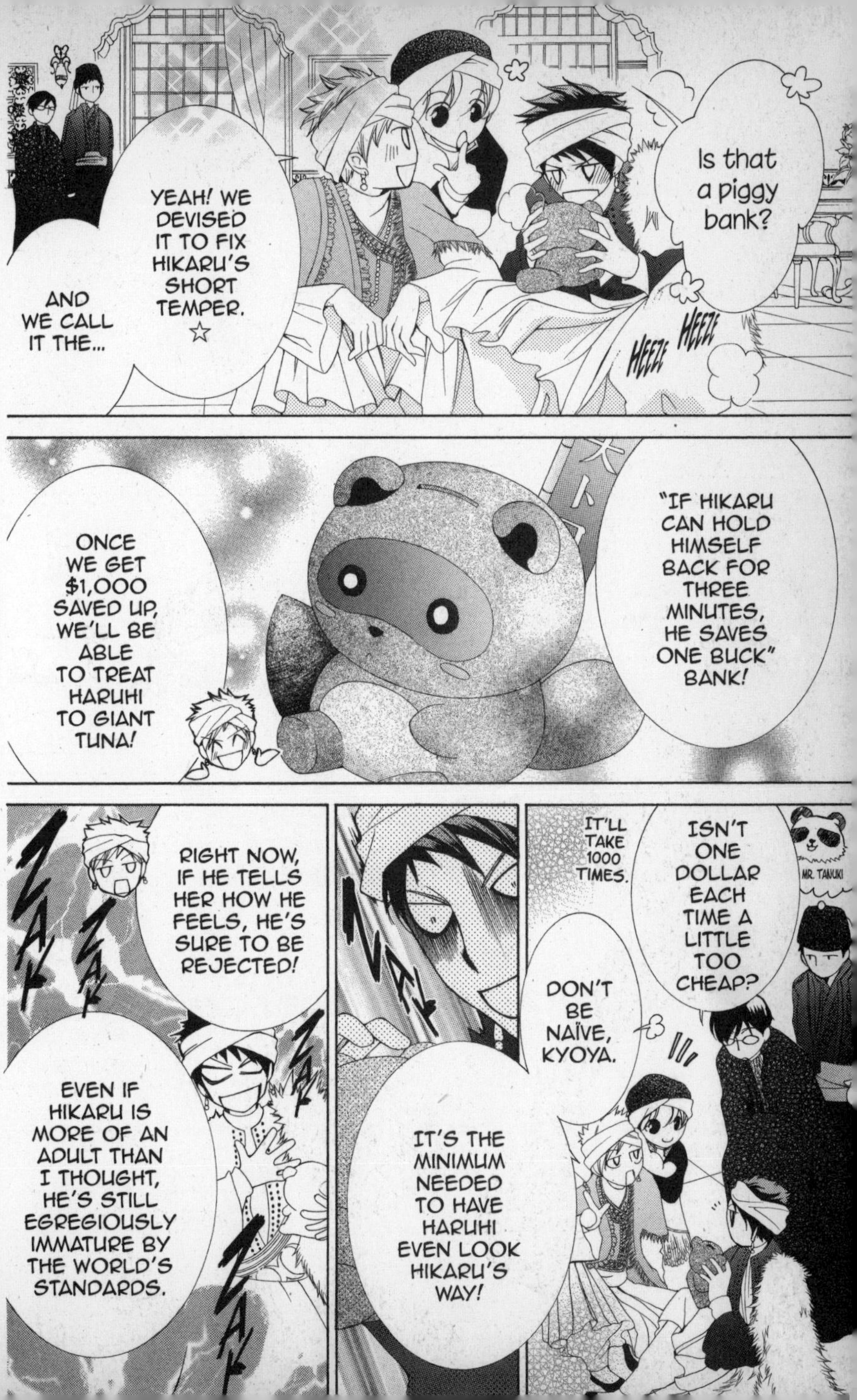
Is that a piggy bank?
YEAH! WE DEVISED IT TO FIX HIKARU'S SHORT TEMPER. ☆
AND WE CALL IT THE...
HEEZE
HEEZE
"IF HIKARU CAN HOLD HIMSELF BACK FOR THREE MINUTES, HE SAVES ONE BUCK" BANK!
ONCE WE GET $1,000 SAVED UP, WE'LL BE ABLE TO TREAT HARUHI TO GIANT TUNA!
MR. TANUKI
ISN'T ONE DOLLAR EACH TIME A LITTLE TOO CHEAP?
IT'LL TAKE 1000 TIMES.
DON'T BE NAÏVE, KYOYA.
IT'S THE MINIMUM NEEDED TO HAVE HARUHI EVEN LOOK HIKARU'S WAY!
RIGHT NOW, IF HE TELLS HER HOW HE FEELS, HE'S SURE TO BE REJECTED!
EVEN IF HIKARU IS MORE OF AN ADULT THAN I THOUGHT, HE'S STILL EGREGIOUSLY IMMATURE BY THE WORLD'S STANDARDS.
ZAK
ZAK
ZAK
ZAK

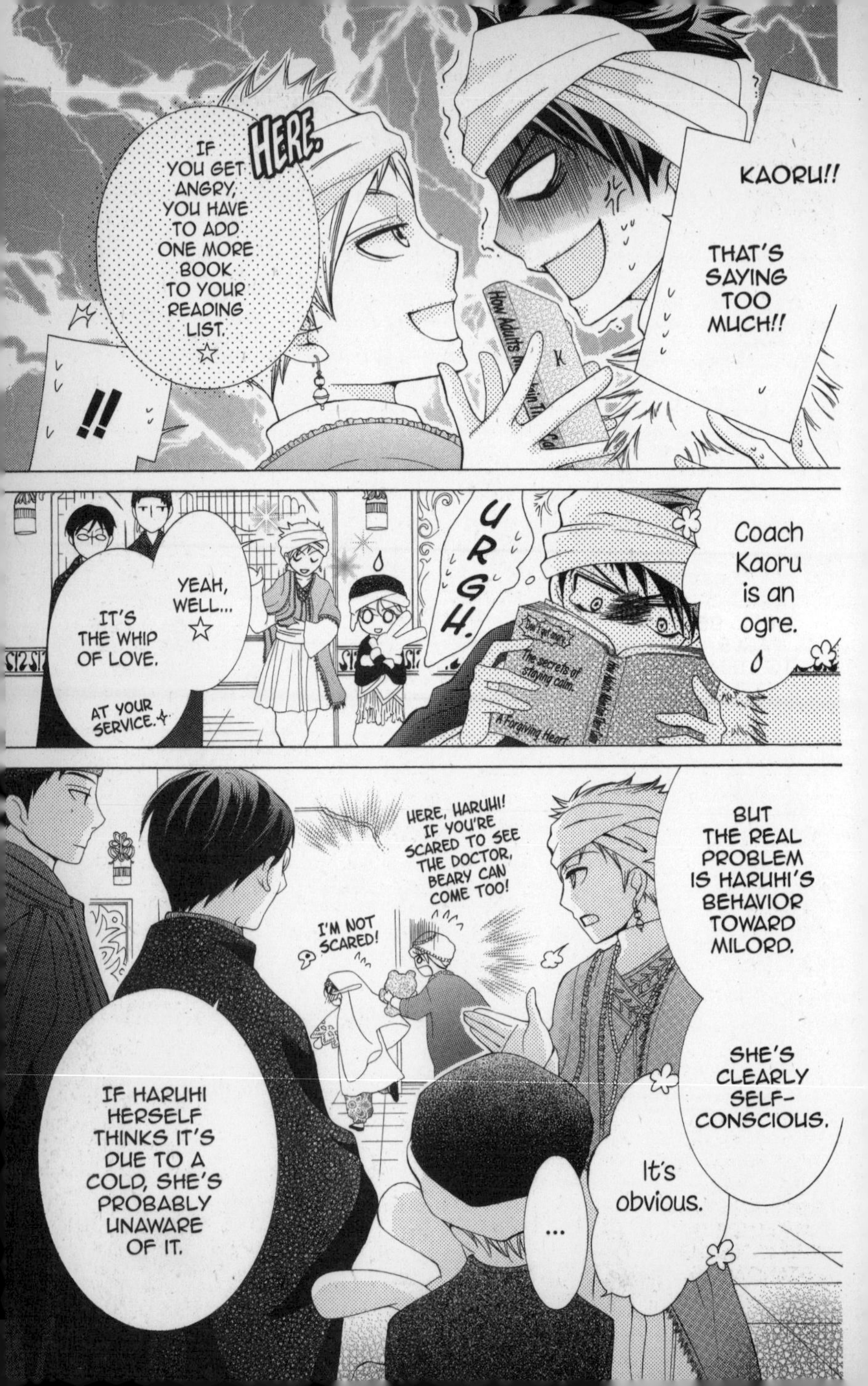
KAORU!!
THAT'S SAYING TOO MUCH!!
HERE.
IF YOU GET ANGRY, YOU HAVE TO ADD ONE MORE BOOK TO YOUR READING LIST. ☆
!!
Coach Kaoru is an ogre.
URGH.
The secrets of staying calm.
A Forgiving Heart
YEAH, WELL... ☆
IT'S THE WHIP OF LOVE.
AT YOUR SERVICE.
BUT THE REAL PROBLEM IS HARUHI'S BEHAVIOR TOWARD MILORD.
HERE, HARUHI! IF YOU'RE SCARED TO SEE THE DOCTOR, BEARY CAN COME TOO!
I'M NOT SCARED!
SHE'S CLEARLY SELF-CONSCIOUS.
It's obvious.
...
IF HARUHI HERSELF THINKS IT'S DUE TO A COLD, SHE'S PROBABLY UNAWARE OF IT.

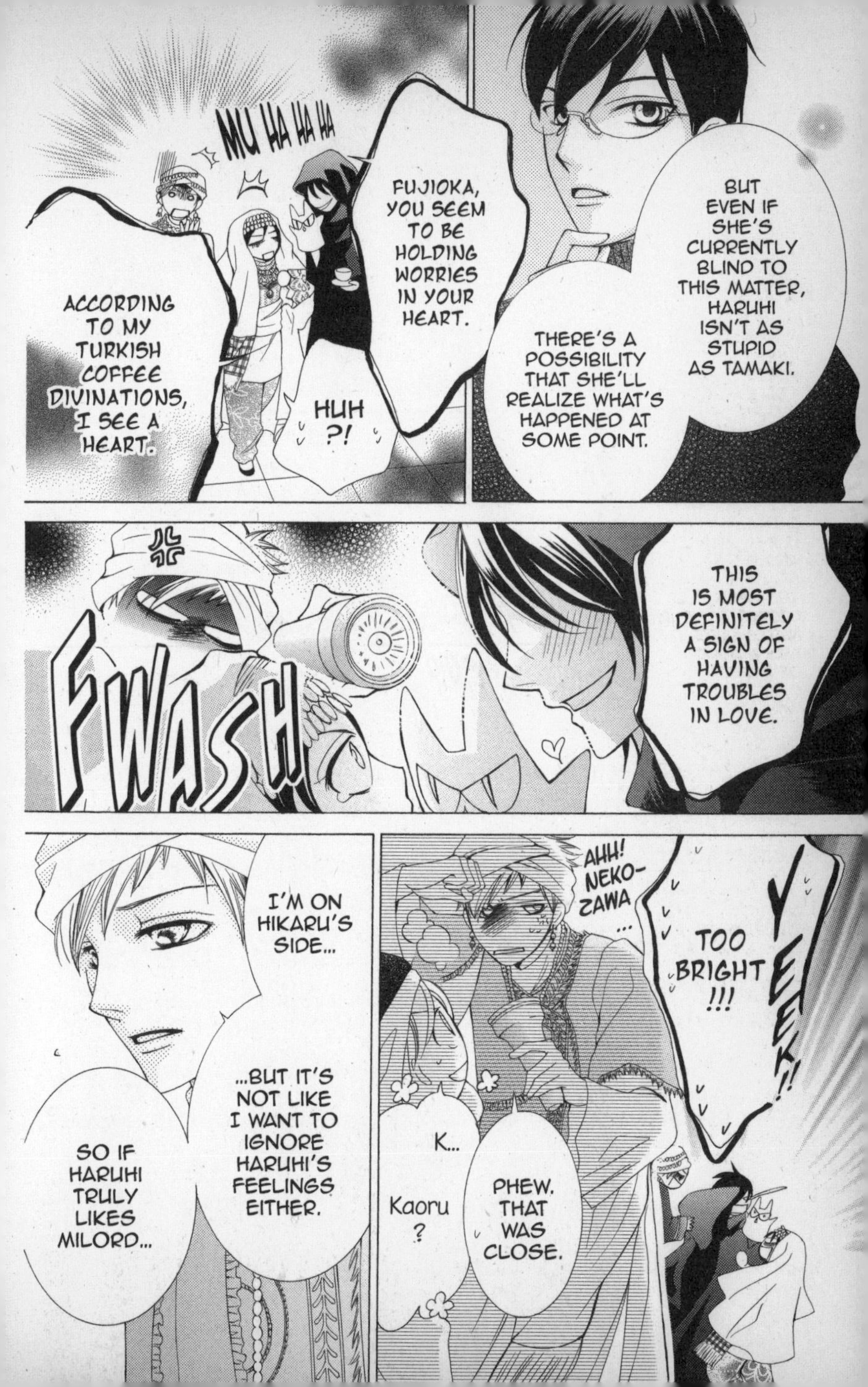
BUT EVEN IF SHE'S CURRENTLY BLIND TO THIS MATTER, HARUHI ISN'T AS STUPID AS TAMAKI.
THERE'S A POSSIBILITY THAT SHE'LL REALIZE WHAT'S HAPPENED AT SOME POINT.
MU HA HA HA
FUJIOKA, YOU SEEM TO BE HOLDING WORRIES IN YOUR HEART.
HUH ?!
ACCORDING TO MY TURKISH COFFEE DIVINATIONS, I SEE A HEART.
THIS IS MOST DEFINITELY A SIGN OF HAVING TROUBLES IN LOVE.
FWASH
YEEK!!
TOO BRIGHT !!!
AHH! NEKO-ZAWA ...
PHEW. THAT WAS CLOSE.
K... Kaoru ?
I'M ON HIKARU'S SIDE...
...BUT IT'S NOT LIKE I WANT TO IGNORE HARUHI'S FEELINGS EITHER.
SO IF HARUHI TRULY LIKES MILORD...

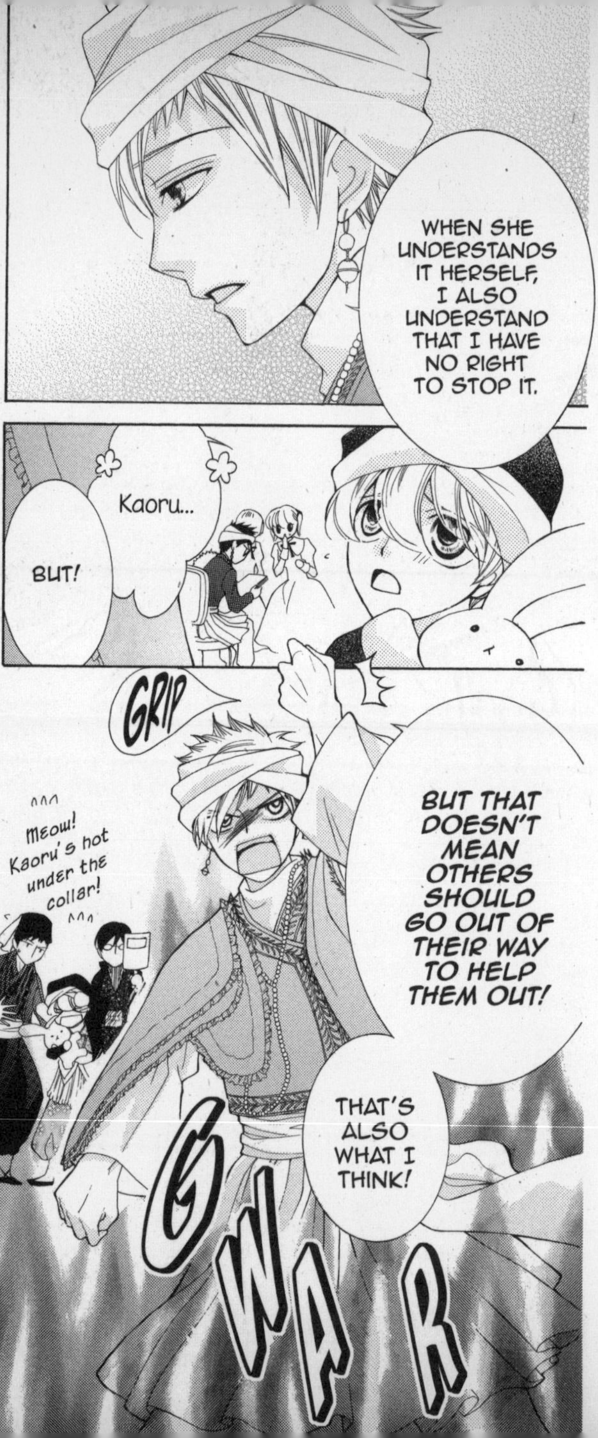
WHEN SHE UNDERSTANDS IT HERSELF, I ALSO UNDERSTAND THAT I HAVE NO RIGHT TO STOP IT.
Kaoru...
BUT!
GRIP
BUT THAT DOESN'T MEAN OTHERS SHOULD GO OUT OF THEIR WAY TO HELP THEM OUT!
THAT'S ALSO WHAT I THINK!
Meow! Kaoru's hot under the collar!
GWAR

1

✿HELLO, EVERYBODY!

HOW HAVE YOU BEEN? THIS IS HATORI. THANK YOU SO MUCH FOR PICKING UP *HOST CLUB* VOLUME 13!!

✿WELL, WELL... THIS IS SUDDEN, BUT HAVE YOU EVER HAD THE EXPERIENCE OF ALMOST FALLING ASLEEP IN CLASS, AND WHEN YOU LOOKED AT YOUR NOTES LATER IT WAS A BUNCH OF WIGGLY, INDECIPHERABLE WRITING?

HATORI DOES. THIS IS ACTUALLY SOMETHING I STILL DO. FOR EXAMPLE, WHEN I AM INKING MY WORK SOMETIMES, I START THINKING, "I'M SO SLEEPY... BUT NOW IS NOT THE TIME TO BE FALLING ASLEEP..." WHEN I COME TO, I REALIZE THE LINES ARE COMPLETELY CROOKED. (AND IN THE END I HAVE TO REDO THE SECTION.)

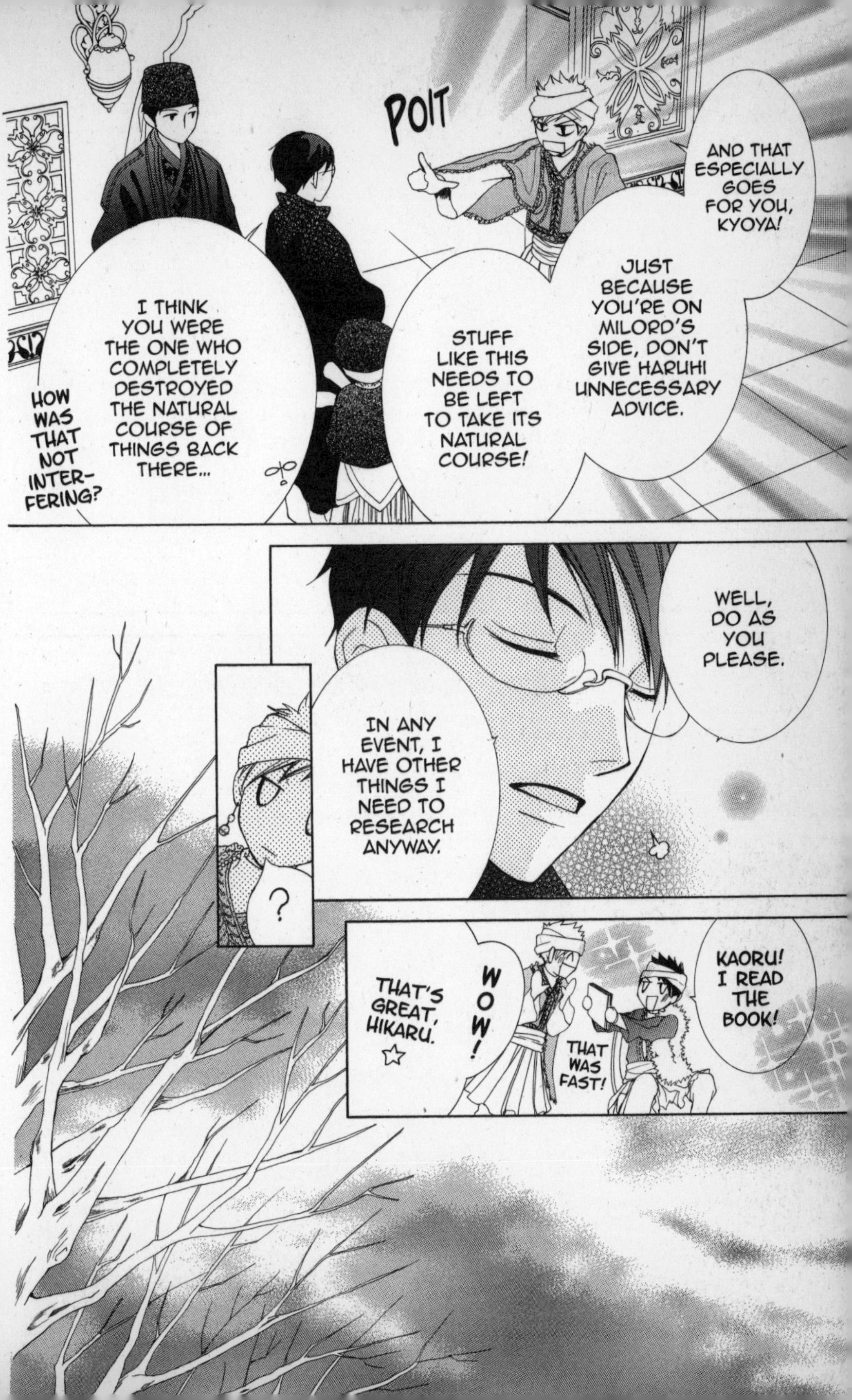
AND THAT ESPECIALLY GOES FOR YOU, KYOYA!
POIT
JUST BECAUSE YOU'RE ON MILORD'S SIDE, DON'T GIVE HARUHI UNNECESSARY ADVICE.
STUFF LIKE THIS NEEDS TO BE LEFT TO TAKE ITS NATURAL COURSE!
I THINK YOU WERE THE ONE WHO COMPLETELY DESTROYED THE NATURAL COURSE OF THINGS BACK THERE...
HOW WAS THAT NOT INTER-FERING?
WELL, DO AS YOU PLEASE.
IN ANY EVENT, I HAVE OTHER THINGS I NEED TO RESEARCH ANYWAY.
?
KAORU! I READ THE BOOK!
THAT WAS FAST!
WOW!
THAT'S GREAT, HIKARU. ☆

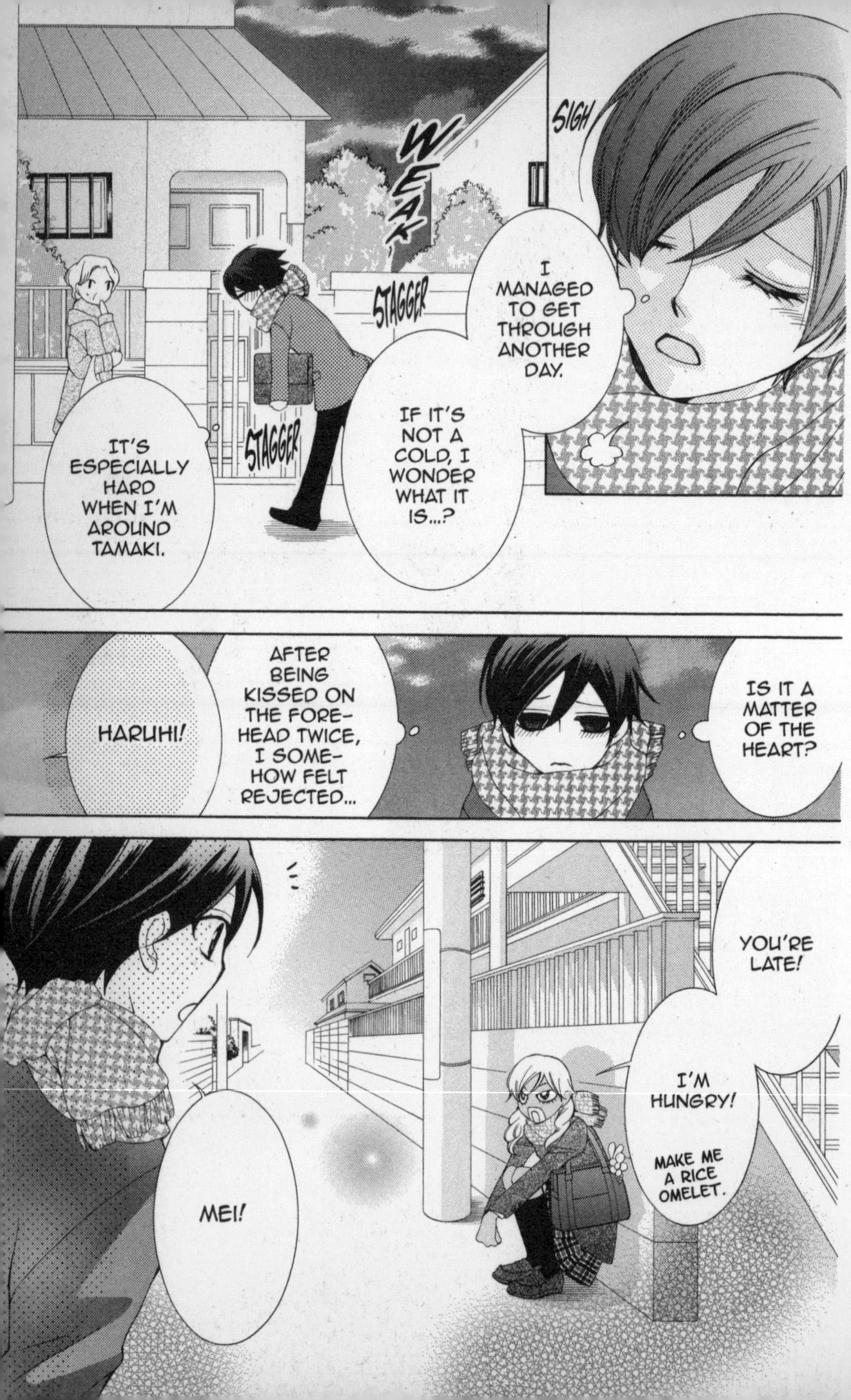
SIGH
I MANAGED TO GET THROUGH ANOTHER DAY.
WEAK
STAGGER
IF IT'S NOT A COLD, I WONDER WHAT IT IS...?
STAGGER
IT'S ESPECIALLY HARD WHEN I'M AROUND TAMAKI.
IS IT A MATTER OF THE HEART?
AFTER BEING KISSED ON THE FORE-HEAD TWICE, I SOME-HOW FELT REJECTED...
HARUHI!
YOU'RE LATE!
I'M HUNGRY!
MAKE ME A RICE OMELET.
MEI!

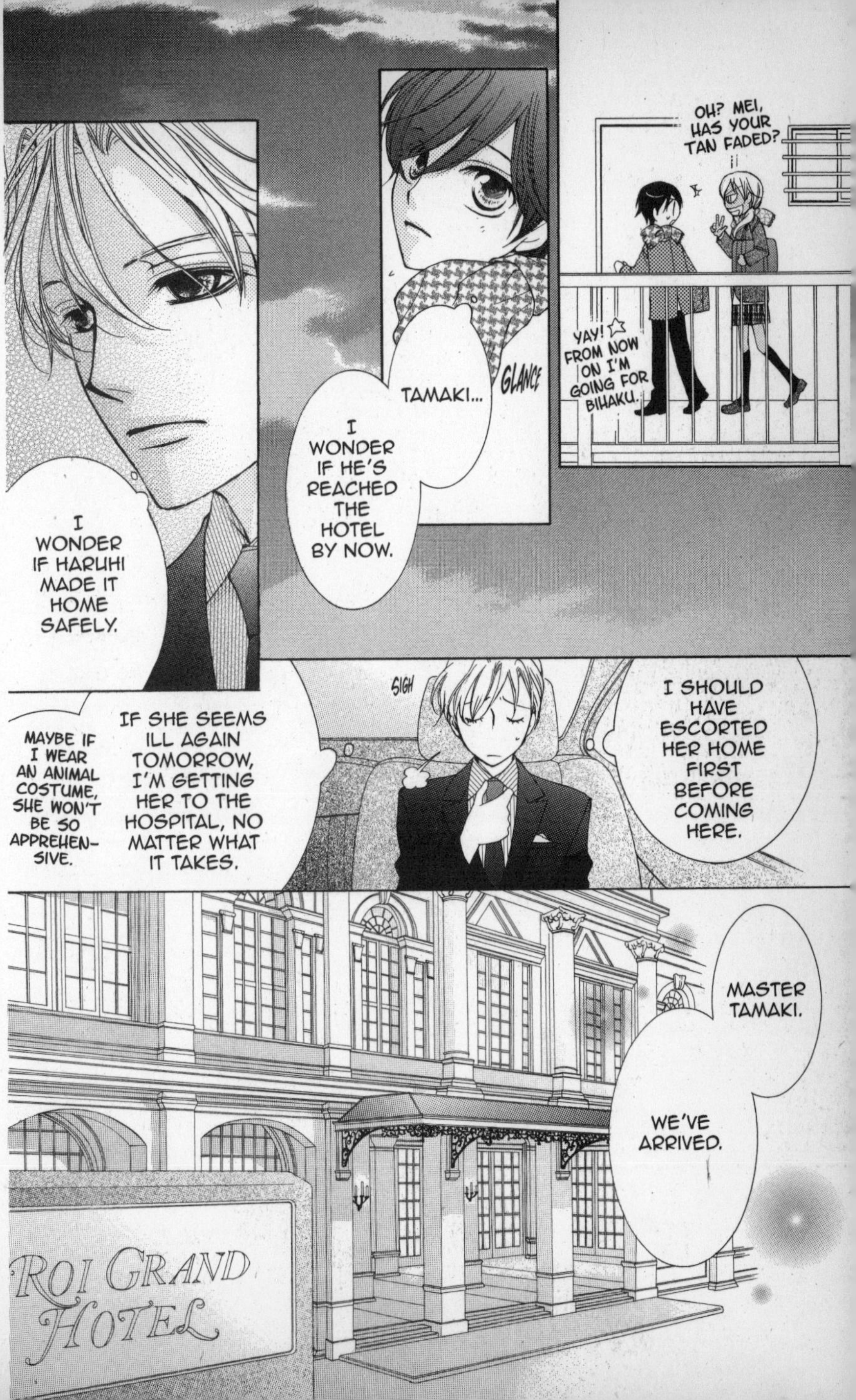
OH? MEI, HAS YOUR TAN FADED?
YAY! FROM NOW ON I'M GOING FOR BIHAKU.
TAMAKI...
GLANCE
I WONDER IF HE'S REACHED THE HOTEL BY NOW.
I WONDER IF HARUHI MADE IT HOME SAFELY.
SIGH
I SHOULD HAVE ESCORTED HER HOME FIRST BEFORE COMING HERE.
IF SHE SEEMS ILL AGAIN TOMORROW, I'M GETTING HER TO THE HOSPITAL, NO MATTER WHAT IT TAKES.
MAYBE IF I WEAR AN ANIMAL COSTUME, SHE WON'T BE SO APPREHENSIVE.
MASTER TAMAKI.
WE'VE ARRIVED.
ROI GRAND HOTEL

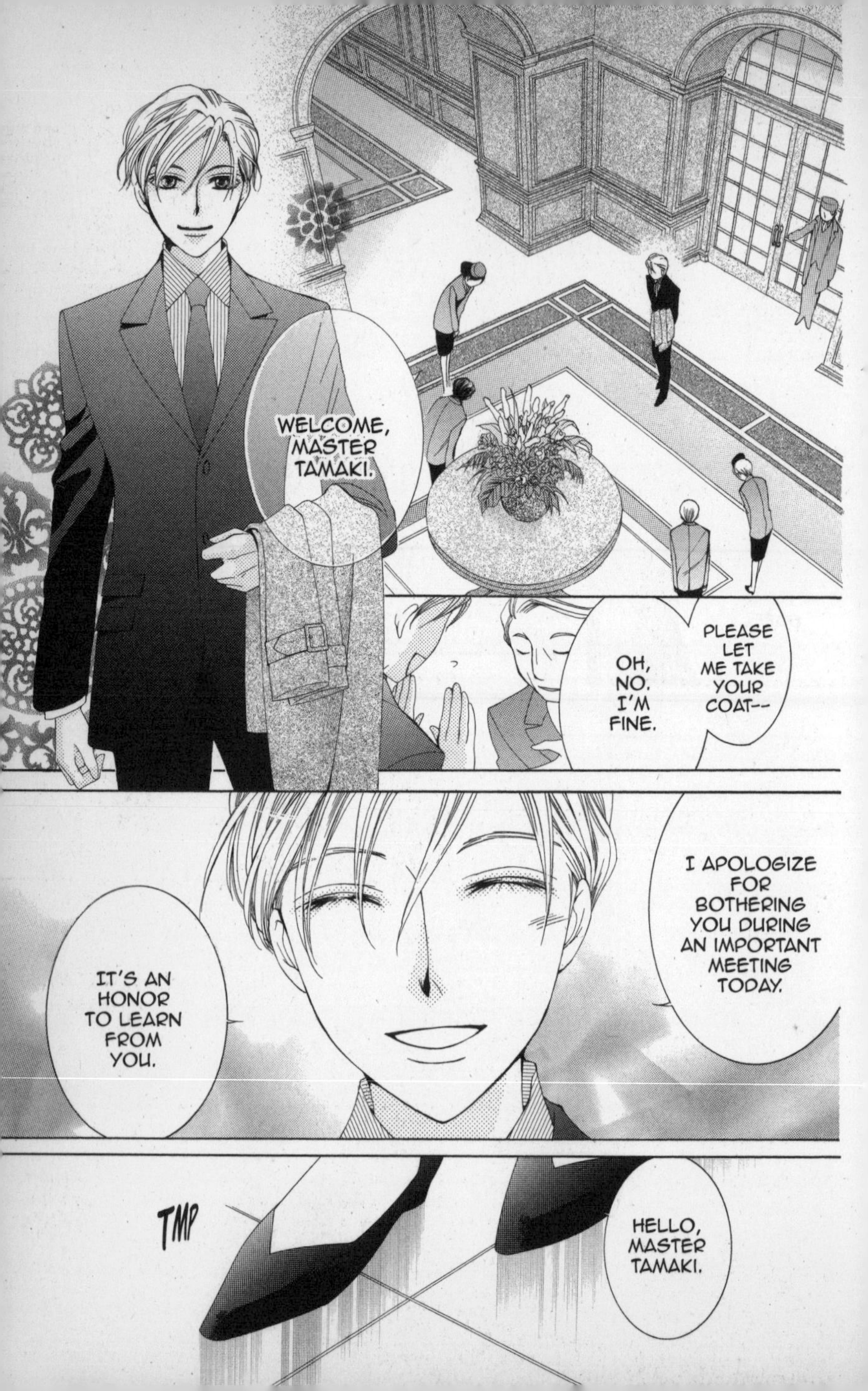
WELCOME, MASTER TAMAKI.
PLEASE LET ME TAKE YOUR COAT--
OH, NO. I'M FINE.
I APOLOGIZE FOR BOTHERING YOU DURING AN IMPORTANT MEETING TODAY.
IT'S AN HONOR TO LEARN FROM YOU.
TMP
HELLO, MASTER TAMAKI.

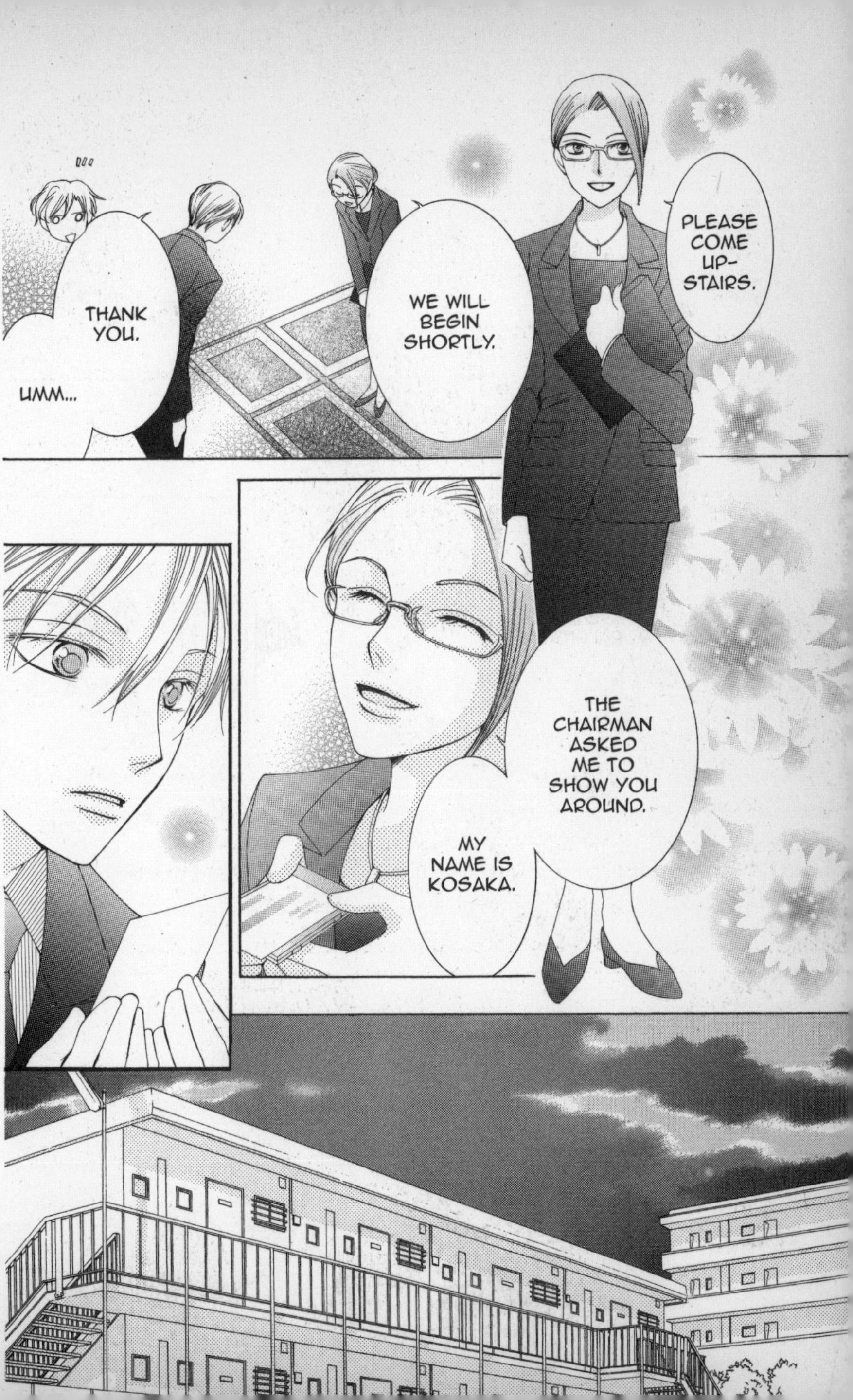
PLEASE COME UP-STAIRS.
WE WILL BEGIN SHORTLY.
THANK YOU.
UMM...
THE CHAIRMAN ASKED ME TO SHOW YOU AROUND.
MY NAME IS KOSAKA.

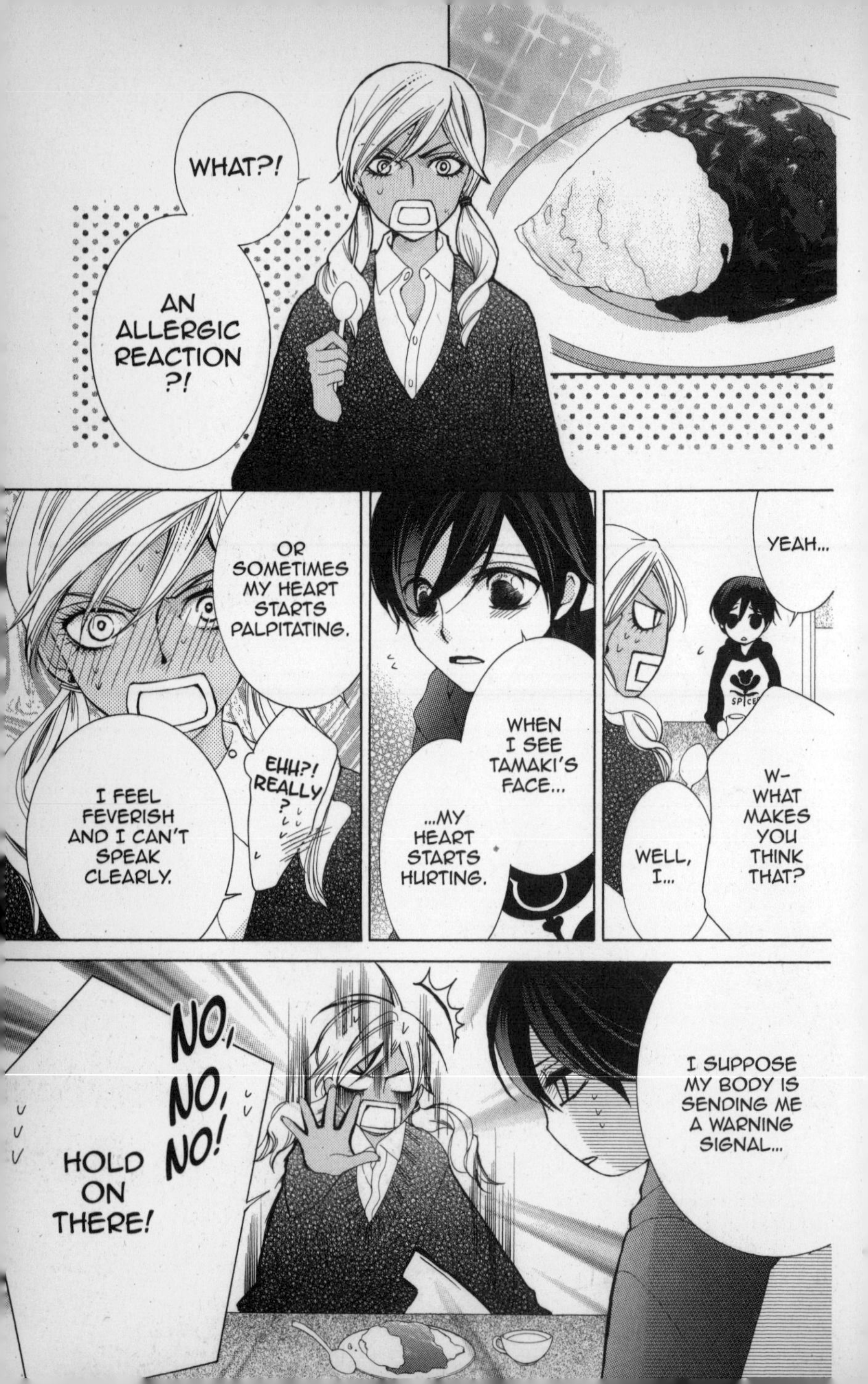
WHAT?!
AN ALLERGIC REACTION?!
YEAH...
W-WHAT MAKES YOU THINK THAT?
WELL, I...
WHEN I SEE TAMAKI'S FACE...
...MY HEART STARTS HURTING.
OR SOMETIMES MY HEART STARTS PALPITATING.
EHH?! REALLY?
I FEEL FEVERISH AND I CAN'T SPEAK CLEARLY.
I SUPPOSE MY BODY IS SENDING ME A WARNING SIGNAL...
NO, NO, NO!
HOLD ON THERE!

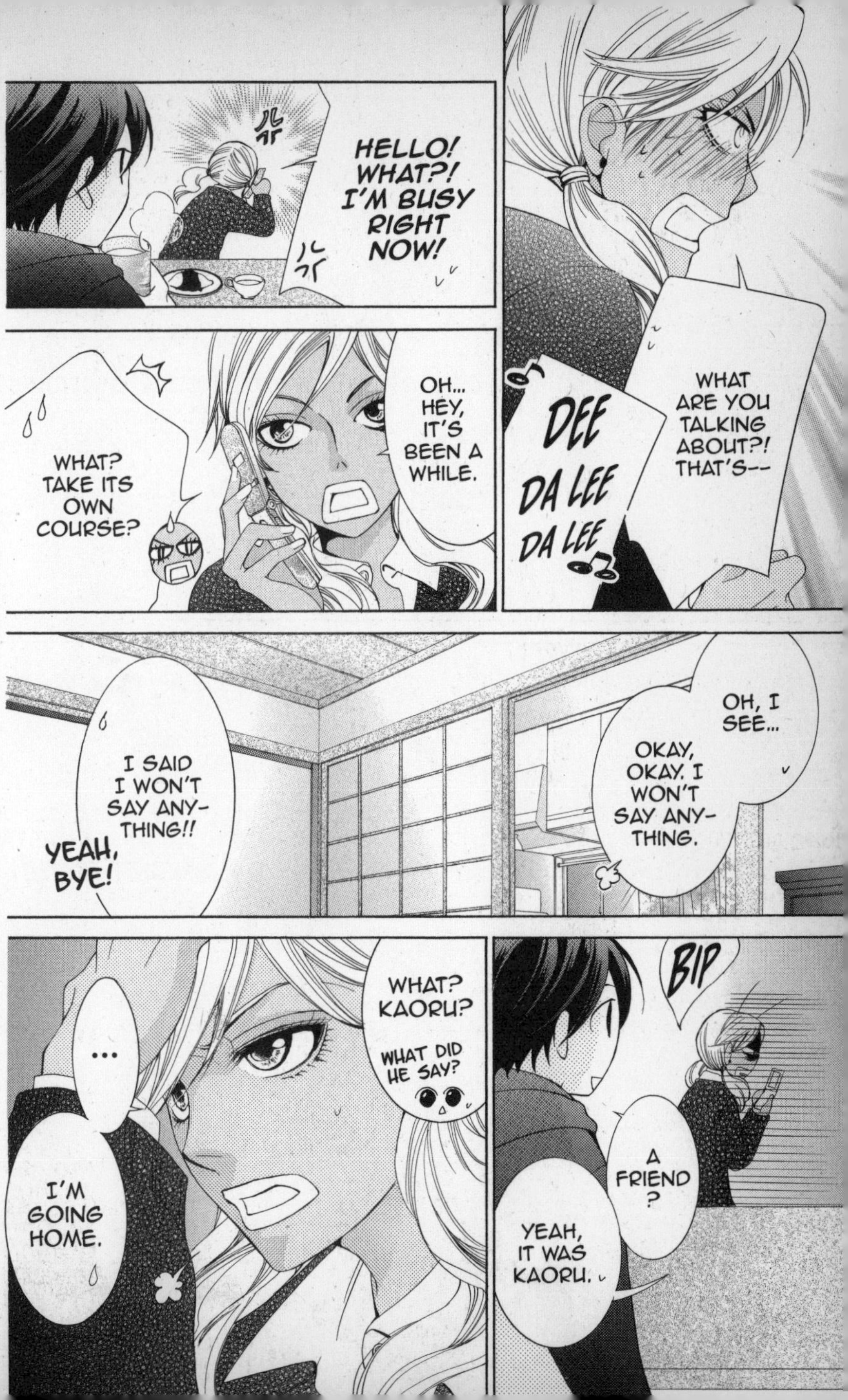
WHAT ARE YOU TALKING ABOUT?! THAT'S--
DEE DA LEE DA LEE
HELLO! WHAT?! I'M BUSY RIGHT NOW!
OH... HEY, IT'S BEEN A WHILE.
WHAT? TAKE ITS OWN COURSE?
OH, I SEE... OKAY, OKAY. I WON'T SAY ANY-THING.
I SAID I WON'T SAY ANY-THING!!
YEAH, BYE!
BIP
A FRIEND?
YEAH, IT WAS KAORU.
WHAT? KAORU?
WHAT DID HE SAY?
...
I'M GOING HOME.

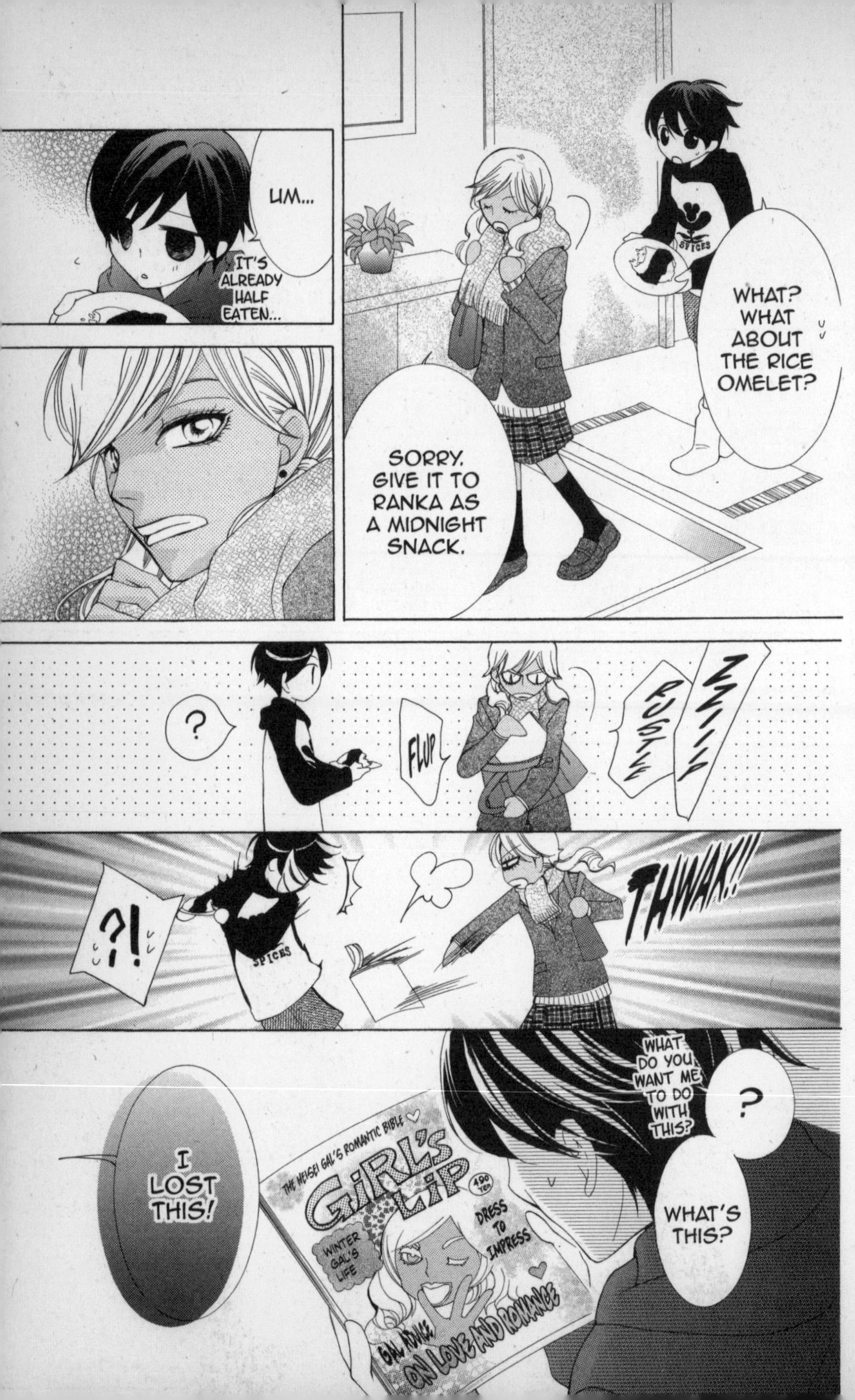
WHAT? WHAT ABOUT THE RICE OMELET?
SORRY. GIVE IT TO RANKA AS A MIDNIGHT SNACK.
UM...
IT'S ALREADY HALF EATEN...
ZZZIIIP
RUSTLE
FLUP
?
THWAK!!
?!
?
WHAT DO YOU WANT ME TO DO WITH THIS?
WHAT'S THIS?
THE HEISEI GAL'S ROMANTIC BIBLE
GIRL'S LIP
490 Yen
DRESS TO IMPRESS
WINTER GAL'S LIFE
GAL ADVICE ON LOVE AND ROMANCE
I LOST THIS!

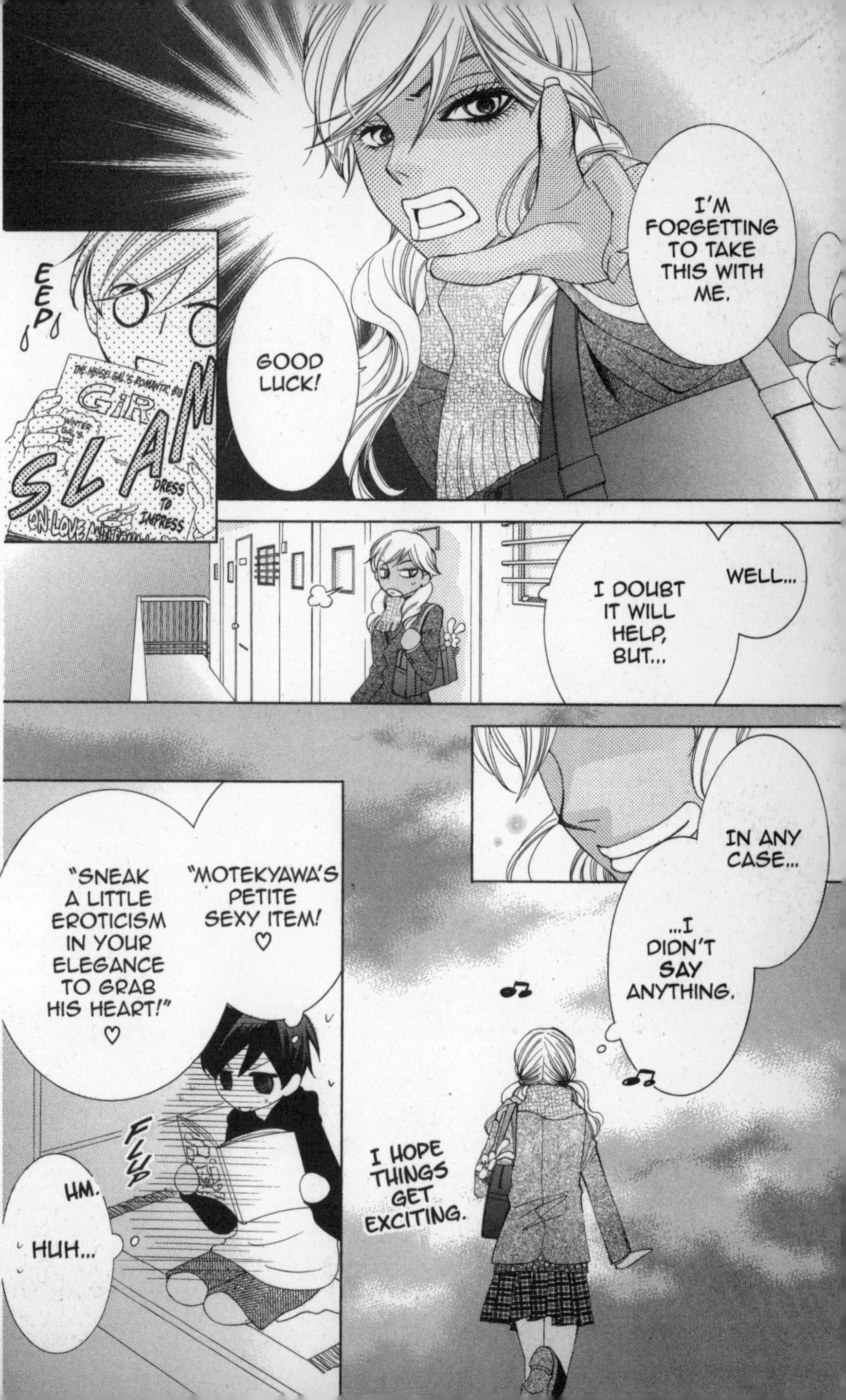
I'M FORGETTING TO TAKE THIS WITH ME.
GOOD LUCK!
EEP
WINTER GAL'S LIFE
DRESS TO IMPRESS
SLAM
WELL...
I DOUBT IT WILL HELP, BUT...
IN ANY CASE...
...I DIDN'T SAY ANYTHING.
I HOPE THINGS GET EXCITING.
"MOTEKYAWA'S PETITE SEXY ITEM! ♡
"SNEAK A LITTLE EROTICISM IN YOUR ELEGANCE TO GRAB HIS HEART!" ♡
FLIP
HM.
HUH...

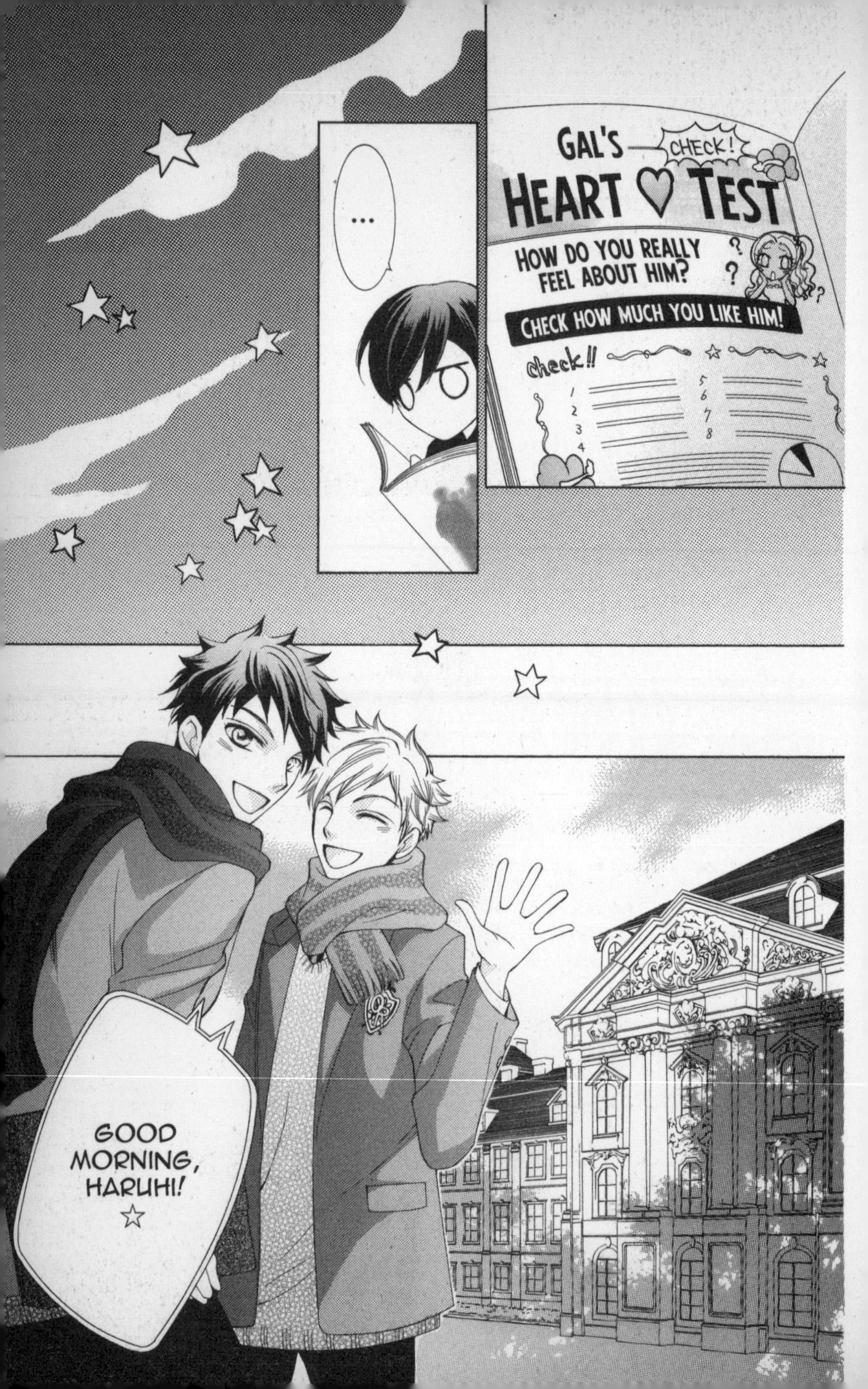
GAL'S
CHECK!
HEART ♡ TEST
HOW DO YOU REALLY FEEL ABOUT HIM?
CHECK HOW MUCH YOU LIKE HIM!
check!!
...
GOOD MORNING, HARUHI! ☆

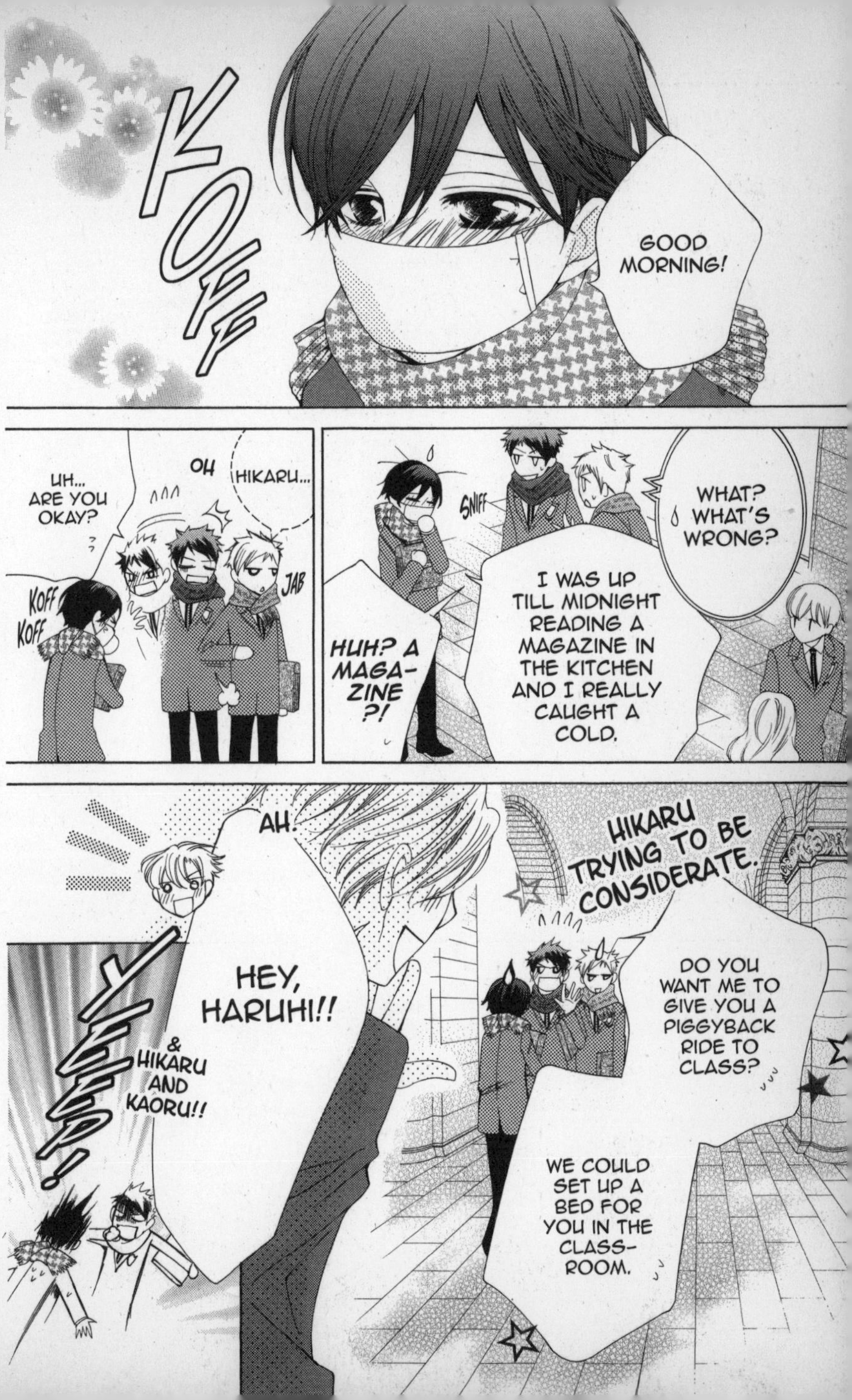
GOOD MORNING!
KOFF
WHAT? WHAT'S WRONG?
SNIFF
I WAS UP TILL MIDNIGHT READING A MAGAZINE IN THE KITCHEN AND I REALLY CAUGHT A COLD.
HUH? A MAGA-ZINE?!
HIKARU...
OH
UH... ARE YOU OKAY?
JAB
KOFF KOFF
HIKARU TRYING TO BE CONSIDERATE.
AH.
DO YOU WANT ME TO GIVE YOU A PIGGYBACK RIDE TO CLASS?
WE COULD SET UP A BED FOR YOU IN THE CLASS-ROOM.
HEY, HARUHI!!
& HIKARU AND KAORU!!

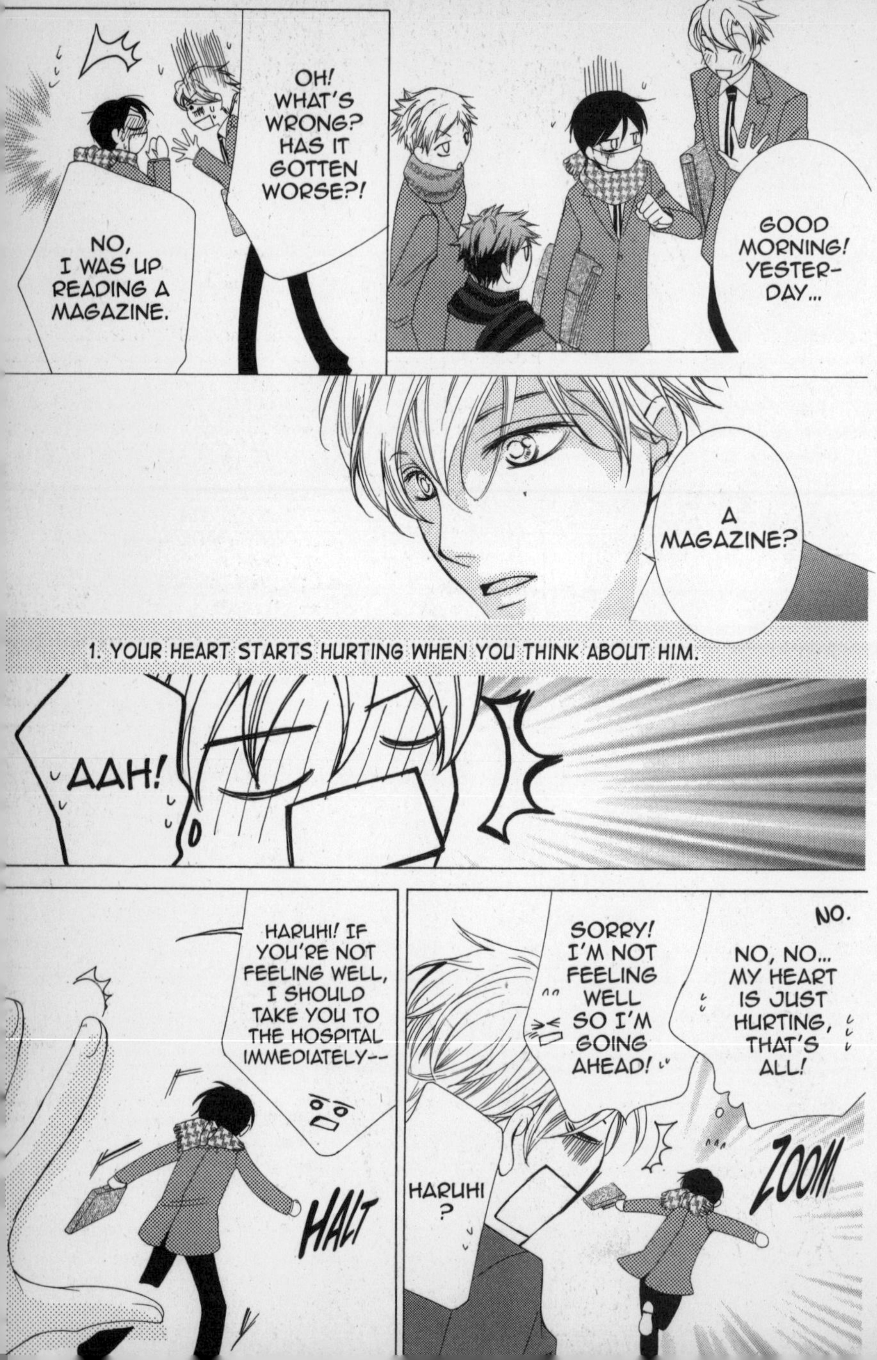
GOOD MORNING! YESTER-DAY...
OH! WHAT'S WRONG? HAS IT GOTTEN WORSE?!
NO, I WAS UP READING A MAGAZINE.
A MAGAZINE?
1. YOUR HEART STARTS HURTING WHEN YOU THINK ABOUT HIM.
AAH!
NO.
NO, NO... MY HEART IS JUST HURTING, THAT'S ALL!
SORRY! I'M NOT FEELING WELL SO I'M GOING AHEAD!
HARUHI?
ZOOM
HARUHI! IF YOU'RE NOT FEELING WELL, I SHOULD TAKE YOU TO THE HOSPITAL IMMEDIATELY--
HALT

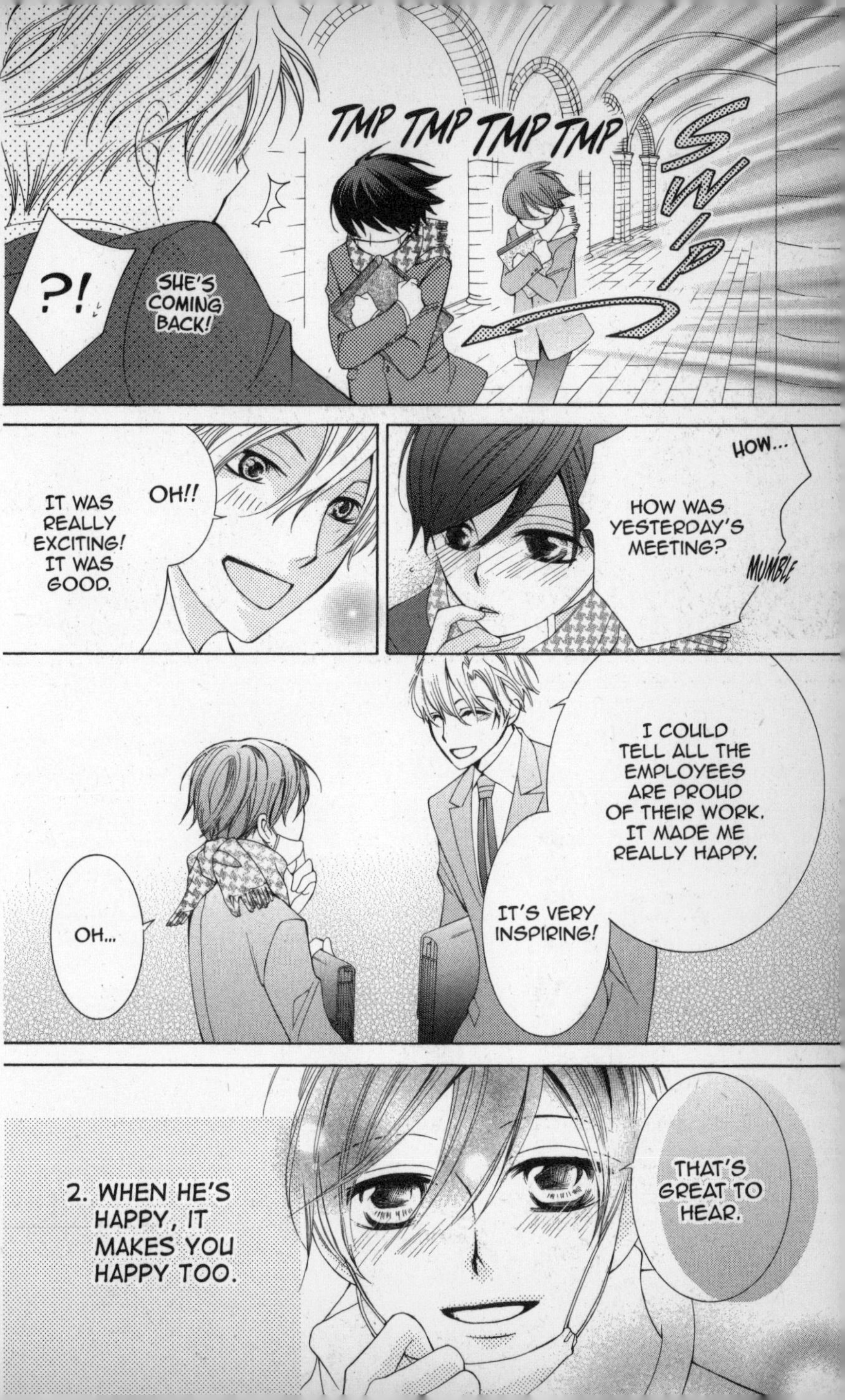
SWIP
TMP TMP TMP TMP
SHE'S COMING BACK!
?!
HOW...
HOW WAS YESTERDAY'S MEETING?
MUMBLE
OH!!
IT WAS REALLY EXCITING! IT WAS GOOD.
I COULD TELL ALL THE EMPLOYEES ARE PROUD OF THEIR WORK. IT MADE ME REALLY HAPPY.
IT'S VERY INSPIRING!
OH...
THAT'S GREAT TO HEAR.
2. WHEN HE'S HAPPY, IT MAKES YOU HAPPY TOO.

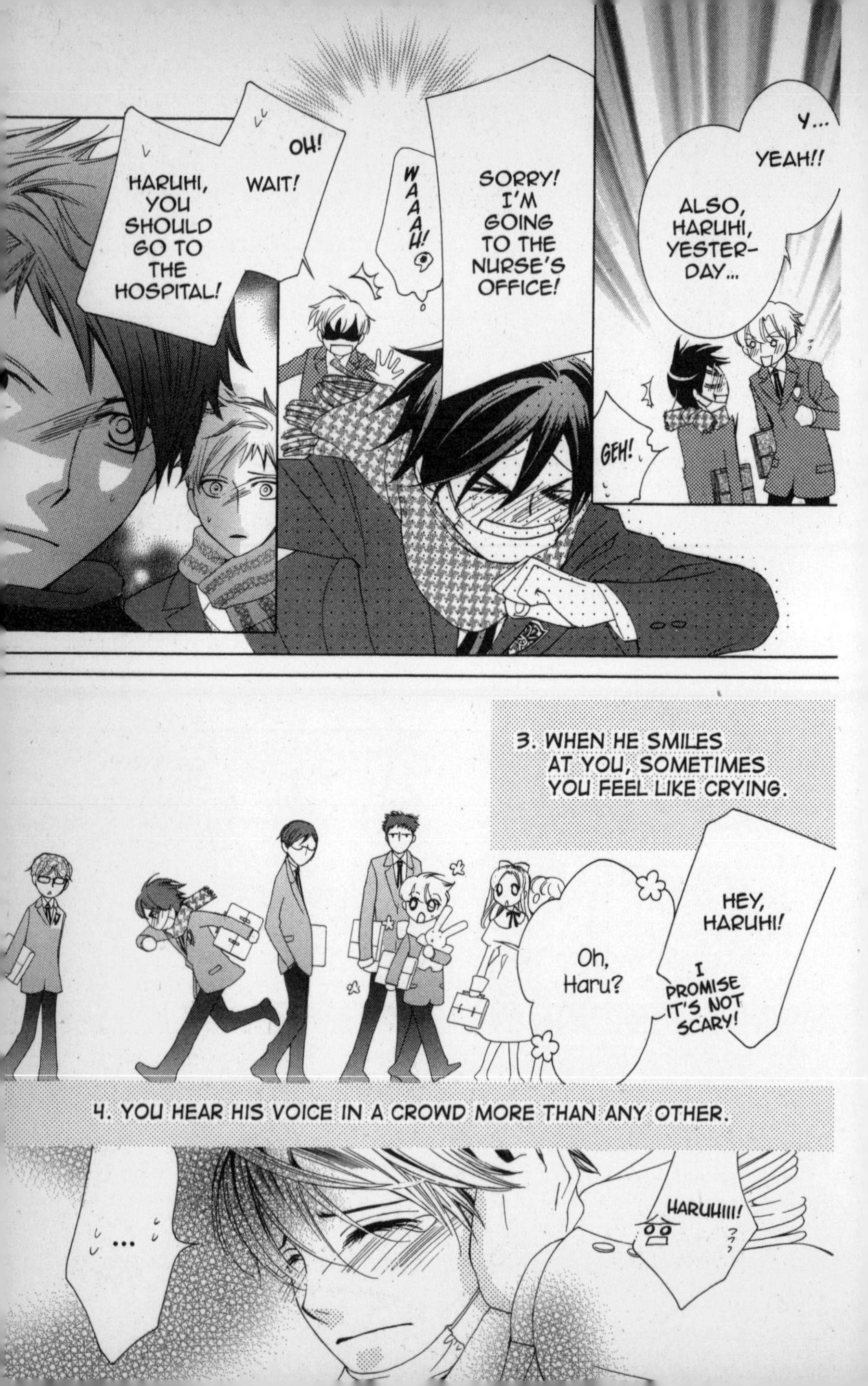
Y... YEAH!!
ALSO, HARUHI, YESTER-DAY...
GEH!
SORRY! I'M GOING TO THE NURSE'S OFFICE!
WAAAAH!
OH! WAIT!
HARUHI, YOU SHOULD GO TO THE HOSPITAL!
3. WHEN HE SMILES AT YOU, SOMETIMES YOU FEEL LIKE CRYING.
HEY, HARUHI!
I PROMISE IT'S NOT SCARY!
Oh, Haru?
4. YOU HEAR HIS VOICE IN A CROWD MORE THAN ANY OTHER.
HARUHIII!
...

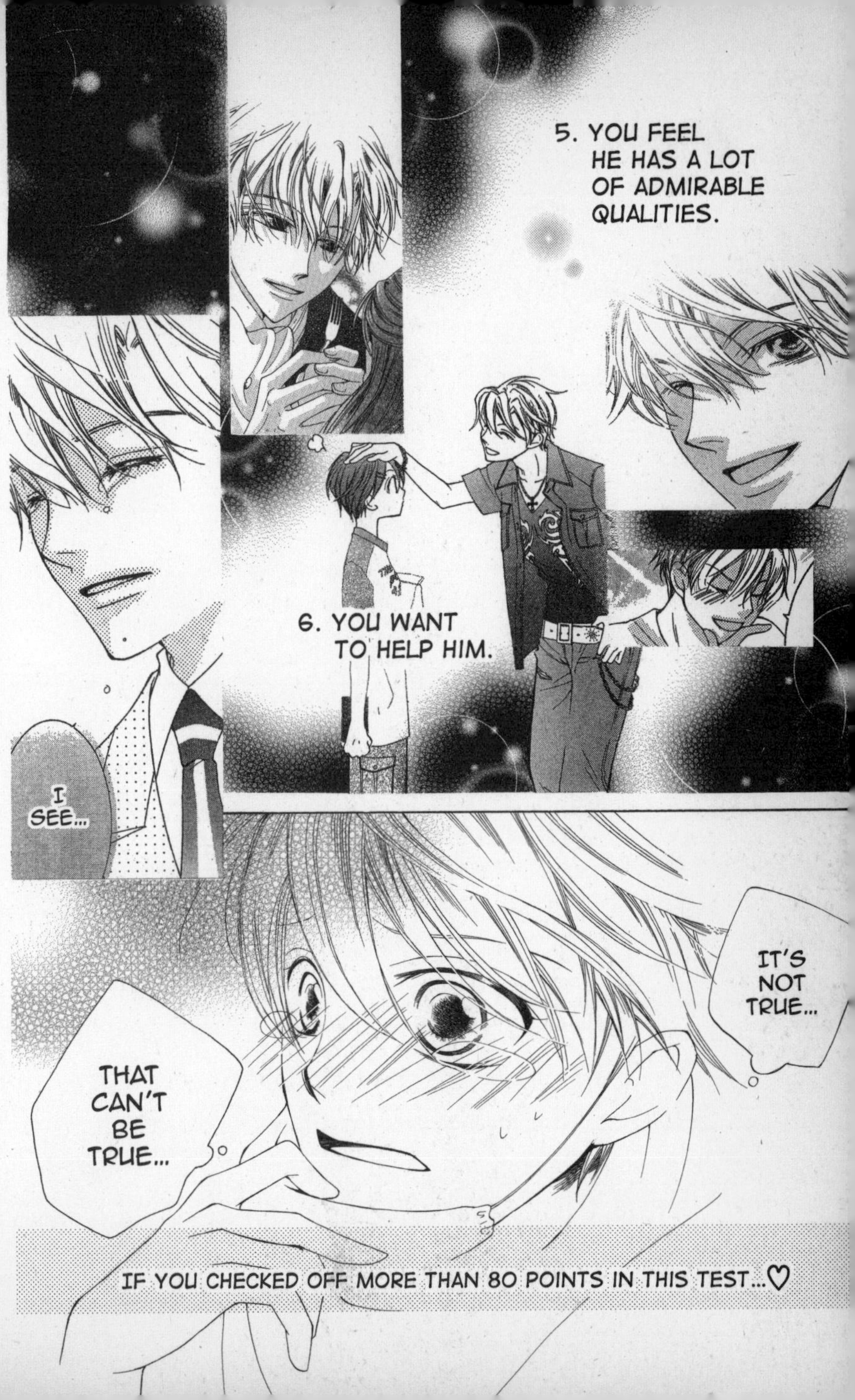
5. YOU FEEL HE HAS A LOT OF ADMIRABLE QUALITIES.
6. YOU WANT TO HELP HIM.
I SEE...
IT'S NOT TRUE...
THAT CAN'T BE TRUE...
IF YOU CHECKED OFF MORE THAN 80 POINTS IN THIS TEST...♡

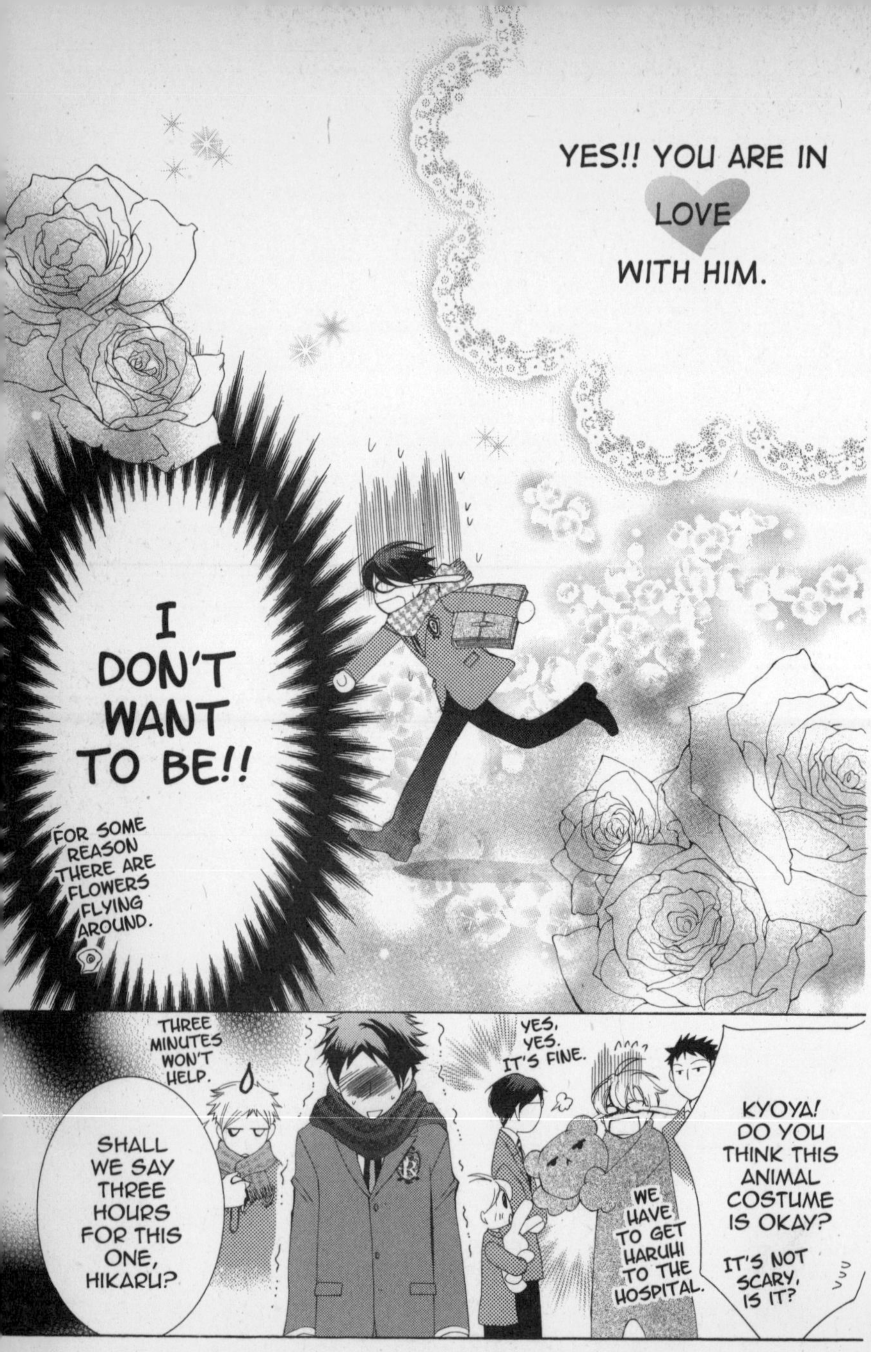
YES!! YOU ARE IN LOVE WITH HIM.
I DON'T WANT TO BE!!
FOR SOME REASON THERE ARE FLOWERS FLYING AROUND.
KYOYA! DO YOU THINK THIS ANIMAL COSTUME IS OKAY?
IT'S NOT SCARY, IS IT?
YES, YES. IT'S FINE.
WE HAVE TO GET HARUHI TO THE HOSPITAL.
THREE MINUTES WON'T HELP.
SHALL WE SAY THREE HOURS FOR THIS ONE, HIKARU?

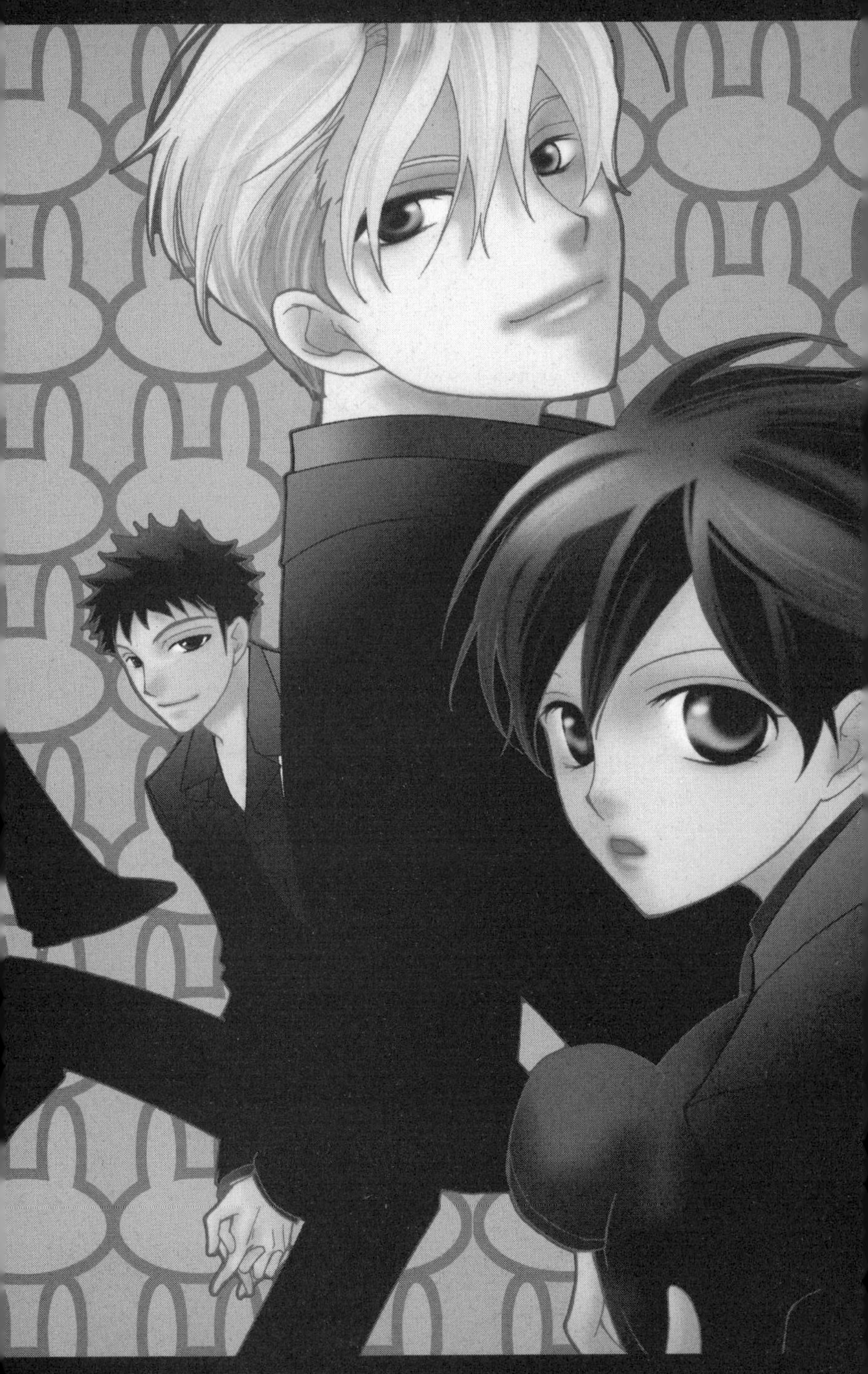

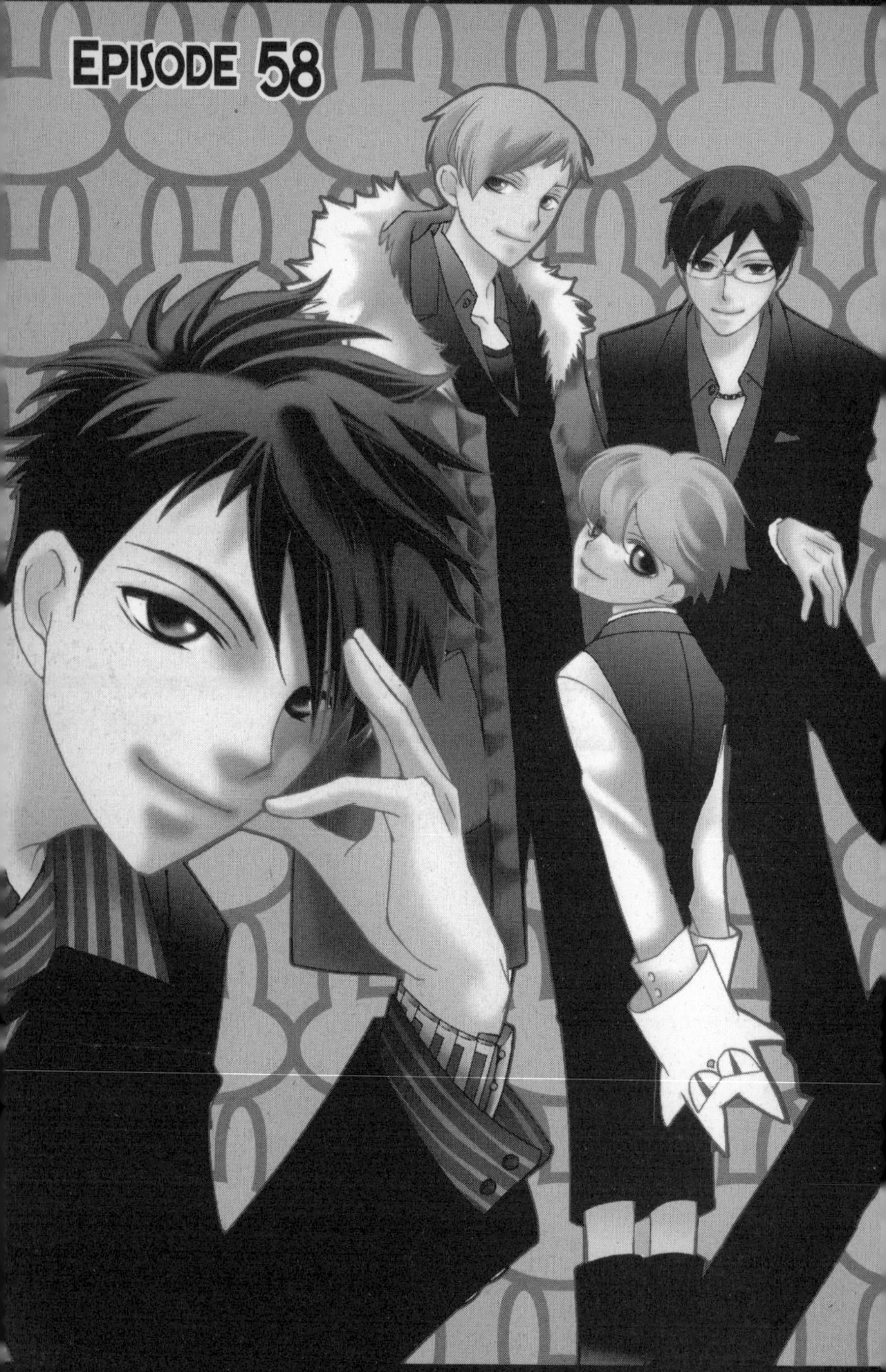
EPISODE 58

GUEST ROOM: FAXES

SPECIAL THANKS TO NARI KUSAKAWA!!
(SECOND APPEARANCE)

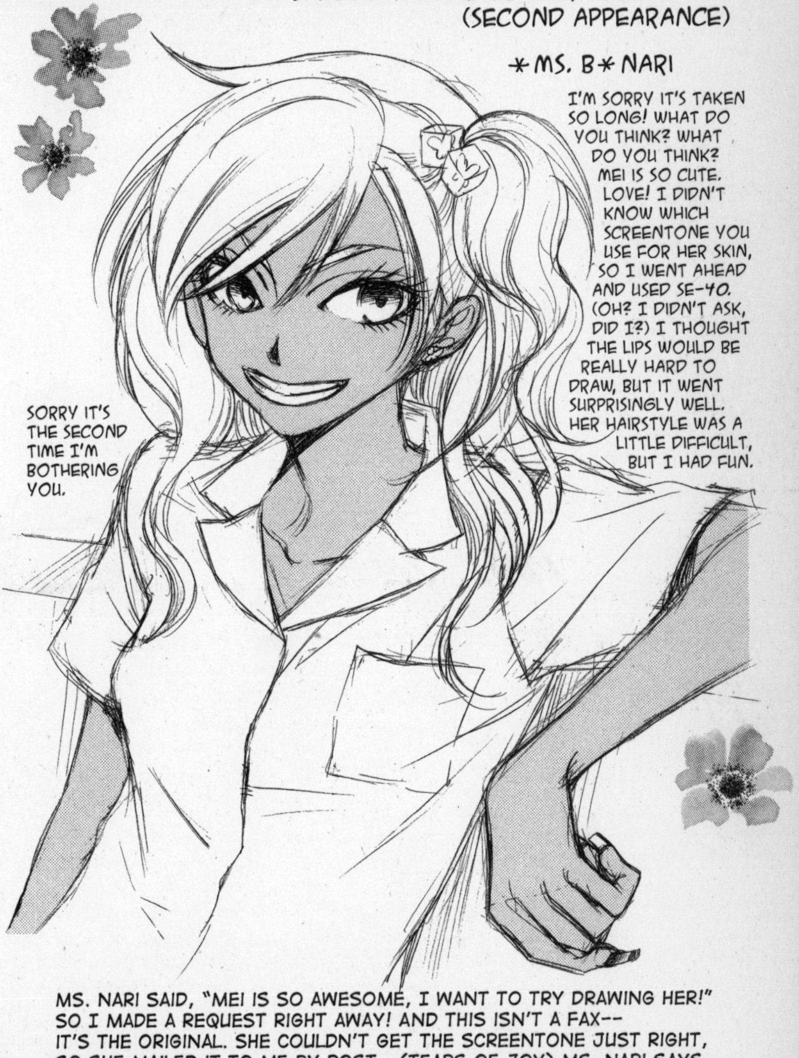
MS. B NARI
I'M SORRY IT'S TAKEN SO LONG! WHAT DO YOU THINK? WHAT DO YOU THINK? MEI IS SO CUTE. LOVE! I DIDN'T KNOW WHICH SCREENTONE YOU USE FOR HER SKIN, SO I WENT AHEAD AND USED SE-40. (OH? I DIDN'T ASK, DID I?) I THOUGHT THE LIPS WOULD BE REALLY HARD TO DRAW, BUT IT WENT SURPRISINGLY WELL. HER HAIRSTYLE WAS A LITTLE DIFFICULT, BUT I HAD FUN.
SORRY IT'S THE SECOND TIME I'M BOTHERING YOU.

MS. NARI SAID, "MEI IS SO AWESOME, I WANT TO TRY DRAWING HER!" SO I MADE A REQUEST RIGHT AWAY! AND THIS ISN'T A FAX-- IT'S THE ORIGINAL. SHE COULDN'T GET THE SCREENTONE JUST RIGHT, SO SHE MAILED IT TO ME BY POST... (TEARS OF JOY) MS. NARI SAYS, "MY PERSONALITY LOST IN THE FACE OF MEI'S UNIQUENESS." THANKS FOR THE CUTE MEI!! BY THE WAY, THE SCREENTONE FOR HER SKIN IS SE-51! (SO CLOSE.)

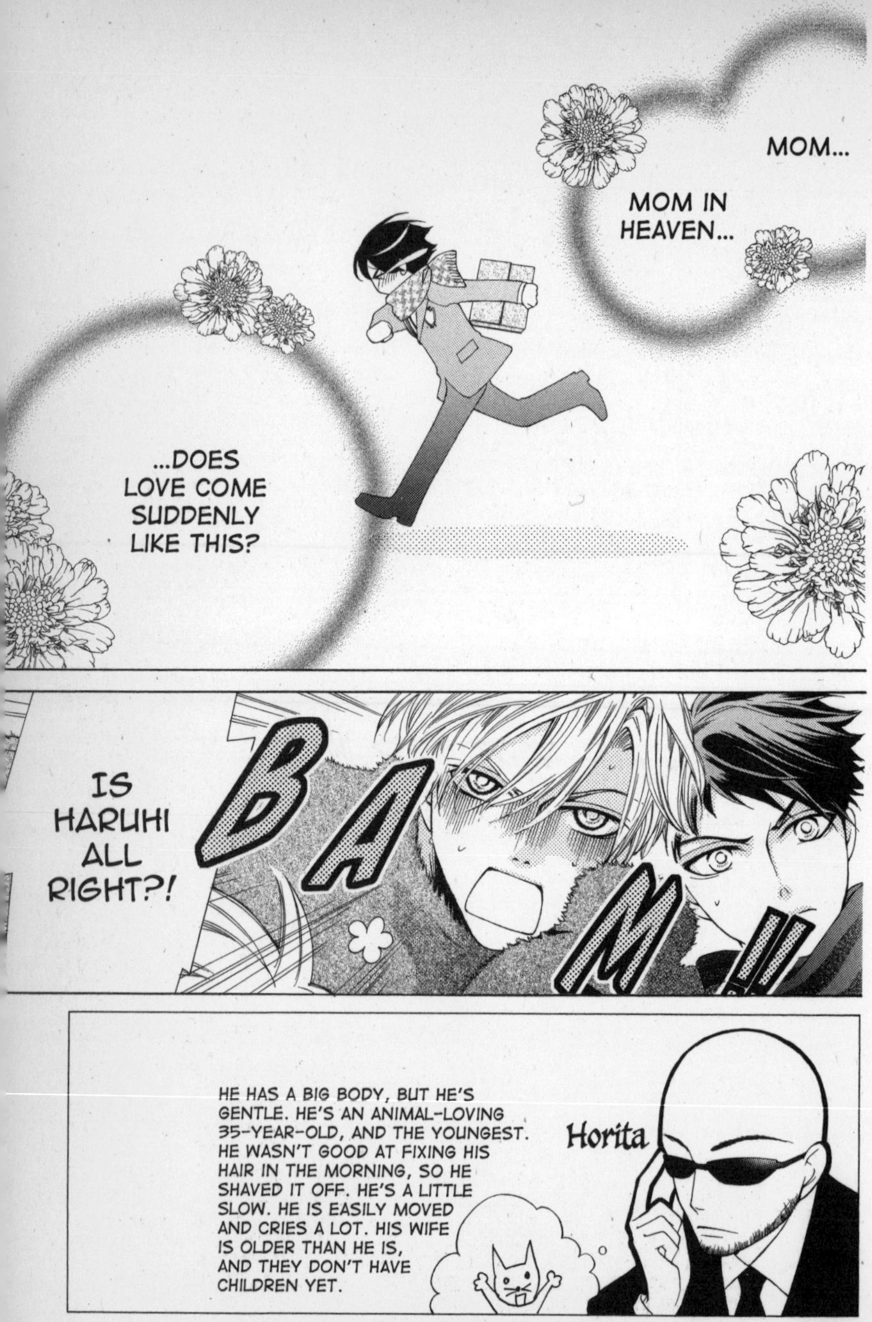
MOM...
MOM IN HEAVEN...
...DOES LOVE COME SUDDENLY LIKE THIS?
BAM!!
IS HARUHI ALL RIGHT?!
Horita
HE HAS A BIG BODY, BUT HE'S GENTLE. HE'S AN ANIMAL-LOVING 35-YEAR-OLD, AND THE YOUNGEST. HE WASN'T GOOD AT FIXING HIS HAIR IN THE MORNING, SO HE SHAVED IT OFF. HE'S A LITTLE SLOW. HE IS EASILY MOVED AND CRIES A LOT. HIS WIFE IS OLDER THAN HE IS, AND THEY DON'T HAVE CHILDREN YET.

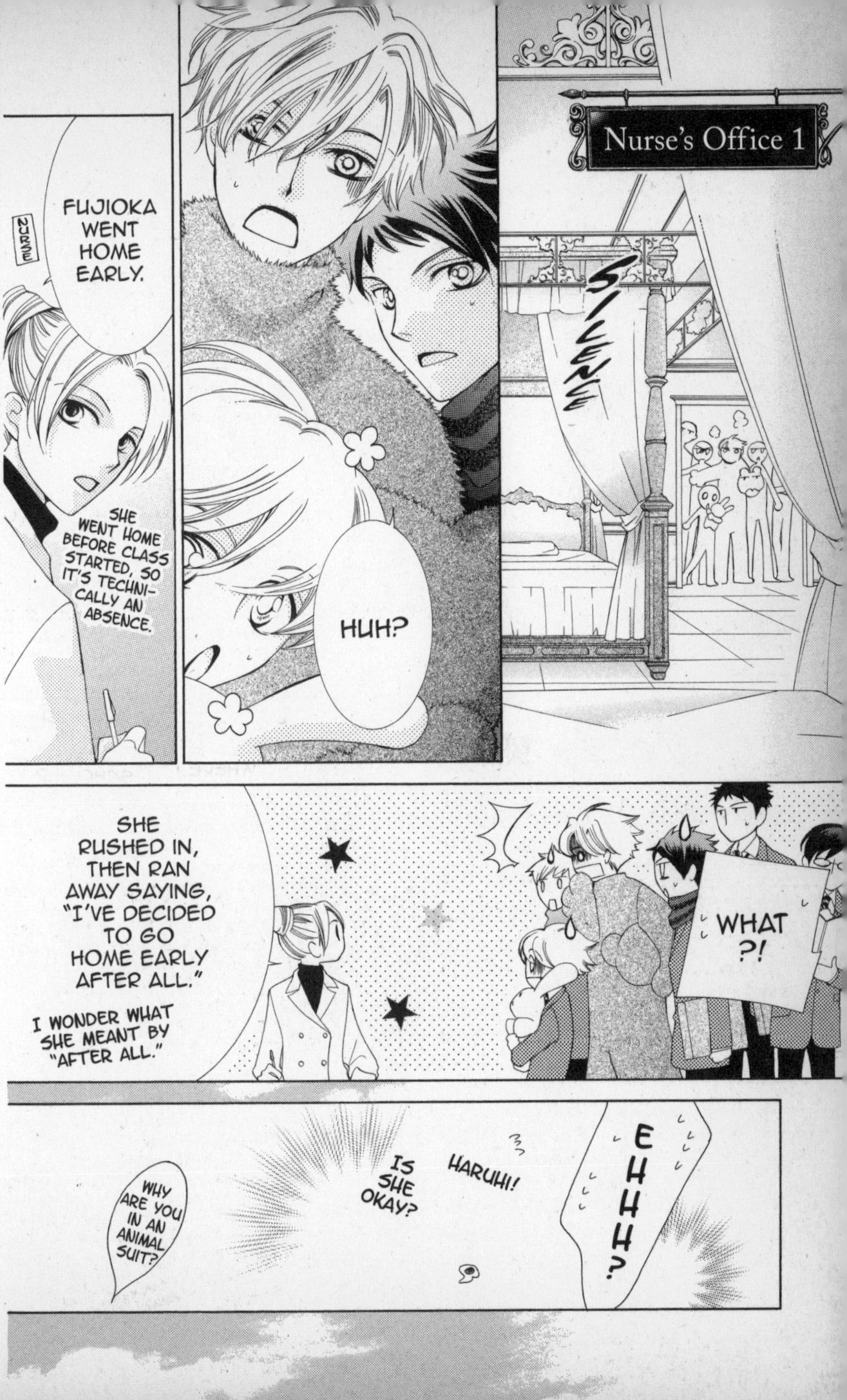
Nurse's Office 1
SILENCE
HUH?
NURSE
FUJIOKA WENT HOME EARLY.
SHE WENT HOME BEFORE CLASS STARTED, SO IT'S TECHNICALLY AN ABSENCE.
WHAT?!
SHE RUSHED IN, THEN RAN AWAY SAYING, "I'VE DECIDED TO GO HOME EARLY AFTER ALL."
I WONDER WHAT SHE MEANT BY "AFTER ALL."
EHHH?
HARUHI!
IS SHE OKAY?
WHY ARE YOU IN AN ANIMAL SUIT?

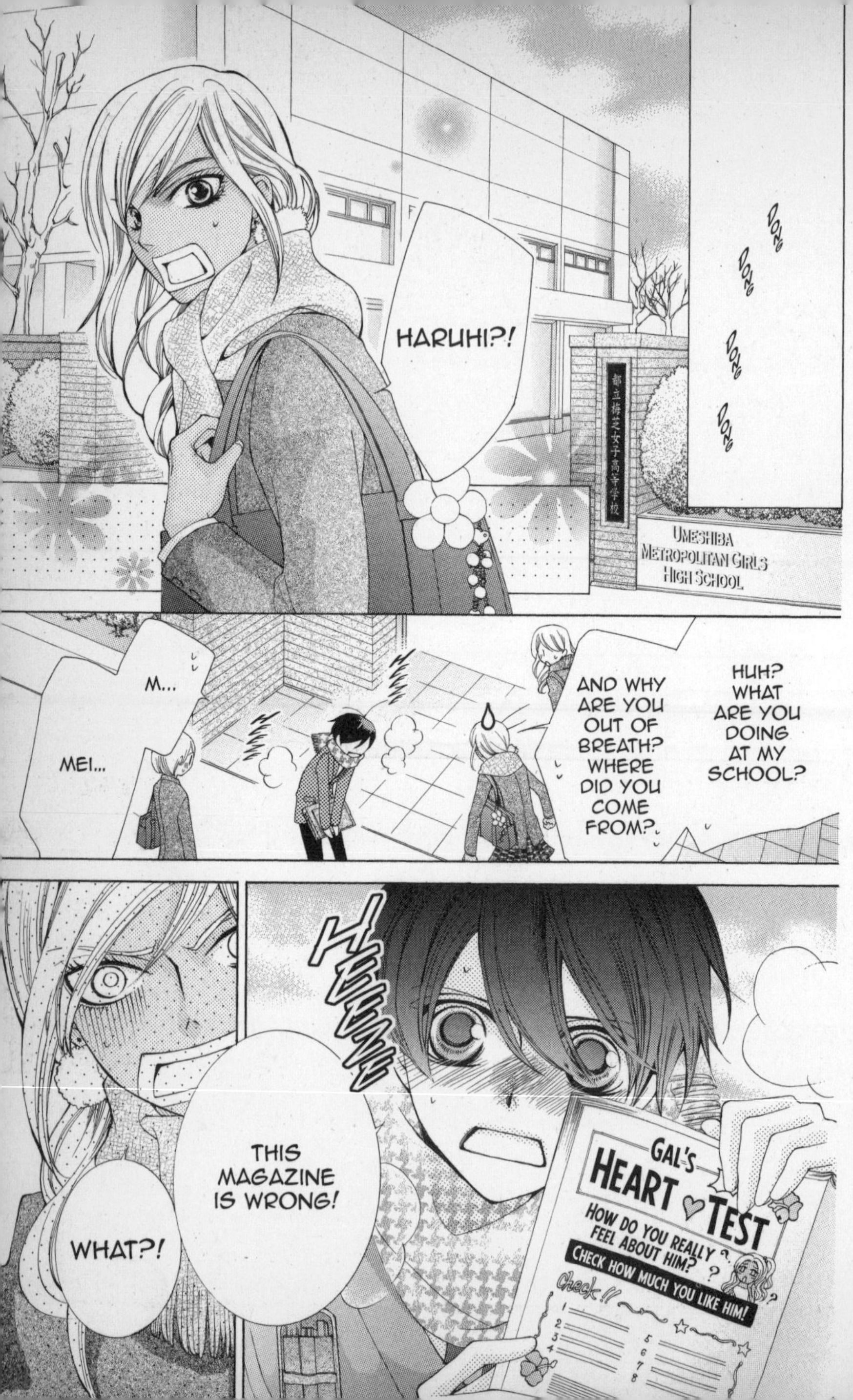
DONG
DONG
DONG
DONG
HARUHI?!
都立梅芝女子高等学校
UMESHIBA METROPOLITAN GIRLS HIGH SCHOOL
HUH? WHAT ARE YOU DOING AT MY SCHOOL?
AND WHY ARE YOU OUT OF BREATH? WHERE DID YOU COME FROM?
M...
MEI...
GAL'S HEART TEST
HOW DO YOU REALLY FEEL ABOUT HIM?
CHECK HOW MUCH YOU LIKE HIM!
Check!!
THIS MAGAZINE IS WRONG!
WHAT?!

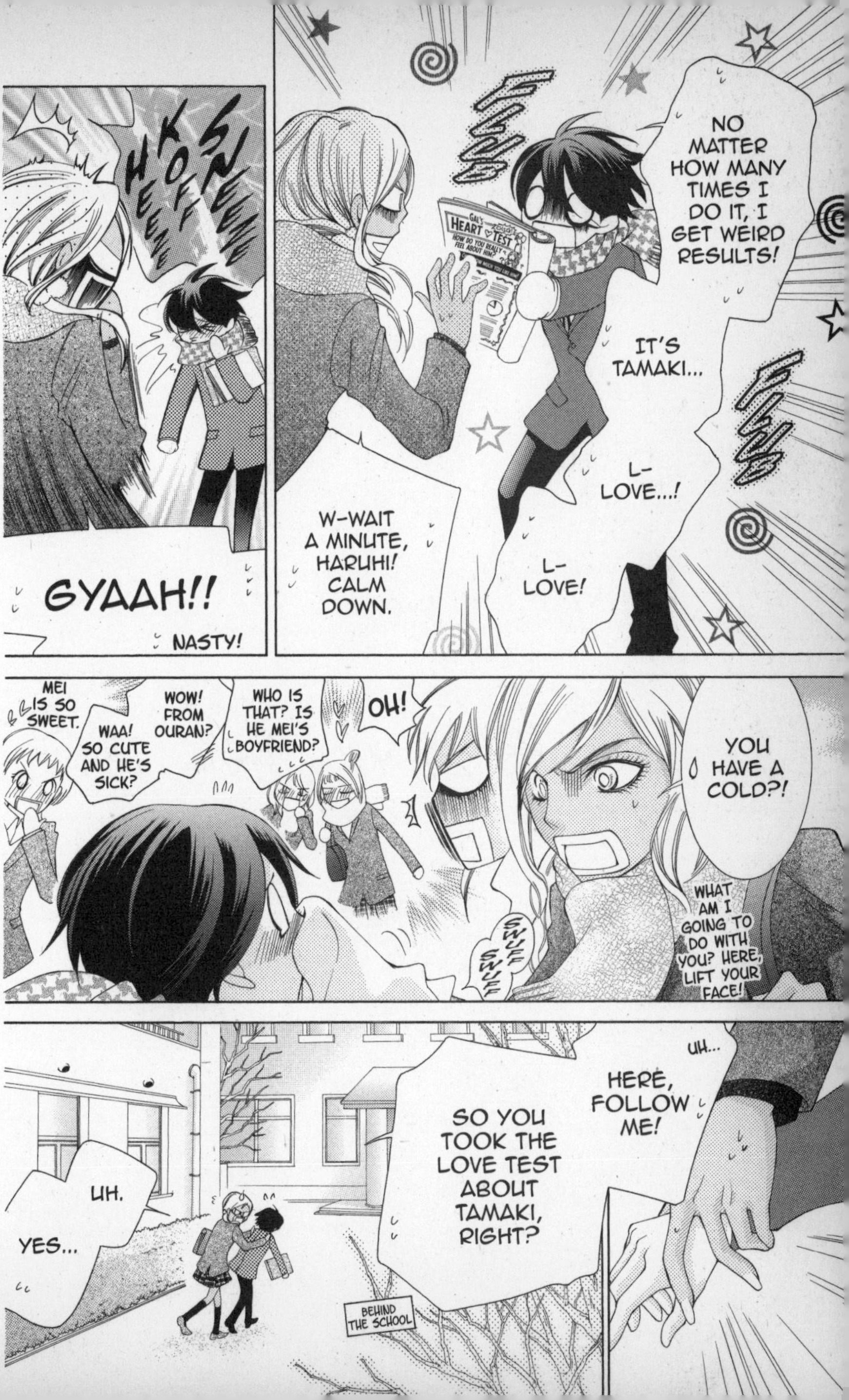
NO MATTER HOW MANY TIMES I DO IT, I GET WEIRD RESULTS!
GAL'S HEART TEST
HOW DO YOU REALLY FEEL ABOUT HIM?
IT'S TAMAKI...
L-LOVE...!
L-LOVE!
W-WAIT A MINUTE, HARUHI! CALM DOWN.
GYAAH!!
NASTY!
YOU HAVE A COLD?!
WHAT AM I GOING TO DO WITH YOU? HERE, LIFT YOUR FACE!
SWUFF SWUFF
OH!
WHO IS THAT? IS HE MEI'S BOYFRIEND?
WOW! FROM OURAN?
WAA! SO CUTE AND HE'S SICK?
MEI IS SO SWEET.
HERE, FOLLOW ME!
UH...
BEHIND THE SCHOOL
SO YOU TOOK THE LOVE TEST ABOUT TAMAKI, RIGHT?
UH.
YES...

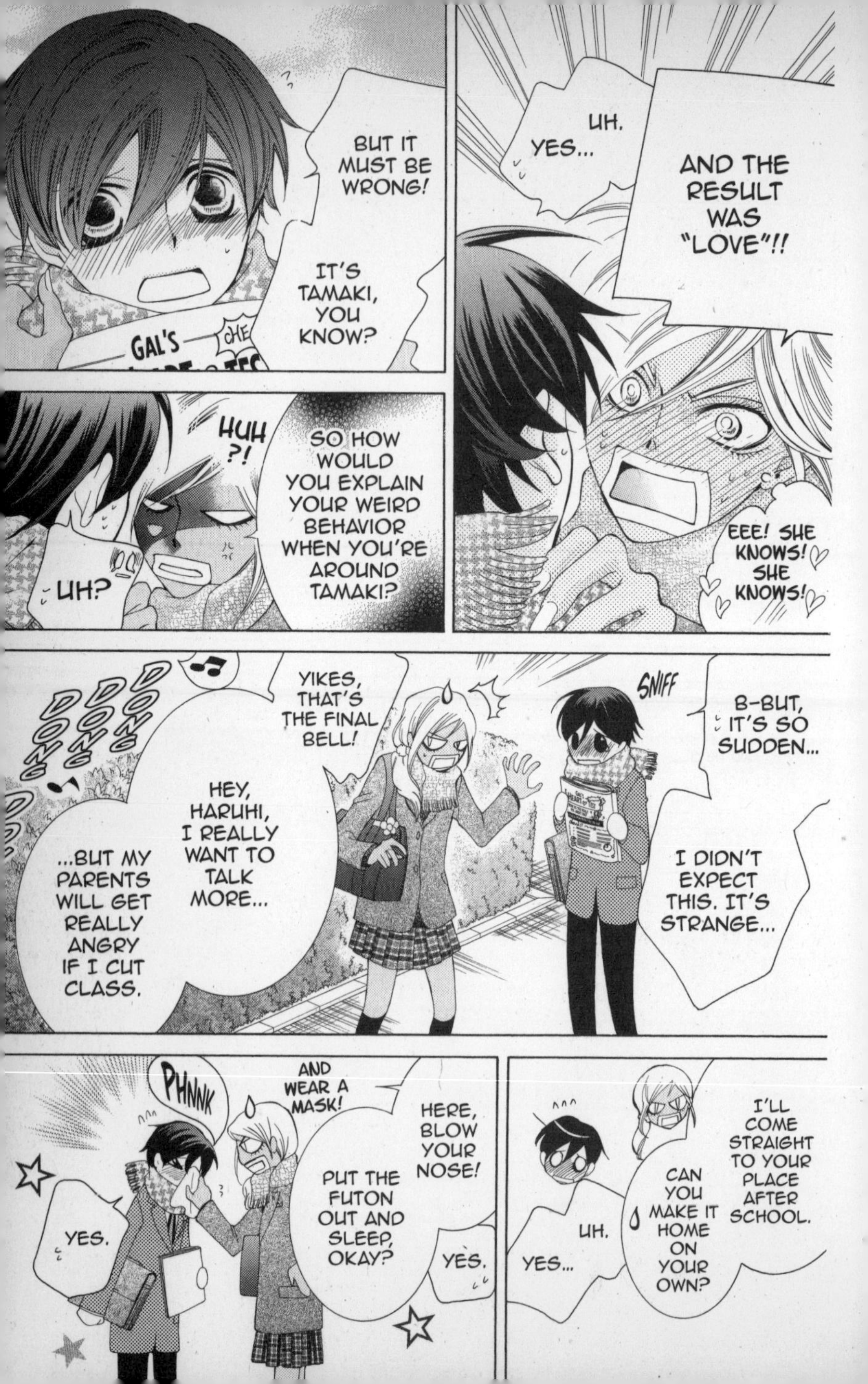
AND THE RESULT WAS "LOVE"!!
UH. YES...
EEE! SHE KNOWS! SHE KNOWS!
BUT IT MUST BE WRONG!
IT'S TAMAKI, YOU KNOW?
GAL'S
SO HOW WOULD YOU EXPLAIN YOUR WEIRD BEHAVIOR WHEN YOU'RE AROUND TAMAKI?
HUH ?!
UH?
SNIFF
B-BUT, IT'S SO SUDDEN...
I DIDN'T EXPECT THIS. IT'S STRANGE...
YIKES, THAT'S THE FINAL BELL!
HEY, HARUHI, I REALLY WANT TO TALK MORE...
...BUT MY PARENTS WILL GET REALLY ANGRY IF I CUT CLASS.
DONG DONG DONG
I'LL COME STRAIGHT TO YOUR PLACE AFTER SCHOOL.
CAN YOU MAKE IT HOME ON YOUR OWN?
UH. YES...
HERE, BLOW YOUR NOSE!
AND WEAR A MASK!
PUT THE FUTON OUT AND SLEEP, OKAY?
YES.
PHNNK
YES.

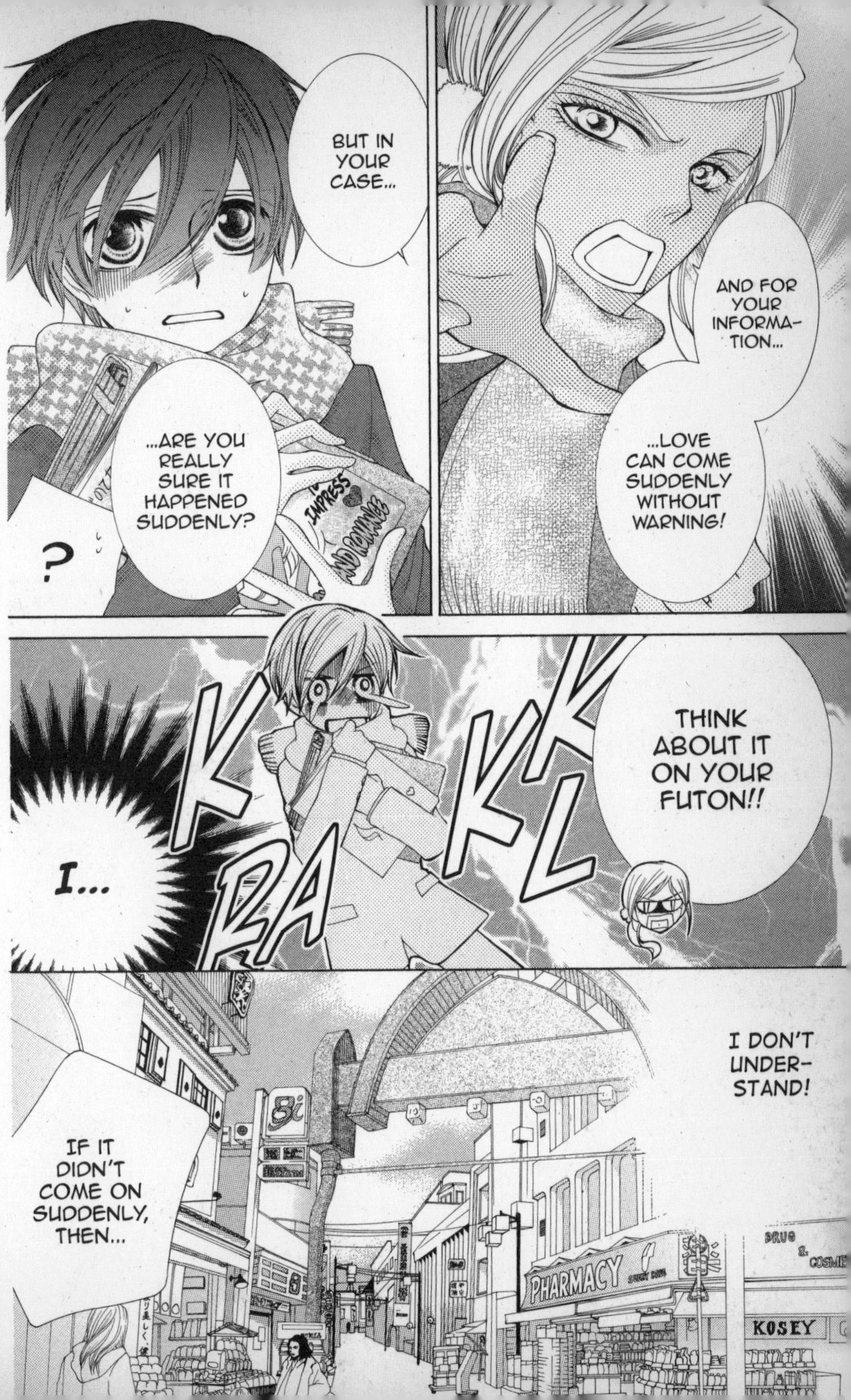
AND FOR YOUR INFORMATION...
...LOVE CAN COME SUDDENLY WITHOUT WARNING!
BUT IN YOUR CASE...
...ARE YOU REALLY SURE IT HAPPENED SUDDENLY?
?
THINK ABOUT IT ON YOUR FUTON!!
KRAKKL
I...
I DON'T UNDERSTAND!
IF IT DIDN'T COME ON SUDDENLY, THEN...
DRUG & COSME
PHARMACY
KOSEY

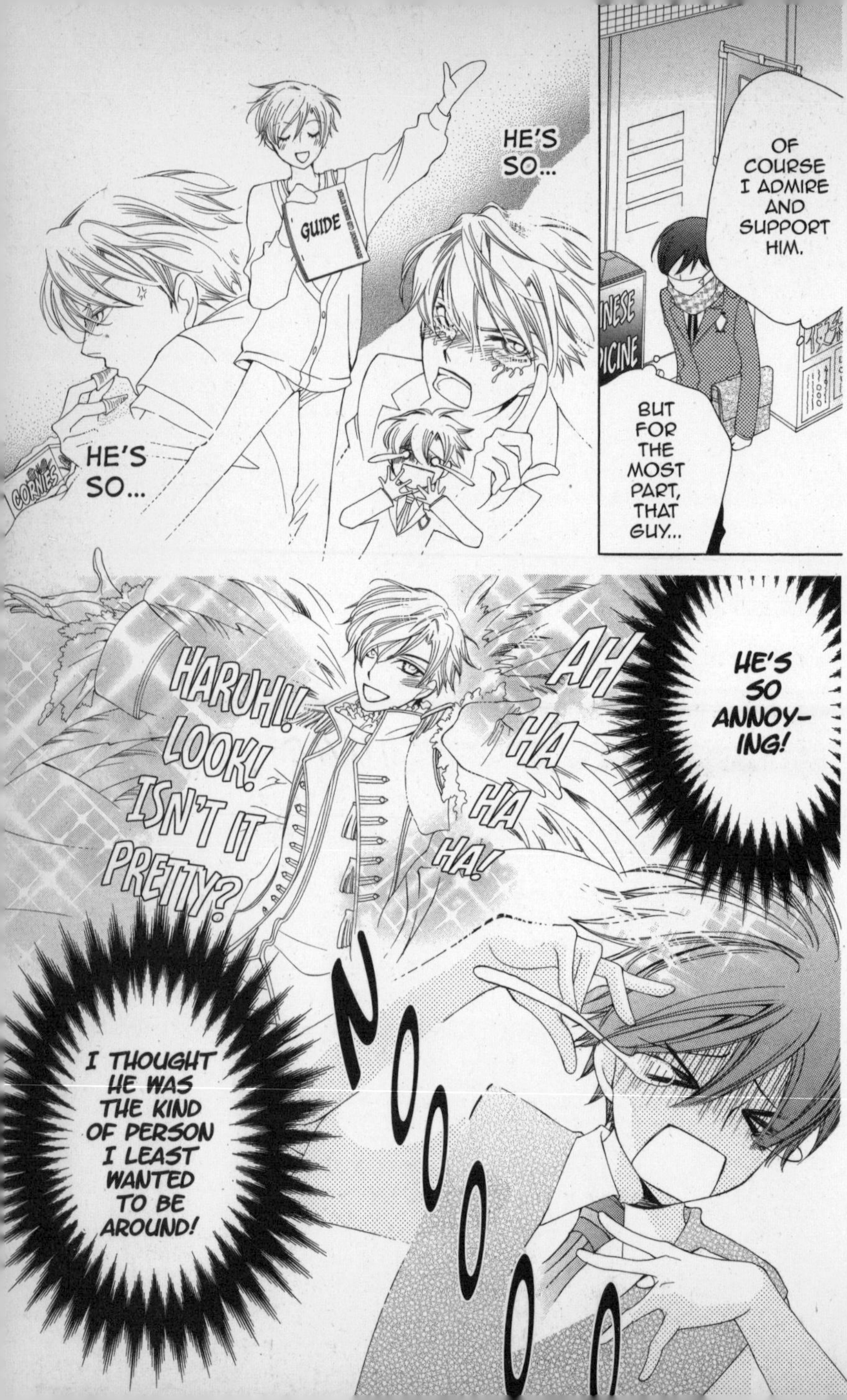

OF COURSE I ADMIRE AND SUPPORT HIM.
BUT FOR THE MOST PART, THAT GUY...
HE'S SO...
GUIDE
HE'S SO...
CORNIES
HE'S SO ANNOY-ING!
AH HA HA HA!
HARUHI! LOOK! ISN'T IT PRETTY?
ZOOOOOOO
I THOUGHT HE WAS THE KIND OF PERSON I LEAST WANTED TO BE AROUND!

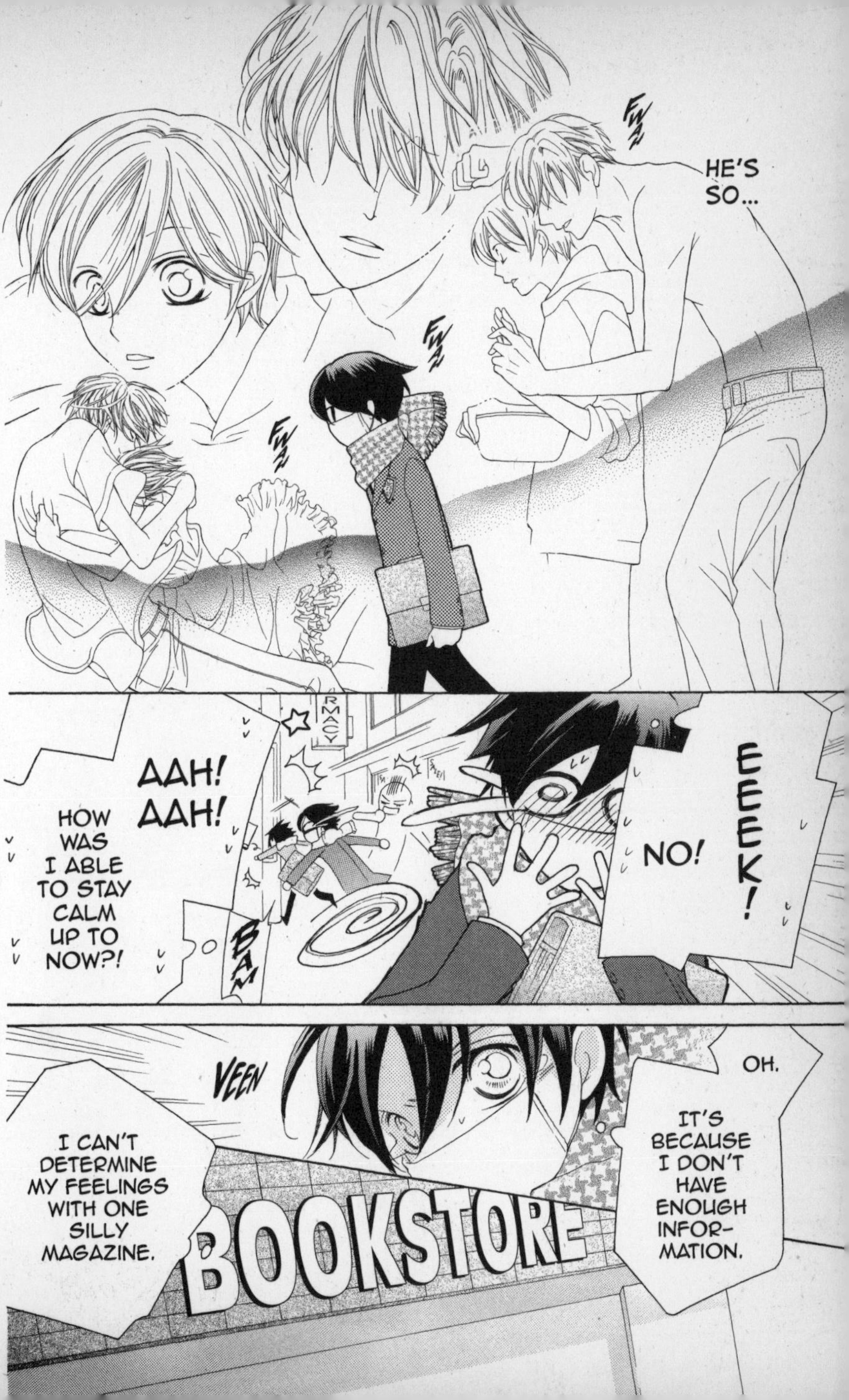
FWA
FWA
FWA
HE'S SO...
EEEK!
NO!
AAH! AAH!
HOW WAS I ABLE TO STAY CALM UP TO NOW?!
BAM
RMACY
VEEN
OH.
IT'S BECAUSE I DON'T HAVE ENOUGH INFOR-MATION.
I CAN'T DETERMINE MY FEELINGS WITH ONE SILLY MAGAZINE.
BOOKSTORE

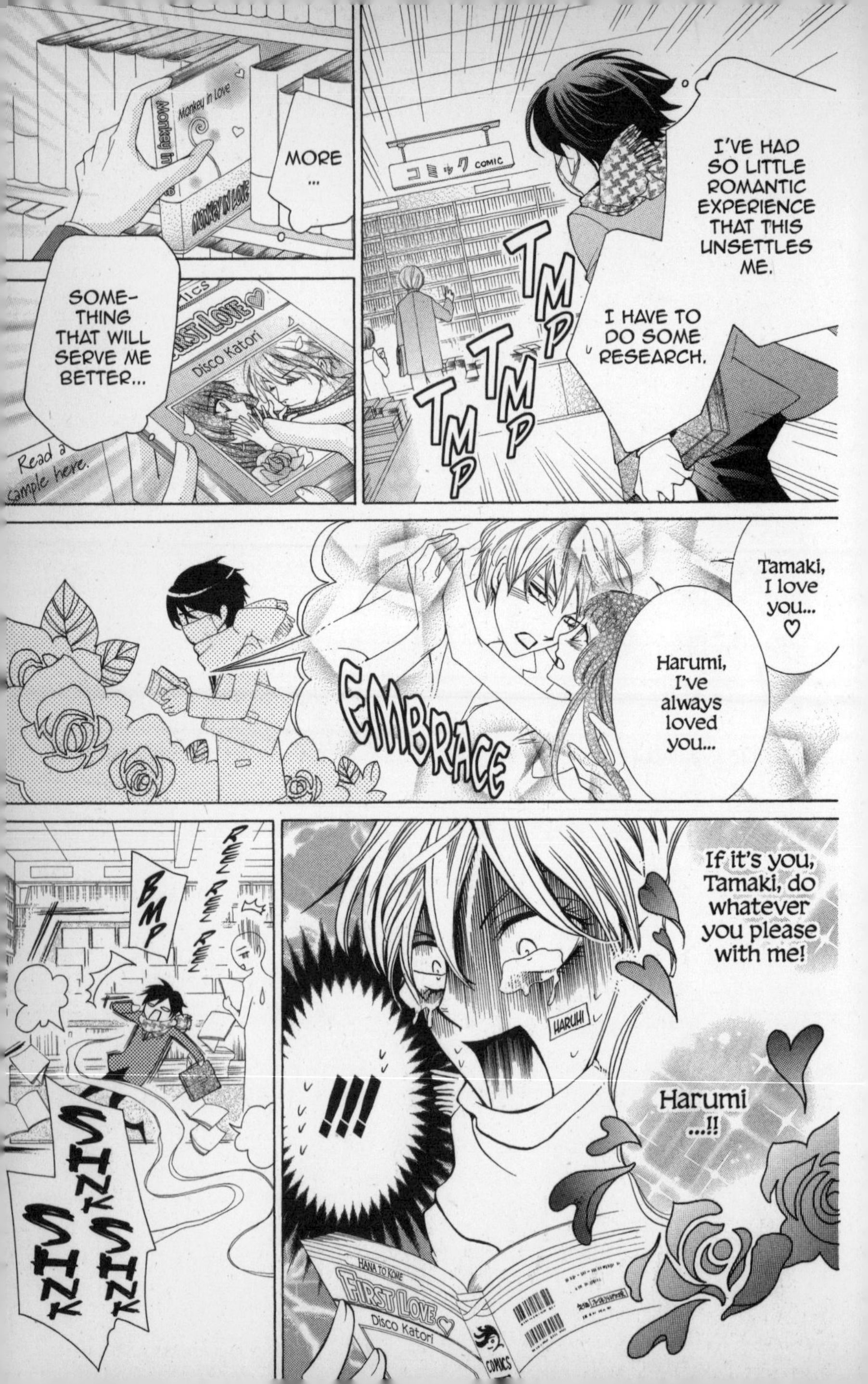
コミック COMIC
I'VE HAD SO LITTLE ROMANTIC EXPERIENCE THAT THIS UNSETTLES ME.
I HAVE TO DO SOME RESEARCH.
TMP TMP TMP
Monkey in Love
MONKEY IN LOVE
MORE ...
SOME-THING THAT WILL SERVE ME BETTER...
FIRST LOVE ♡
Disco Katori
Read a sample here.
Tamaki, I love you... ♡
Harumi, I've always loved you...
EMBRACE
If it's you, Tamaki, do whatever you please with me!
Harumi ...!!
!!!
HARUHI
HANA TO KOME
FIRST LOVE ♡
Disco Katori
COMICS
REE REE REE
BMP
SHINK SHINK SHINK

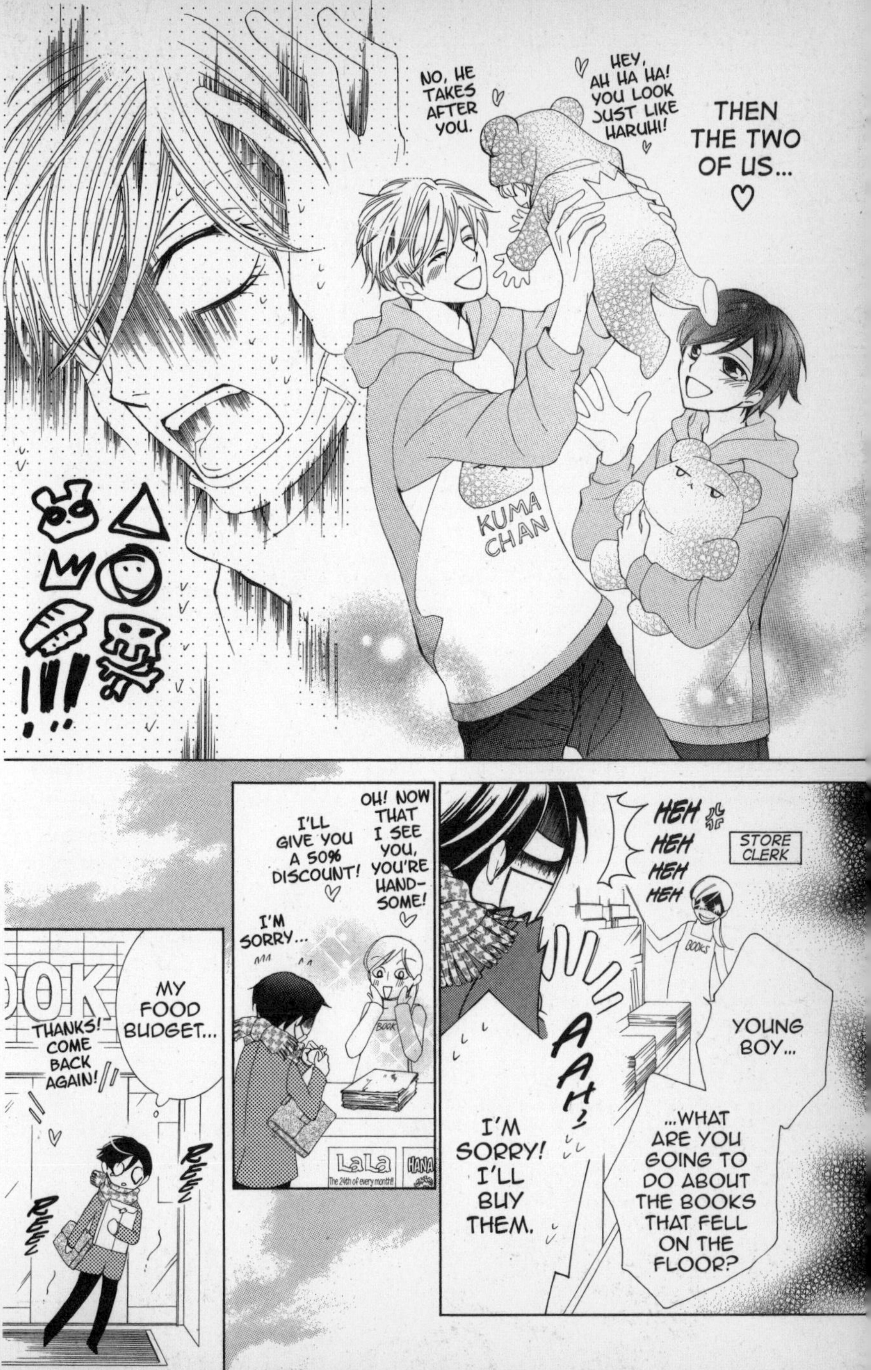
THEN THE TWO OF US... ♡
HEY, AH HA HA! YOU LOOK JUST LIKE HARUHI!
NO, HE TAKES AFTER YOU.
KUMA CHAN
!!!
HEH HEH HEH HEH
STORE CLERK
BOOKS
YOUNG BOY...
...WHAT ARE YOU GOING TO DO ABOUT THE BOOKS THAT FELL ON THE FLOOR?
AAAH!
I'M SORRY! I'LL BUY THEM.
OH! NOW THAT I SEE YOU, YOU'RE HAND-SOME!
I'LL GIVE YOU A 50% DISCOUNT!
I'M SORRY...
LaLa
The 24th of every month!!
HANA
MY FOOD BUDGET...
THANKS! COME BACK AGAIN!

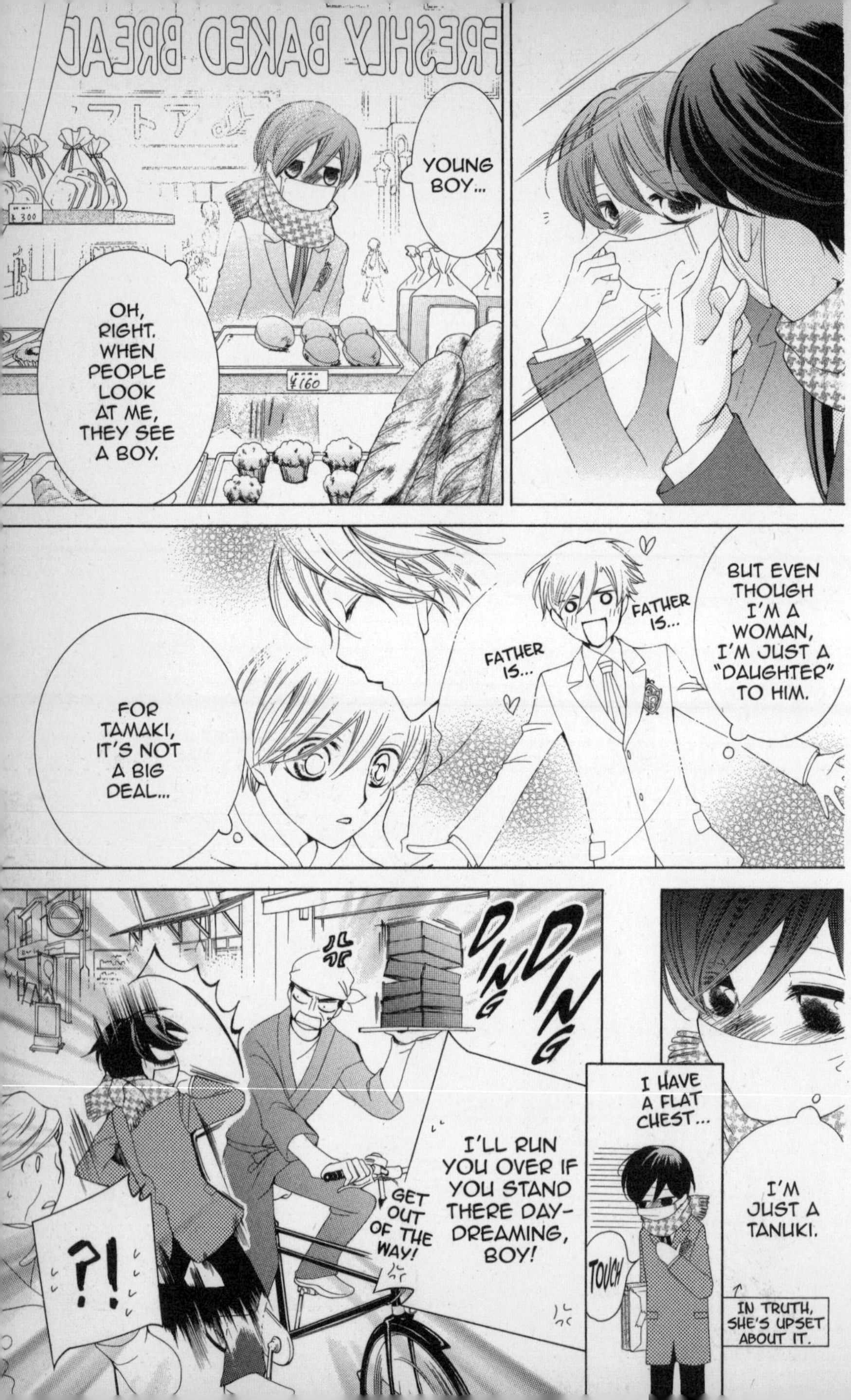
FRESHLY BAKED BREAD
YOUNG BOY...
OH, RIGHT. WHEN PEOPLE LOOK AT ME, THEY SEE A BOY.
BUT EVEN THOUGH I'M A WOMAN, I'M JUST A "DAUGHTER" TO HIM.
FATHER IS...
FATHER IS...
FOR TAMAKI, IT'S NOT A BIG DEAL...
I'M JUST A TANUKI.
IN TRUTH, SHE'S UPSET ABOUT IT.
I HAVE A FLAT CHEST...
TOUCH
DING DING
I'LL RUN YOU OVER IF YOU STAND THERE DAY-DREAMING, BOY!
GET OUT OF THE WAY!
?!

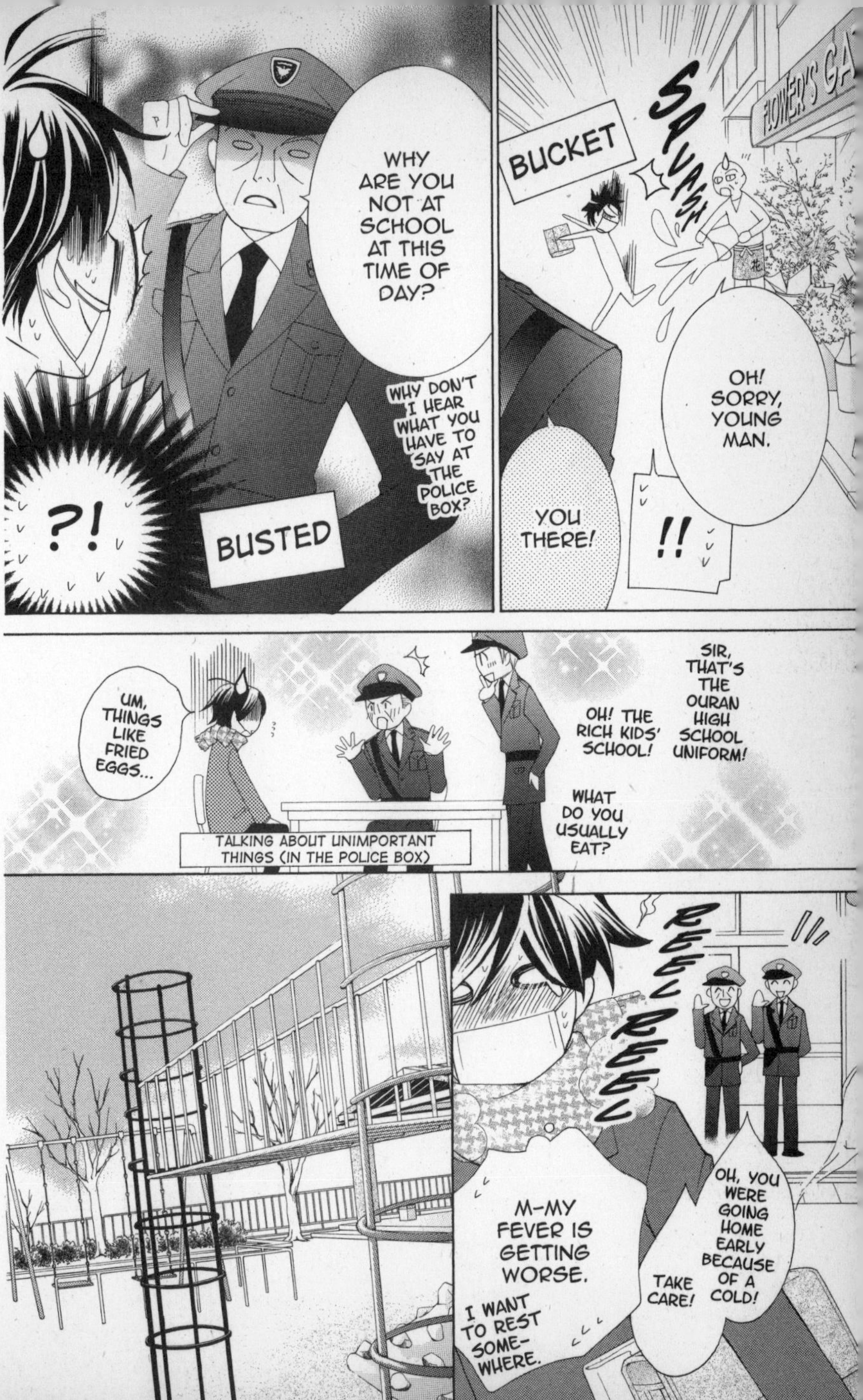
SPLASH
BUCKET
OH! SORRY, YOUNG MAN.
!!
YOU THERE!
WHY ARE YOU NOT AT SCHOOL AT THIS TIME OF DAY?
WHY DON'T I HEAR WHAT YOU HAVE TO SAY AT THE POLICE BOX?
BUSTED
?!
SIR, THAT'S THE OURAN HIGH SCHOOL UNIFORM!
OH! THE RICH KIDS' SCHOOL!
WHAT DO YOU USUALLY EAT?
UM, THINGS LIKE FRIED EGGS...
TALKING ABOUT UNIMPORTANT THINGS (IN THE POLICE BOX)
REEL REEL
OH, YOU WERE GOING HOME EARLY BECAUSE OF A COLD!
TAKE CARE!
M-MY FEVER IS GETTING WORSE.
I WANT TO REST SOME-WHERE.

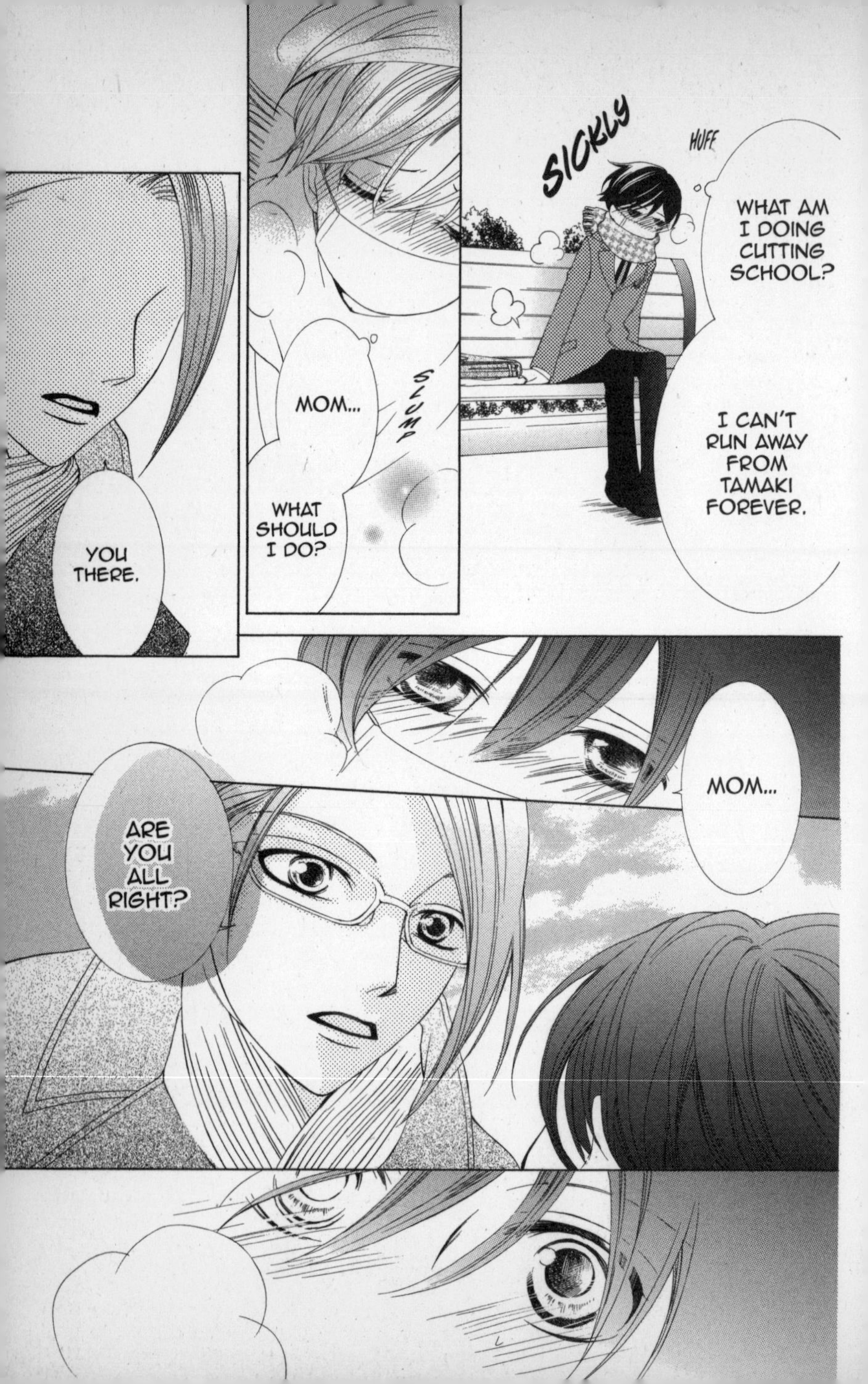
SICKLY
HUFF
WHAT AM I DOING CUTTING SCHOOL?
I CAN'T RUN AWAY FROM TAMAKI FOREVER.
SLUMP
MOM...
WHAT SHOULD I DO?
YOU THERE.
MOM...
ARE YOU ALL RIGHT?

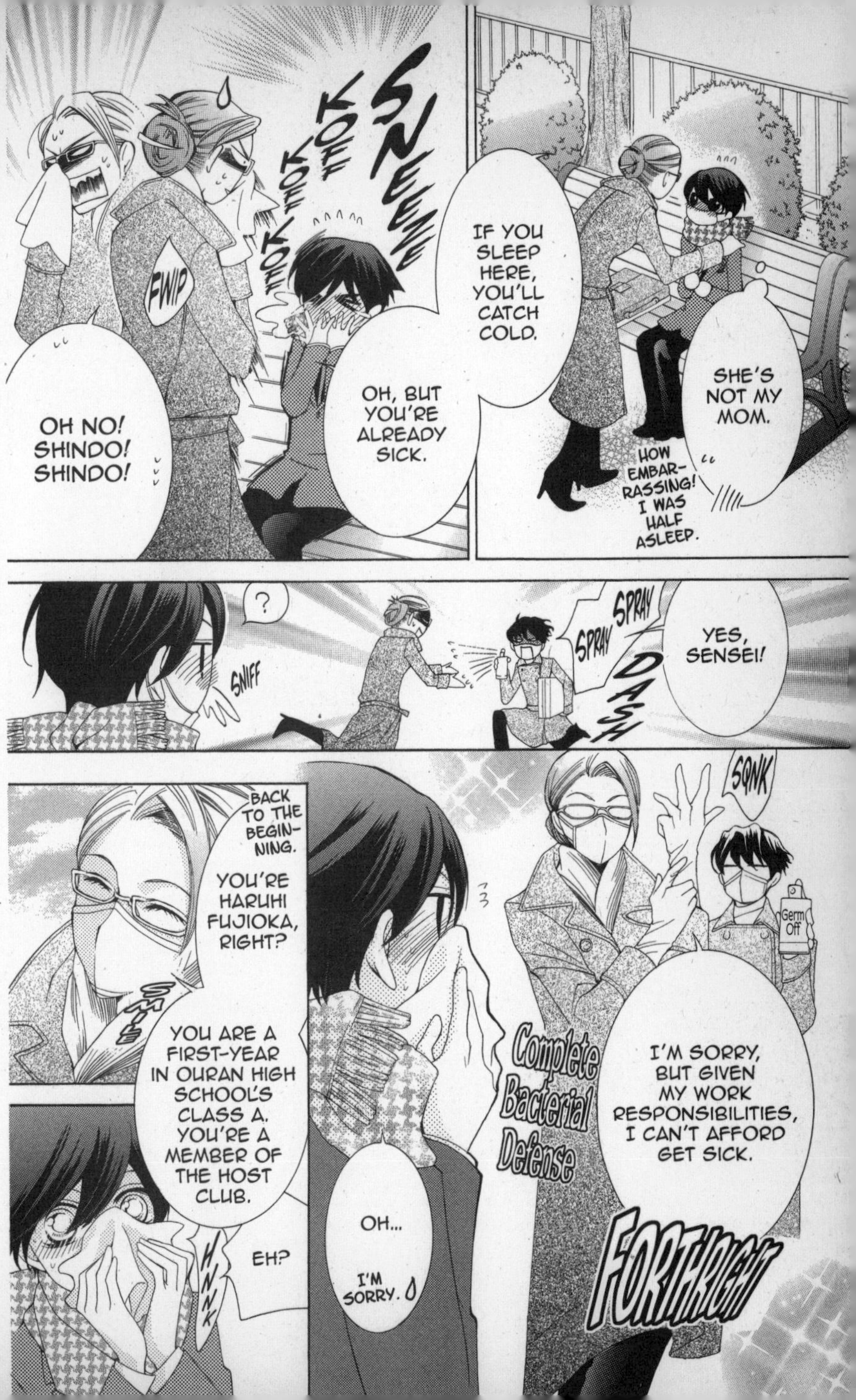
IF YOU SLEEP HERE, YOU'LL CATCH COLD.
SHE'S NOT MY MOM.
HOW EMBARRASSING! I WAS HALF ASLEEP.
SNEEEZE
KOFF KOFF KOFF KOFF
OH, BUT YOU'RE ALREADY SICK.
FWIP
OH NO! SHINDO! SHINDO!
YES, SENSEI!
SPRAY SPRAY
DASH
?
SNIFF
SQNK
Germ Off
I'M SORRY, BUT GIVEN MY WORK RESPONSIBILITIES, I CAN'T AFFORD GET SICK.
Complete Bacterial Defense
OH...
I'M SORRY.
BACK TO THE BEGIN-NING.
YOU'RE HARUHI FUJIOKA, RIGHT?
SMILE
YOU ARE A FIRST-YEAR IN OURAN HIGH SCHOOL'S CLASS A. YOU'RE A MEMBER OF THE HOST CLUB.
EH?
HNNK

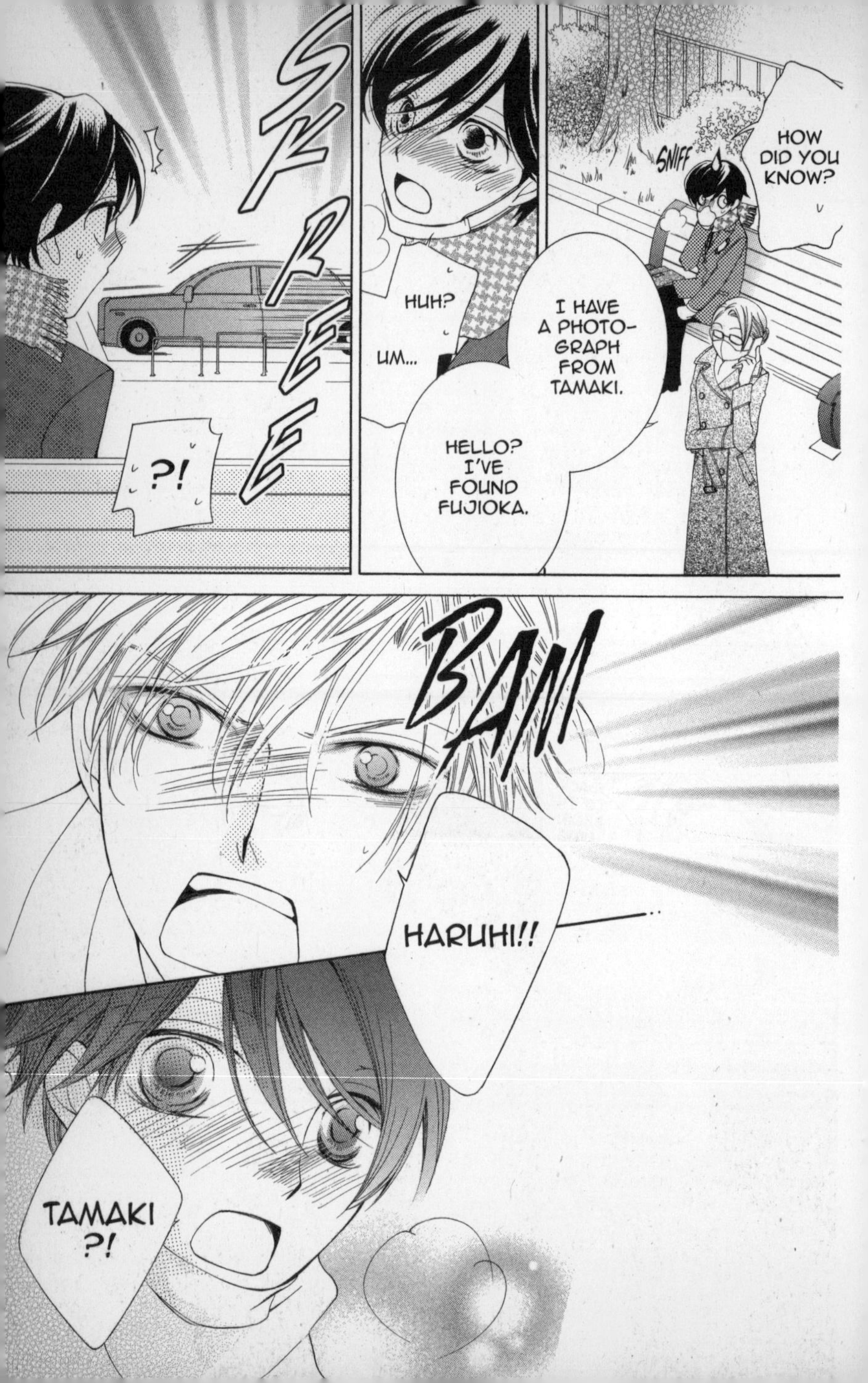
HOW DID YOU KNOW?
SNIFF
I HAVE A PHOTOGRAPH FROM TAMAKI.
HELLO? I'VE FOUND FUJIOKA.
HUH?
UM...
SKREEE
?!
BAM
HARUHI!!
TAMAKI ?!

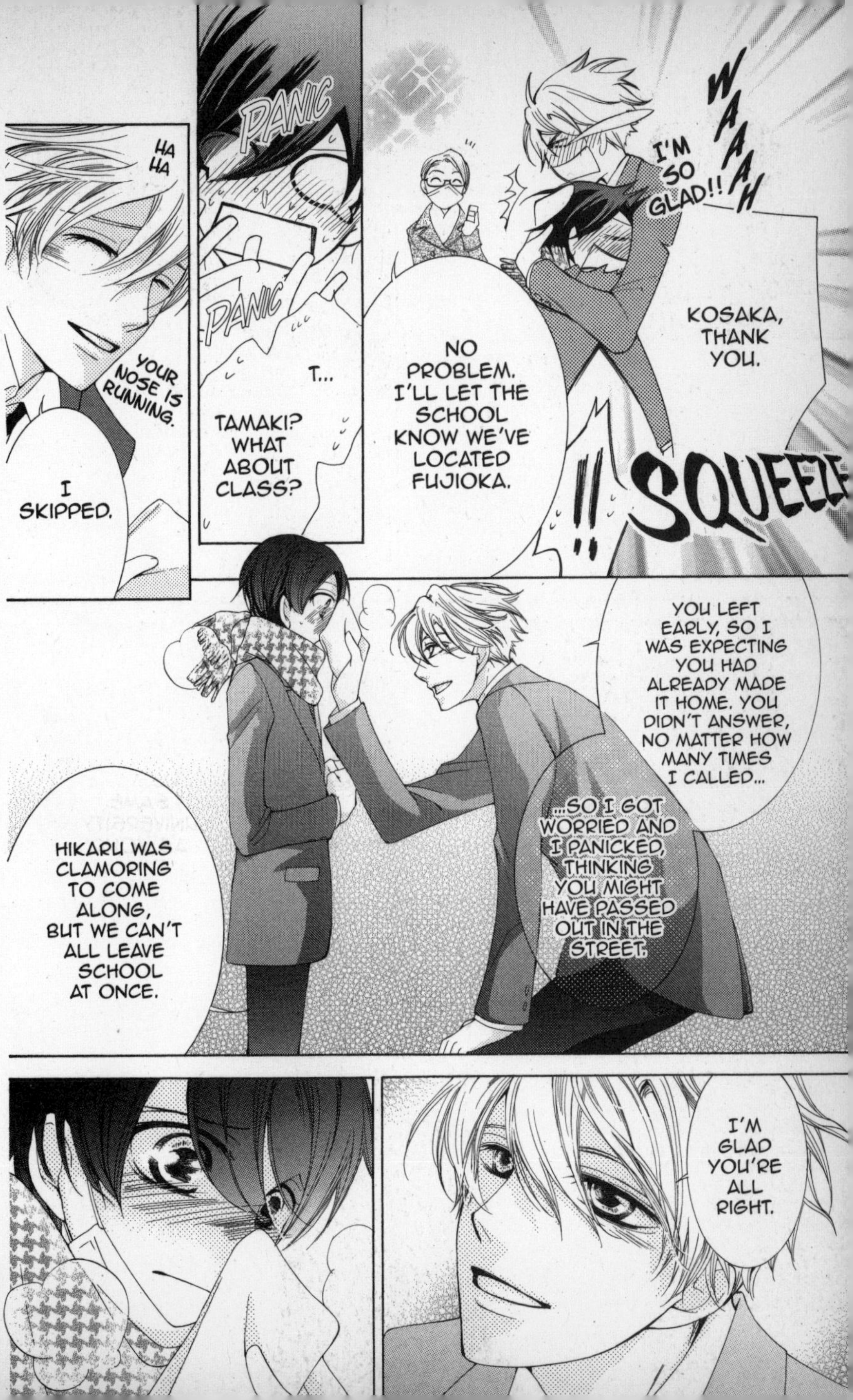
WAAAAH
I'M SO GLAD!!
KOSAKA, THANK YOU.
!!
SQUEEZE
NO PROBLEM. I'LL LET THE SCHOOL KNOW WE'VE LOCATED FUJIOKA.
PANIC
PANIC
T...
TAMAKI? WHAT ABOUT CLASS?
HA HA
YOUR NOSE IS RUNNING.
I SKIPPED.
YOU LEFT EARLY, SO I WAS EXPECTING YOU HAD ALREADY MADE IT HOME. YOU DIDN'T ANSWER, NO MATTER HOW MANY TIMES I CALLED...
...SO I GOT WORRIED AND I PANICKED, THINKING YOU MIGHT HAVE PASSED OUT IN THE STREET.
HIKARU WAS CLAMORING TO COME ALONG, BUT WE CAN'T ALL LEAVE SCHOOL AT ONCE.
I'M GLAD YOU'RE ALL RIGHT.

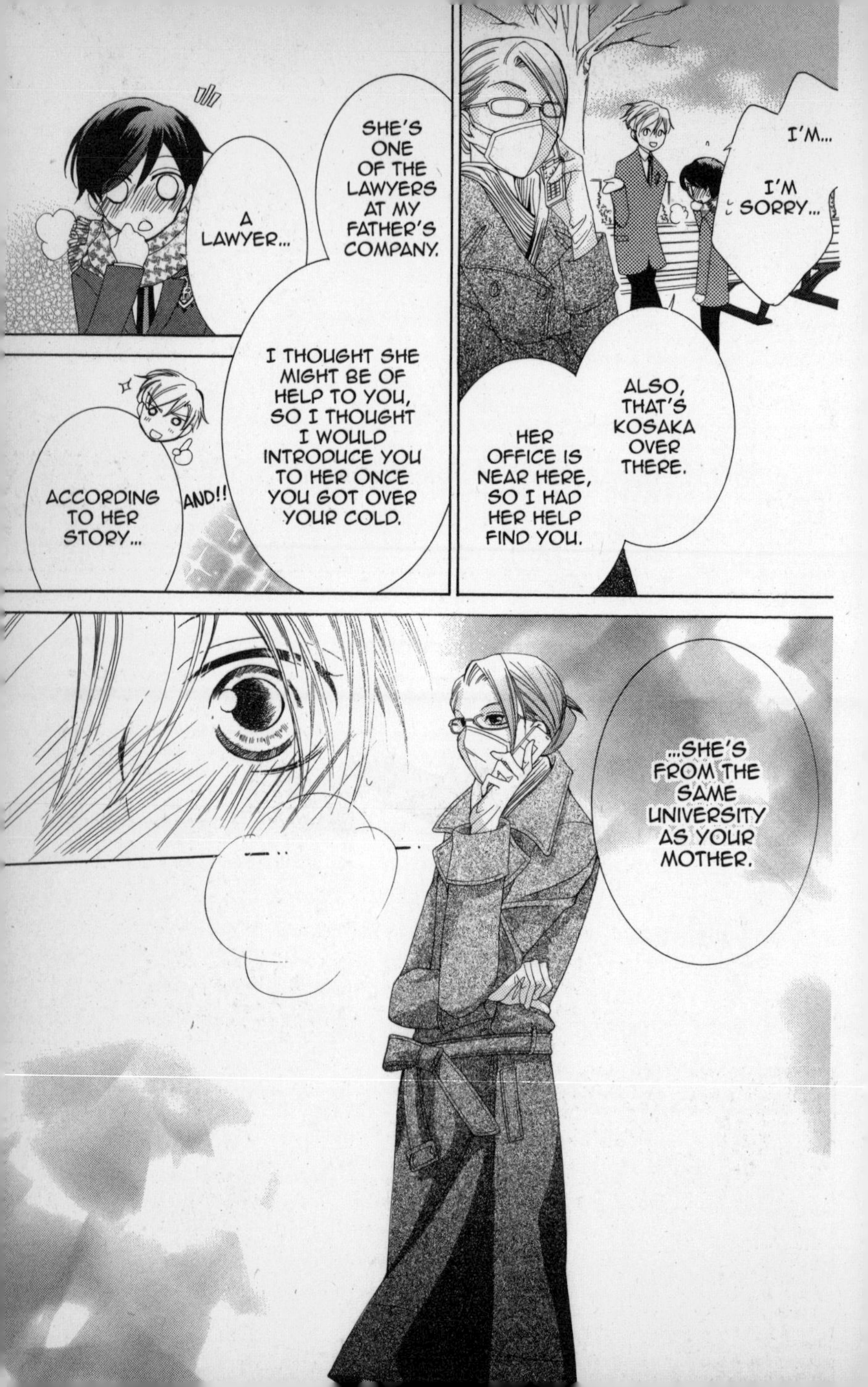
I'M...
I'M SORRY...
ALSO, THAT'S KOSAKA OVER THERE.
HER OFFICE IS NEAR HERE, SO I HAD HER HELP FIND YOU.
SHE'S ONE OF THE LAWYERS AT MY FATHER'S COMPANY.
A LAWYER...
I THOUGHT SHE MIGHT BE OF HELP TO YOU, SO I THOUGHT I WOULD INTRODUCE YOU TO HER ONCE YOU GOT OVER YOUR COLD.
AND!!
ACCORDING TO HER STORY...
...SHE'S FROM THE SAME UNIVERSITY AS YOUR MOTHER.
—...

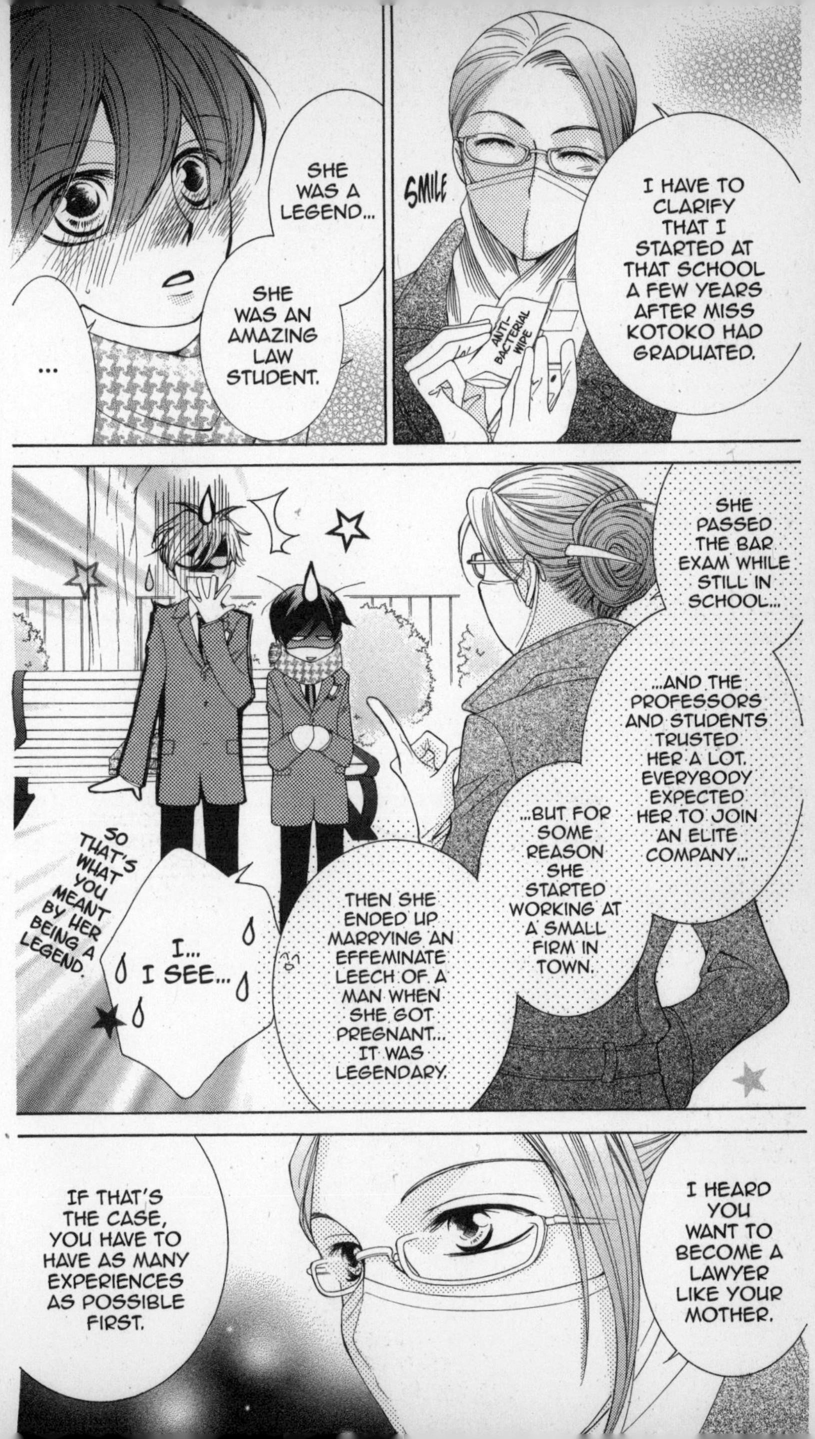
I HAVE TO CLARIFY THAT I STARTED AT THAT SCHOOL A FEW YEARS AFTER MISS KOTOKO HAD GRADUATED.
SMILE
ANTI-BACTERIAL WIPE
SHE WAS A LEGEND...
SHE WAS AN AMAZING LAW STUDENT.
...
SHE PASSED THE BAR EXAM WHILE STILL IN SCHOOL...
...AND THE PROFESSORS AND STUDENTS TRUSTED HER A LOT. EVERYBODY EXPECTED HER TO JOIN AN ELITE COMPANY...
...BUT FOR SOME REASON SHE STARTED WORKING AT A SMALL FIRM IN TOWN.
THEN SHE ENDED UP MARRYING AN EFFEMINATE LEECH OF A MAN WHEN SHE GOT PREGNANT... IT WAS LEGENDARY.
I... I SEE...
SO THAT'S WHAT YOU MEANT BY HER BEING A LEGEND.
I HEARD YOU WANT TO BECOME A LAWYER LIKE YOUR MOTHER.
IF THAT'S THE CASE, YOU HAVE TO HAVE AS MANY EXPERIENCES AS POSSIBLE FIRST.

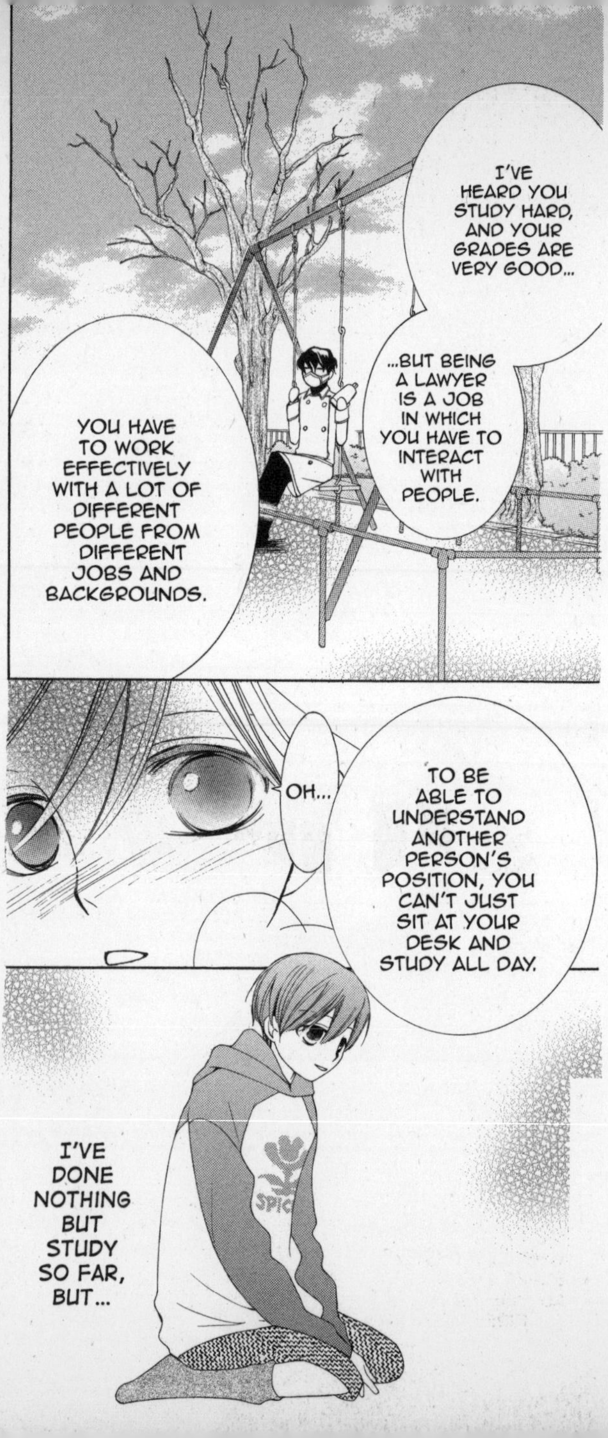
I'VE HEARD YOU STUDY HARD, AND YOUR GRADES ARE VERY GOOD...
...BUT BEING A LAWYER IS A JOB IN WHICH YOU HAVE TO INTERACT WITH PEOPLE.
YOU HAVE TO WORK EFFECTIVELY WITH A LOT OF DIFFERENT PEOPLE FROM DIFFERENT JOBS AND BACKGROUNDS.
OH...
TO BE ABLE TO UNDERSTAND ANOTHER PERSON'S POSITION, YOU CAN'T JUST SIT AT YOUR DESK AND STUDY ALL DAY.
I'VE DONE NOTHING BUT STUDY SO FAR, BUT...

2

✿SO THINGS LIKE THIS HAVE BEEN ALMOST A DAILY ROUTINE FOR ME, BUT RECENTLY I DID SOMETHING EVEN CRAZIER.

I WAS INKING THE MANGA, AND I WAS SO TIRED THAT I STARTED DOZING OFF AND DREAMING.

THIS HAPPENED UNDER THE STRESS OF THE DEADLINE APPROACHING, AND THE GIST OF MY DREAM WAS THAT I KEPT CRYING, "WE NEED MORE HANDS, WE NEED MORE HANDS!" ONE OF THE NEW STAFF MEMBERS, SUBARU, THEN SAID, "WE DO HAVE A BACKSCRATCHER."

I THOUGHT, "THAT WON'T DO!" IN MY DREAM, BUT RIGHT AFTER THAT I WOKE UP AND LOOKED DOWN AND SAW I HAD DRAWN...

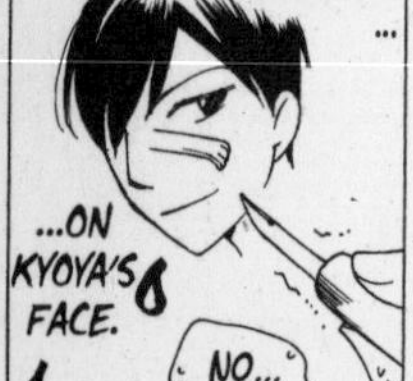
A BACK-SCRATCHER ...
...ON KYOYA'S FACE.
NO...
A TRUE STORY.

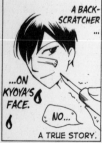

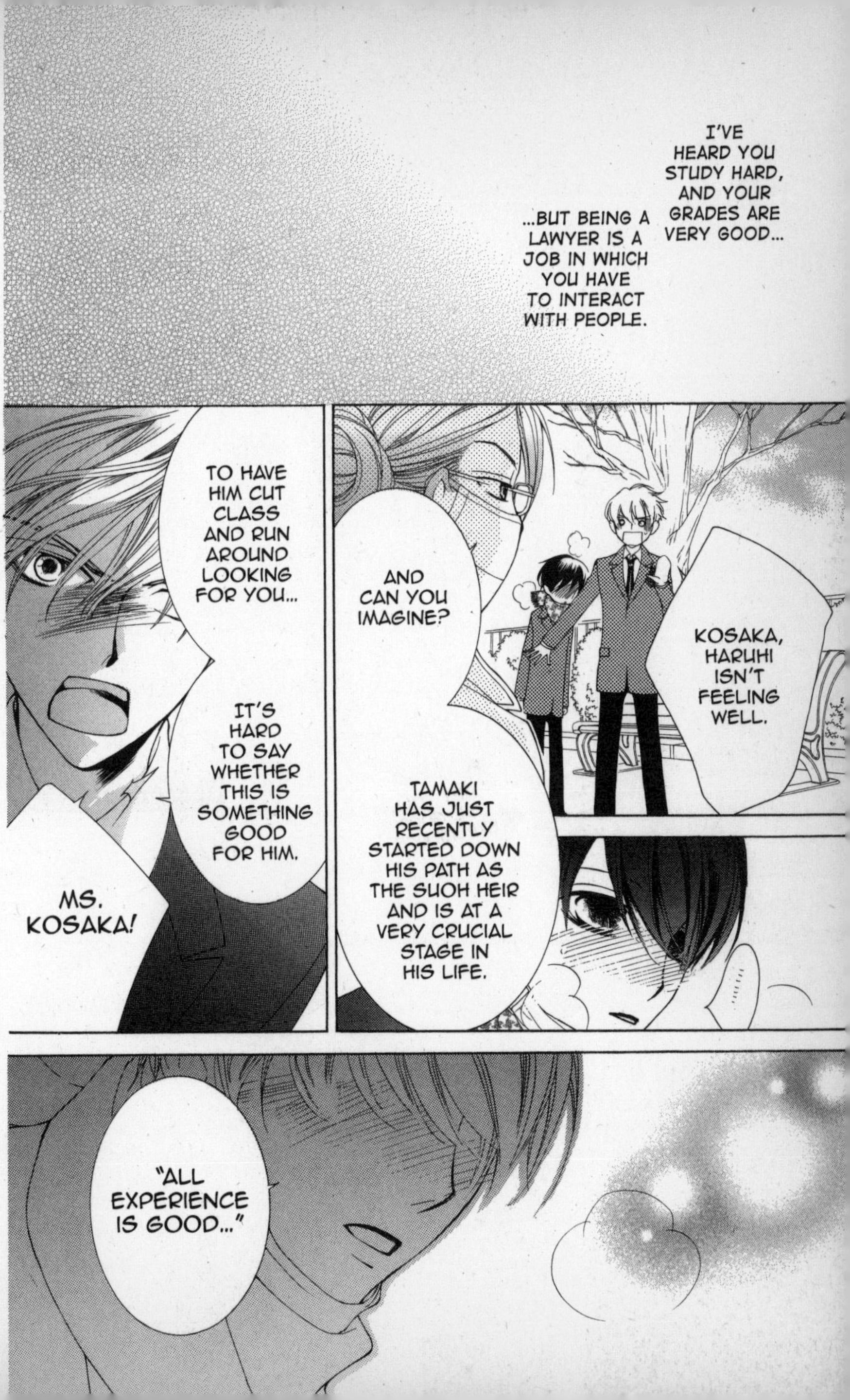
I'VE HEARD YOU STUDY HARD, AND YOUR GRADES ARE VERY GOOD...
...BUT BEING A LAWYER IS A JOB IN WHICH YOU HAVE TO INTERACT WITH PEOPLE.
KOSAKA, HARUHI ISN'T FEELING WELL.
AND CAN YOU IMAGINE?
TAMAKI HAS JUST RECENTLY STARTED DOWN HIS PATH AS THE SUOH HEIR AND IS AT A VERY CRUCIAL STAGE IN HIS LIFE.
TO HAVE HIM CUT CLASS AND RUN AROUND LOOKING FOR YOU...
IT'S HARD TO SAY WHETHER THIS IS SOMETHING GOOD FOR HIM.
MS. KOSAKA!
"ALL EXPERIENCE IS GOOD..."

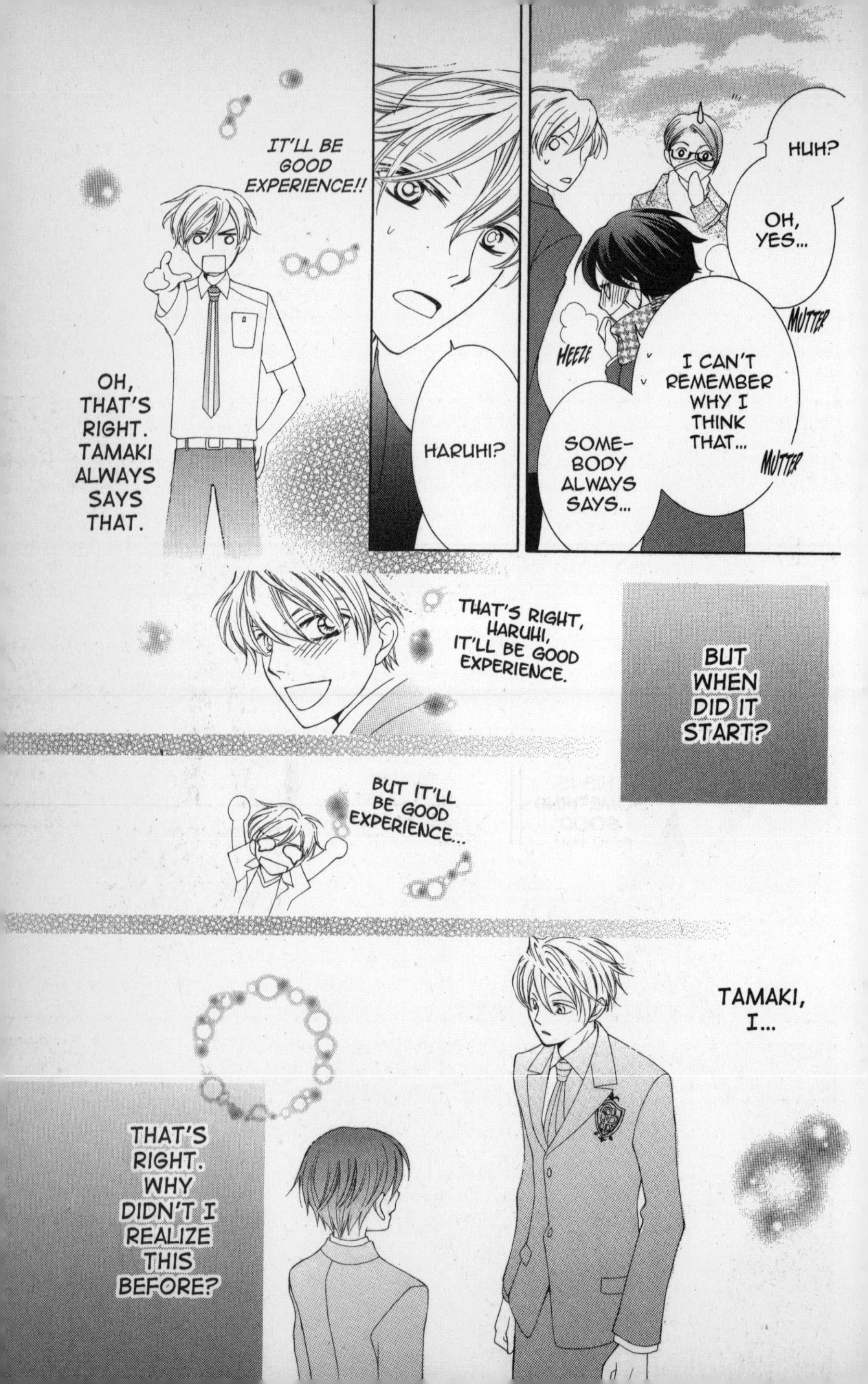
HUH?
OH, YES...
MUTTER
I CAN'T REMEMBER WHY I THINK THAT...
MUTTER
HEEZE
SOME-BODY ALWAYS SAYS...
HARUHI?
IT'LL BE GOOD EXPERIENCE!!
OH, THAT'S RIGHT. TAMAKI ALWAYS SAYS THAT.
BUT WHEN DID IT START?
THAT'S RIGHT, HARUHI, IT'LL BE GOOD EXPERIENCE.
BUT IT'LL BE GOOD EXPERIENCE...
TAMAKI, I...
THAT'S RIGHT. WHY DIDN'T I REALIZE THIS BEFORE?

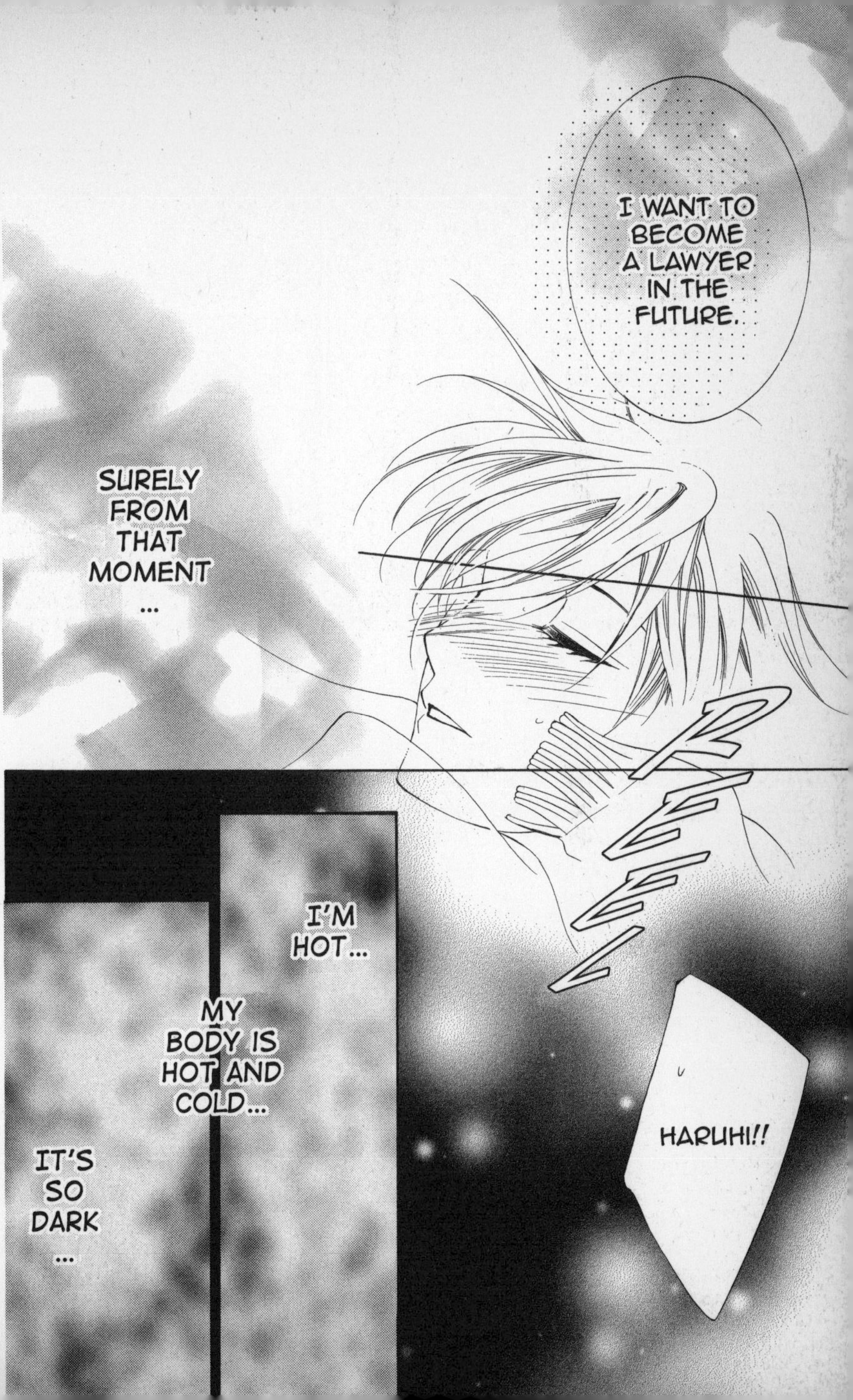

I WANT TO BECOME A LAWYER IN THE FUTURE.
SURELY FROM THAT MOMENT ...
HARUHI!!
I'M HOT...
MY BODY IS HOT AND COLD...
IT'S SO DARK ...

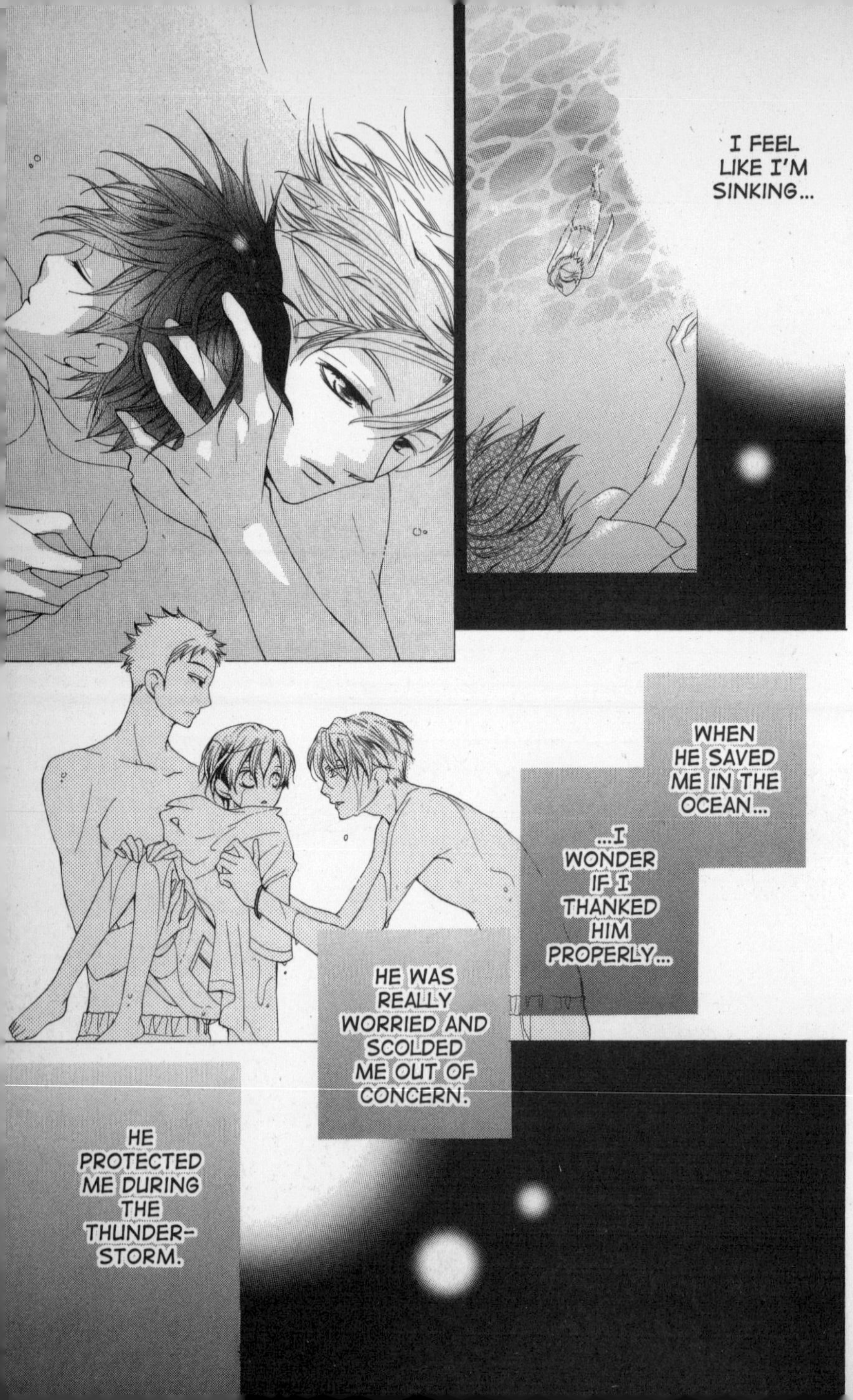
I FEEL LIKE I'M SINKING...
WHEN HE SAVED ME IN THE OCEAN...
...I WONDER IF I THANKED HIM PROPERLY...
HE WAS REALLY WORRIED AND SCOLDED ME OUT OF CONCERN.
HE PROTECTED ME DURING THE THUNDER-STORM.

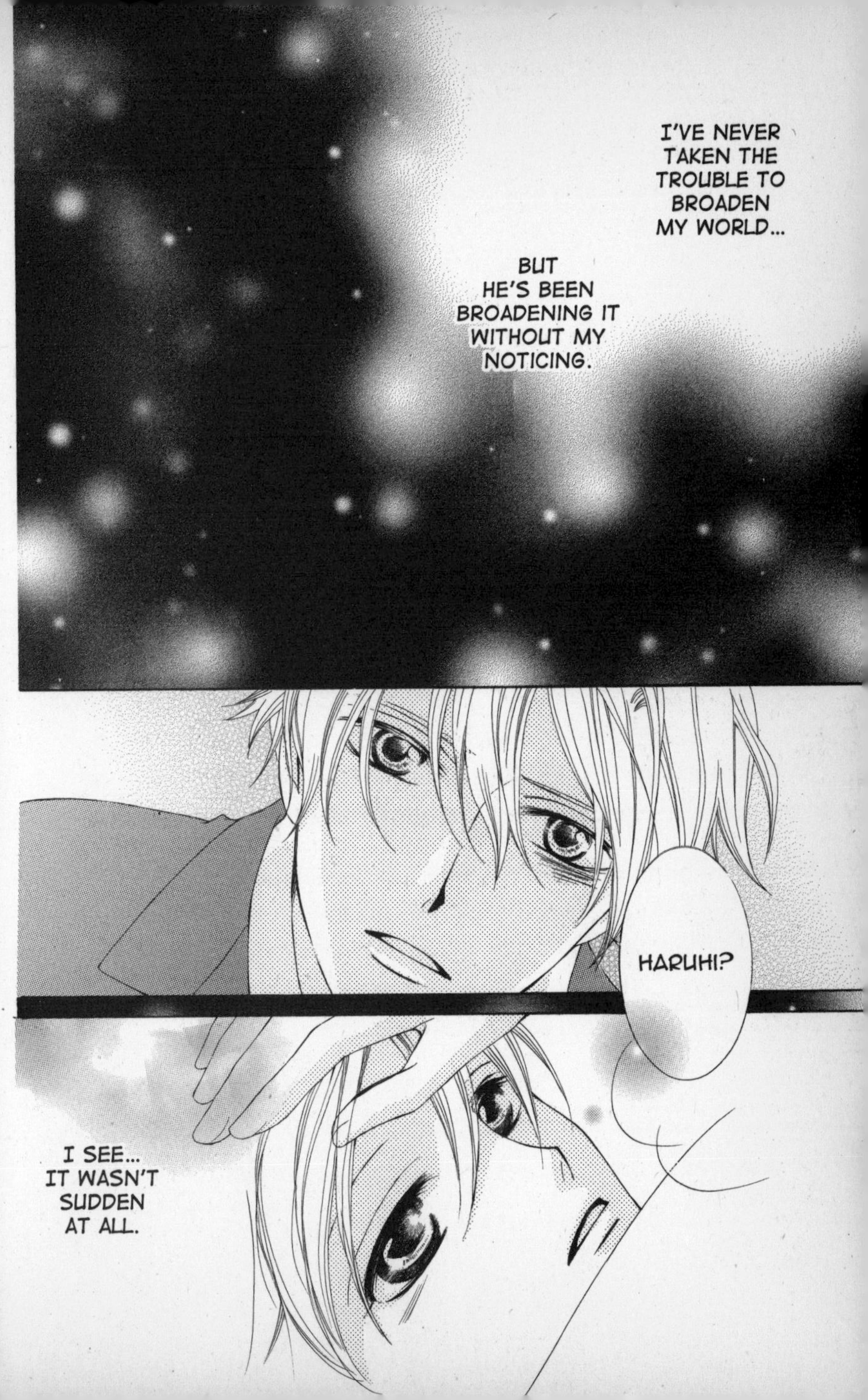
I'VE NEVER TAKEN THE TROUBLE TO BROADEN MY WORLD...
BUT HE'S BEEN BROADENING IT WITHOUT MY NOTICING.
HARUHI?
I SEE... IT WASN'T SUDDEN AT ALL.

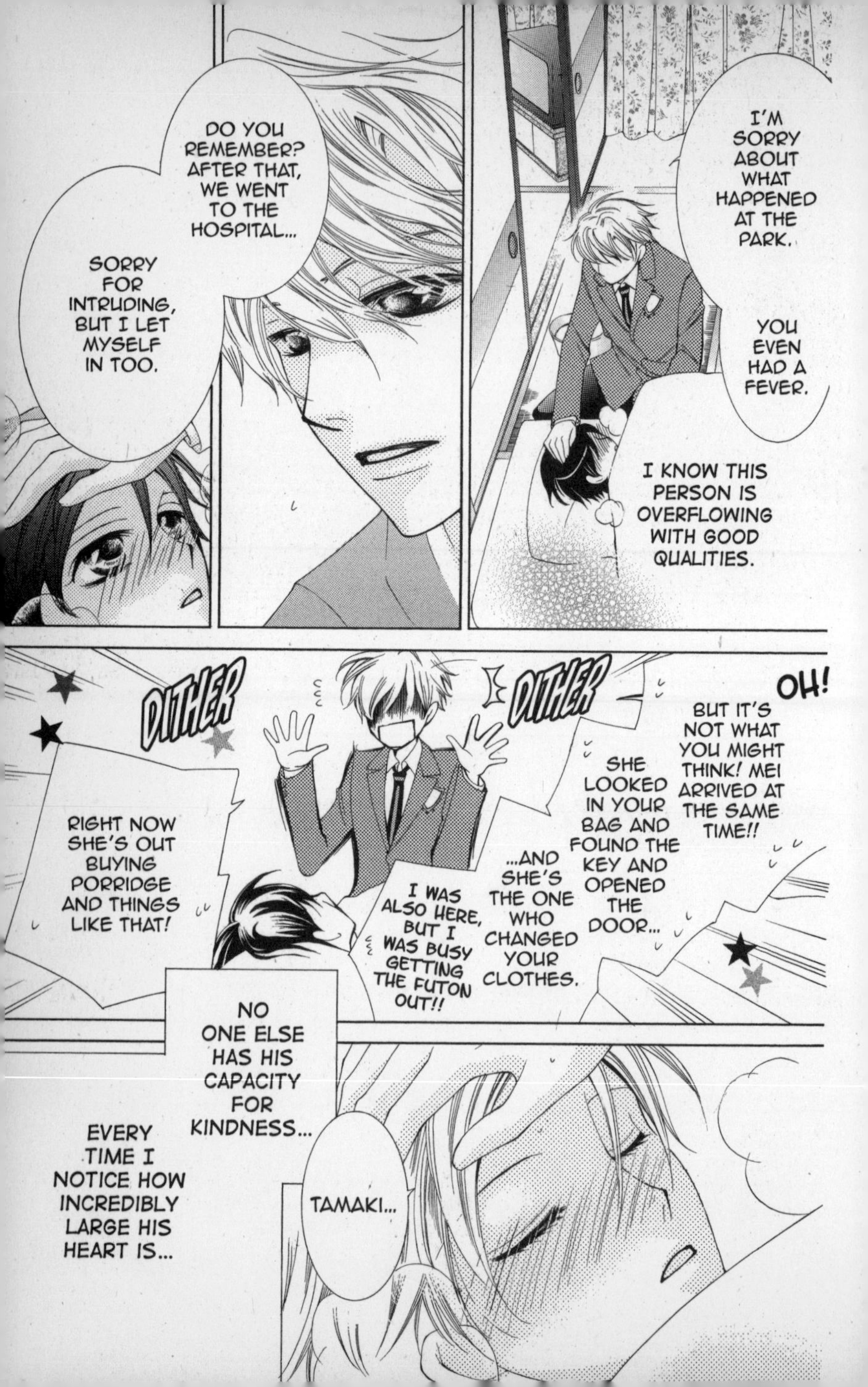
I'M SORRY ABOUT WHAT HAPPENED AT THE PARK.
YOU EVEN HAD A FEVER.
I KNOW THIS PERSON IS OVERFLOWING WITH GOOD QUALITIES.
DO YOU REMEMBER? AFTER THAT, WE WENT TO THE HOSPITAL...
SORRY FOR INTRUDING, BUT I LET MYSELF IN TOO.
OH!
BUT IT'S NOT WHAT YOU MIGHT THINK! MEI ARRIVED AT THE SAME TIME!!
DITHER
SHE LOOKED IN YOUR BAG AND FOUND THE KEY AND OPENED THE DOOR...
...AND SHE'S THE ONE WHO CHANGED YOUR CLOTHES.
I WAS ALSO HERE, BUT I WAS BUSY GETTING THE FUTON OUT!!
DITHER
RIGHT NOW SHE'S OUT BUYING PORRIDGE AND THINGS LIKE THAT!
NO ONE ELSE HAS HIS CAPACITY FOR KINDNESS...
TAMAKI...
EVERY TIME I NOTICE HOW INCREDIBLY LARGE HIS HEART IS...

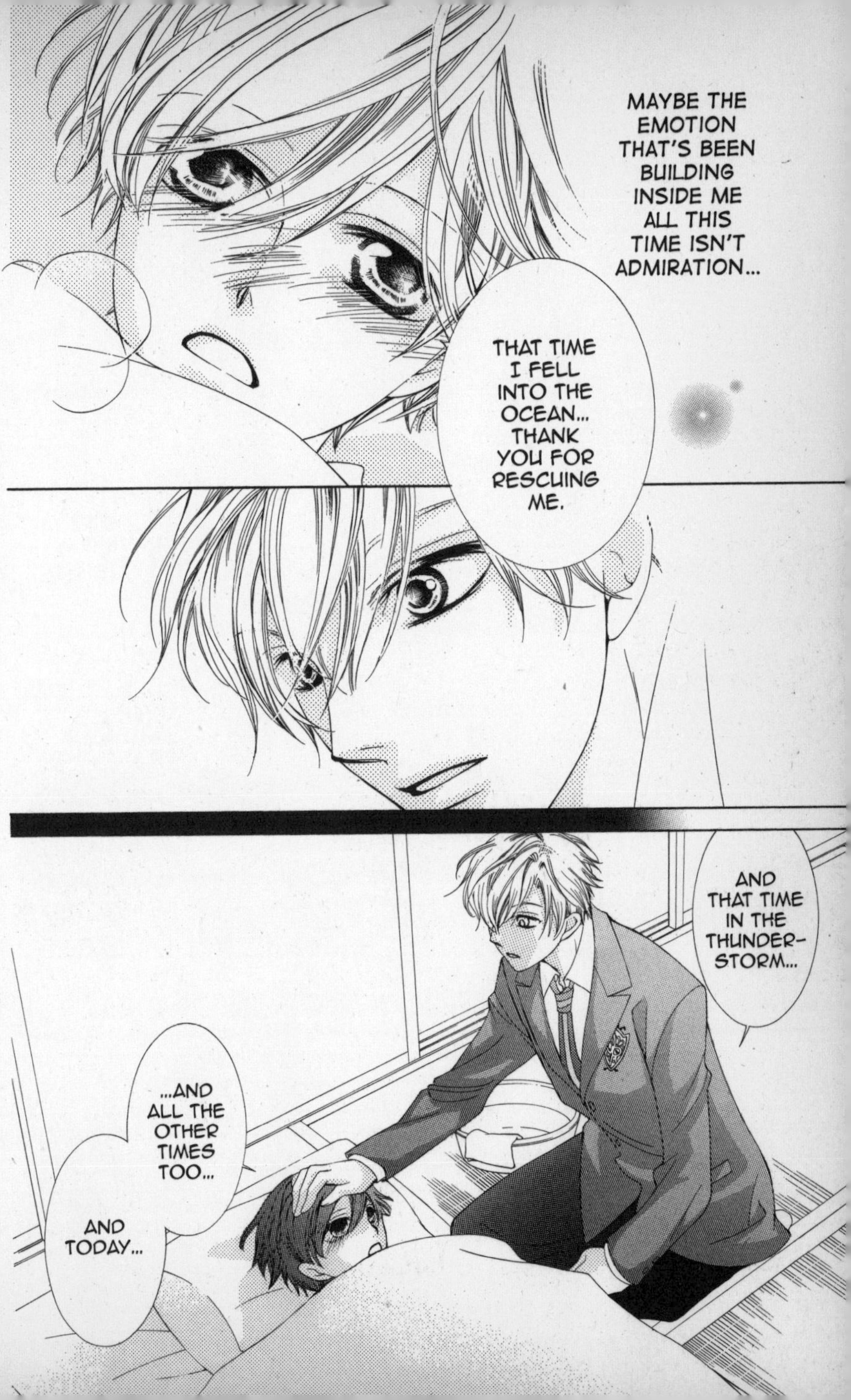
MAYBE THE EMOTION THAT'S BEEN BUILDING INSIDE ME ALL THIS TIME ISN'T ADMIRATION...
THAT TIME I FELL INTO THE OCEAN... THANK YOU FOR RESCUING ME.
AND THAT TIME IN THE THUNDER-STORM...
...AND ALL THE OTHER TIMES TOO...
AND TODAY...

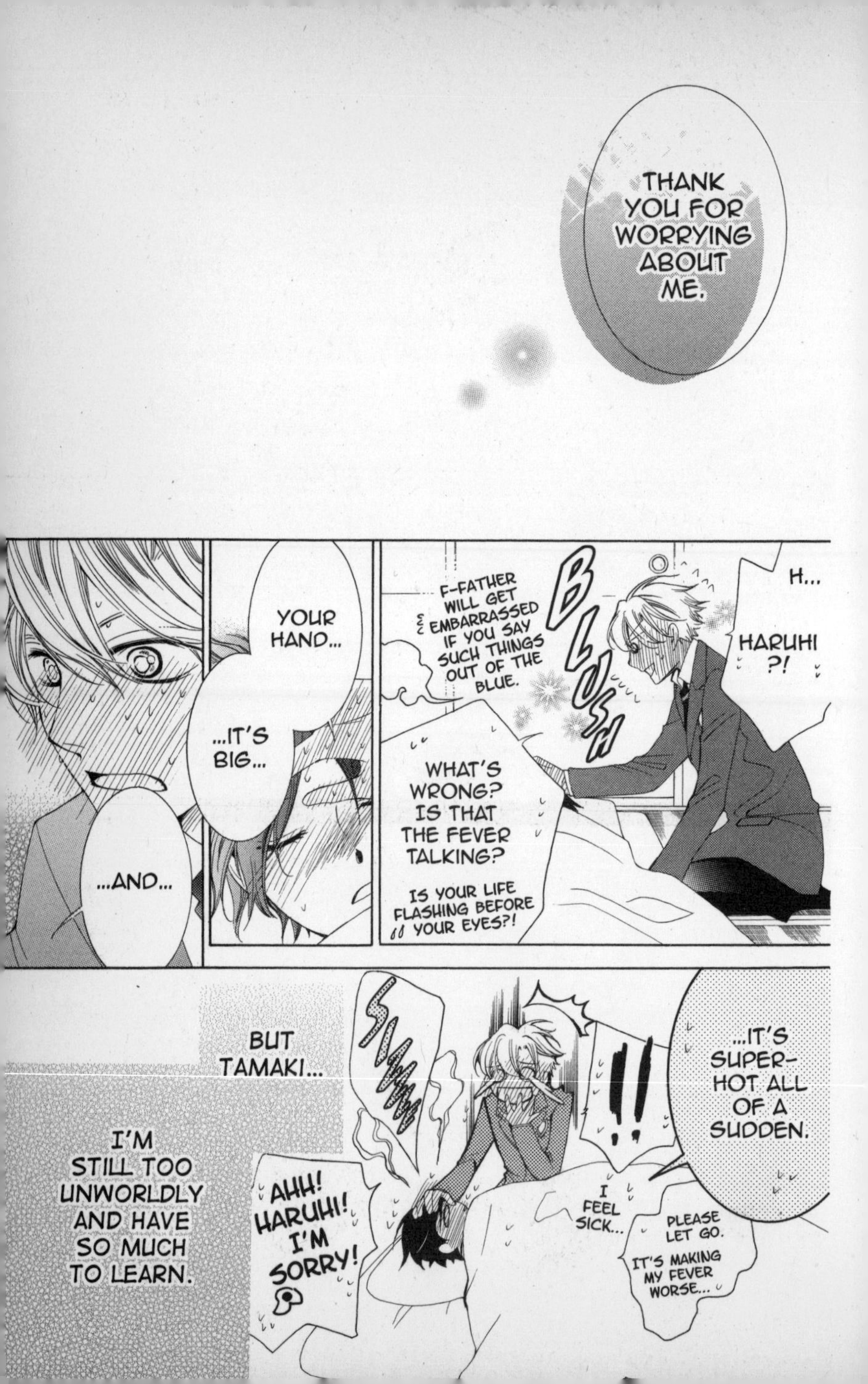

THANK YOU FOR WORRYING ABOUT ME.
H... HARUHI?!
BLUSH
F-FATHER WILL GET EMBARRASSED IF YOU SAY SUCH THINGS OUT OF THE BLUE.
WHAT'S WRONG? IS THAT THE FEVER TALKING?
IS YOUR LIFE FLASHING BEFORE YOUR EYES?!
YOUR HAND...
...IT'S BIG...
...AND...
...IT'S SUPER-HOT ALL OF A SUDDEN.
!!
I FEEL SICK...
PLEASE LET GO.
IT'S MAKING MY FEVER WORSE...
AHH! HARUHI! I'M SORRY!
BUT TAMAKI...
I'M STILL TOO UNWORLDLY AND HAVE SO MUCH TO LEARN.

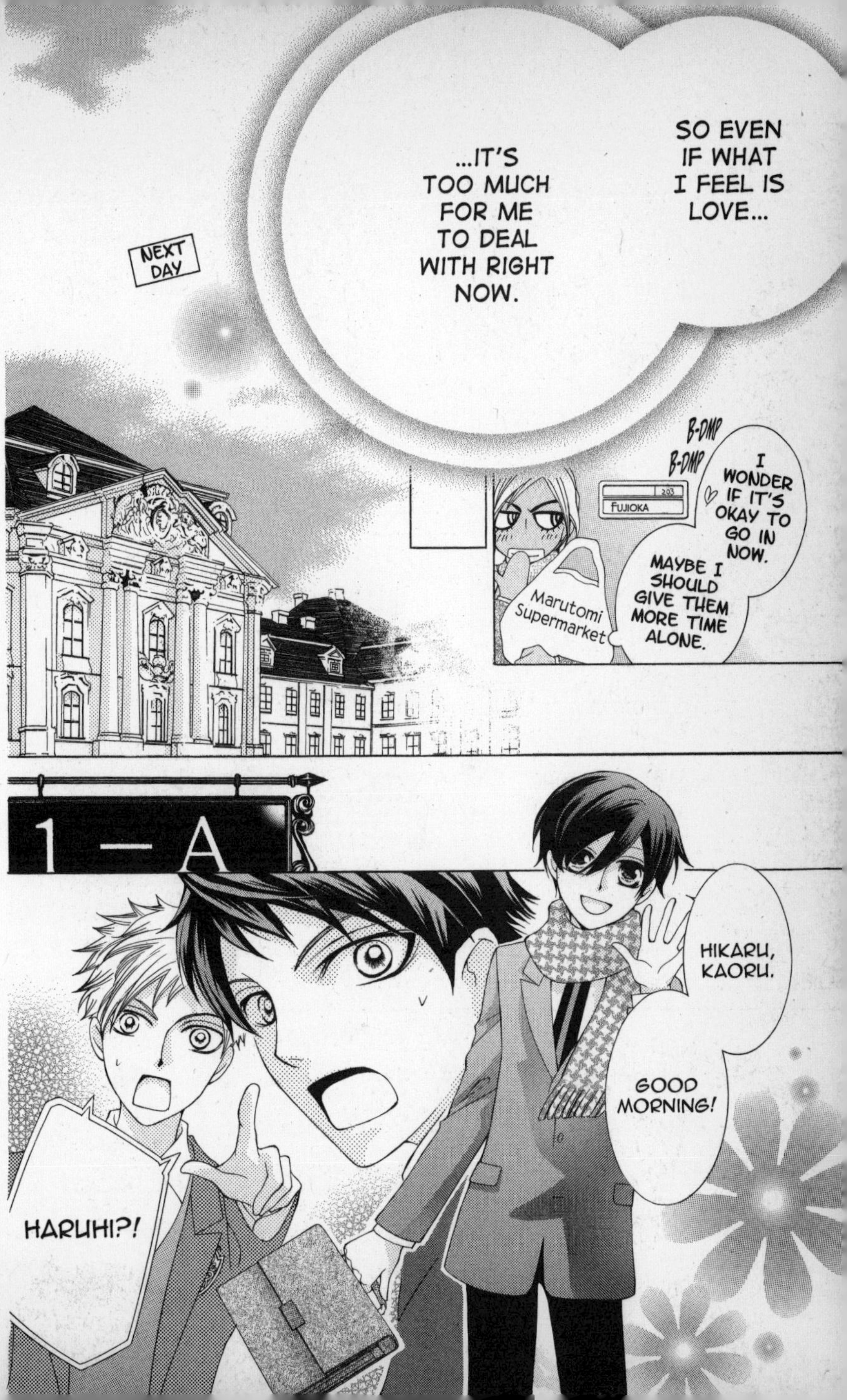
SO EVEN IF WHAT I FEEL IS LOVE...
...IT'S TOO MUCH FOR ME TO DEAL WITH RIGHT NOW.
NEXT DAY
B-DMP B-DMP
I WONDER IF IT'S OKAY TO GO IN NOW.
FUJIOKA
203
MAYBE I SHOULD GIVE THEM MORE TIME ALONE.
Marutomi Supermarket
1—A
HIKARU, KAORU.
GOOD MORNING!
HARUHI?!

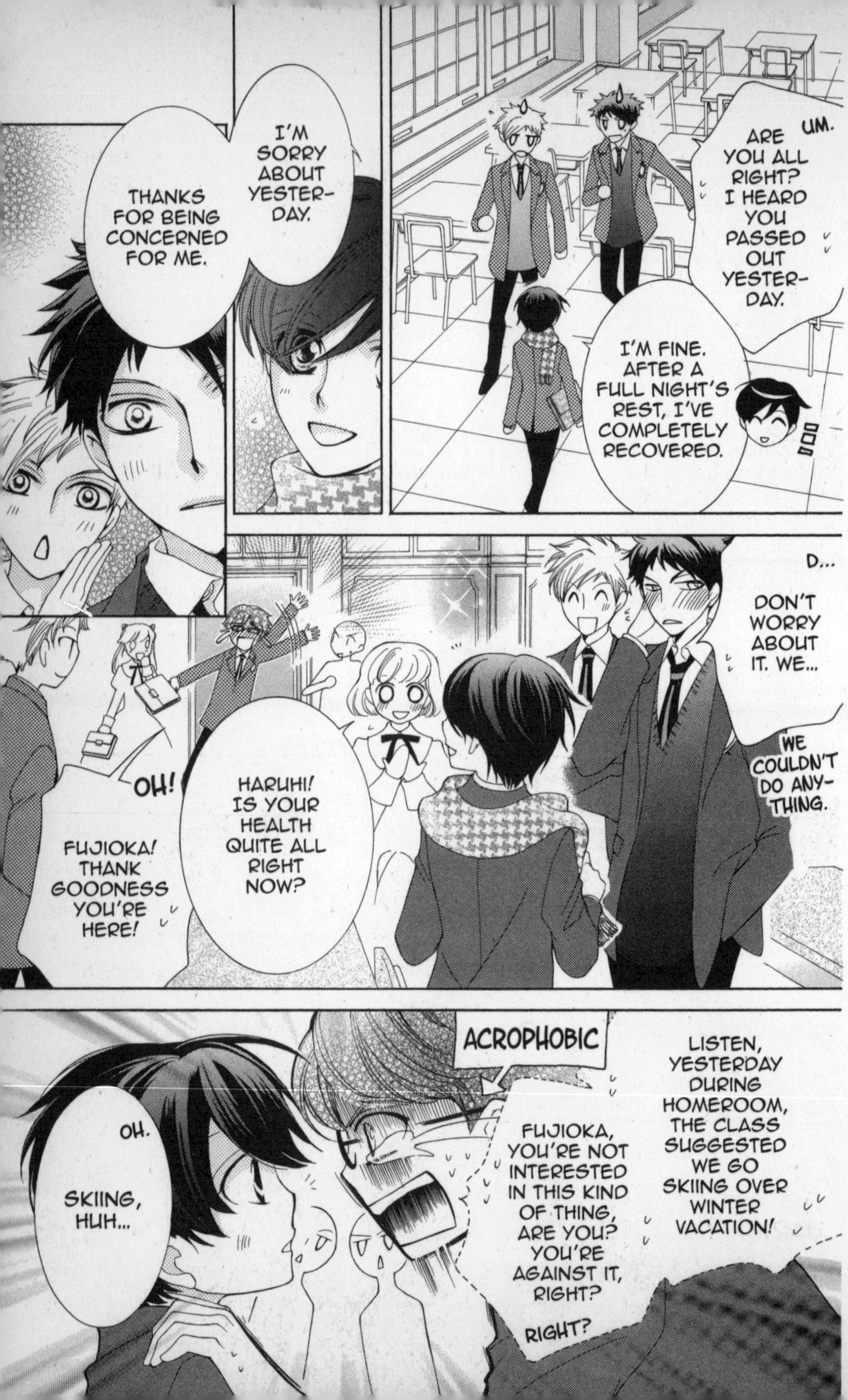
UM.
ARE YOU ALL RIGHT? I HEARD YOU PASSED OUT YESTER-DAY.
I'M FINE. AFTER A FULL NIGHT'S REST, I'VE COMPLETELY RECOVERED.
I'M SORRY ABOUT YESTER-DAY.
THANKS FOR BEING CONCERNED FOR ME.
D...
DON'T WORRY ABOUT IT. WE...
WE COULDN'T DO ANY-THING.
HARUHI! IS YOUR HEALTH QUITE ALL RIGHT NOW?
OH!
FUJIOKA! THANK GOODNESS YOU'RE HERE!
LISTEN, YESTERDAY DURING HOMEROOM, THE CLASS SUGGESTED WE GO SKIING OVER WINTER VACATION!
ACROPHOBIC
FUJIOKA, YOU'RE NOT INTERESTED IN THIS KIND OF THING, ARE YOU? YOU'RE AGAINST IT, RIGHT?
RIGHT?
OH.
SKIING, HUH...

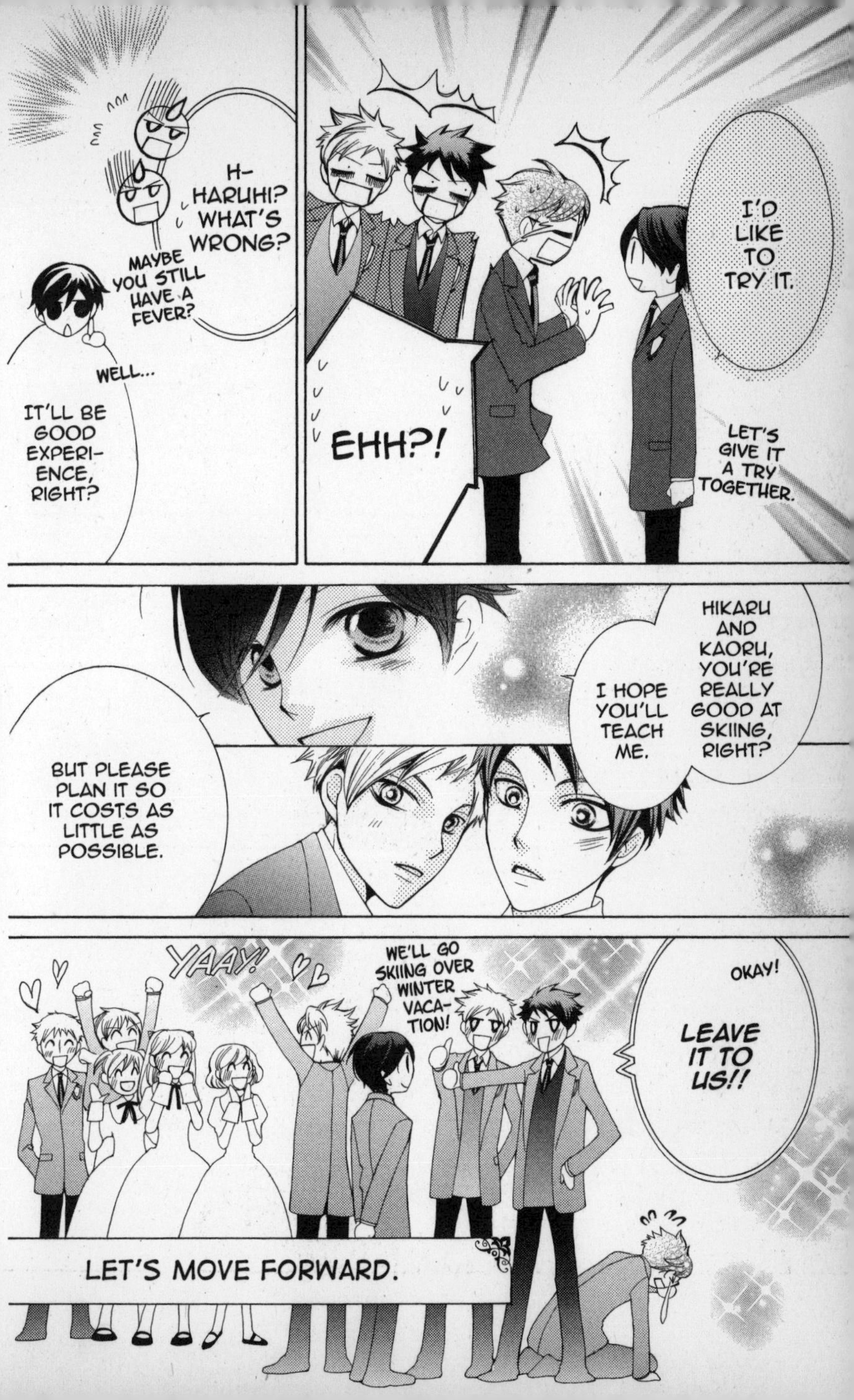
I'D LIKE TO TRY IT.
LET'S GIVE IT A TRY TOGETHER.
EHH?!
H-HARUHI? WHAT'S WRONG?
MAYBE YOU STILL HAVE A FEVER?
WELL...
IT'LL BE GOOD EXPERIENCE, RIGHT?
HIKARU AND KAORU, YOU'RE REALLY GOOD AT SKIING, RIGHT?
I HOPE YOU'LL TEACH ME.
BUT PLEASE PLAN IT SO IT COSTS AS LITTLE AS POSSIBLE.
OKAY!
LEAVE IT TO US!!
WE'LL GO SKIING OVER WINTER VACATION!
YAAY!
LET'S MOVE FORWARD.

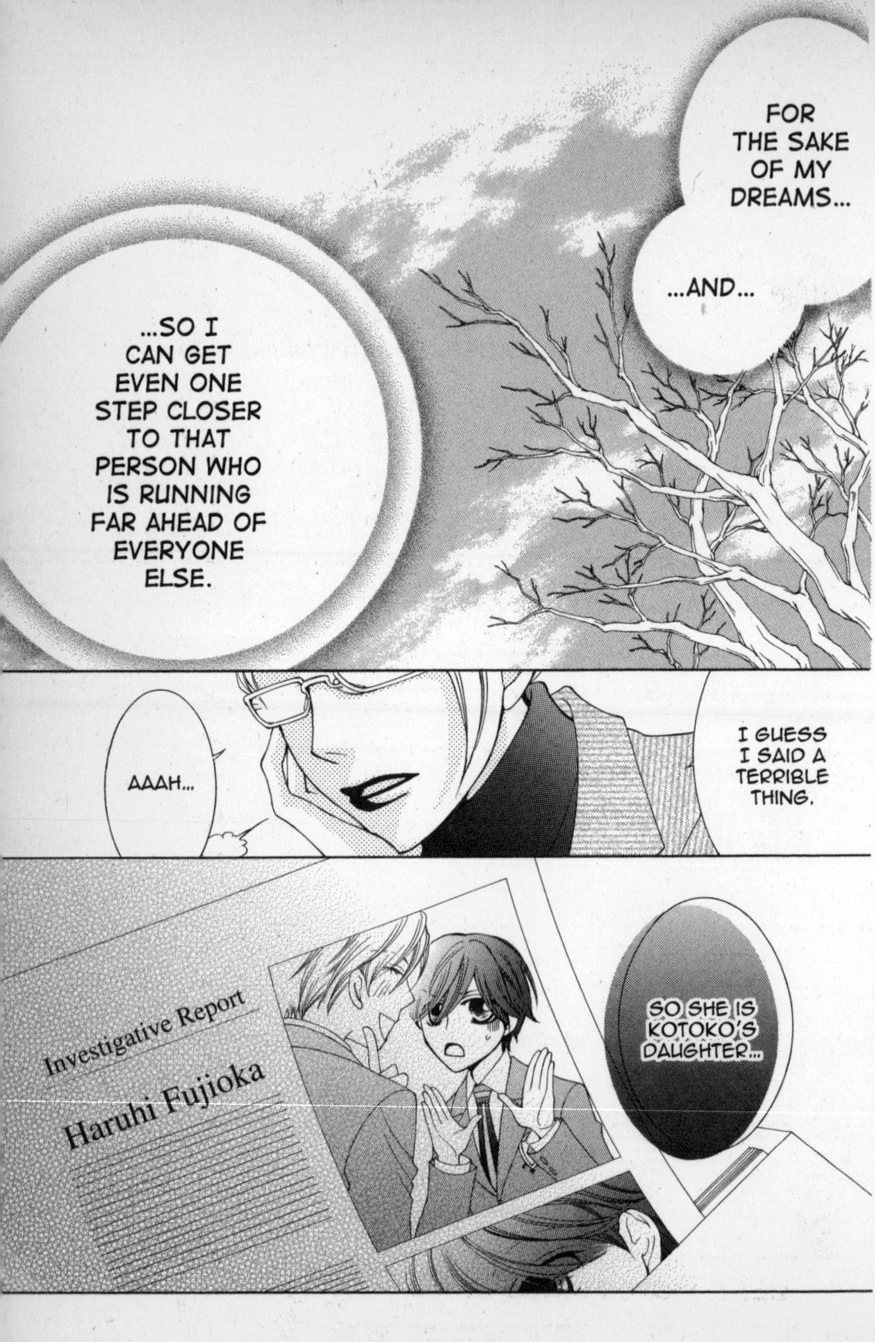
FOR THE SAKE OF MY DREAMS...
...AND...
...SO I CAN GET EVEN ONE STEP CLOSER TO THAT PERSON WHO IS RUNNING FAR AHEAD OF EVERYONE ELSE.
I GUESS I SAID A TERRIBLE THING.
AAAH...
SO SHE IS KOTOKO'S DAUGHTER...
Investigative Report
Haruhi Fujioka

GUEST ROOM: FAXES

SPECIAL THANKS TO
SHIGEYOSHI TAKAGI!

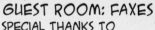

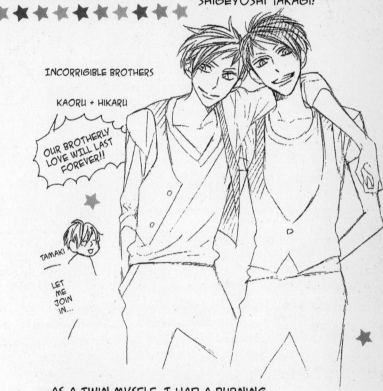

INCORRIGIBLE BROTHERS
KAORU + HIKARU
OUR BROTHERLY LOVE WILL LAST FOREVER!!
TAMAKI
LET ME JOIN IN...

AS A TWIN MYSELF, I HAD A BURNING COMPULSION TO DRAW THE TWINS. I WISH HAPPINESS FOR BOTH OF THEM!! (TAMAKI TOO...)

SHIGEYOSHI TAKAGI

SHIGEYOSHI TAKAGI, WHOM I LIKE A LOT, DREW A PICTURE FOR ME! IT LOOKS SO COOL!! THANK YOU!! TAMAKI ON THE LEFT IS SO CUTE... (TEARS) PLEASE LET HIM JOIN! TAKAGI'S TWIN SISTER IS THE ARTIST SATOSHI MORIE WHO IS ACTIVE IN *HANA TO YUME*. THE TWINS' TALENT IS AMAZING!!

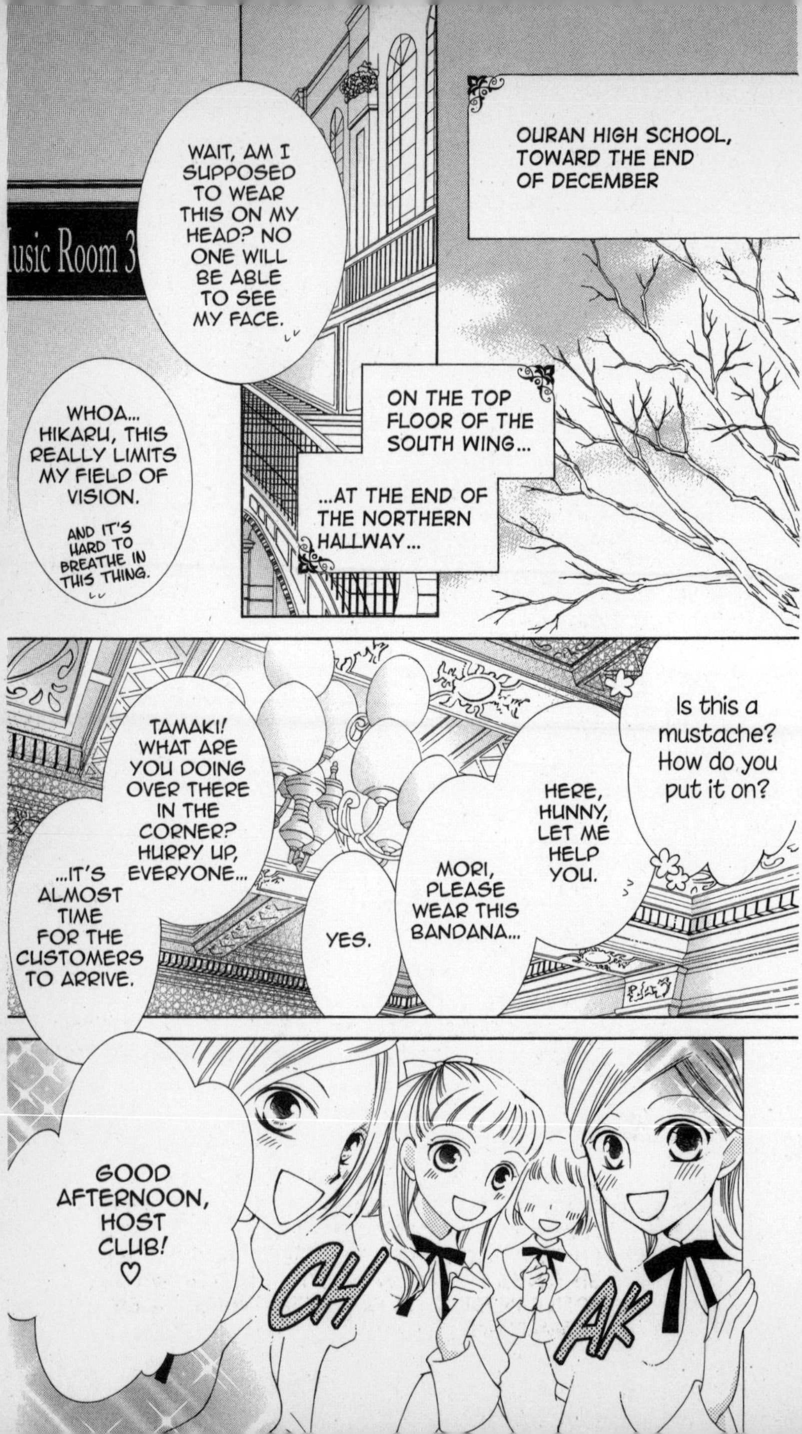
OURAN HIGH SCHOOL, TOWARD THE END OF DECEMBER
ON THE TOP FLOOR OF THE SOUTH WING...
...AT THE END OF THE NORTHERN HALLWAY...
usic Room 3
WAIT, AM I SUPPOSED TO WEAR THIS ON MY HEAD? NO ONE WILL BE ABLE TO SEE MY FACE.
WHOA... HIKARU, THIS REALLY LIMITS MY FIELD OF VISION.
AND IT'S HARD TO BREATHE IN THIS THING.
Is this a mustache? How do you put it on?
HERE, HUNNY, LET ME HELP YOU.
MORI, PLEASE WEAR THIS BANDANA...
YES.
TAMAKI! WHAT ARE YOU DOING OVER THERE IN THE CORNER? HURRY UP, EVERYONE...
...IT'S ALMOST TIME FOR THE CUSTOMERS TO ARRIVE.
GOOD AFTERNOON, HOST CLUB! ♡
CHAK

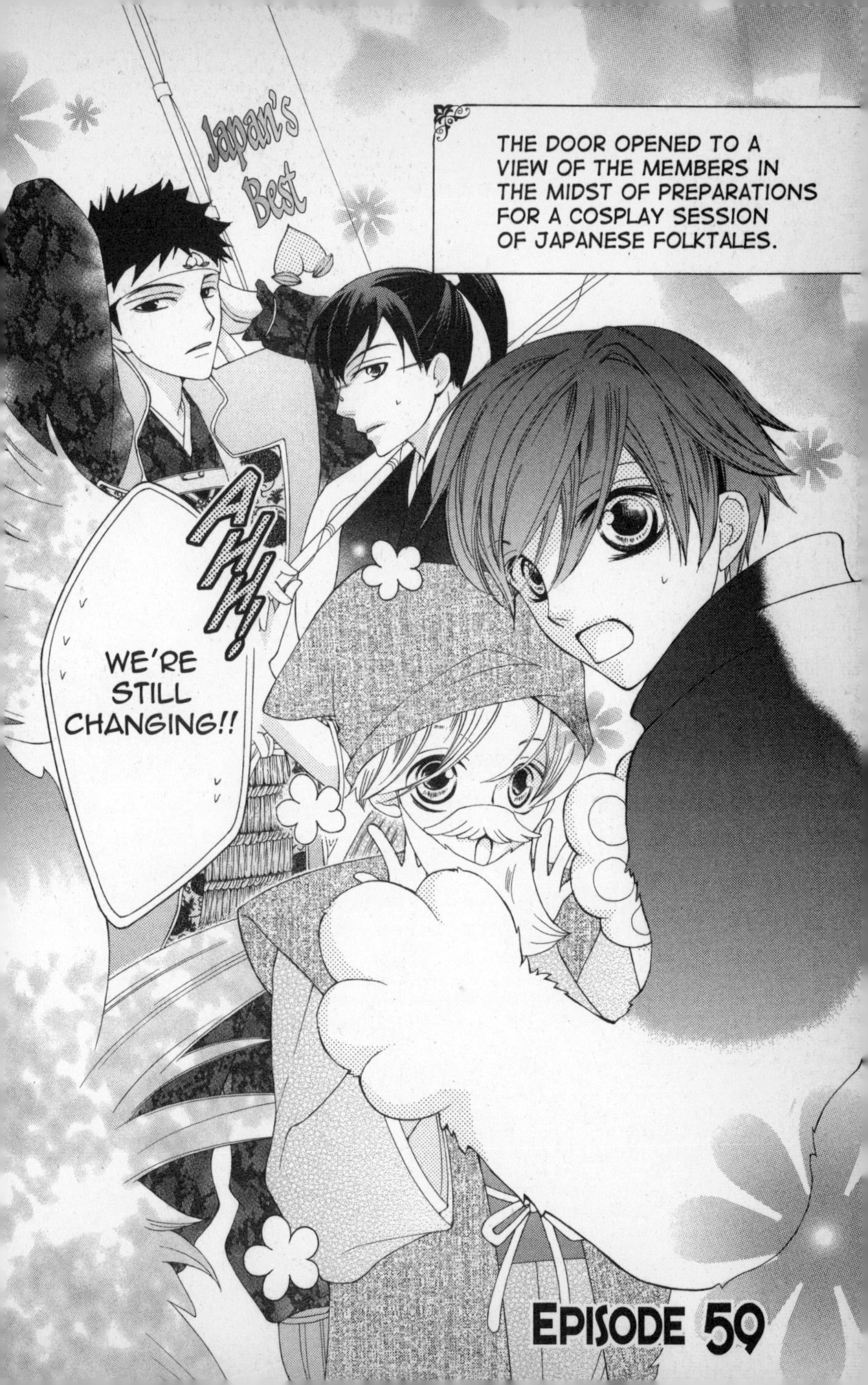
THE DOOR OPENED TO A VIEW OF THE MEMBERS IN THE MIDST OF PREPARATIONS FOR A COSPLAY SESSION OF JAPANESE FOLKTALES.
Japan's Best
AHH!
WE'RE STILL CHANGING!!
EPISODE 59

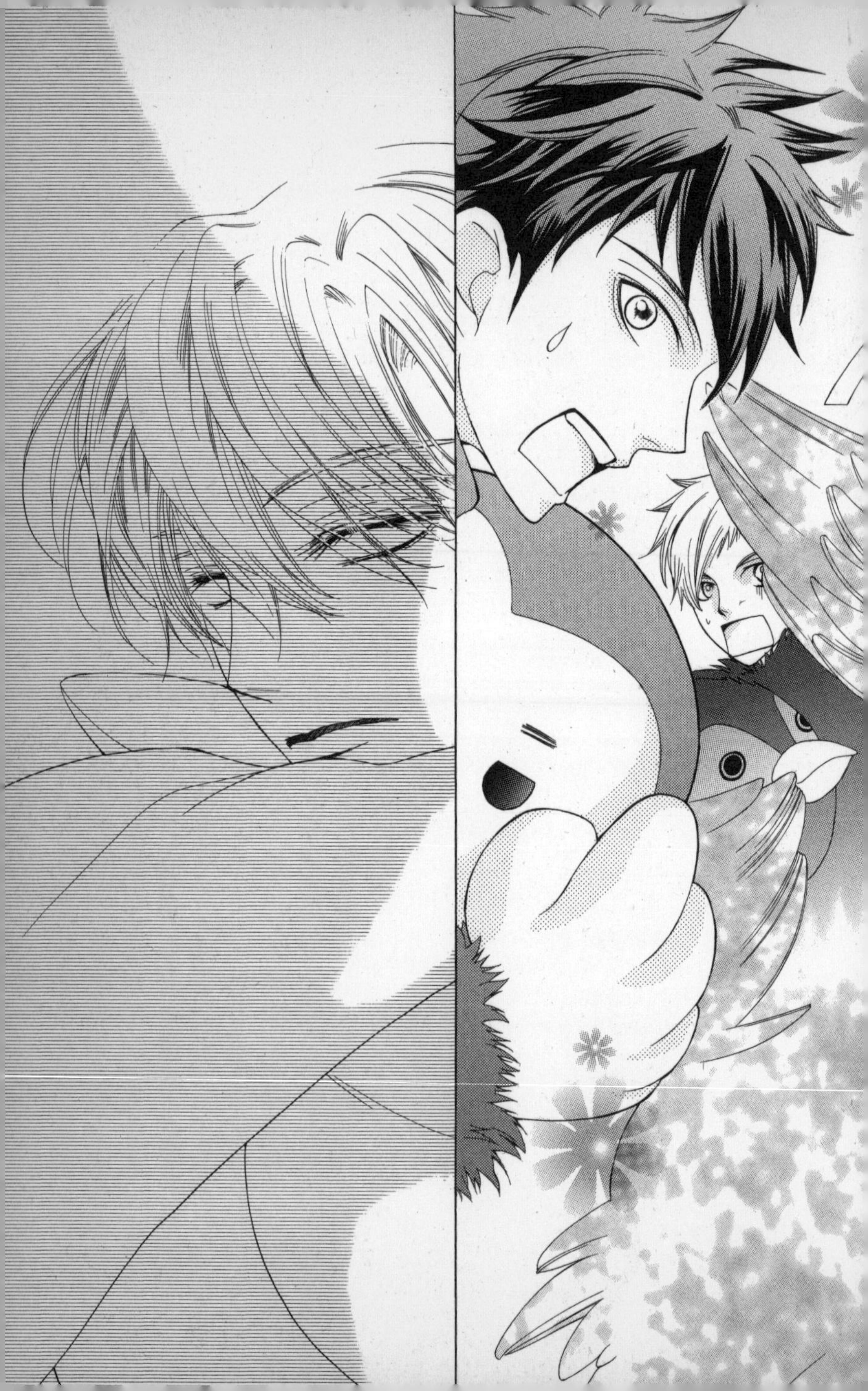

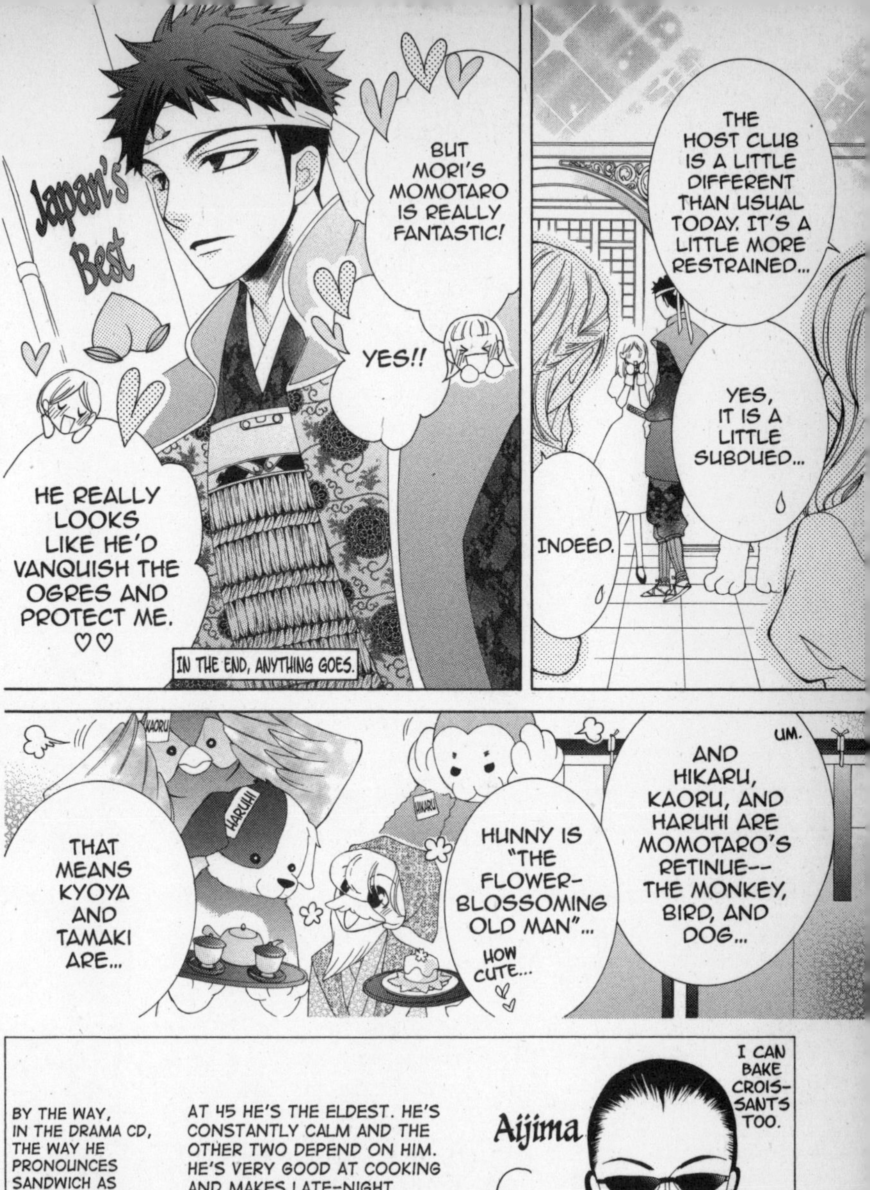
THE HOST CLUB IS A LITTLE DIFFERENT THAN USUAL TODAY. IT'S A LITTLE MORE RESTRAINED...
YES, IT IS A LITTLE SUBDUED...
INDEED.
BUT MORI'S MOMOTARO IS REALLY FANTASTIC!
YES!!
Japan's Best
HE REALLY LOOKS LIKE HE'D VANQUISH THE OGRES AND PROTECT ME. ♡♡
IN THE END, ANYTHING GOES.
UM.
AND HIKARU, KAORU, AND HARUHI ARE MOMOTARO'S RETINUE-- THE MONKEY, BIRD, AND DOG...
HIKARU
KAORU
HUNNY IS "THE FLOWER-BLOSSOMING OLD MAN"...
HOW CUTE...
HARUHI
THAT MEANS KYOYA AND TAMAKI ARE...

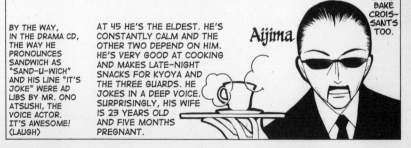

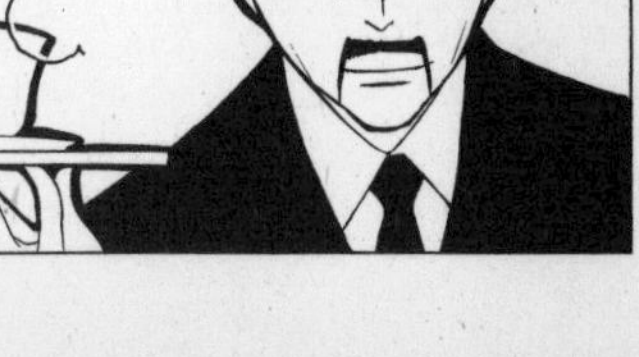
I CAN BAKE CROIS-SANTS TOO.
Aijima

AT 45 HE'S THE ELDEST. HE'S CONSTANTLY CALM AND THE OTHER TWO DEPEND ON HIM. HE'S VERY GOOD AT COOKING AND MAKES LATE-NIGHT SNACKS FOR KYOYA AND THE THREE GUARDS. HE JOKES IN A DEEP VOICE. SURPRISINGLY, HIS WIFE IS 23 YEARS OLD AND FIVE MONTHS PREGNANT.

BY THE WAY, IN THE DRAMA CD, THE WAY HE PRONOUNCES SANDWICH AS "SAND-U-WICH" AND HIS LINE "IT'S JOKE" WERE AD LIBS BY MR. ONO ATSUSHI, THE VOICE ACTOR. IT'S AWESOME! (LAUGH)

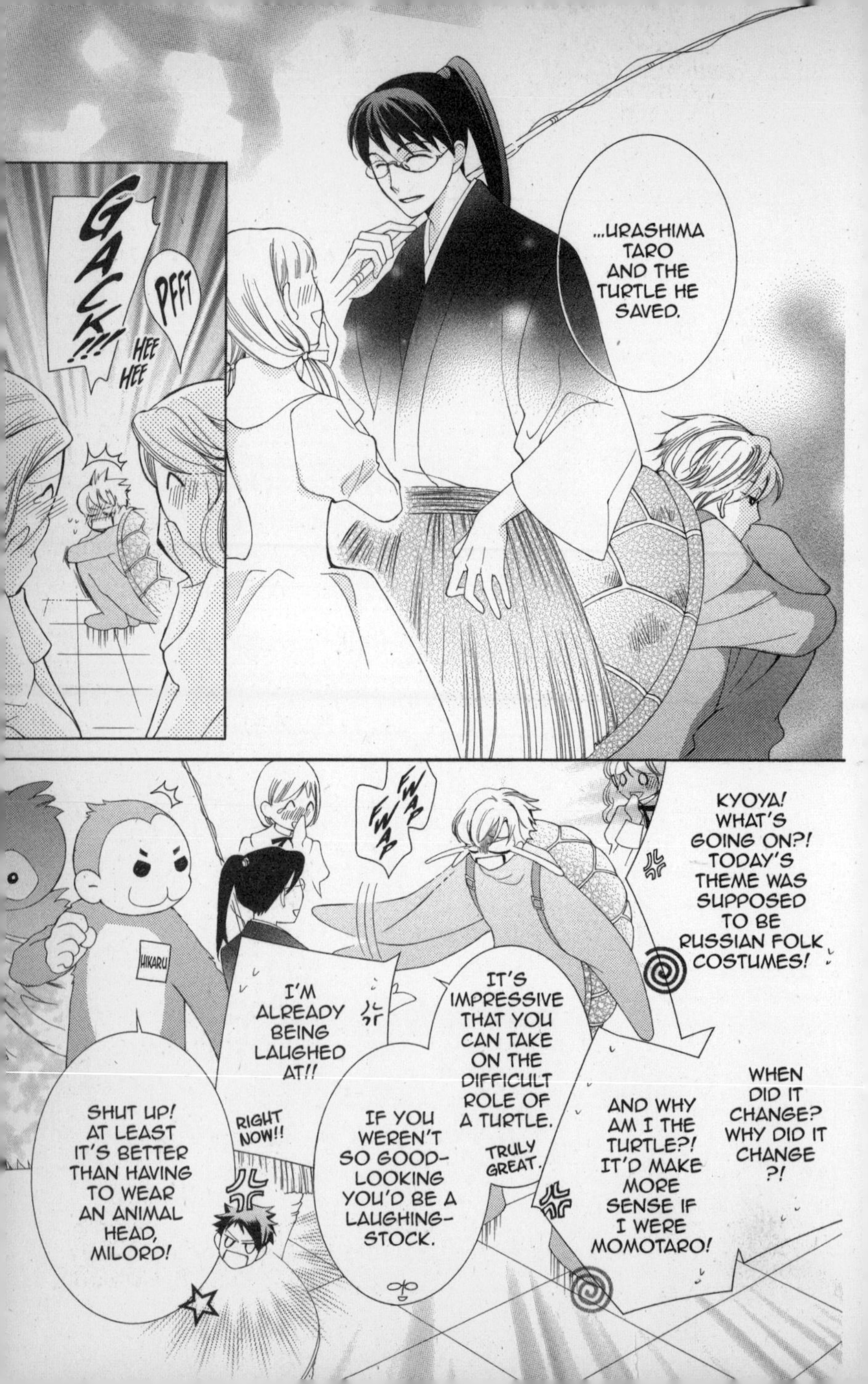
...URASHIMA TARO AND THE TURTLE HE SAVED.
GACK!!!
PFFT
HEE HEE
KYOYA! WHAT'S GOING ON?! TODAY'S THEME WAS SUPPOSED TO BE RUSSIAN FOLK COSTUMES!
WHEN DID IT CHANGE? WHY DID IT CHANGE?!
AND WHY AM I THE TURTLE?! IT'D MAKE MORE SENSE IF I WERE MOMOTARO!
IT'S IMPRESSIVE THAT YOU CAN TAKE ON THE DIFFICULT ROLE OF A TURTLE.
TRULY GREAT.
FWAP FWAP
I'M ALREADY BEING LAUGHED AT!!
IF YOU WEREN'T SO GOOD-LOOKING YOU'D BE A LAUGHING-STOCK.
RIGHT NOW!!
SHUT UP! AT LEAST IT'S BETTER THAN HAVING TO WEAR AN ANIMAL HEAD, MILORD!
HIKARU

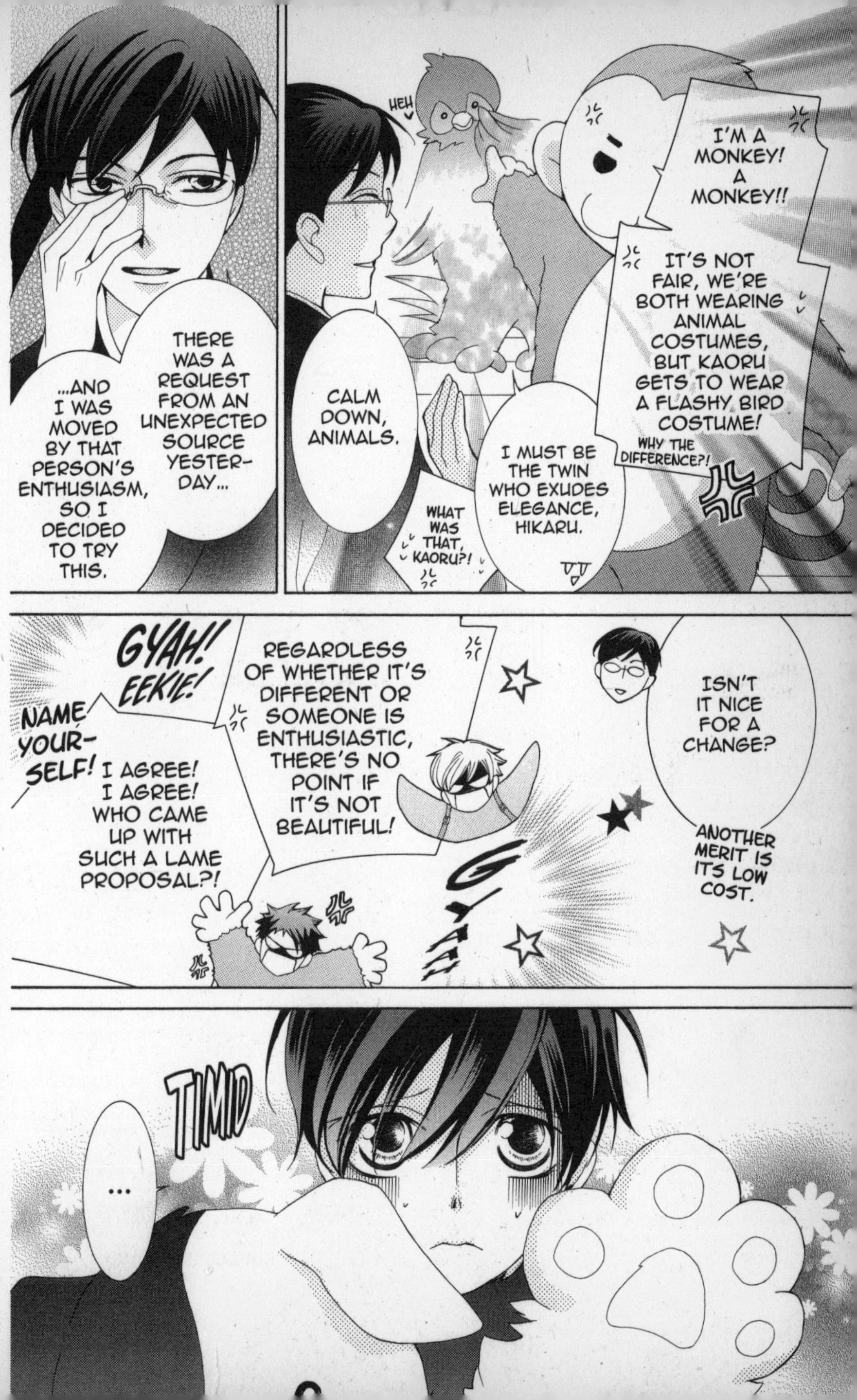
I'M A MONKEY! A MONKEY!!
IT'S NOT FAIR, WE'RE BOTH WEARING ANIMAL COSTUMES, BUT KAORU GETS TO WEAR A FLASHY BIRD COSTUME!
WHY THE DIFFERENCE?!
HEH
I MUST BE THE TWIN WHO EXUDES ELEGANCE, HIKARU.
WHAT WAS THAT, KAORU?!
CALM DOWN, ANIMALS.
THERE WAS A REQUEST FROM AN UNEXPECTED SOURCE YESTERDAY...
...AND I WAS MOVED BY THAT PERSON'S ENTHUSIASM, SO I DECIDED TO TRY THIS.
ISN'T IT NICE FOR A CHANGE?
ANOTHER MERIT IS ITS LOW COST.
REGARDLESS OF WHETHER IT'S DIFFERENT OR SOMEONE IS ENTHUSIASTIC, THERE'S NO POINT IF IT'S NOT BEAUTIFUL!
GYAH! EEKIE!
NAME YOURSELF!
I AGREE! I AGREE! WHO CAME UP WITH SUCH A LAME PROPOSAL?!
TIMID
...

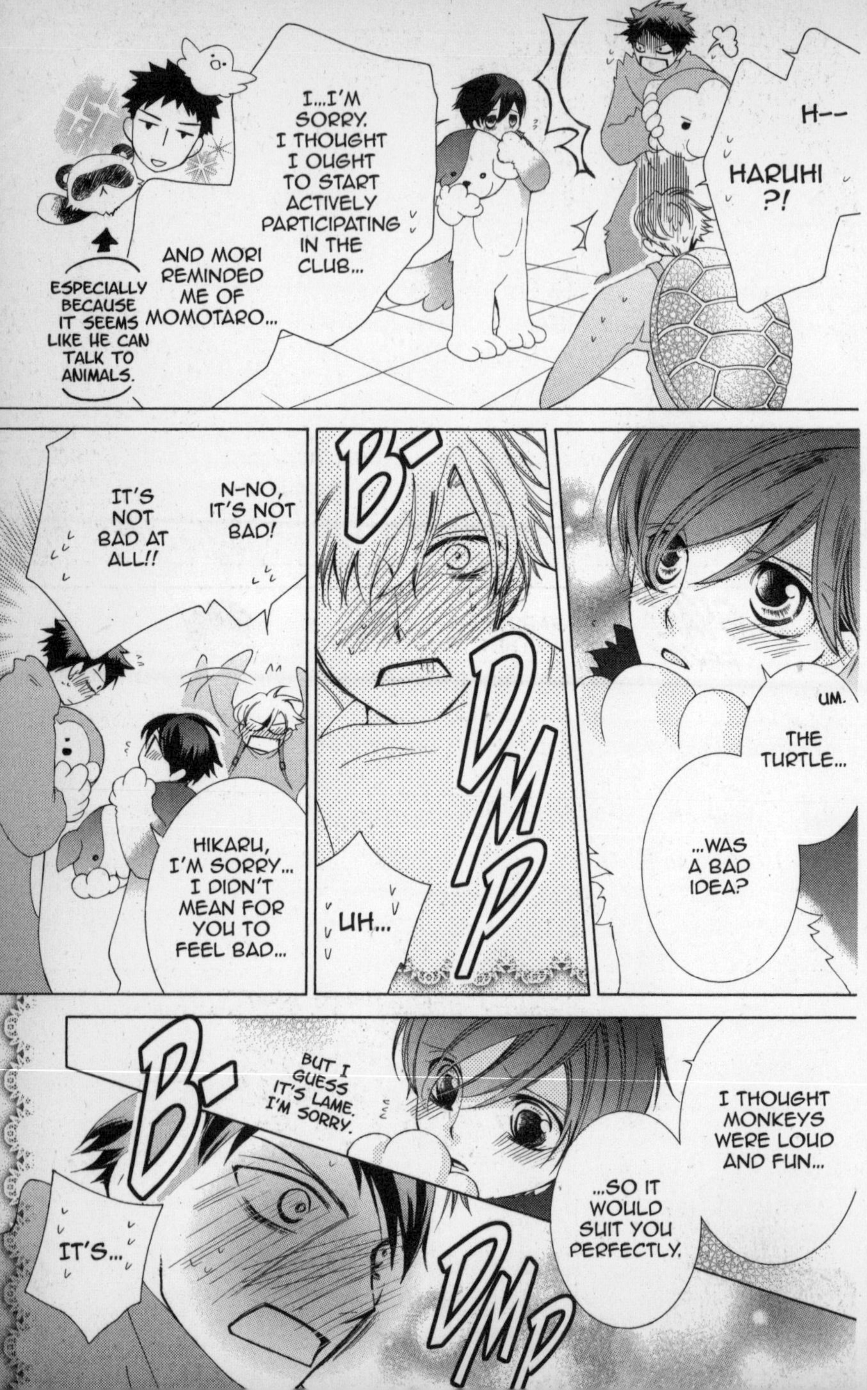
H--
HARUHI?!
I...I'M SORRY. I THOUGHT I OUGHT TO START ACTIVELY PARTICIPATING IN THE CLUB...
AND MORI REMINDED ME OF MOMOTARO...
ESPECIALLY BECAUSE IT SEEMS LIKE HE CAN TALK TO ANIMALS.
UM.
THE TURTLE...
...WAS A BAD IDEA?
B-
DMP
UH...
N-NO, IT'S NOT BAD!
IT'S NOT BAD AT ALL!!
HIKARU, I'M SORRY... I DIDN'T MEAN FOR YOU TO FEEL BAD...
I THOUGHT MONKEYS WERE LOUD AND FUN...
...SO IT WOULD SUIT YOU PERFECTLY.
BUT I GUESS IT'S LAME. I'M SORRY.
B-
DMP
IT'S...

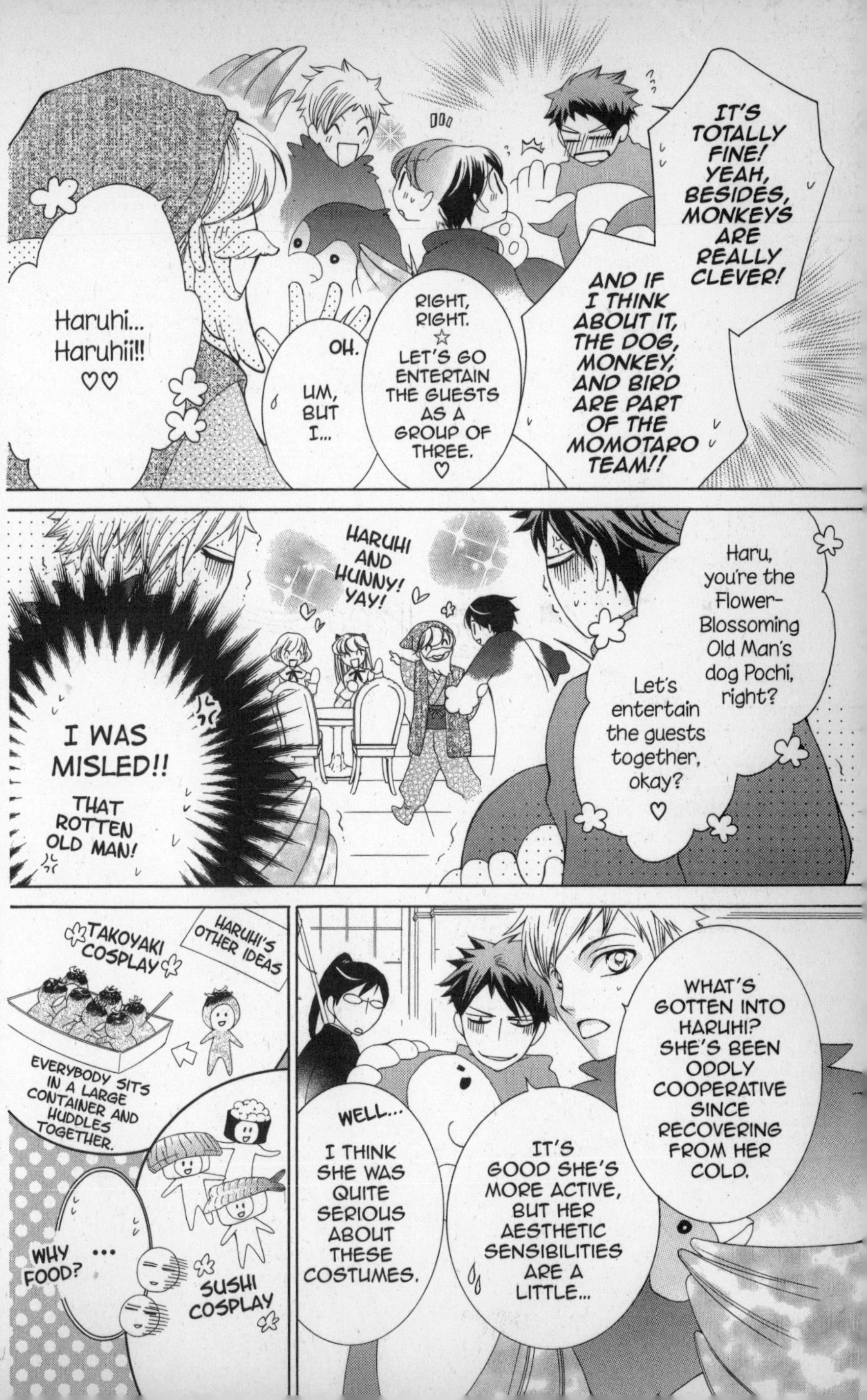
IT'S TOTALLY FINE! YEAH, BESIDES, MONKEYS ARE REALLY CLEVER!
AND IF I THINK ABOUT IT, THE DOG, MONKEY, AND BIRD ARE PART OF THE MOMOTARO TEAM!!
RIGHT, RIGHT. ☆ LET'S GO ENTERTAIN THE GUESTS AS A GROUP OF THREE. ♡
OH.
UM, BUT I...
Haruhi... Haruhii!! ♡♡
Haru, you're the Flower-Blossoming Old Man's dog Pochi, right?
Let's entertain the guests together, okay? ♡
HARUHI AND HUNNY! YAY!
I WAS MISLED!!
THAT ROTTEN OLD MAN!
WHAT'S GOTTEN INTO HARUHI? SHE'S BEEN ODDLY COOPERATIVE SINCE RECOVERING FROM HER COLD.
IT'S GOOD SHE'S MORE ACTIVE, BUT HER AESTHETIC SENSIBILITIES ARE A LITTLE...
WELL...
I THINK SHE WAS QUITE SERIOUS ABOUT THESE COSTUMES.
HARUHI'S OTHER IDEAS
TAKOYAKI COSPLAY
EVERYBODY SITS IN A LARGE CONTAINER AND HUDDLES TOGETHER.
SUSHI COSPLAY
...
WHY FOOD?

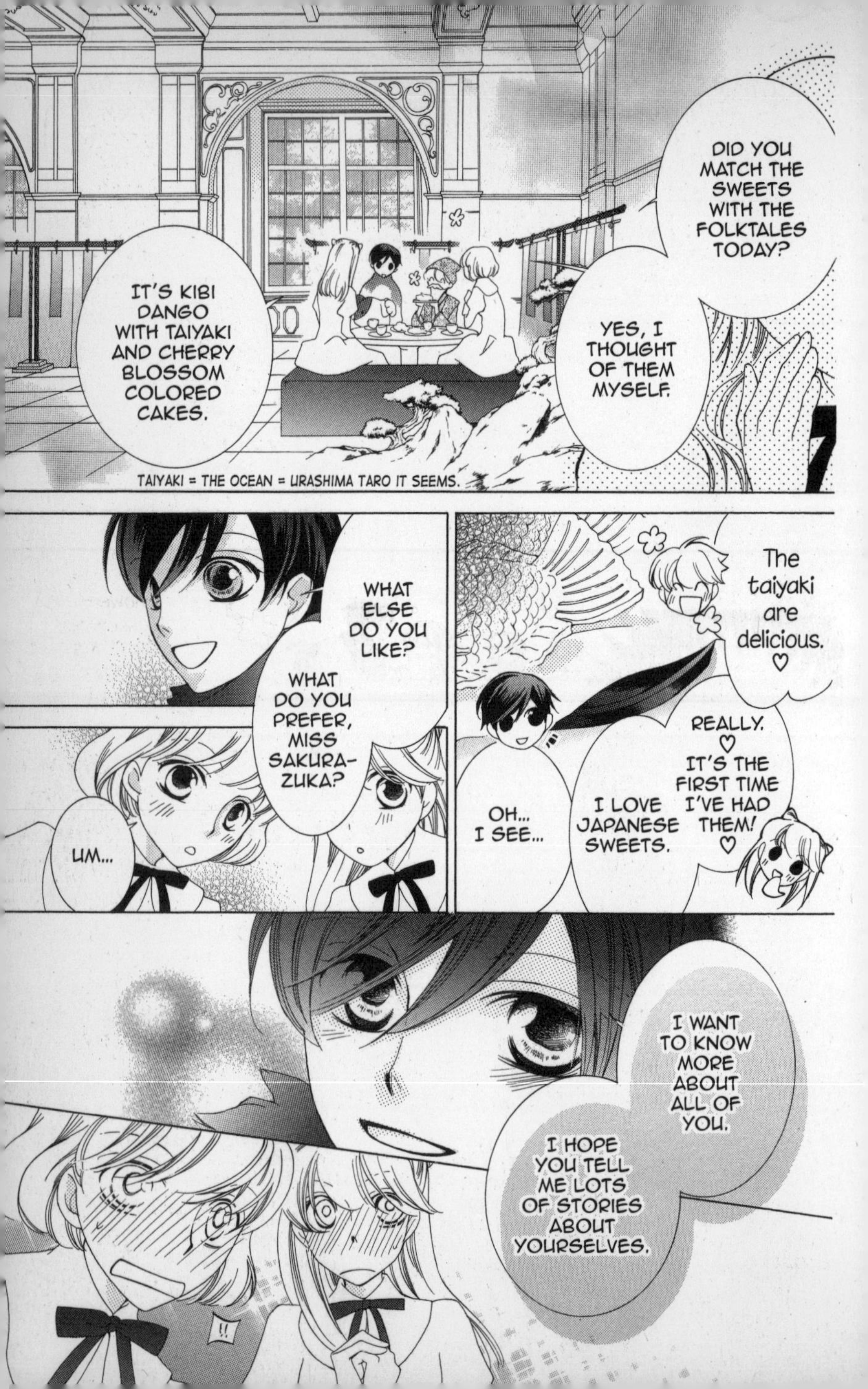
DID YOU MATCH THE SWEETS WITH THE FOLKTALES TODAY?
YES, I THOUGHT OF THEM MYSELF.
IT'S KIBI DANGO WITH TAIYAKI AND CHERRY BLOSSOM COLORED CAKES.
TAIYAKI = THE OCEAN = URASHIMA TARO IT SEEMS.
The taiyaki are delicious. ♡
REALLY. ♡ IT'S THE FIRST TIME I'VE HAD THEM! ♡
I LOVE JAPANESE SWEETS.
OH... I SEE...
WHAT ELSE DO YOU LIKE?
WHAT DO YOU PREFER, MISS SAKURAZUKA?
UM...
I WANT TO KNOW MORE ABOUT ALL OF YOU.
I HOPE YOU TELL ME LOTS OF STORIES ABOUT YOURSELVES.
!!

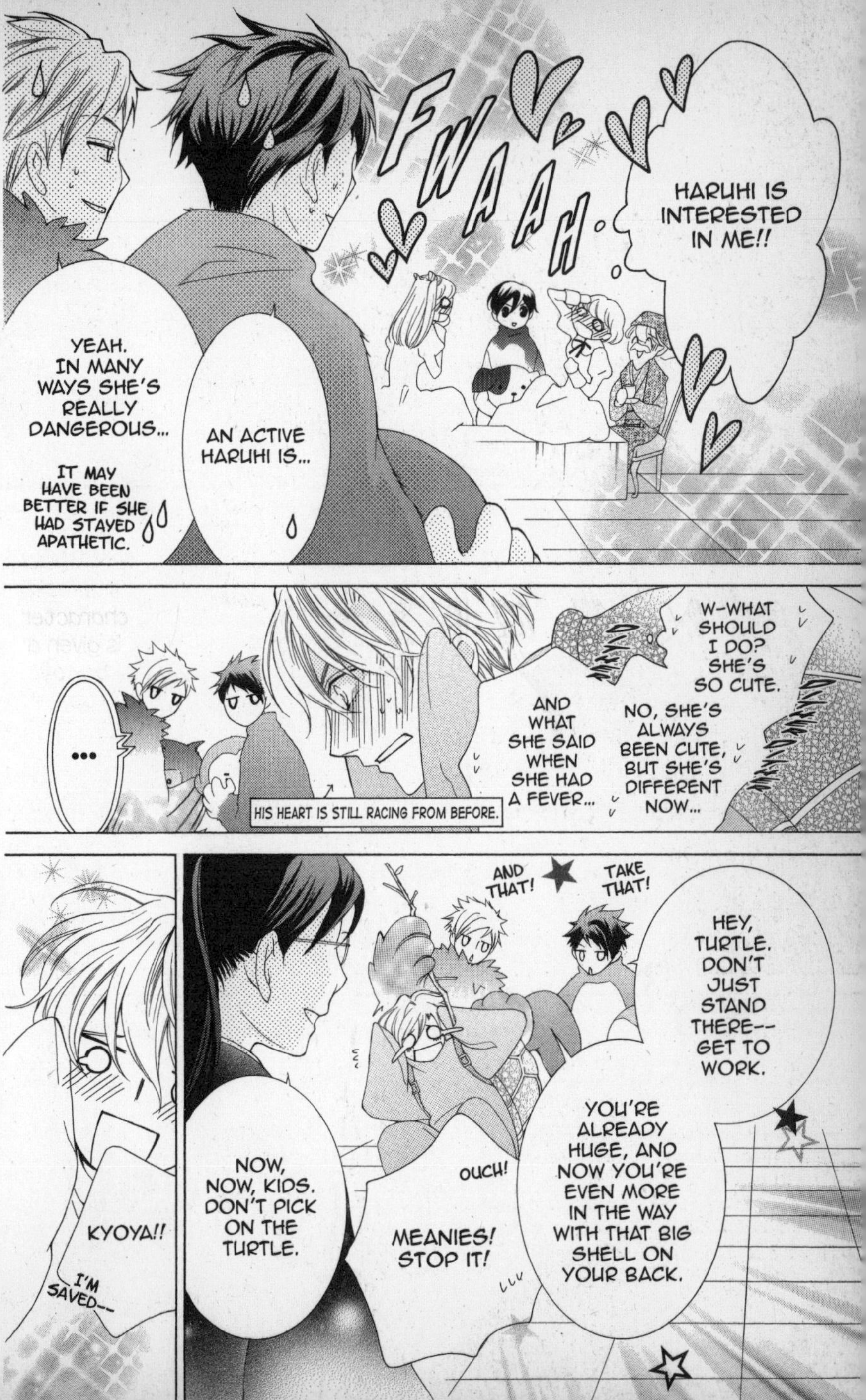
FWAAAH
HARUHI IS INTERESTED IN ME!!
AN ACTIVE HARUHI IS...
YEAH. IN MANY WAYS SHE'S REALLY DANGEROUS...
IT MAY HAVE BEEN BETTER IF SHE HAD STAYED APATHETIC.
W-WHAT SHOULD I DO? SHE'S SO CUTE.
NO, SHE'S ALWAYS BEEN CUTE, BUT SHE'S DIFFERENT NOW...
AND WHAT SHE SAID WHEN SHE HAD A FEVER...
HIS HEART IS STILL RACING FROM BEFORE.
...
TAKE THAT!
AND THAT!
HEY, TURTLE. DON'T JUST STAND THERE--GET TO WORK.
YOU'RE ALREADY HUGE, AND NOW YOU'RE EVEN MORE IN THE WAY WITH THAT BIG SHELL ON YOUR BACK.
OUCH!
MEANIES! STOP IT!
NOW, NOW, KIDS. DON'T PICK ON THE TURTLE.
KYOYA!!
I'M SAVED--

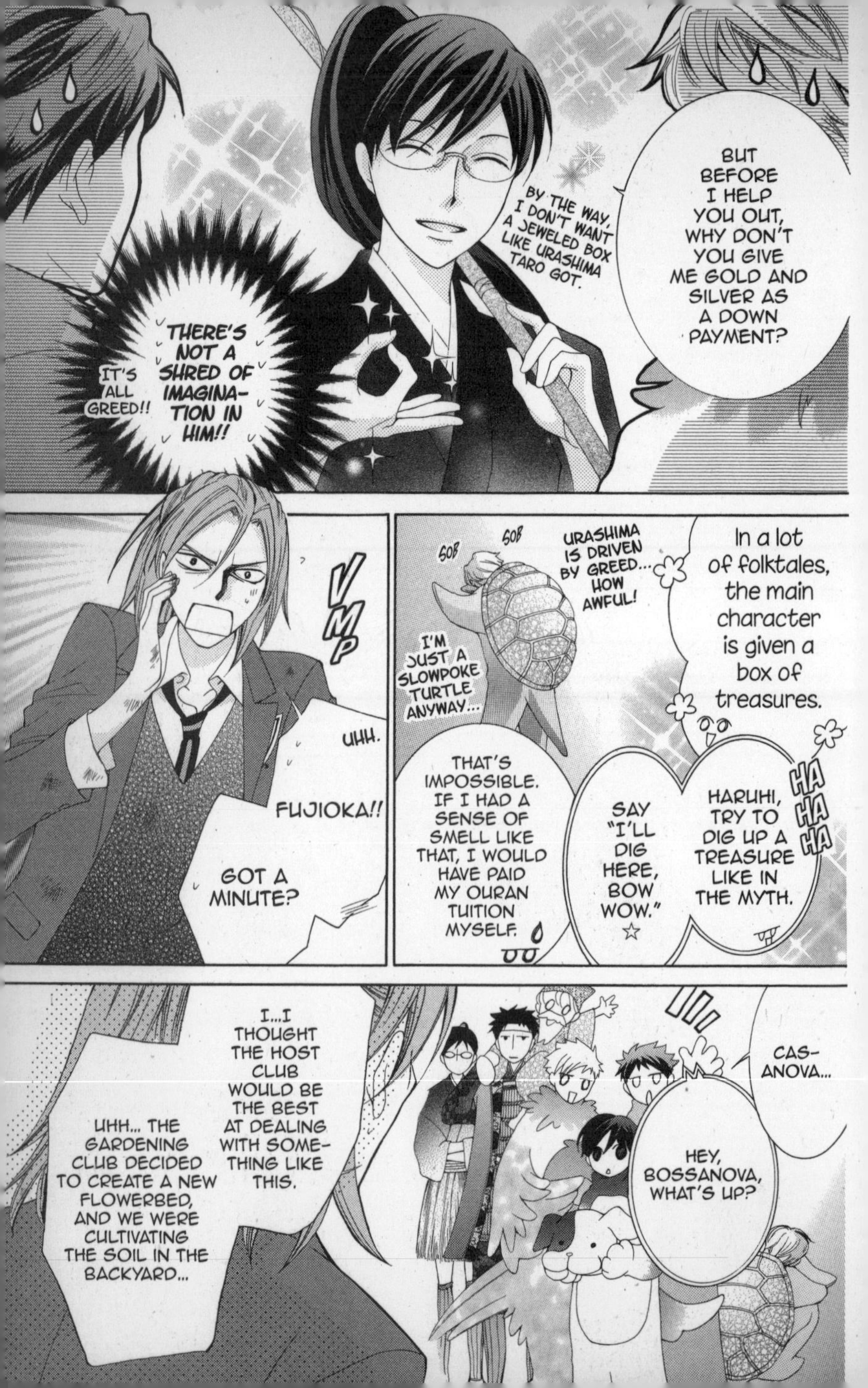
BUT BEFORE I HELP YOU OUT, WHY DON'T YOU GIVE ME GOLD AND SILVER AS A DOWN PAYMENT?
BY THE WAY, I DON'T WANT A JEWELED BOX LIKE URASHIMA TARO GOT.
THERE'S NOT A SHRED OF IMAGINATION IN HIM!!
IT'S ALL GREED!!
In a lot of folktales, the main character is given a box of treasures.
URASHIMA IS DRIVEN BY GREED... HOW AWFUL!
SOB
SOB
I'M JUST A SLOWPOKE TURTLE ANYWAY...
HARUHI, TRY TO DIG UP A TREASURE LIKE IN THE MYTH.
HA HA HA
SAY "I'LL DIG HERE, BOW WOW." ☆
THAT'S IMPOSSIBLE. IF I HAD A SENSE OF SMELL LIKE THAT, I WOULD HAVE PAID MY OURAN TUITION MYSELF.
VMP
UHH.
FUJIOKA!!
GOT A MINUTE?
CAS-ANOVA...
HEY, BOSSANOVA, WHAT'S UP?
I...I THOUGHT THE HOST CLUB WOULD BE THE BEST AT DEALING WITH SOME-THING LIKE THIS.
UHH... THE GARDENING CLUB DECIDED TO CREATE A NEW FLOWERBED, AND WE WERE CULTIVATING THE SOIL IN THE BACKYARD...

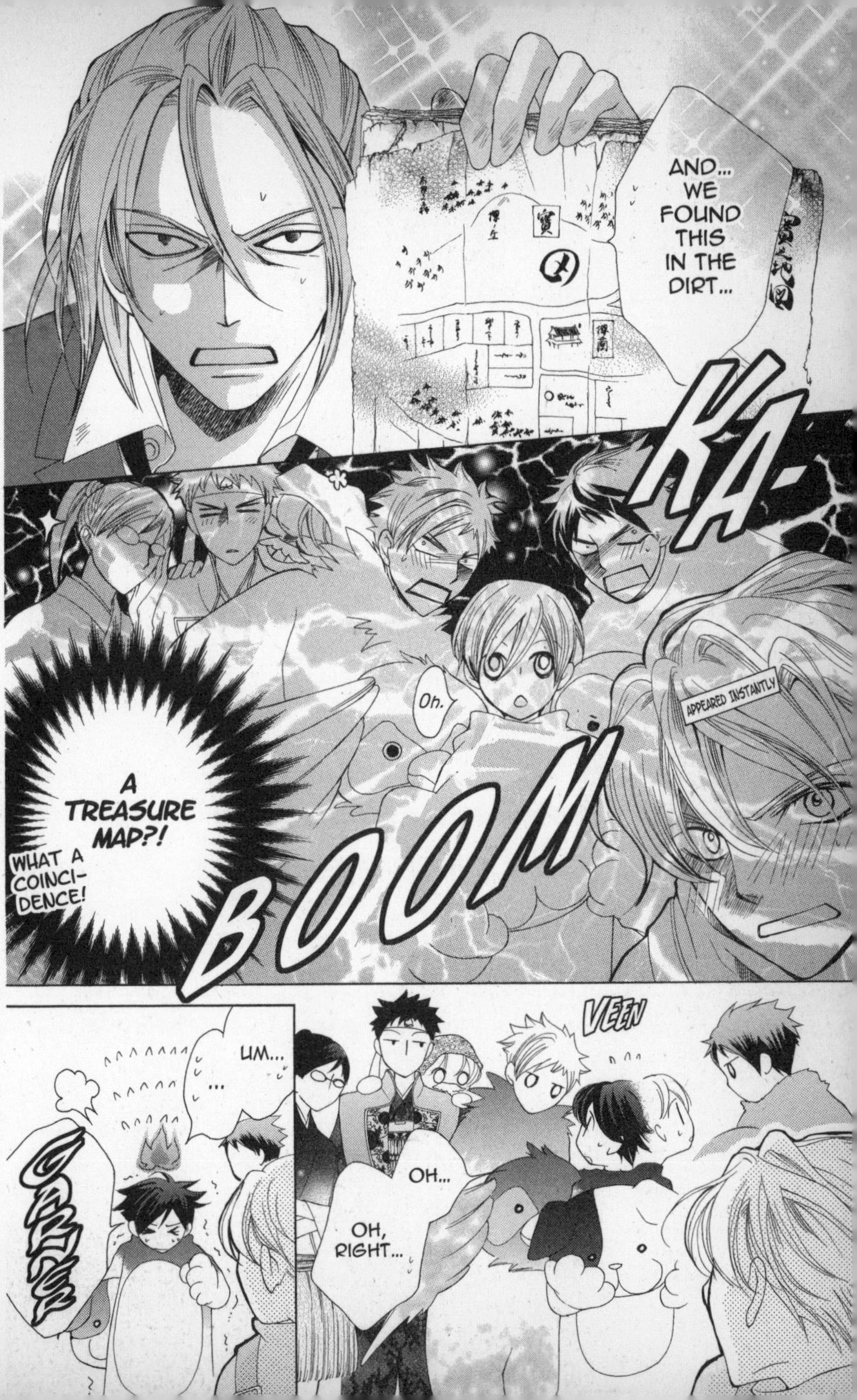

AND... WE FOUND THIS IN THE DIRT...
KA-
APPEARED INSTANTLY
Oh.
BOOM
A TREASURE MAP?!
WHAT A COINCI-DENCE!
VEEN
OH...
OH, RIGHT...
UM...
...

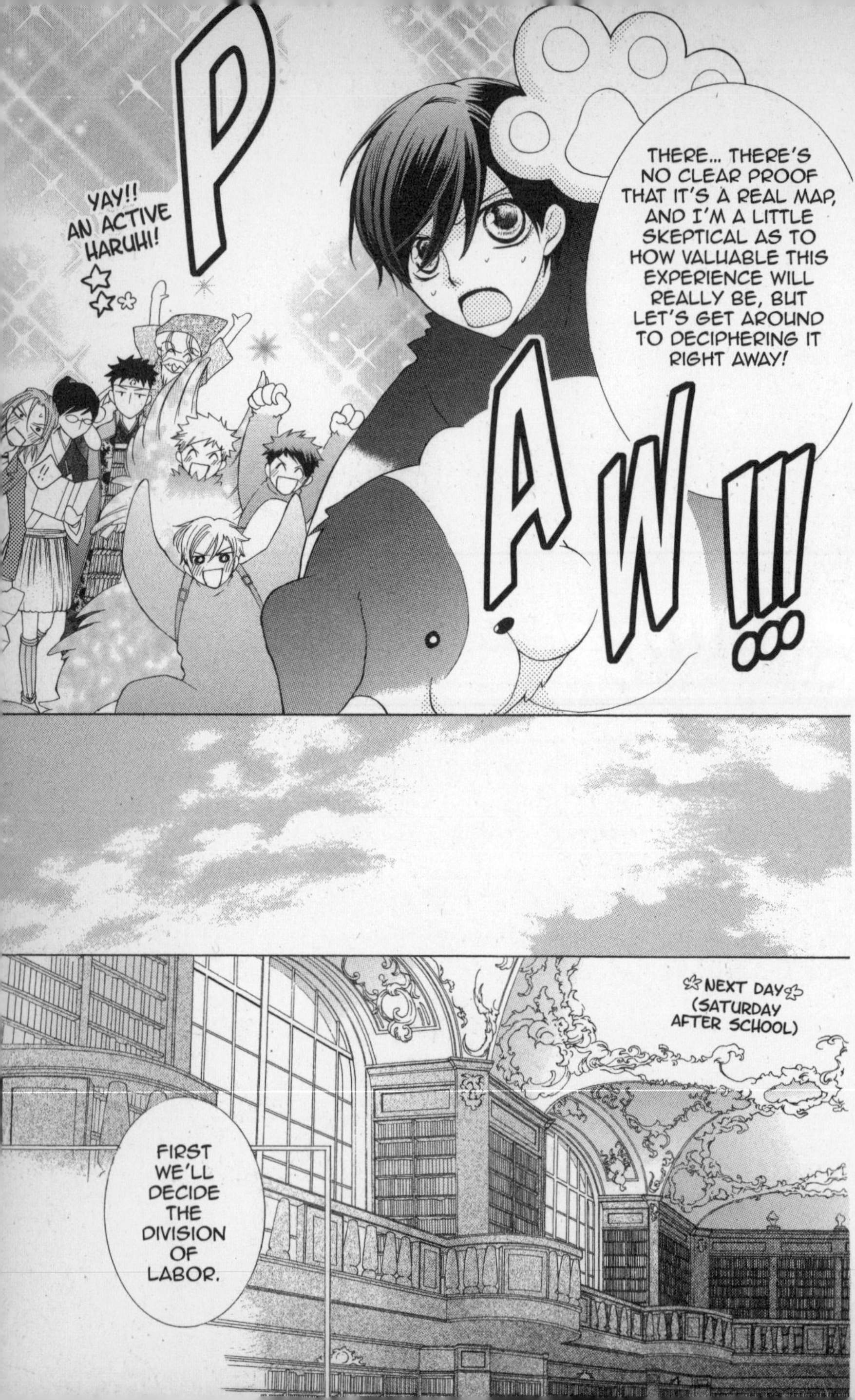
THERE... THERE'S NO CLEAR PROOF THAT IT'S A REAL MAP, AND I'M A LITTLE SKEPTICAL AS TO HOW VALUABLE THIS EXPERIENCE WILL REALLY BE, BUT LET'S GET AROUND TO DECIPHERING IT RIGHT AWAY!
PAW!!!...
YAY!! AN ACTIVE HARUHI!
NEXT DAY (SATURDAY AFTER SCHOOL)
FIRST WE'LL DECIDE THE DIVISION OF LABOR.

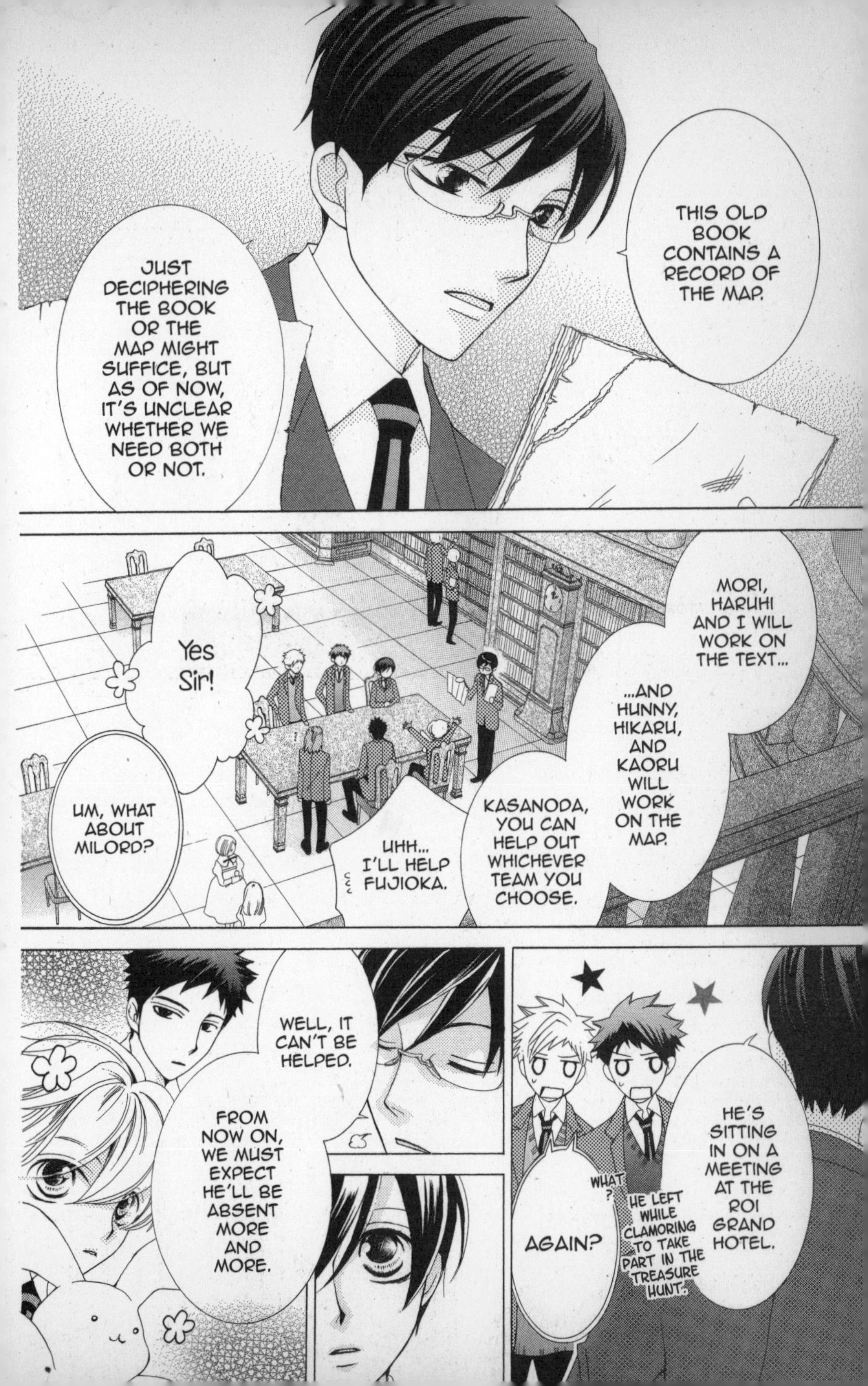
THIS OLD BOOK CONTAINS A RECORD OF THE MAP.
JUST DECIPHERING THE BOOK OR THE MAP MIGHT SUFFICE, BUT AS OF NOW, IT'S UNCLEAR WHETHER WE NEED BOTH OR NOT.
MORI, HARUHI AND I WILL WORK ON THE TEXT...
...AND HUNNY, HIKARU, AND KAORU WILL WORK ON THE MAP.
KASANODA, YOU CAN HELP OUT WHICHEVER TEAM YOU CHOOSE.
UHH... I'LL HELP FUJIOKA.
Yes Sir!
UM, WHAT ABOUT MILORD?
HE'S SITTING IN ON A MEETING AT THE ROI GRAND HOTEL.
HE LEFT WHILE CLAMORING TO TAKE PART IN THE TREASURE HUNT.
WHAT?
AGAIN?
WELL, IT CAN'T BE HELPED.
FROM NOW ON, WE MUST EXPECT HE'LL BE ABSENT MORE AND MORE.

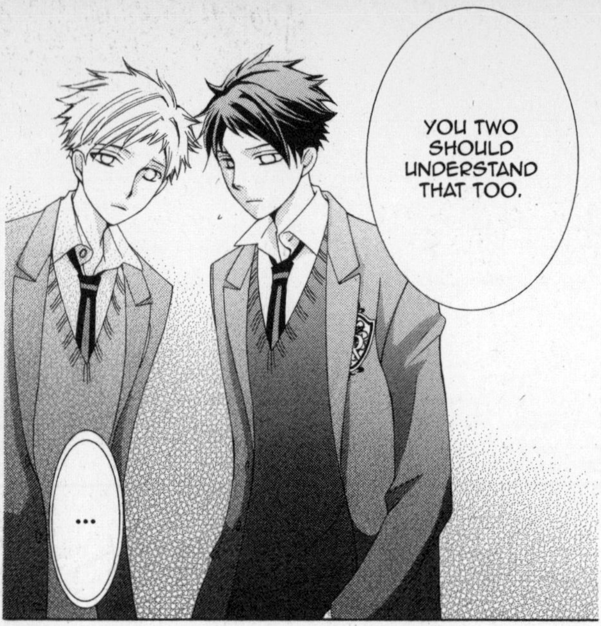
YOU TWO SHOULD UNDERSTAND THAT TOO.
...

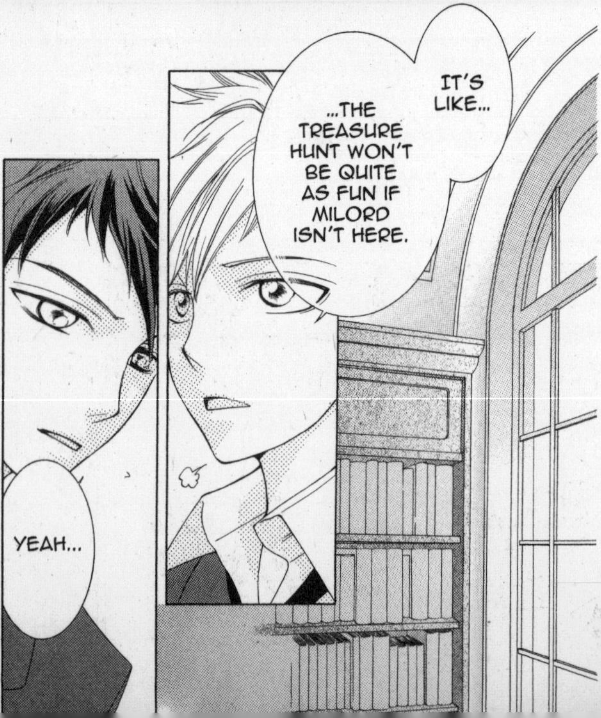
IT'S LIKE...
...THE TREASURE HUNT WON'T BE QUITE AS FUN IF MILORD ISN'T HERE.
YEAH...

3

✿WELL, STUFF LIKE THIS HAPPENS. WHEN IT HAPPENED I WAS REALLY TAKEN ABACK. I WAS.

✿MOVING ON... H/K (CHANGING THE SUBJECT). ABOUT THE RESEARCH TRIP TO THE SNOWY MOUNTAINS...

FOR THIS VOLUME, WE VISITED IWATE PREFECTURE'S APPI PLAINS AND HACHIMANTAI WHERE KANA OF THE NIZAKANA PAIR (MANGA CREATORS) LIVES.

KANA DROVE FOR US, AND WE TOURED THE HOT SPRINGS AND THE SKI RESORTS! OH BOY.

IT WAS QUITE A TRIP. KANA WROTE ABOUT THE DETAILS IN *LA LA DX*, SO MANY OF YOU ALREADY KNOW ABOUT IT, BUT I WANTED TO TALK A LITTLE ABOUT IT TOO.

① AT THE SKI RESORT, WE REACHED THE SUMMIT BY CABLE CAR AND SKI LIFT, BUT THERE WAS A SNOWSTORM AND THE LIFT STOPPED WORKING. THE SNOWMOBILE EMERGENCY CREW HELPED US OUT. THE SNOWMOBILES ARE REALLY FRIGHTENING...

BUT IT WAS ALSO REALLY FUN!!

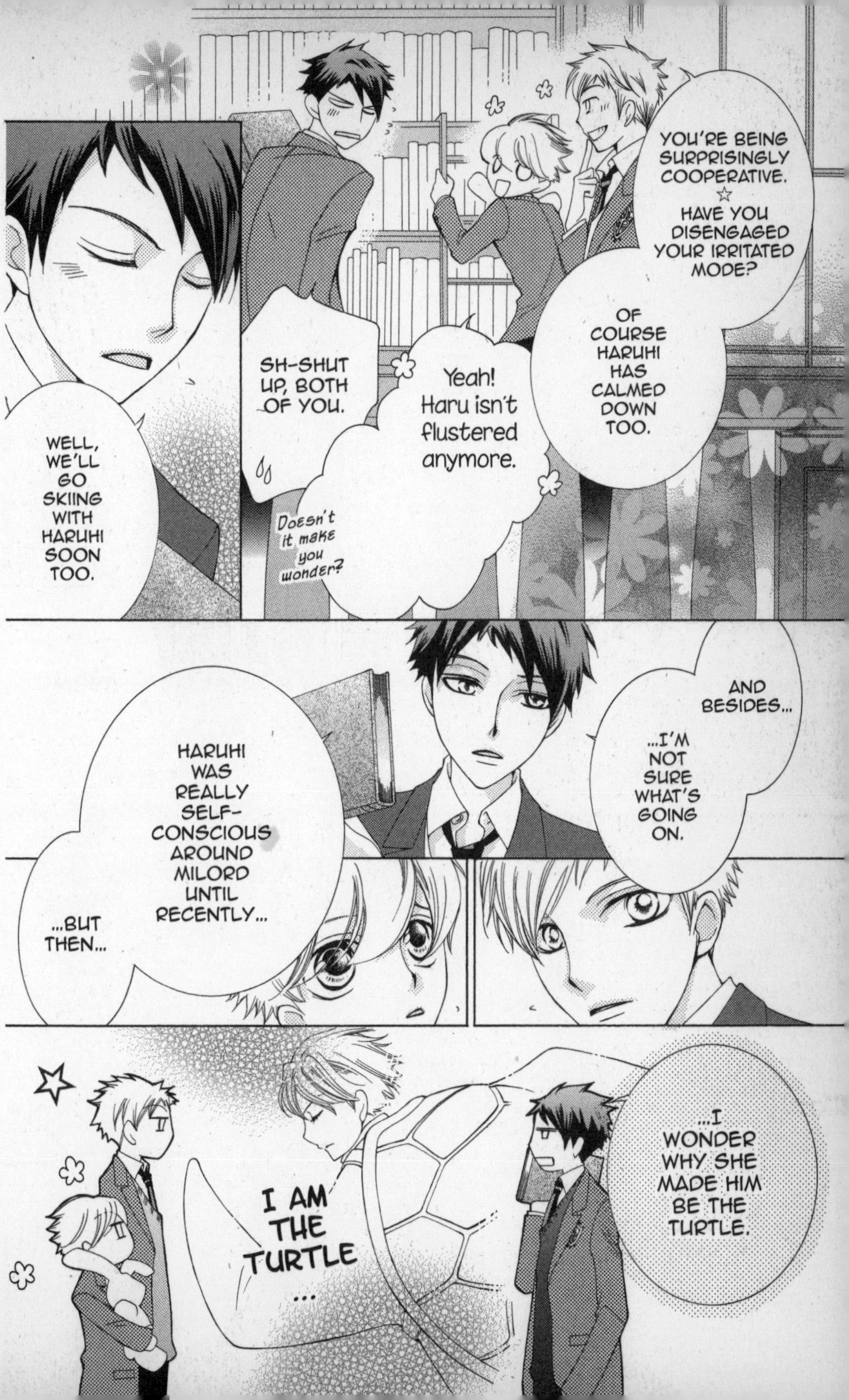
YOU'RE BEING SURPRISINGLY COOPERATIVE. ☆ HAVE YOU DISENGAGED YOUR IRRITATED MODE?
OF COURSE HARUHI HAS CALMED DOWN TOO.
Yeah! Haru isn't flustered anymore.
SH-SHUT UP, BOTH OF YOU.
Doesn't it make you wonder?
WELL, WE'LL GO SKIING WITH HARUHI SOON TOO.
AND BESIDES...
...I'M NOT SURE WHAT'S GOING ON.
HARUHI WAS REALLY SELF-CONSCIOUS AROUND MILORD UNTIL RECENTLY...
...BUT THEN...
...I WONDER WHY SHE MADE HIM BE THE TURTLE.
I AM THE TURTLE...

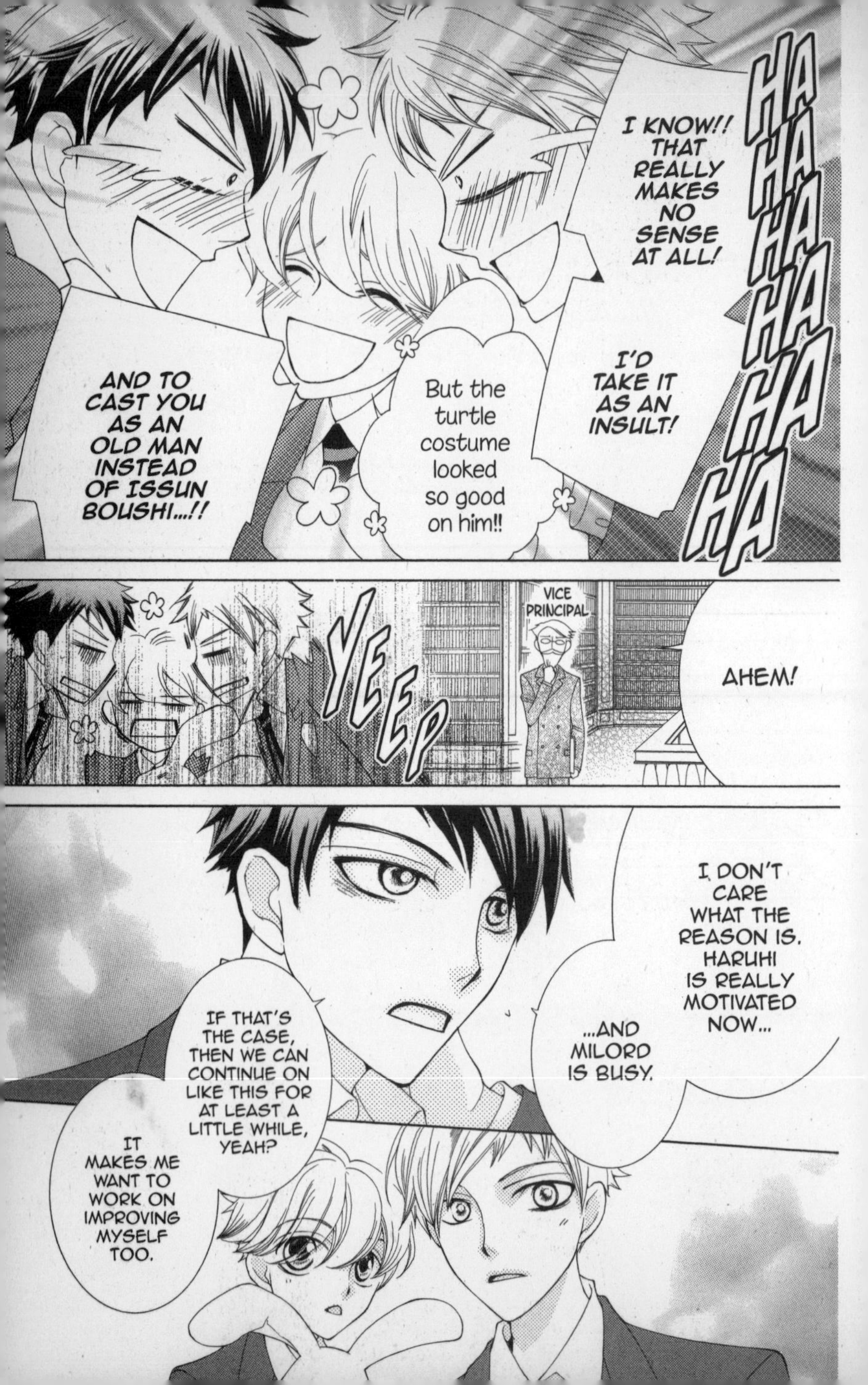
HA HA HA HA HA HA HA HA
I KNOW!! THAT REALLY MAKES NO SENSE AT ALL!
I'D TAKE IT AS AN INSULT!
But the turtle costume looked so good on him!!
AND TO CAST YOU AS AN OLD MAN INSTEAD OF ISSUN BOUSHI...!!
AHEM!
VICE PRINCIPAL
YEEP
I DON'T CARE WHAT THE REASON IS. HARUHI IS REALLY MOTIVATED NOW...
...AND MILORD IS BUSY.
IF THAT'S THE CASE, THEN WE CAN CONTINUE ON LIKE THIS FOR AT LEAST A LITTLE WHILE, YEAH?
IT MAKES ME WANT TO WORK ON IMPROVING MYSELF TOO.

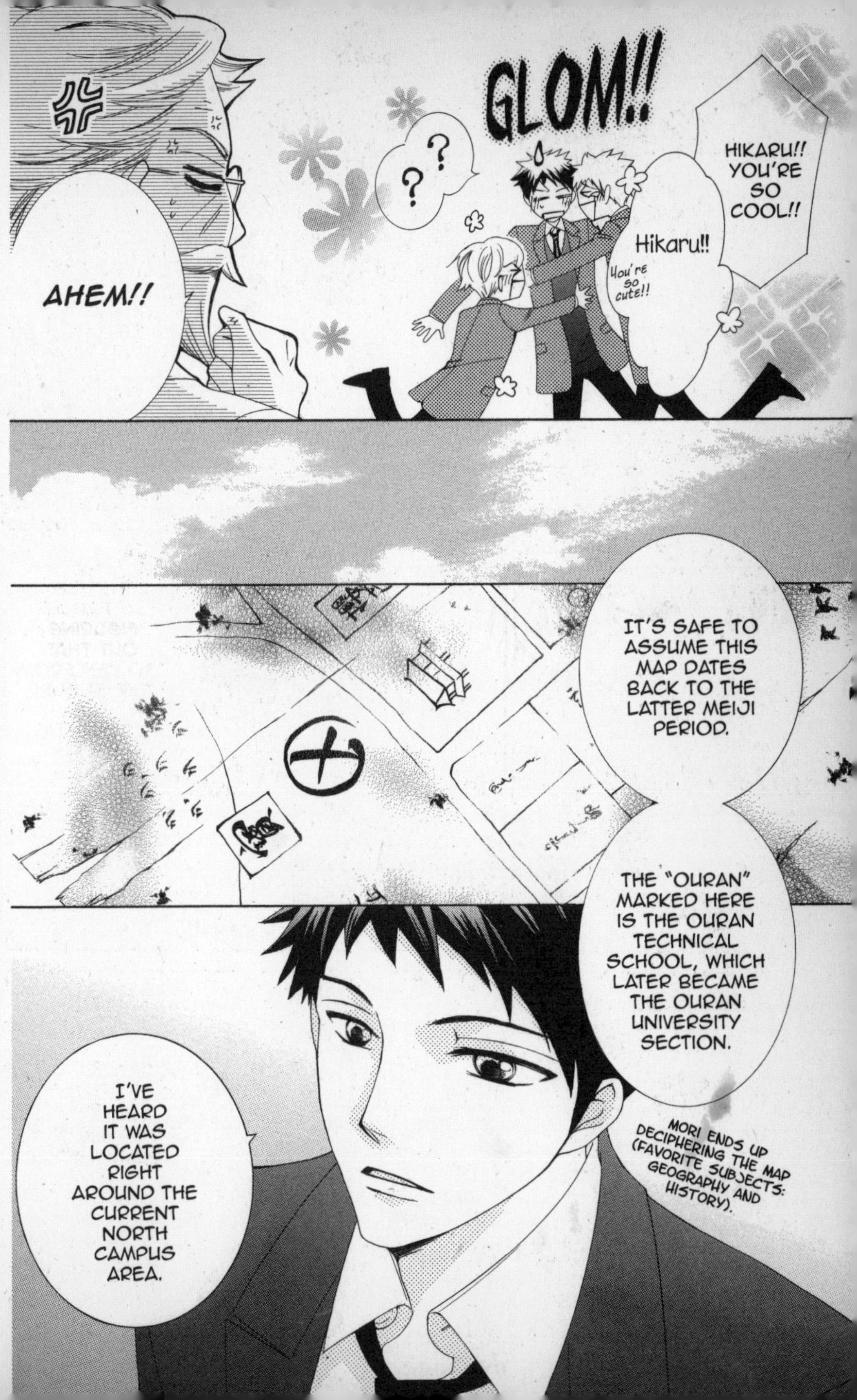
GLOM!!
HIKARU!! YOU'RE SO COOL!!
Hikaru!!
You're so cute!!
? ?
AHEM!!
IT'S SAFE TO ASSUME THIS MAP DATES BACK TO THE LATTER MEIJI PERIOD.
THE "OURAN" MARKED HERE IS THE OURAN TECHNICAL SCHOOL, WHICH LATER BECAME THE OURAN UNIVERSITY SECTION.
MORI ENDS UP DECIPHERING THE MAP (FAVORITE SUBJECTS: GEOGRAPHY AND HISTORY).
I'VE HEARD IT WAS LOCATED RIGHT AROUND THE CURRENT NORTH CAMPUS AREA.

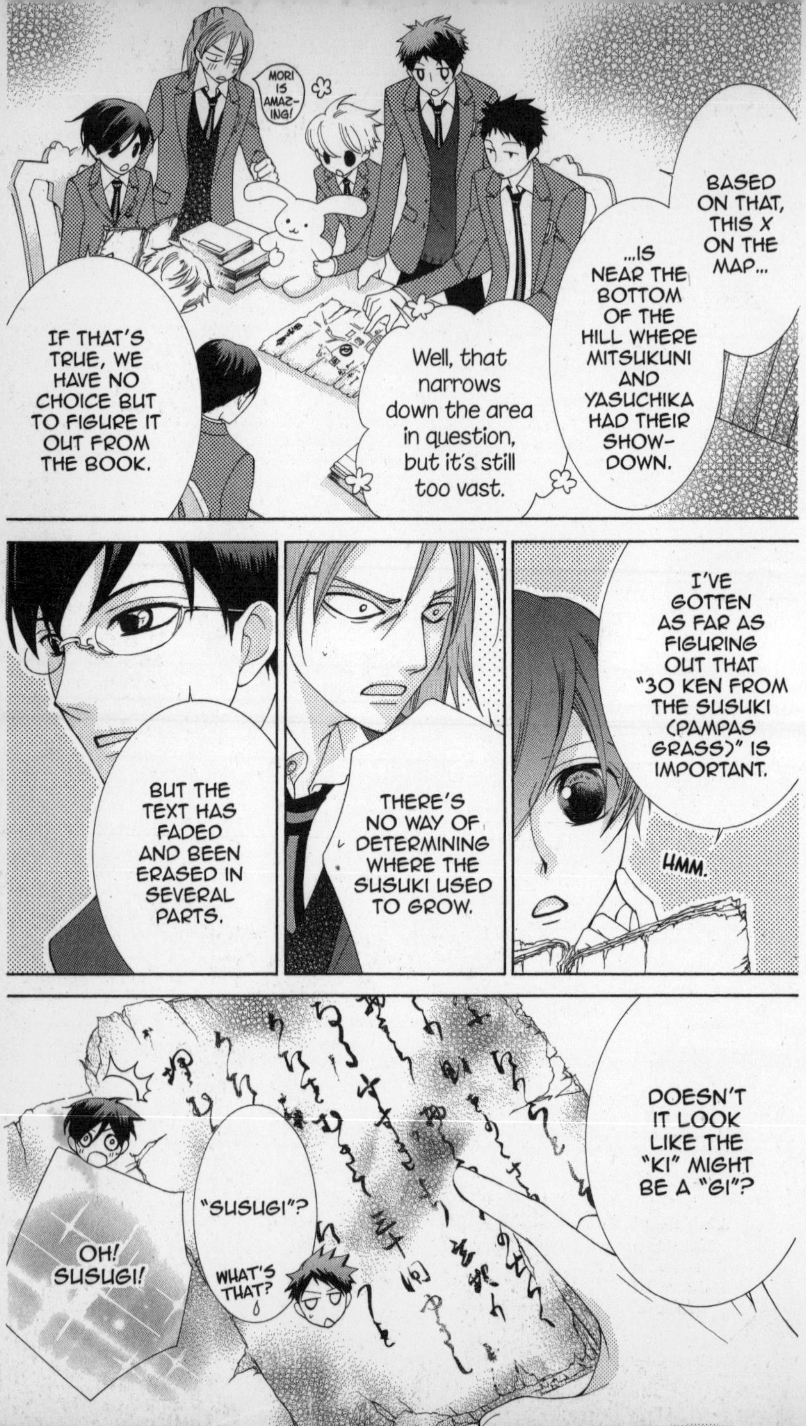
BASED ON THAT, THIS X ON THE MAP...
...IS NEAR THE BOTTOM OF THE HILL WHERE MITSUKUNI AND YASUCHIKA HAD THEIR SHOW-DOWN.
MORI IS AMAZ-ING!
Well, that narrows down the area in question, but it's still too vast.
IF THAT'S TRUE, WE HAVE NO CHOICE BUT TO FIGURE IT OUT FROM THE BOOK.
I'VE GOTTEN AS FAR AS FIGURING OUT THAT "30 KEN FROM THE SUSUKI (PAMPAS GRASS)" IS IMPORTANT.
HMM.
THERE'S NO WAY OF DETERMINING WHERE THE SUSUKI USED TO GROW.
BUT THE TEXT HAS FADED AND BEEN ERASED IN SEVERAL PARTS.
DOESN'T IT LOOK LIKE THE "KI" MIGHT BE A "GI"?
"SUSUGI"?
WHAT'S THAT?
OH! SUSUGI!

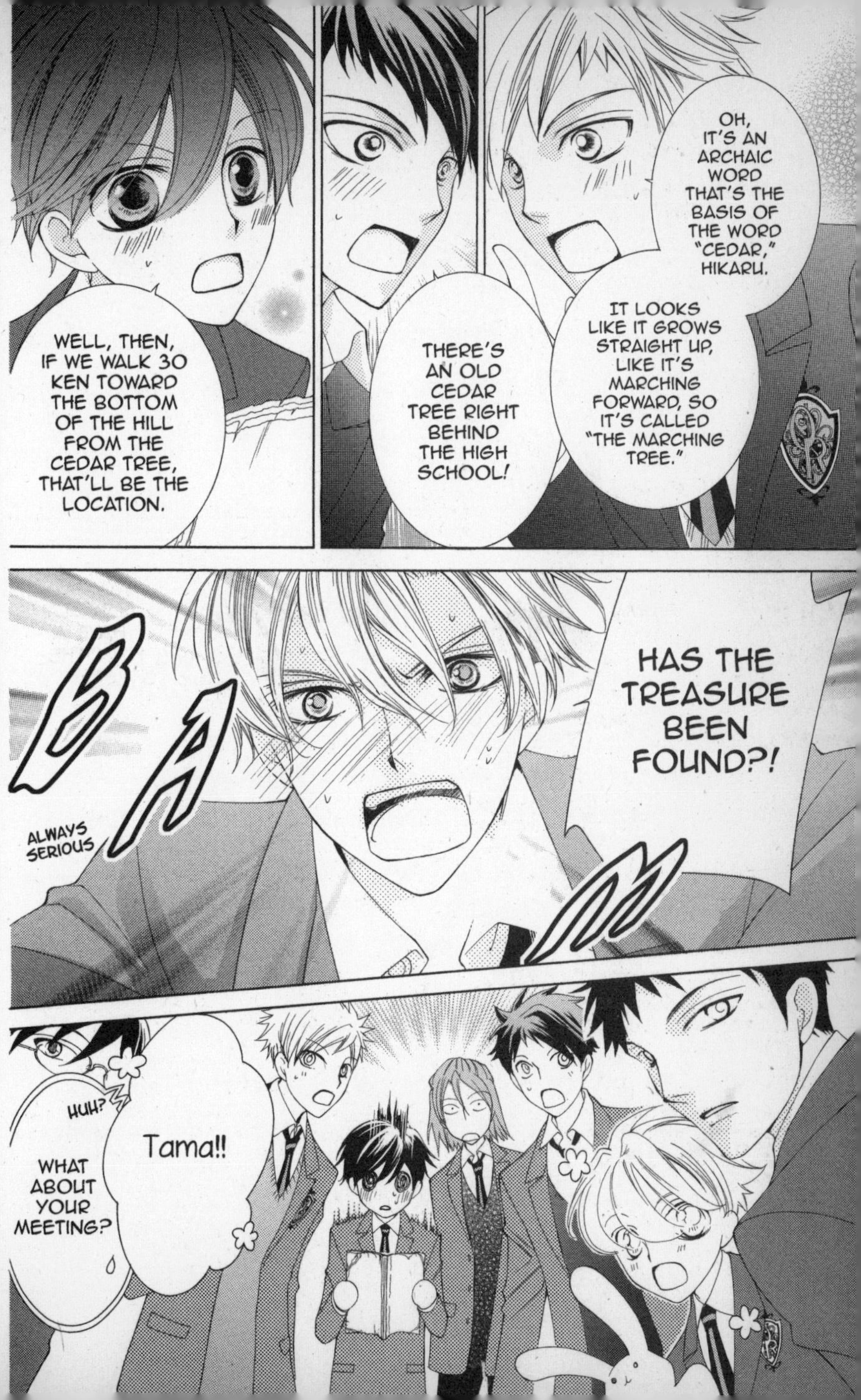
OH, IT'S AN ARCHAIC WORD THAT'S THE BASIS OF THE WORD "CEDAR," HIKARU.
IT LOOKS LIKE IT GROWS STRAIGHT UP, LIKE IT'S MARCHING FORWARD, SO IT'S CALLED "THE MARCHING TREE."
THERE'S AN OLD CEDAR TREE RIGHT BEHIND THE HIGH SCHOOL!
WELL, THEN, IF WE WALK 30 KEN TOWARD THE BOTTOM OF THE HILL FROM THE CEDAR TREE, THAT'LL BE THE LOCATION.
HAS THE TREASURE BEEN FOUND?!
BAM
ALWAYS SERIOUS
Tama!!
HUH?
WHAT ABOUT YOUR MEETING?

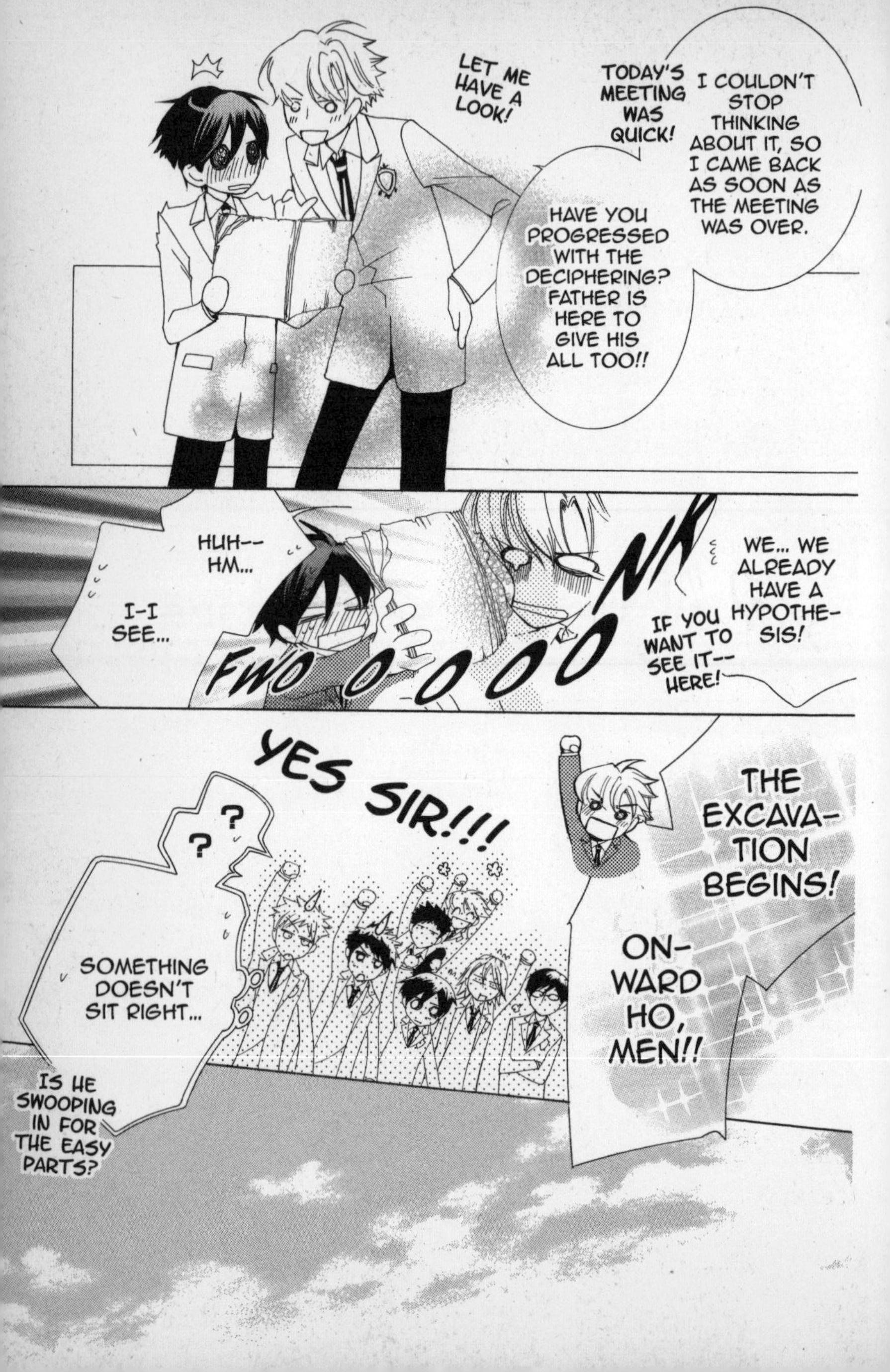
TODAY'S MEETING WAS QUICK!
I COULDN'T STOP THINKING ABOUT IT, SO I CAME BACK AS SOON AS THE MEETING WAS OVER.
HAVE YOU PROGRESSED WITH THE DECIPHERING? FATHER IS HERE TO GIVE HIS ALL TOO!!
LET ME HAVE A LOOK!
WE... WE ALREADY HAVE A HYPOTHE-SIS!
IF YOU WANT TO SEE IT-- HERE!
NK
FWOOOOO
HUH-- HM...
I-I SEE...
THE EXCAVA-TION BEGINS!
ON-WARD HO, MEN!!
YES SIR!!!
??
SOMETHING DOESN'T SIT RIGHT...
IS HE SWOOPING IN FOR THE EASY PARTS?

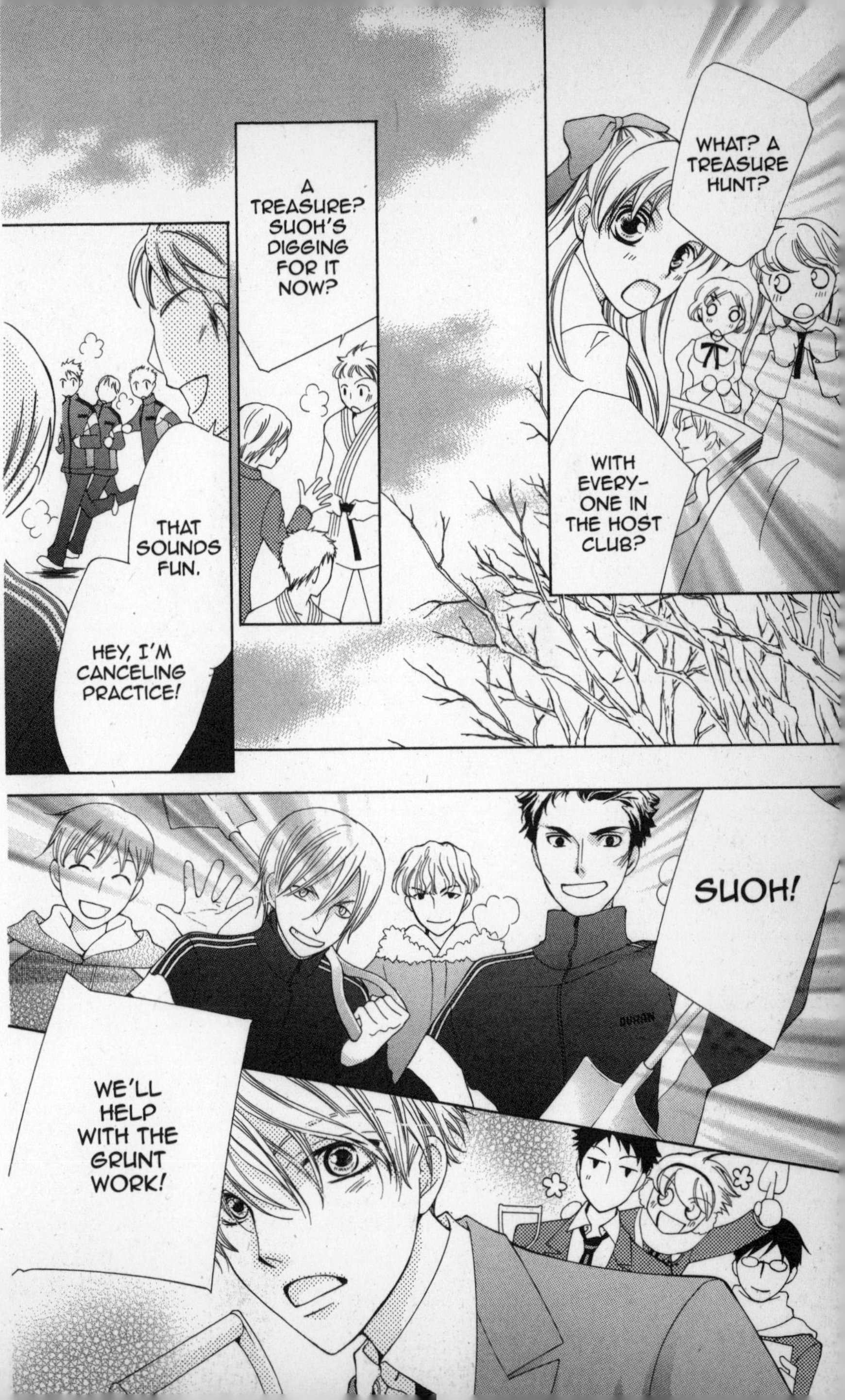
WHAT? A TREASURE HUNT?
WITH EVERYONE IN THE HOST CLUB?
A TREASURE? SUOH'S DIGGING FOR IT NOW?
THAT SOUNDS FUN.
HEY, I'M CANCELING PRACTICE!
SUOH!
WE'LL HELP WITH THE GRUNT WORK!

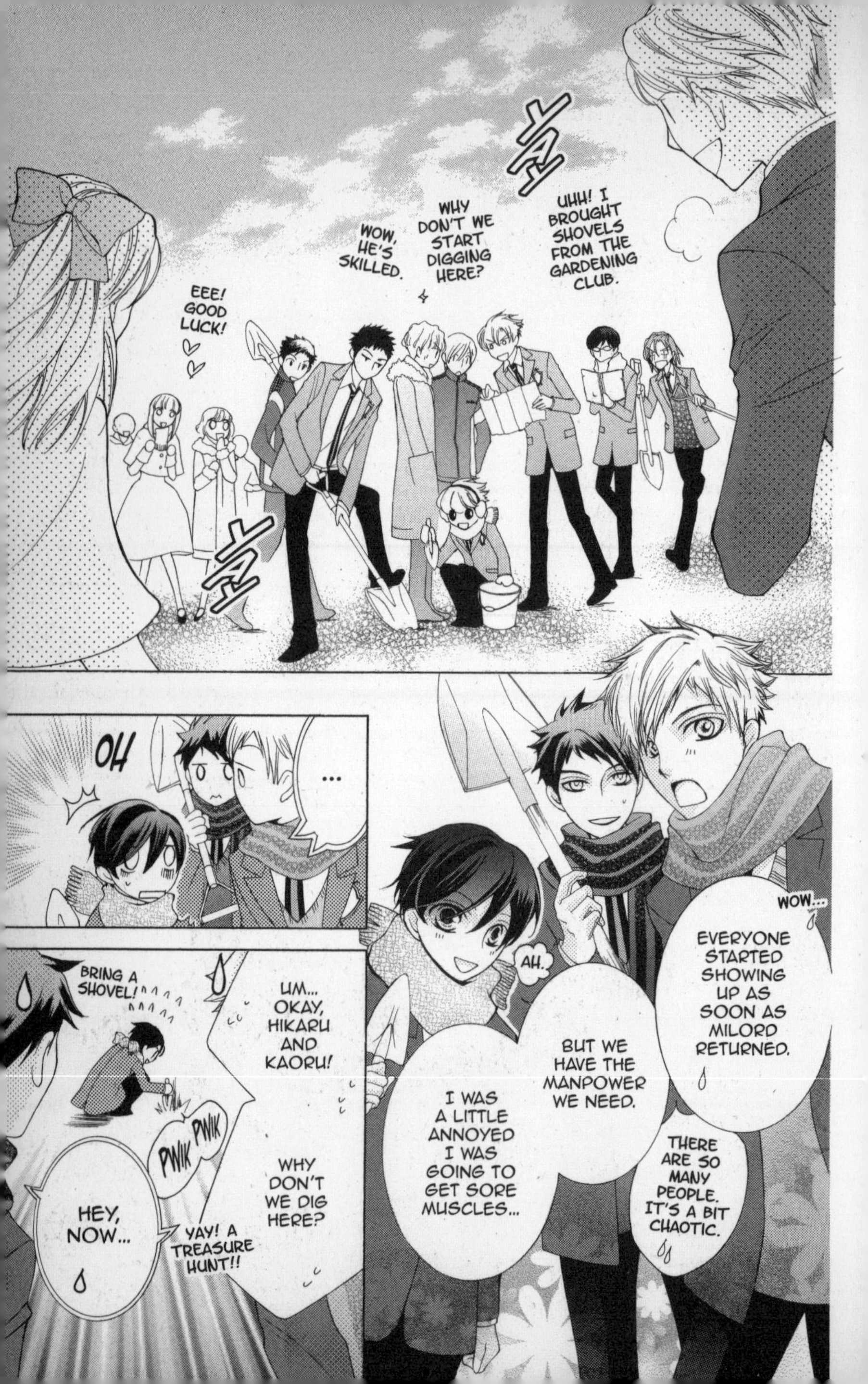
UHH! I BROUGHT SHOVELS FROM THE GARDENING CLUB.
YAY
WHY DON'T WE START DIGGING HERE?
WOW, HE'S SKILLED.
EEE! GOOD LUCK!
YAY
WOW...
EVERYONE STARTED SHOWING UP AS SOON AS MILORD RETURNED.
THERE ARE SO MANY PEOPLE. IT'S A BIT CHAOTIC.
AH.
BUT WE HAVE THE MANPOWER WE NEED.
I WAS A LITTLE ANNOYED I WAS GOING TO GET SORE MUSCLES...
...
OH
UM... OKAY, HIKARU AND KAORU!
WHY DON'T WE DIG HERE?
BRING A SHOVEL!
PWIK PWIK
YAY! A TREASURE HUNT!!
HEY, NOW...

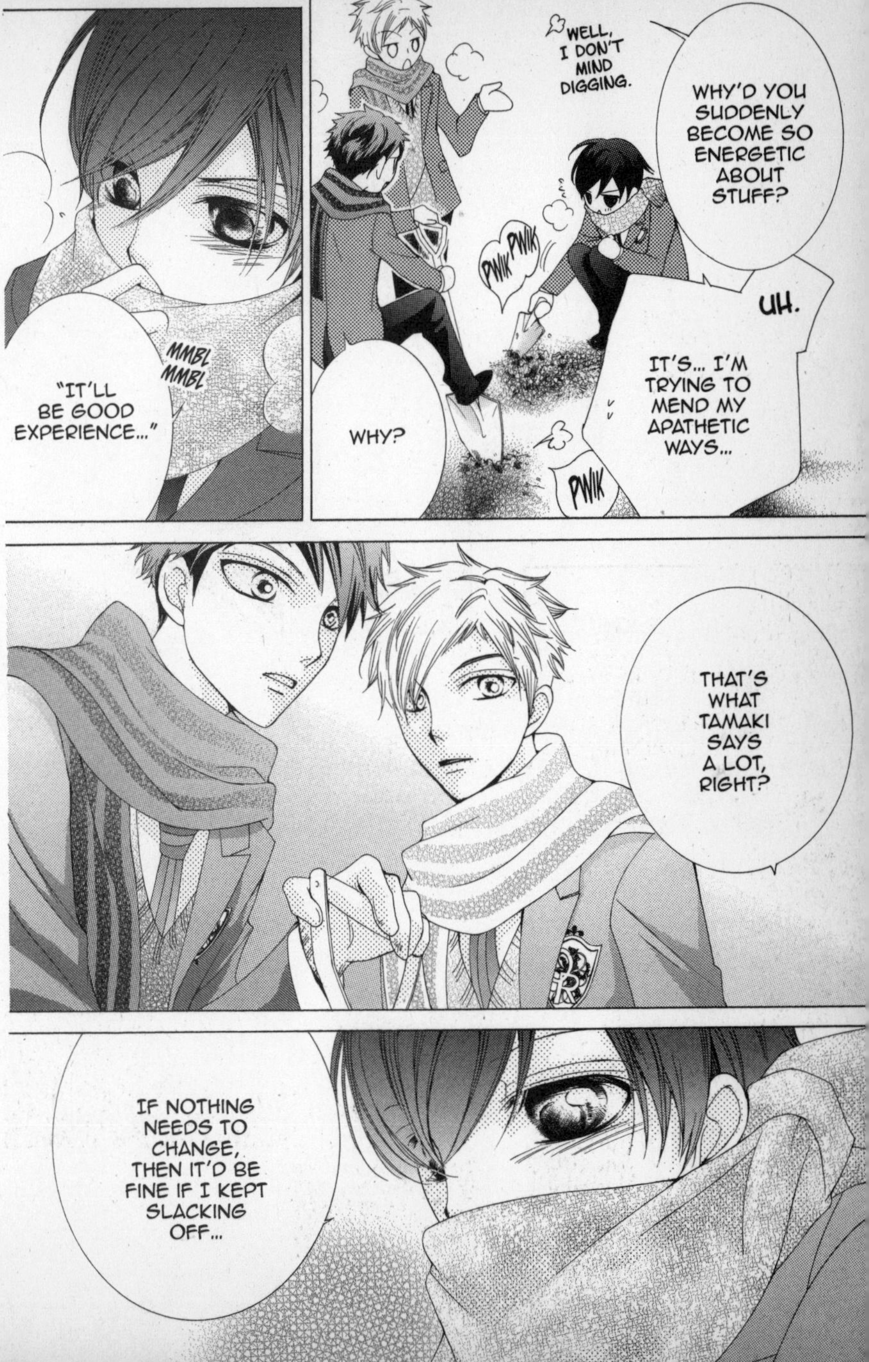
WHY'D YOU SUDDENLY BECOME SO ENERGETIC ABOUT STUFF?
WELL, I DON'T MIND DIGGING.
UH.
PWIK PWIK
PWIK
IT'S... I'M TRYING TO MEND MY APATHETIC WAYS...
PWIK
WHY?
MMBL MMBL
"IT'LL BE GOOD EXPERIENCE..."
THAT'S WHAT TAMAKI SAYS A LOT, RIGHT?
IF NOTHING NEEDS TO CHANGE, THEN IT'D BE FINE IF I KEPT SLACKING OFF...

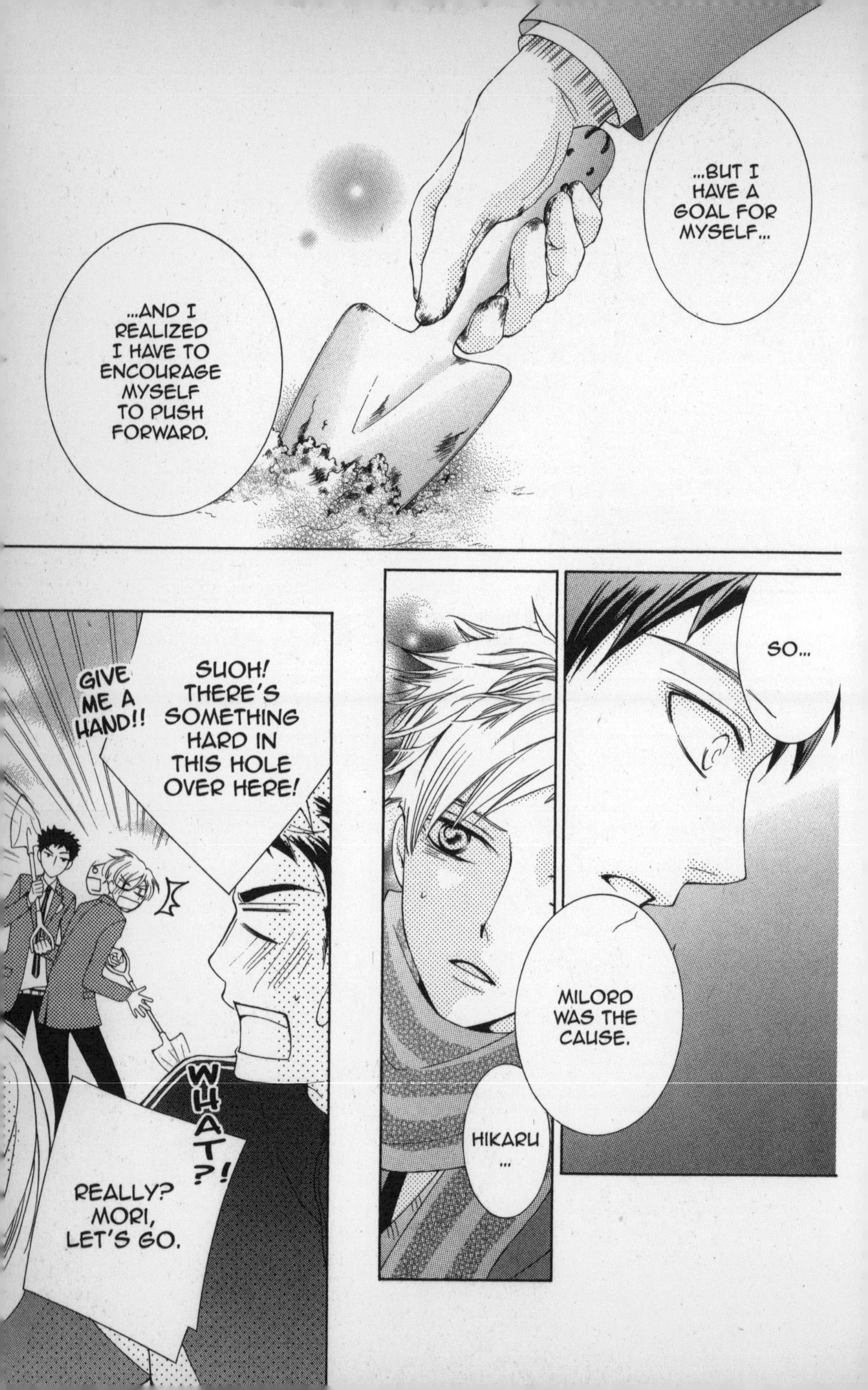
...BUT I HAVE A GOAL FOR MYSELF...
...AND I REALIZED I HAVE TO ENCOURAGE MYSELF TO PUSH FORWARD.
SO...
MILORD WAS THE CAUSE.
HIKARU ...
SUOH! THERE'S SOMETHING HARD IN THIS HOLE OVER HERE!
GIVE ME A HAND!!
WHAT?!
REALLY? MORI, LET'S GO.

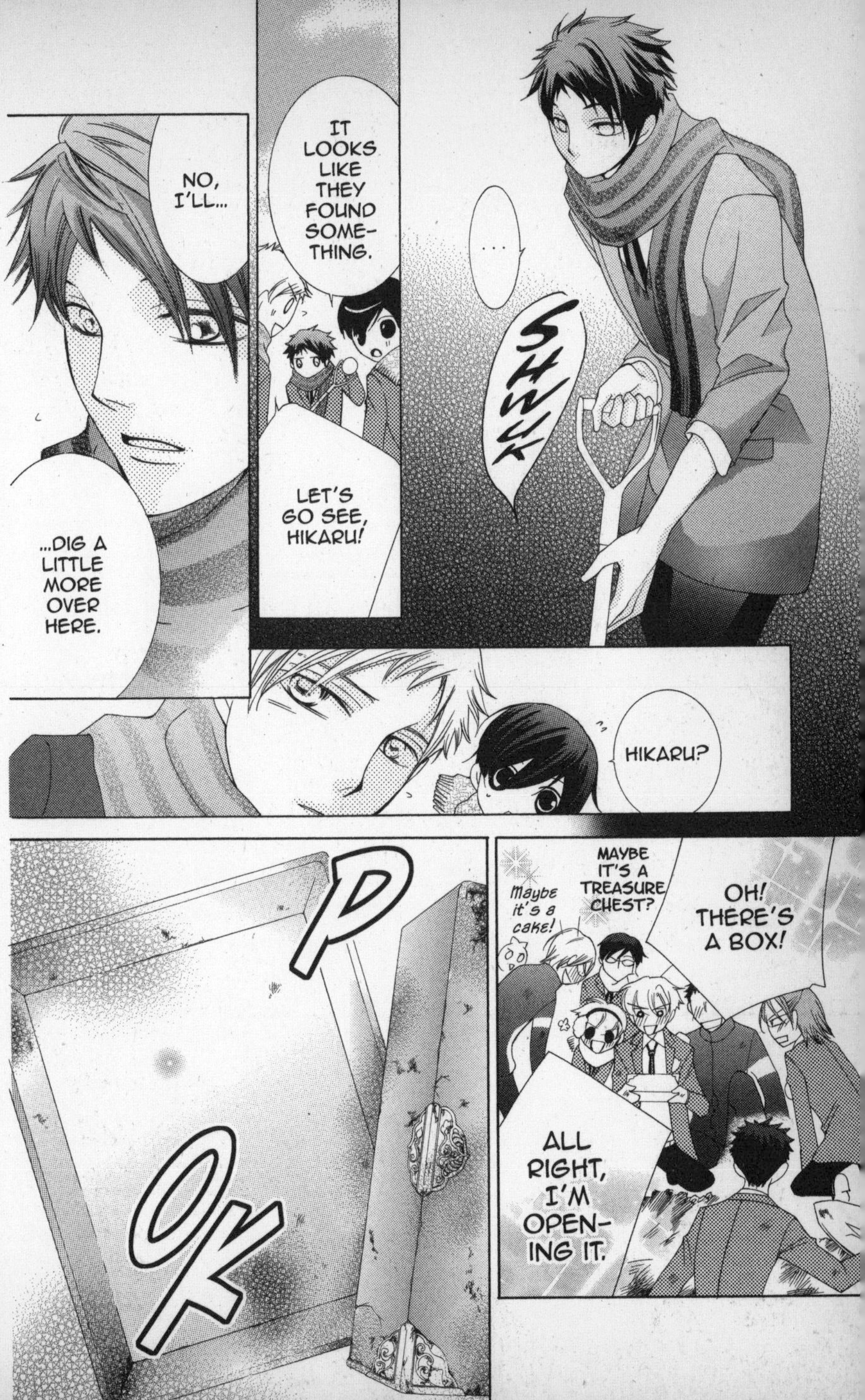
. . .
SHWUK
IT LOOKS LIKE THEY FOUND SOMETHING.
LET'S GO SEE, HIKARU!
NO, I'LL...
...DIG A LITTLE MORE OVER HERE.
HIKARU?
OH! THERE'S A BOX!
MAYBE IT'S A TREASURE CHEST?
Maybe it's a cake!
ALL RIGHT, I'M OPENING IT.
POK

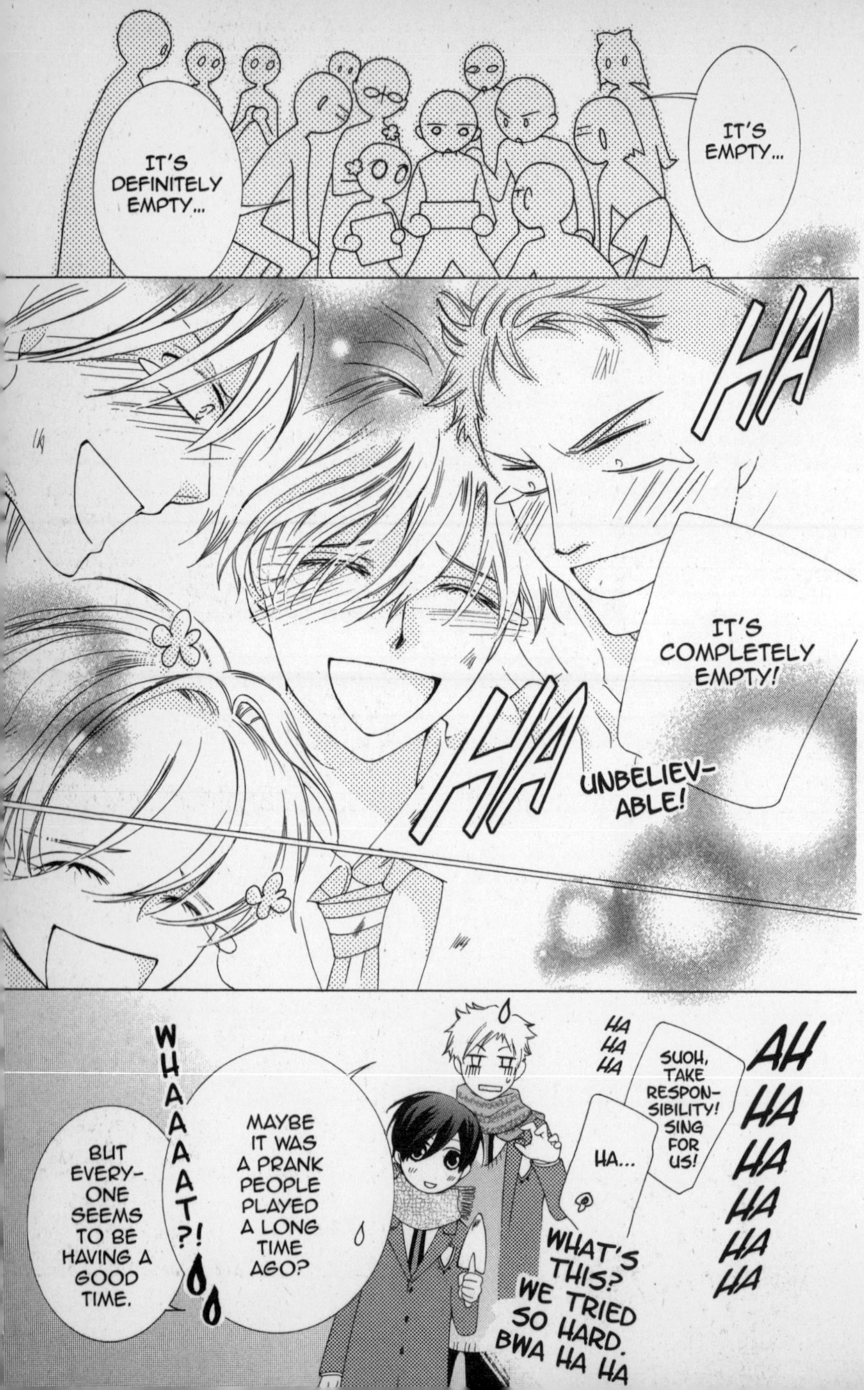
IT'S EMPTY...
IT'S DEFINITELY EMPTY...
HA
IT'S COMPLETELY EMPTY!
HA
UNBELIEV-ABLE!
AH HA HA HA HA HA HA
HA HA HA
SUOH, TAKE RESPON-SIBILITY! SING FOR US!
HA...
WHAT'S THIS? WE TRIED SO HARD. BWA HA HA
MAYBE IT WAS A PRANK PEOPLE PLAYED A LONG TIME AGO?
WHAAAAT?!
BUT EVERY-ONE SEEMS TO BE HAVING A GOOD TIME.

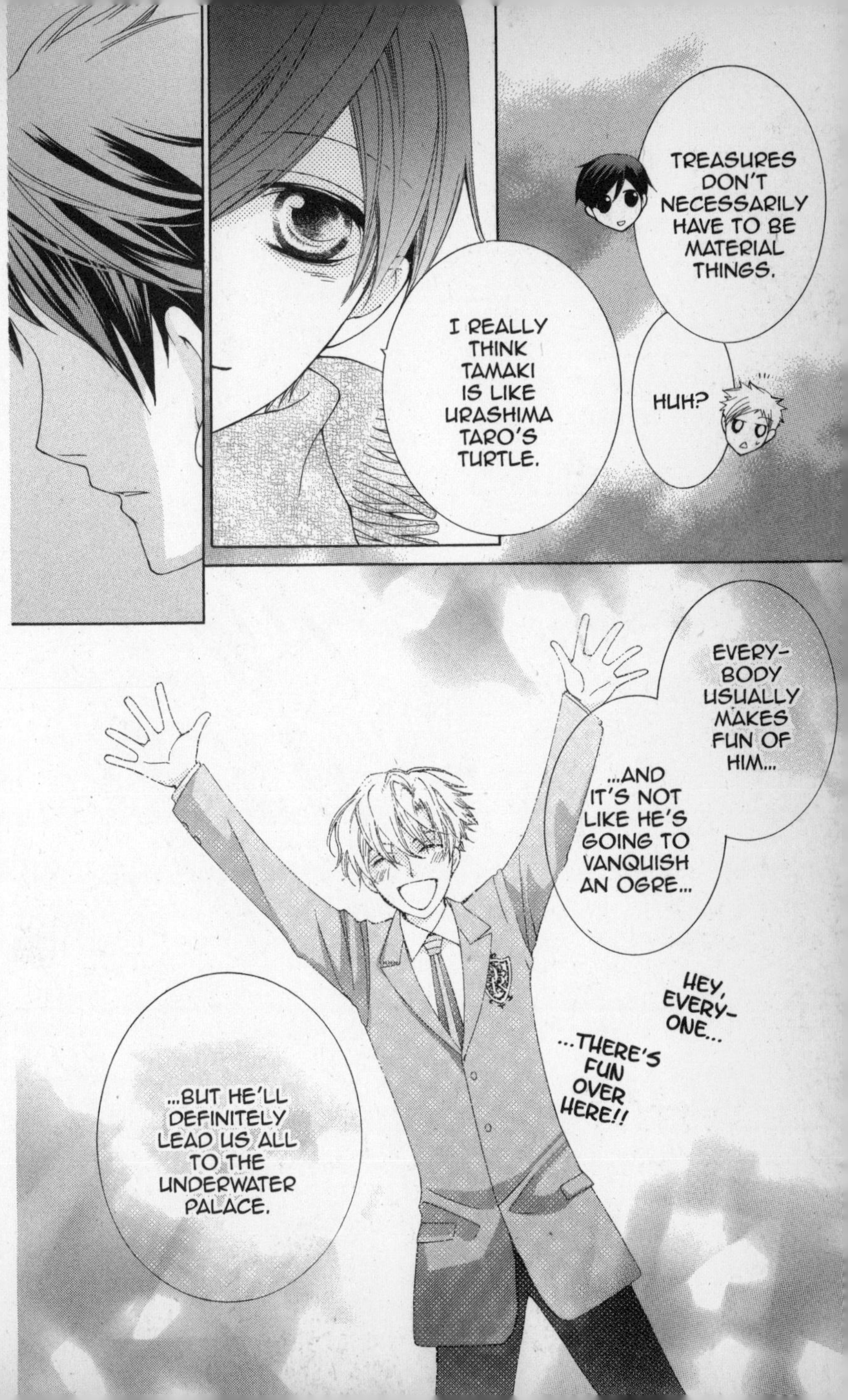
TREASURES DON'T NECESSARILY HAVE TO BE MATERIAL THINGS.
HUH?
I REALLY THINK TAMAKI IS LIKE URASHIMA TARO'S TURTLE.
EVERY-BODY USUALLY MAKES FUN OF HIM...
...AND IT'S NOT LIKE HE'S GOING TO VANQUISH AN OGRE...
HEY, EVERY-ONE...
...THERE'S FUN OVER HERE!!
...BUT HE'LL DEFINITELY LEAD US ALL TO THE UNDERWATER PALACE.

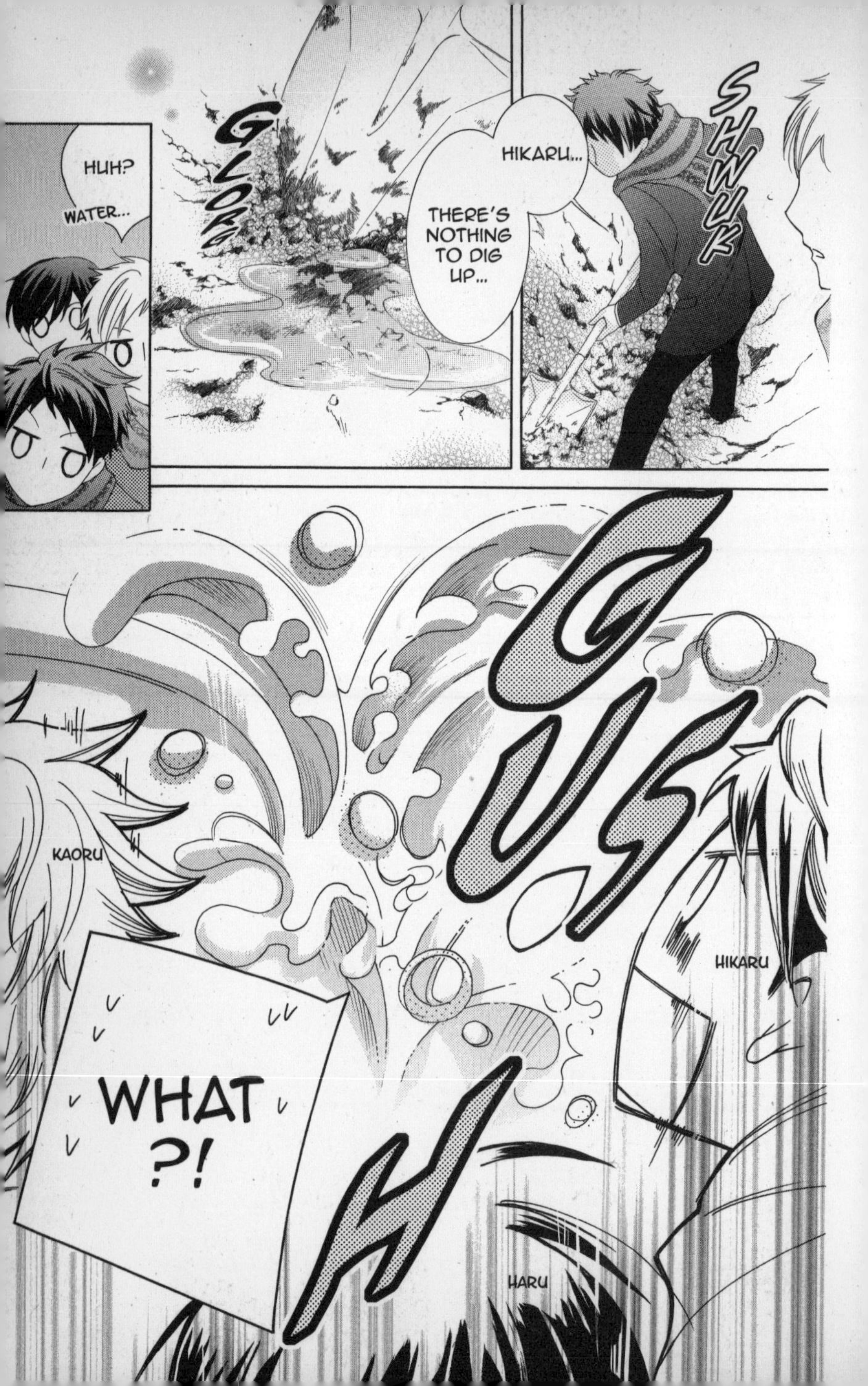
SHWUK
HIKARU...
THERE'S NOTHING TO DIG UP...
GLORG
HUH?
WATER...
GUSH
HIKARU
KAORU
HARU
WHAT?!

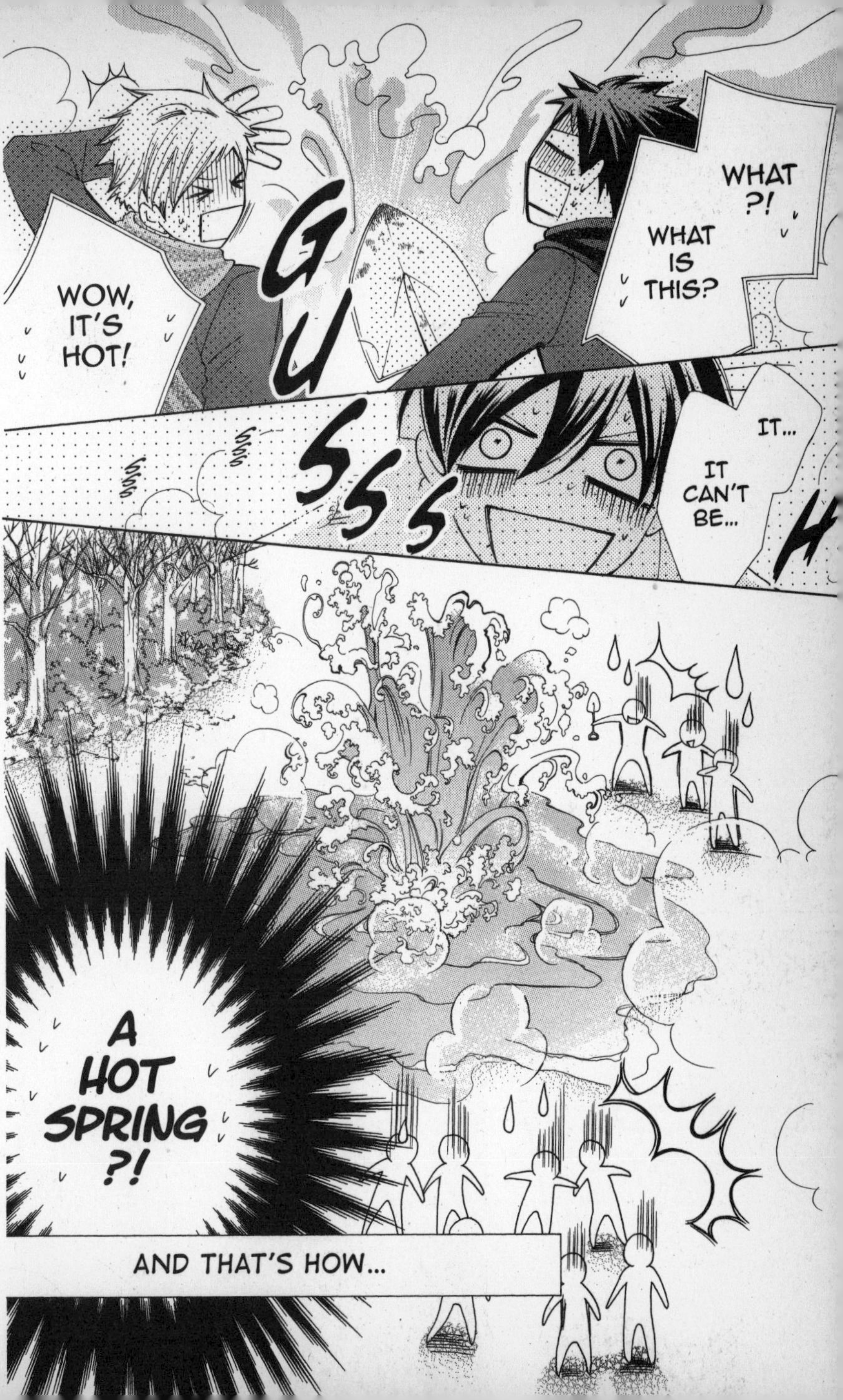
WHAT ?!
WHAT IS THIS?
WOW, IT'S HOT!
GUSSSSH
IT... IT CAN'T BE...
A HOT SPRING ?!
AND THAT'S HOW...

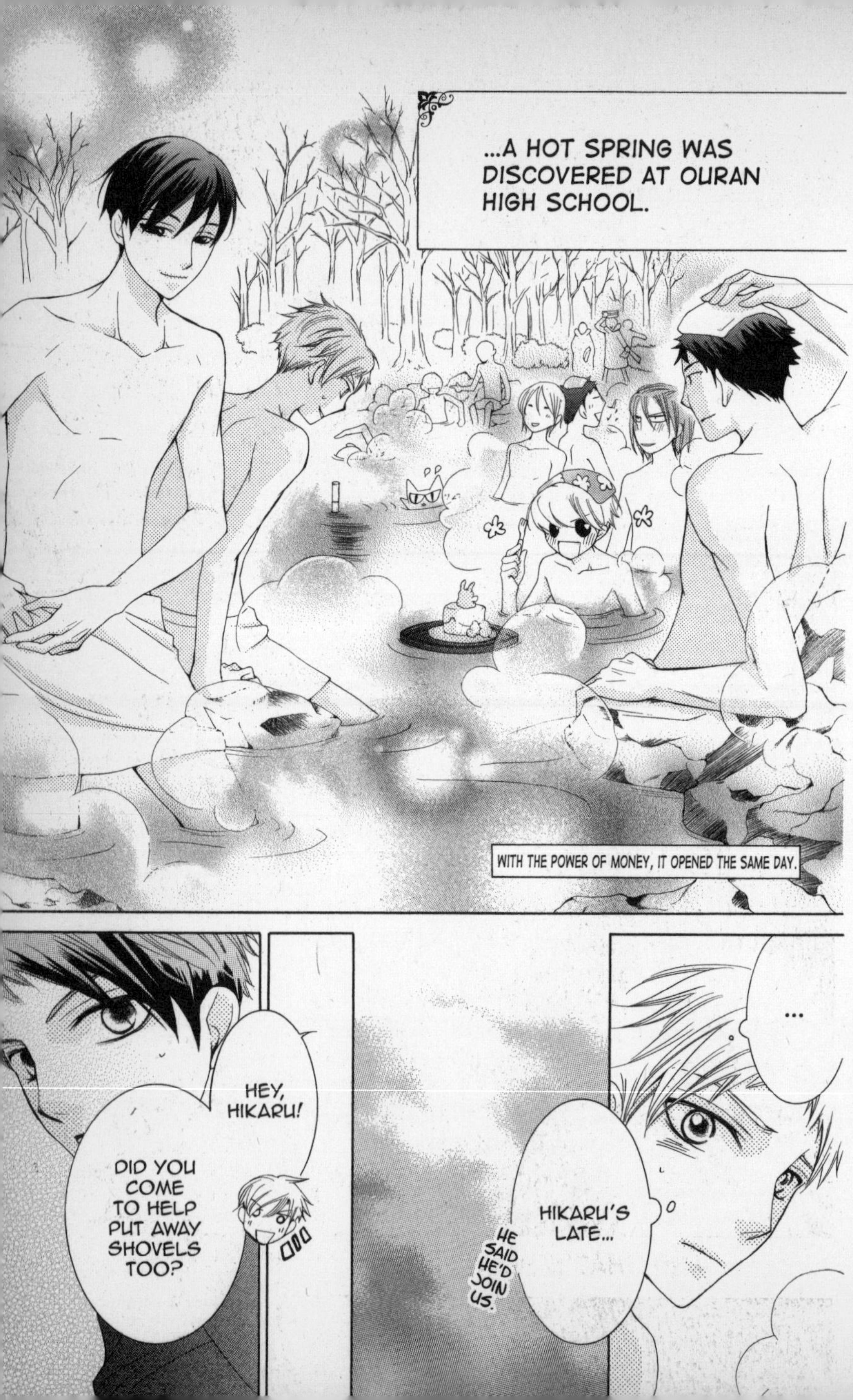
...A HOT SPRING WAS DISCOVERED AT OURAN HIGH SCHOOL.
WITH THE POWER OF MONEY, IT OPENED THE SAME DAY.
...
HIKARU'S LATE...
HE SAID HE'D JOIN US.
HEY, HIKARU!
DID YOU COME TO HELP PUT AWAY SHOVELS TOO?

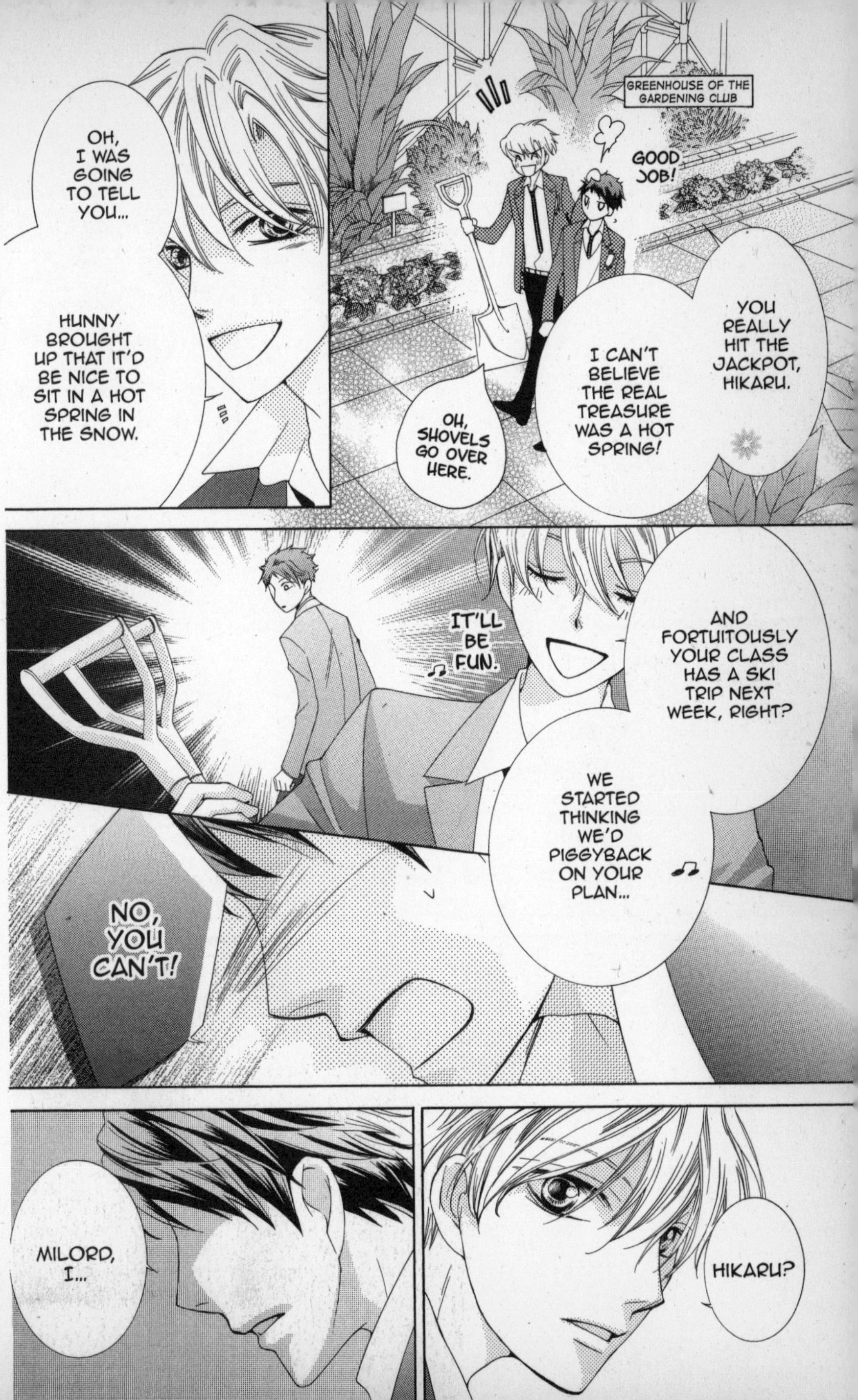
GREENHOUSE OF THE GARDENING CLUB
GOOD JOB!
YOU REALLY HIT THE JACKPOT, HIKARU.
I CAN'T BELIEVE THE REAL TREASURE WAS A HOT SPRING!
OH, SHOVELS GO OVER HERE.
OH, I WAS GOING TO TELL YOU...
HUNNY BROUGHT UP THAT IT'D BE NICE TO SIT IN A HOT SPRING IN THE SNOW.
AND FORTUITOUSLY YOUR CLASS HAS A SKI TRIP NEXT WEEK, RIGHT?
IT'LL BE FUN.
WE STARTED THINKING WE'D PIGGYBACK ON YOUR PLAN...
NO, YOU CAN'T!
HIKARU?
MILORD, I...

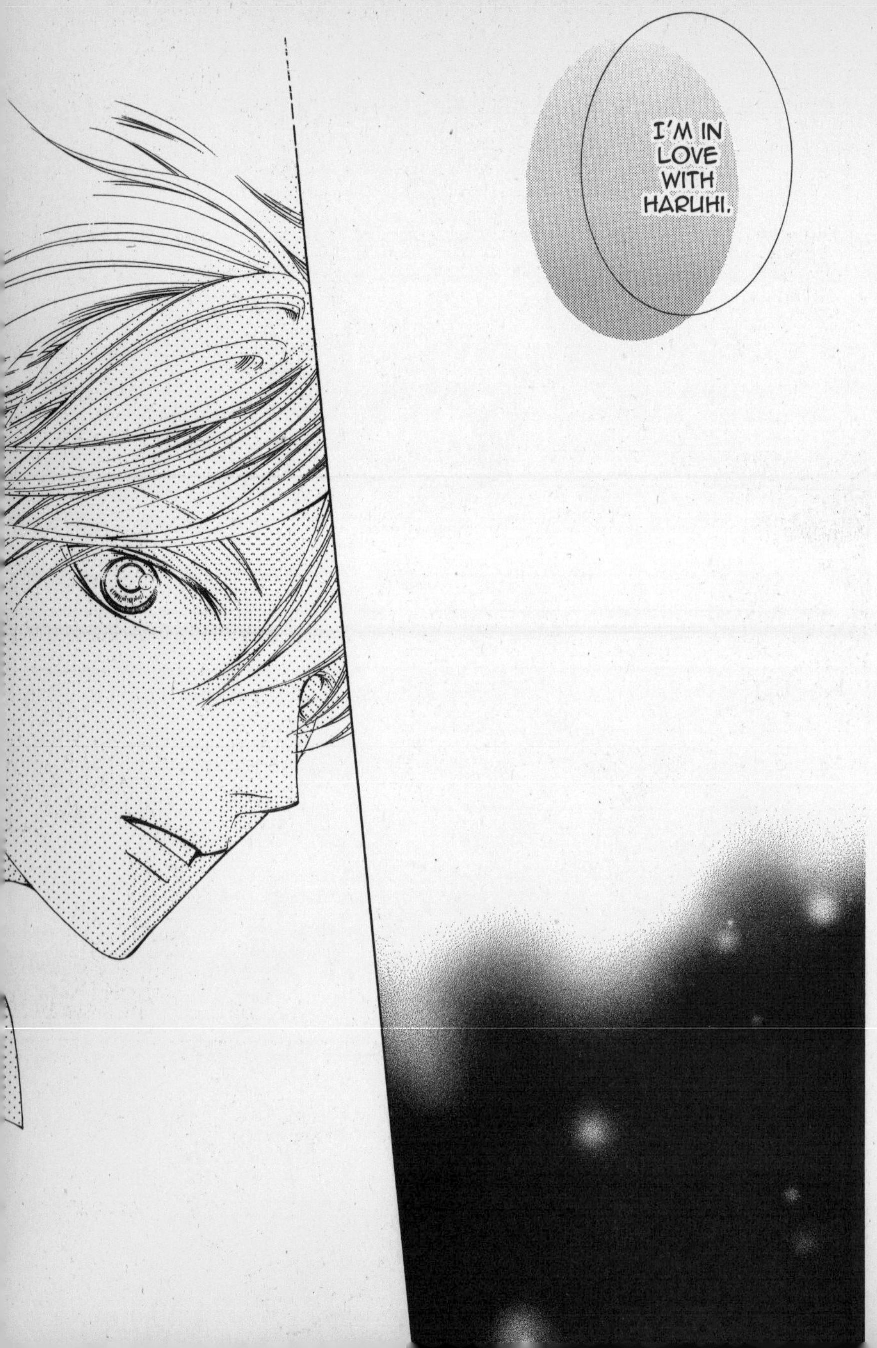
I'M IN LOVE WITH HARUHI.

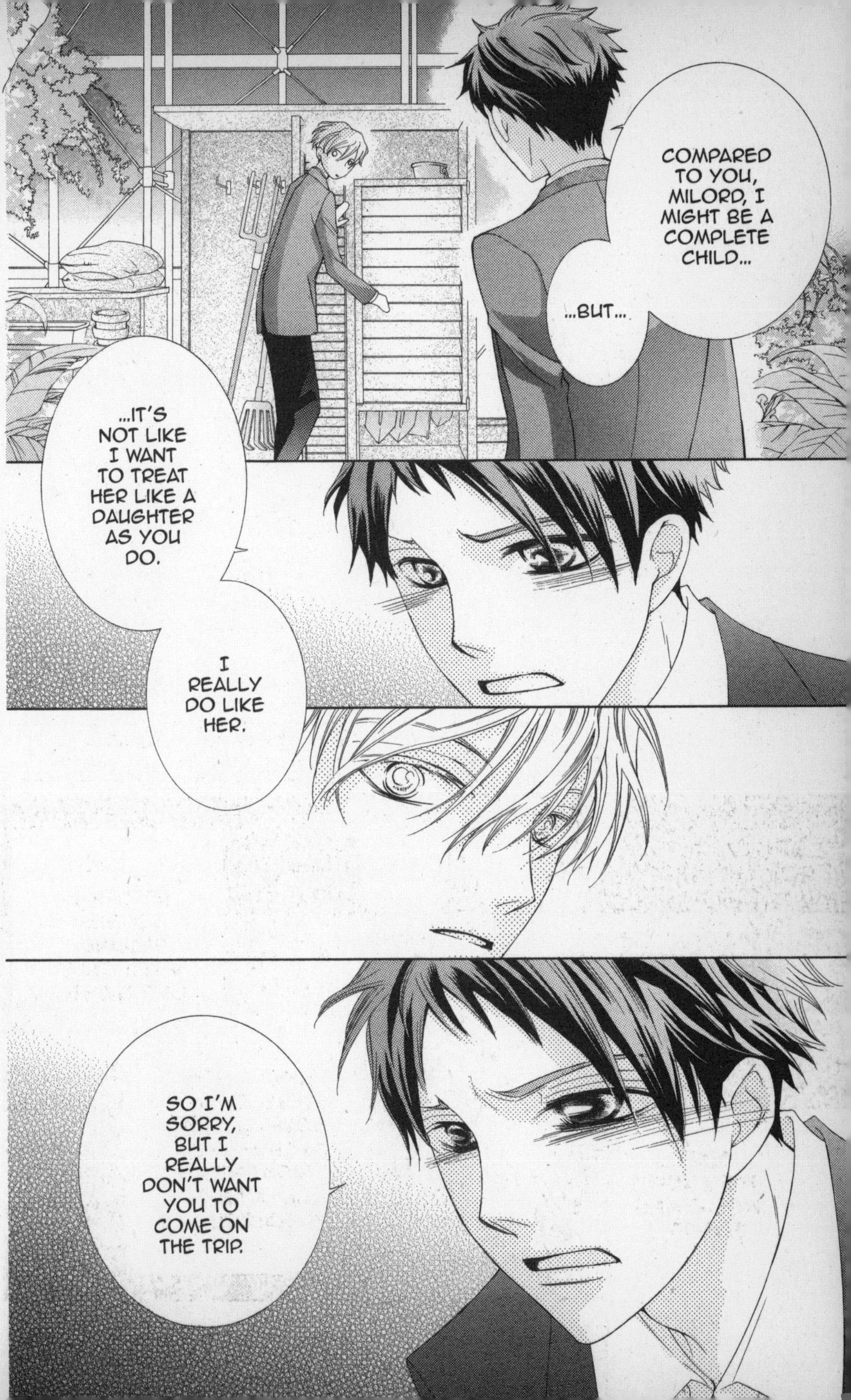
COMPARED TO YOU, MILORD, I MIGHT BE A COMPLETE CHILD...
...BUT...
...IT'S NOT LIKE I WANT TO TREAT HER LIKE A DAUGHTER AS YOU DO.
I REALLY DO LIKE HER.
SO I'M SORRY, BUT I REALLY DON'T WANT YOU TO COME ON THE TRIP.

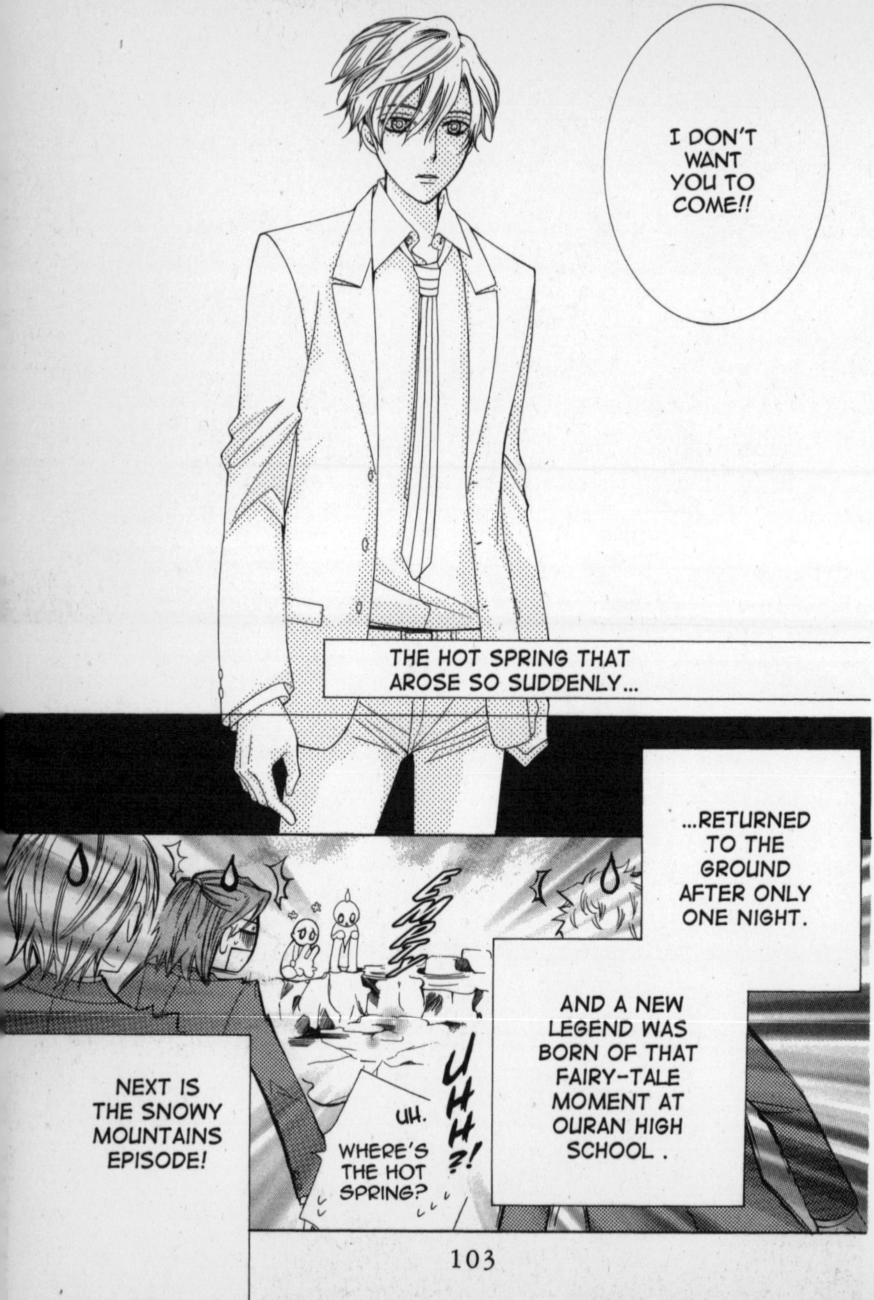
I DON'T WANT YOU TO COME!!
THE HOT SPRING THAT AROSE SO SUDDENLY...
...RETURNED TO THE GROUND AFTER ONLY ONE NIGHT.
AND A NEW LEGEND WAS BORN OF THAT FAIRY-TALE MOMENT AT OURAN HIGH SCHOOL.
UHHH?!
UH. WHERE'S THE HOT SPRING?
NEXT IS THE SNOWY MOUNTAINS EPISODE!

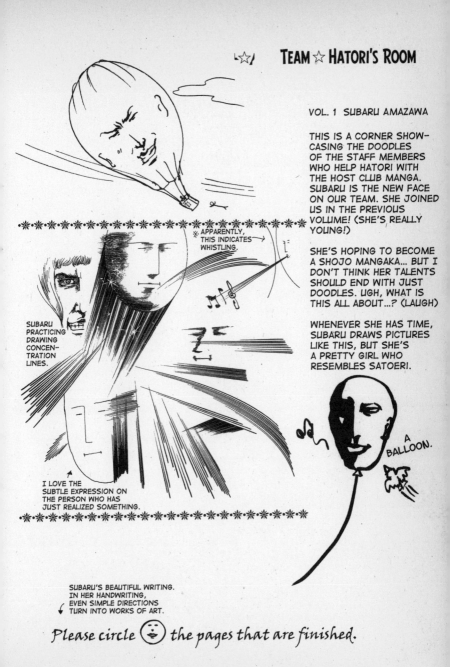

VOL. 1 SUBARU AMAZAWA

THIS IS A CORNER SHOW-CASING THE DOODLES OF THE STAFF MEMBERS WHO HELP HATORI WITH THE HOST CLUB MANGA. SUBARU IS THE NEW FACE ON OUR TEAM. SHE JOINED US IN THE PREVIOUS VOLUME! (SHE'S REALLY YOUNG!)

SHE'S HOPING TO BECOME A SHOJO MANGAKA... BUT I DON'T THINK HER TALENTS SHOULD END WITH JUST DOODLES. UGH, WHAT IS THIS ALL ABOUT...? (LAUGH)

WHENEVER SHE HAS TIME, SUBARU DRAWS PICTURES LIKE THIS, BUT SHE'S A PRETTY GIRL WHO RESEMBLES SATOERI.

* APPARENTLY, THIS INDICATES WHISTLING.

SUBARU PRACTICING DRAWING CONCEN-TRATION LINES.

I LOVE THE SUBTLE EXPRESSION ON THE PERSON WHO HAS JUST REALIZED SOMETHING.

A BALLOON.

SUBARU'S BEAUTIFUL WRITING. IN HER HANDWRITING, EVEN SIMPLE DIRECTIONS TURN INTO WORKS OF ART.

Please circle ☺ the pages that are finished.

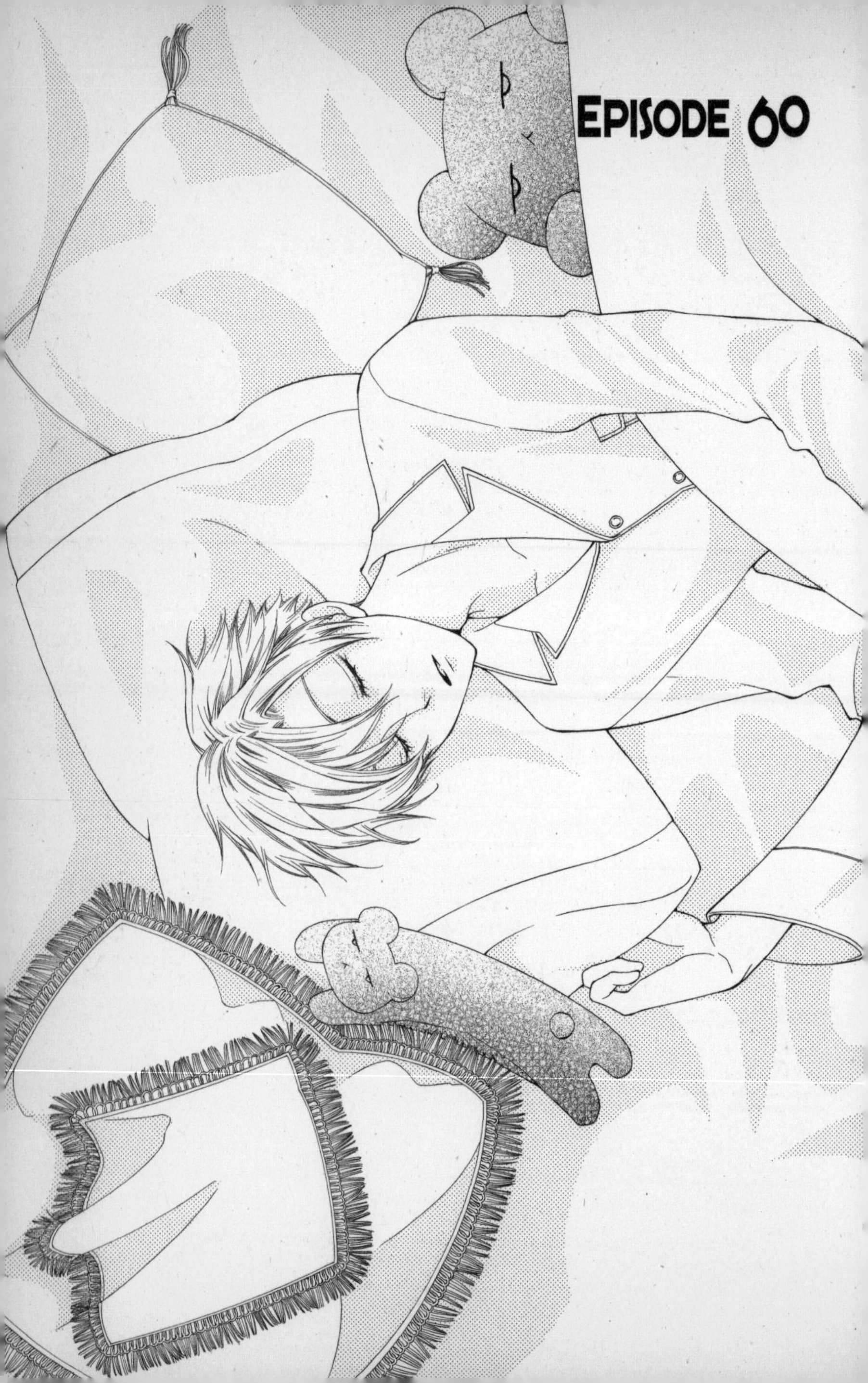
EPISODE 60

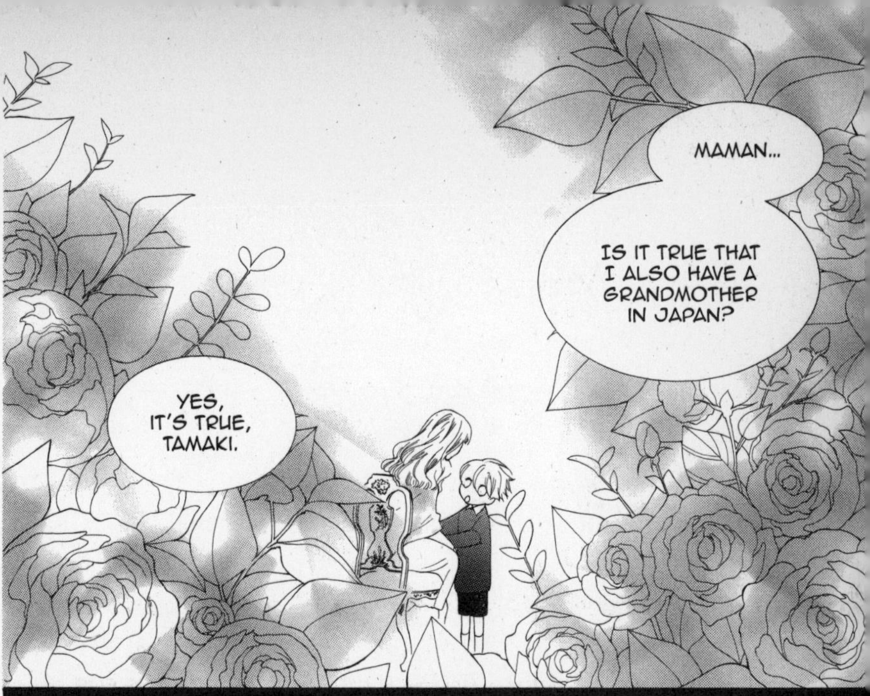
MAMAN...
IS IT TRUE THAT I ALSO HAVE A GRANDMOTHER IN JAPAN?
YES, IT'S TRUE, TAMAKI.

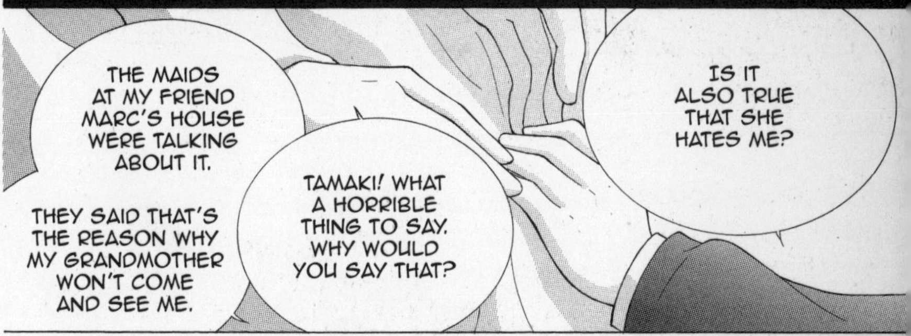
IS IT ALSO TRUE THAT SHE HATES ME?
TAMAKI! WHAT A HORRIBLE THING TO SAY. WHY WOULD YOU SAY THAT?
THE MAIDS AT MY FRIEND MARC'S HOUSE WERE TALKING ABOUT IT.
THEY SAID THAT'S THE REASON WHY MY GRANDMOTHER WON'T COME AND SEE ME.

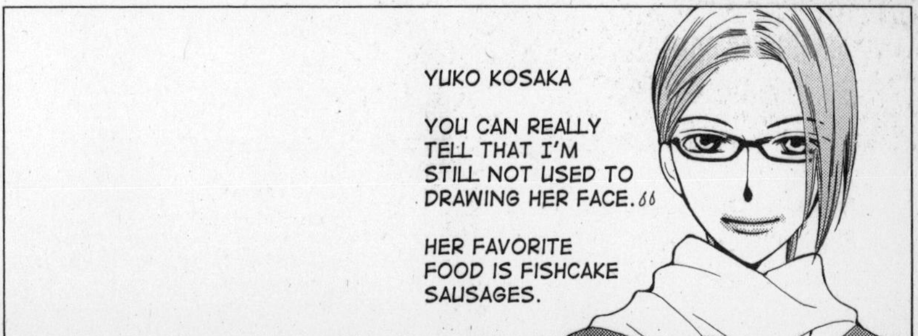
YUKO KOSAKA
YOU CAN REALLY TELL THAT I'M STILL NOT USED TO DRAWING HER FACE.
HER FAVORITE FOOD IS FISHCAKE SAUSAGES.

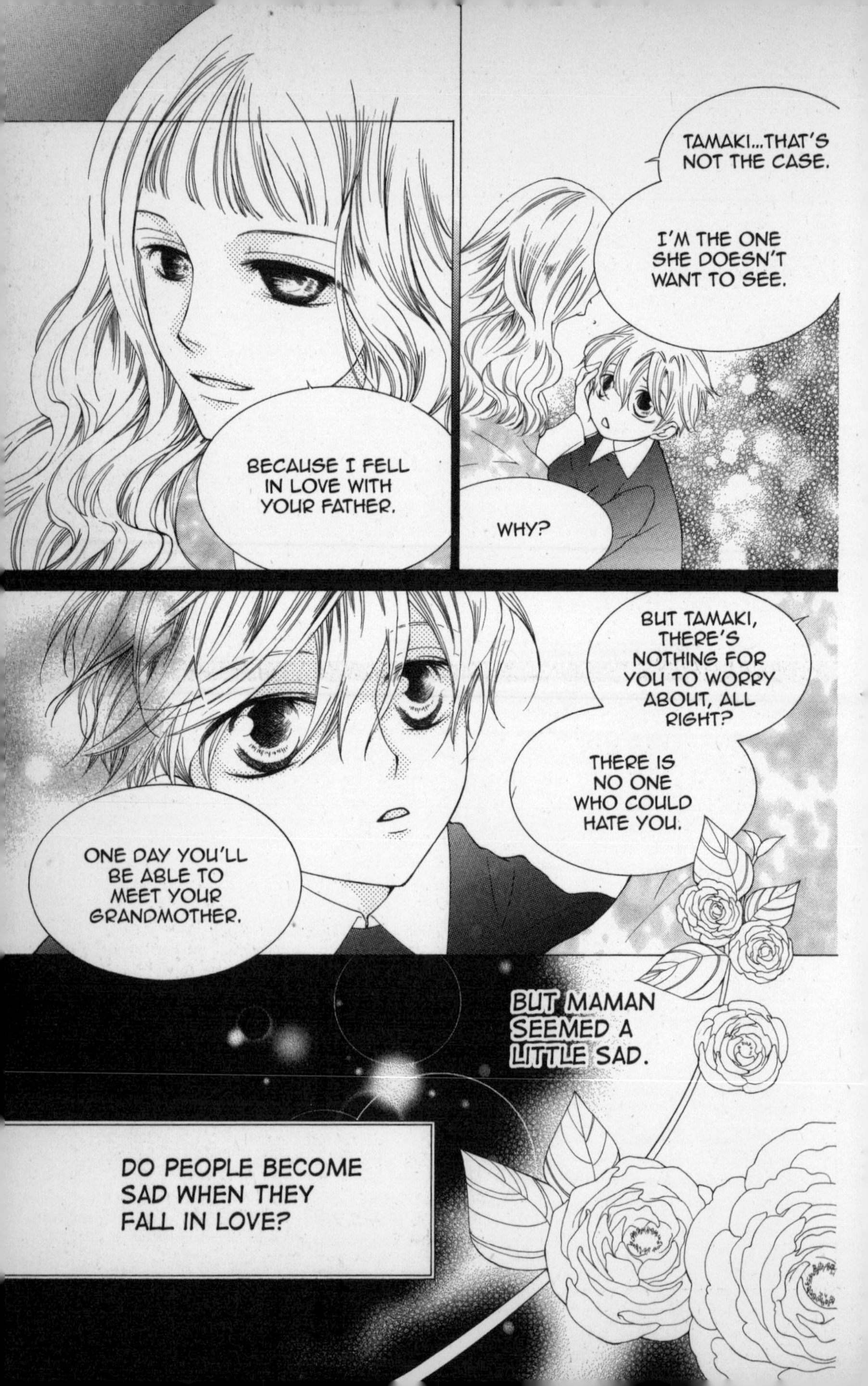
TAMAKI...THAT'S NOT THE CASE.
I'M THE ONE SHE DOESN'T WANT TO SEE.
WHY?
BECAUSE I FELL IN LOVE WITH YOUR FATHER.
BUT TAMAKI, THERE'S NOTHING FOR YOU TO WORRY ABOUT, ALL RIGHT?
THERE IS NO ONE WHO COULD HATE YOU.
ONE DAY YOU'LL BE ABLE TO MEET YOUR GRANDMOTHER.
BUT MAMAN SEEMED A LITTLE SAD.
DO PEOPLE BECOME SAD WHEN THEY FALL IN LOVE?

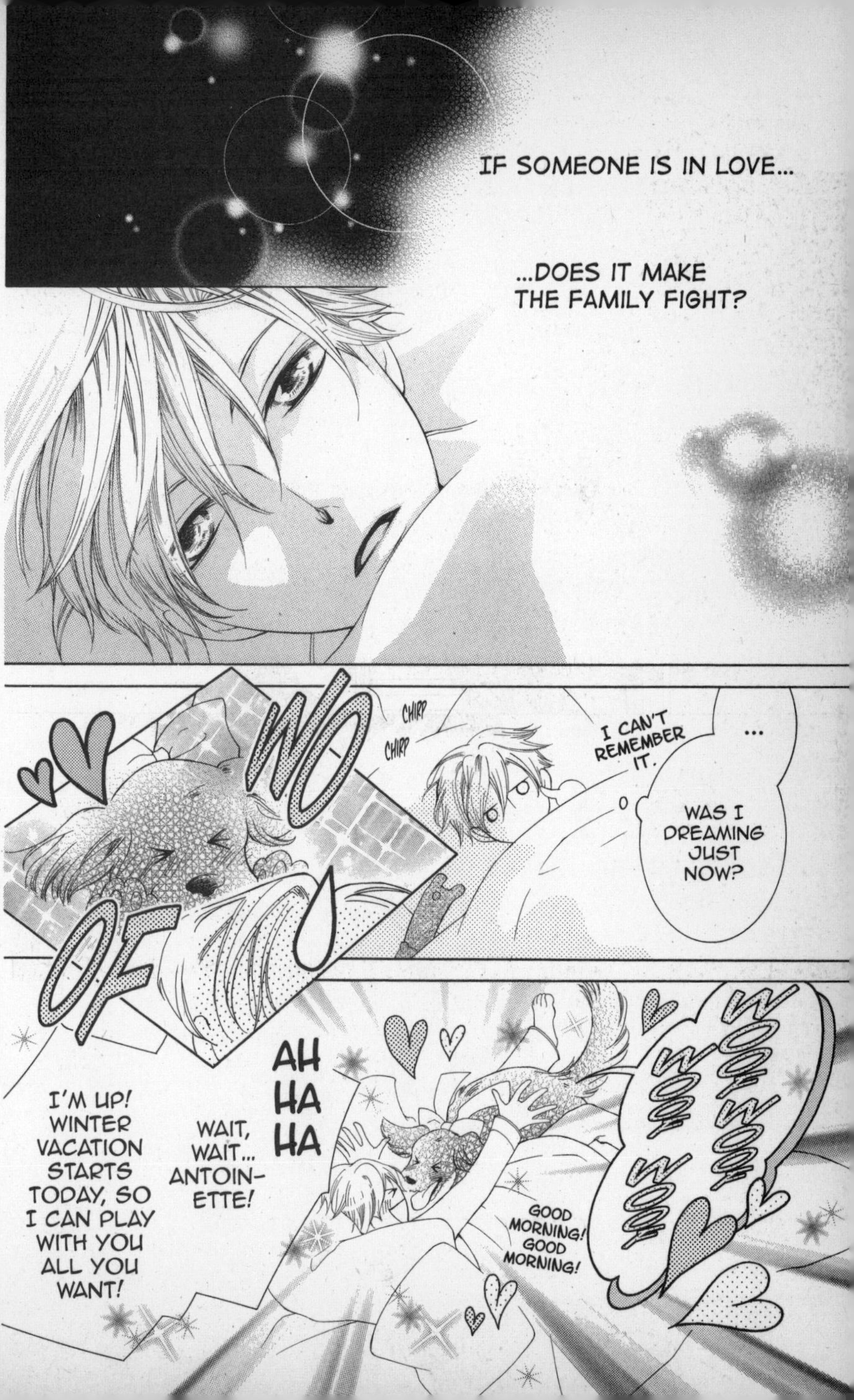
IF SOMEONE IS IN LOVE...
...DOES IT MAKE THE FAMILY FIGHT?
...
WAS I DREAMING JUST NOW?
I CAN'T REMEMBER IT.
CHIRP
CHIRP
WOOF
WOOF WOOF WOOF WOOF
GOOD MORNING! GOOD MORNING!
AH HA HA
WAIT, WAIT... ANTOIN-ETTE!
I'M UP! WINTER VACATION STARTS TODAY, SO I CAN PLAY WITH YOU ALL YOU WANT!

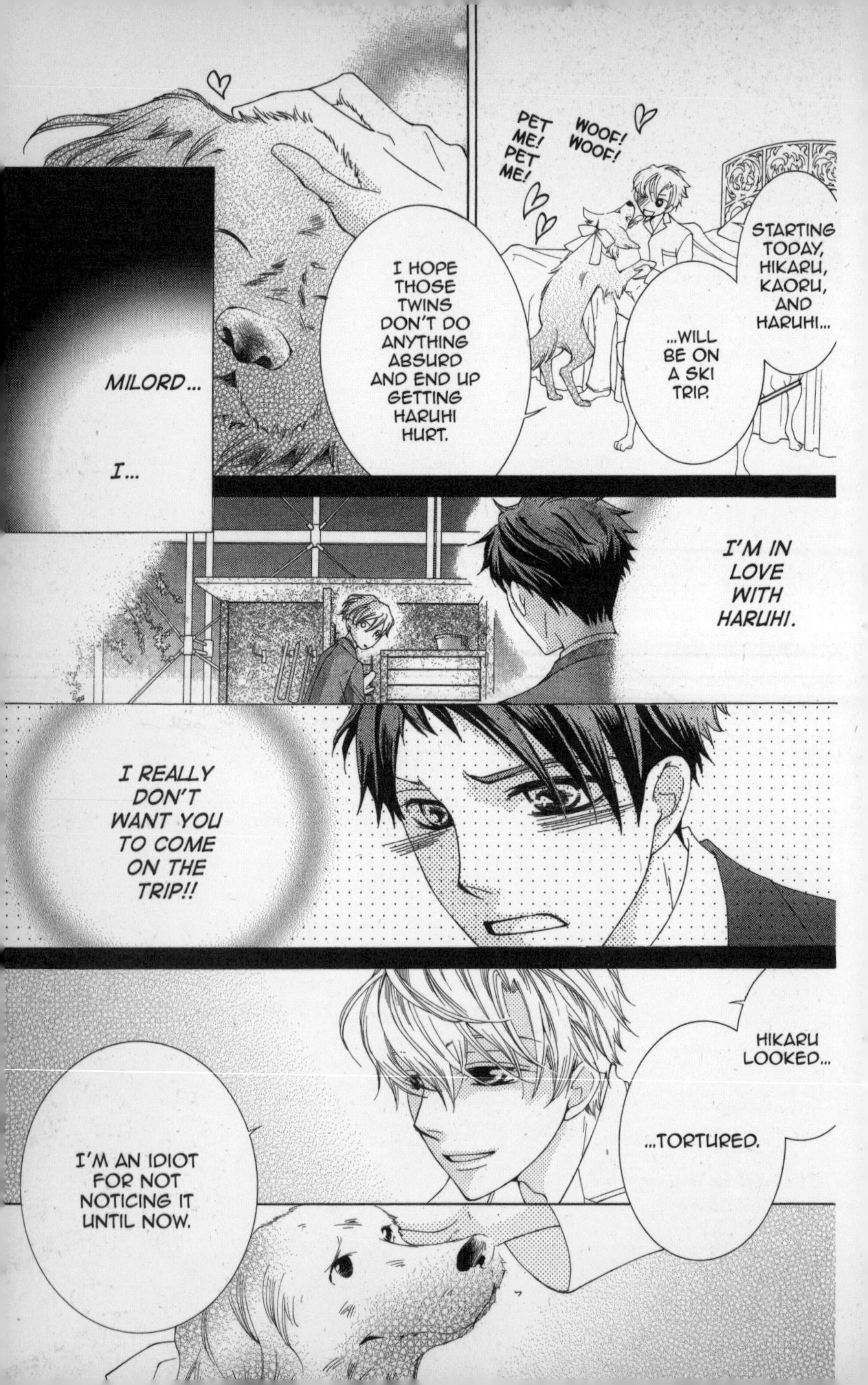
STARTING TODAY, HIKARU, KAORU, AND HARUHI...
...WILL BE ON A SKI TRIP.
WOOF! WOOF!
PET ME! PET ME!
I HOPE THOSE TWINS DON'T DO ANYTHING ABSURD AND END UP GETTING HARUHI HURT.
MILORD...
I...
I'M IN LOVE WITH HARUHI.
I REALLY DON'T WANT YOU TO COME ON THE TRIP!!
HIKARU LOOKED...
...TORTURED.
I'M AN IDIOT FOR NOT NOTICING IT UNTIL NOW.

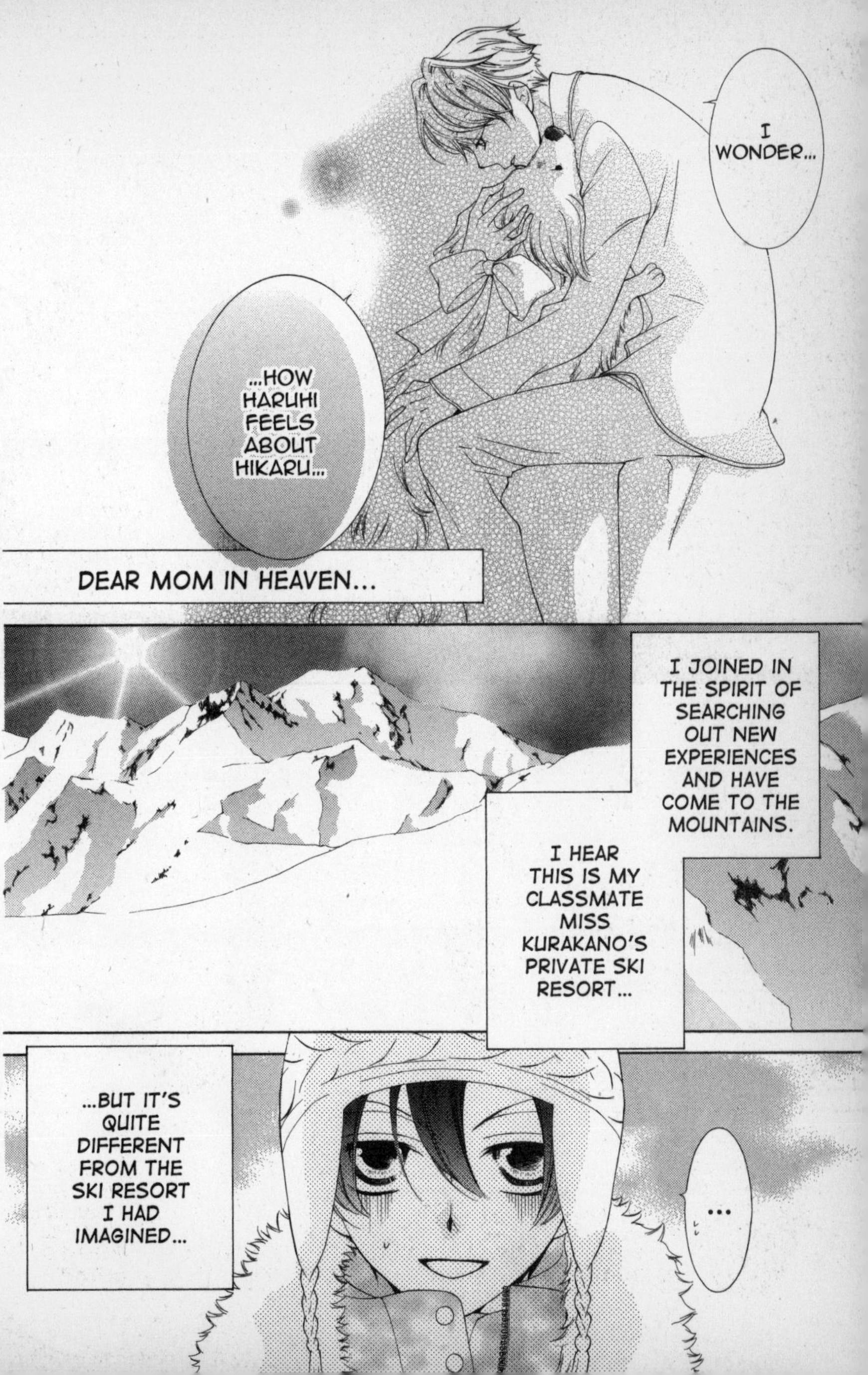
I WONDER...
...HOW HARUHI FEELS ABOUT HIKARU...
DEAR MOM IN HEAVEN...
I JOINED IN THE SPIRIT OF SEARCHING OUT NEW EXPERIENCES AND HAVE COME TO THE MOUNTAINS.
I HEAR THIS IS MY CLASSMATE MISS KURAKANO'S PRIVATE SKI RESORT...
...
...BUT IT'S QUITE DIFFERENT FROM THE SKI RESORT I HAD IMAGINED...

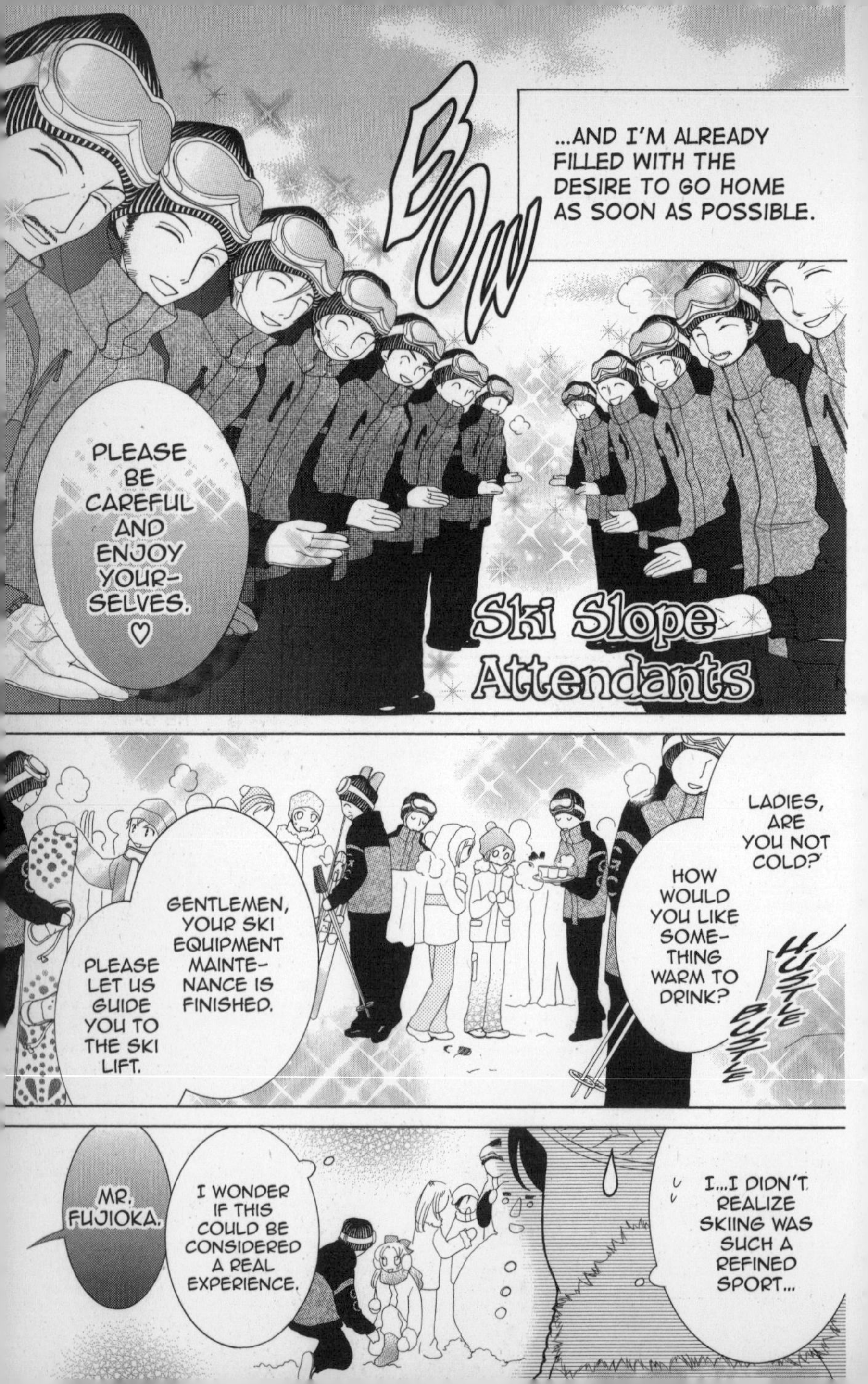
...AND I'M ALREADY FILLED WITH THE DESIRE TO GO HOME AS SOON AS POSSIBLE.
BOW
PLEASE BE CAREFUL AND ENJOY YOUR-SELVES. ♡
Ski Slope Attendants
LADIES, ARE YOU NOT COLD?
HOW WOULD YOU LIKE SOME-THING WARM TO DRINK?
HUSTLE BUSTLE
GENTLEMEN, YOUR SKI EQUIPMENT MAINTE-NANCE IS FINISHED.
PLEASE LET US GUIDE YOU TO THE SKI LIFT.
I...I DIDN'T REALIZE SKIING WAS SUCH A REFINED SPORT...
I WONDER IF THIS COULD BE CONSIDERED A REAL EXPERIENCE.
MR. FUJIOKA.

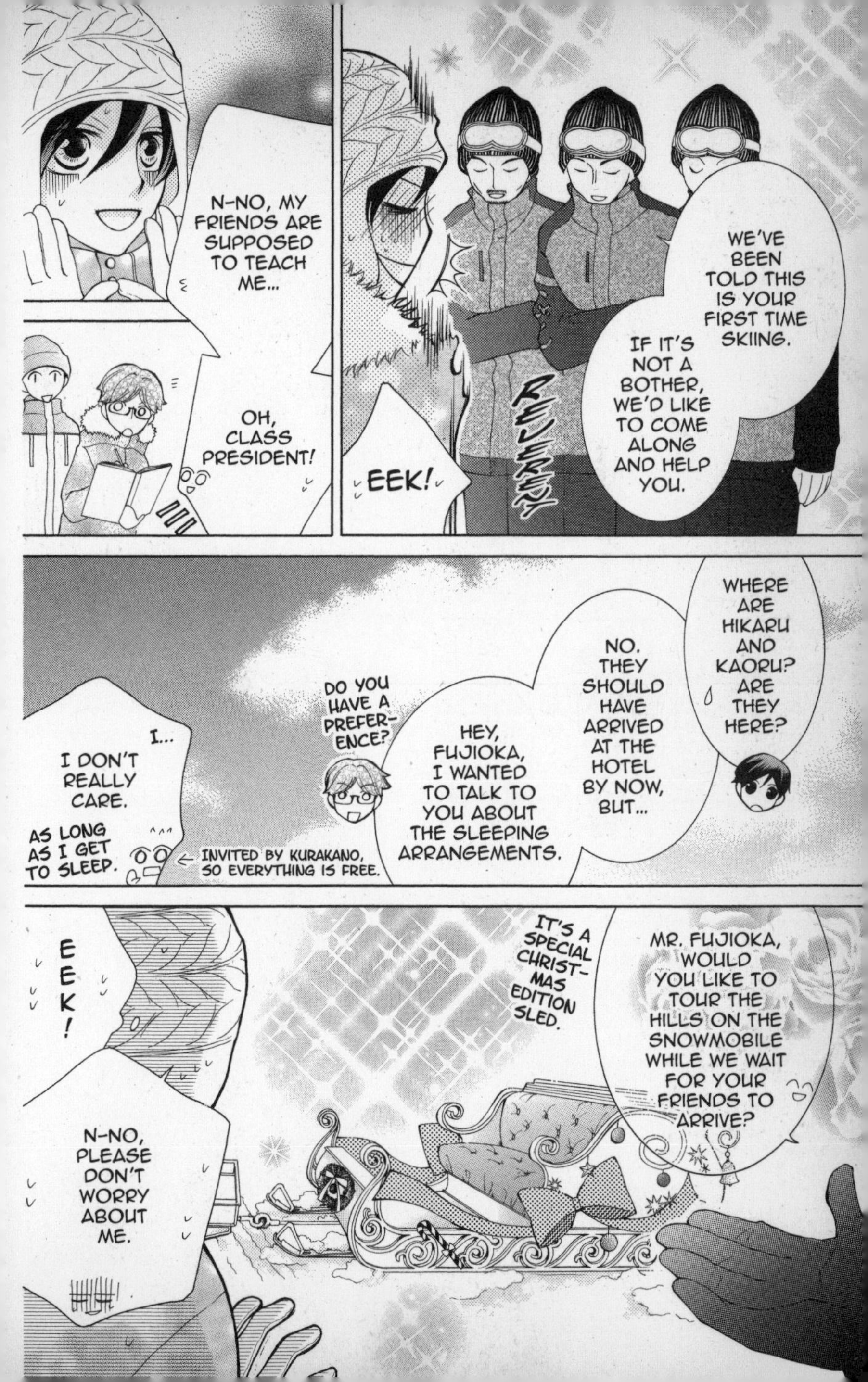
WE'VE BEEN TOLD THIS IS YOUR FIRST TIME SKIING.
IF IT'S NOT A BOTHER, WE'D LIKE TO COME ALONG AND HELP YOU.
EEK!
N-NO, MY FRIENDS ARE SUPPOSED TO TEACH ME...
OH, CLASS PRESIDENT!
WHERE ARE HIKARU AND KAORU? ARE THEY HERE?
NO. THEY SHOULD HAVE ARRIVED AT THE HOTEL BY NOW, BUT...
HEY, FUJIOKA, I WANTED TO TALK TO YOU ABOUT THE SLEEPING ARRANGEMENTS.
DO YOU HAVE A PREFERENCE?
I...
I DON'T REALLY CARE.
AS LONG AS I GET TO SLEEP.
INVITED BY KURAKANO, SO EVERYTHING IS FREE.
MR. FUJIOKA, WOULD YOU LIKE TO TOUR THE HILLS ON THE SNOWMOBILE WHILE WE WAIT FOR YOUR FRIENDS TO ARRIVE?
IT'S A SPECIAL CHRIST-MAS EDITION SLED.
EEK!
N-NO, PLEASE DON'T WORRY ABOUT ME.

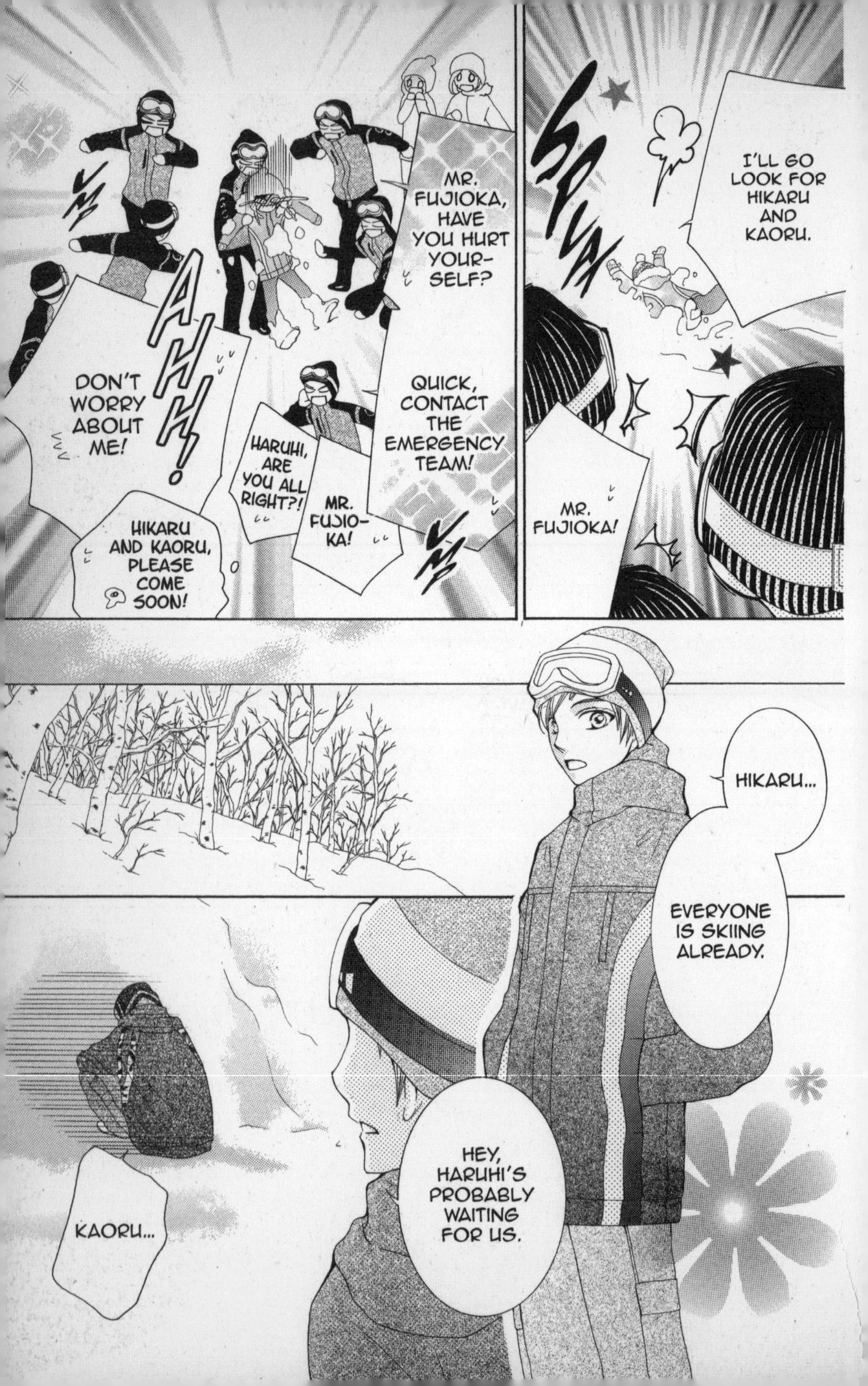
I'LL GO LOOK FOR HIKARU AND KAORU.
SPLUNK
MR. FUJIOKA!
MR. FUJIOKA, HAVE YOU HURT YOURSELF?
QUICK, CONTACT THE EMERGENCY TEAM!
MR. FUJIOKA!
HARUHI, ARE YOU ALL RIGHT?!
AHHH!
DON'T WORRY ABOUT ME!
HIKARU AND KAORU, PLEASE COME SOON!
HIKARU...
EVERYONE IS SKIING ALREADY.
HEY, HARUHI'S PROBABLY WAITING FOR US.
KAORU...

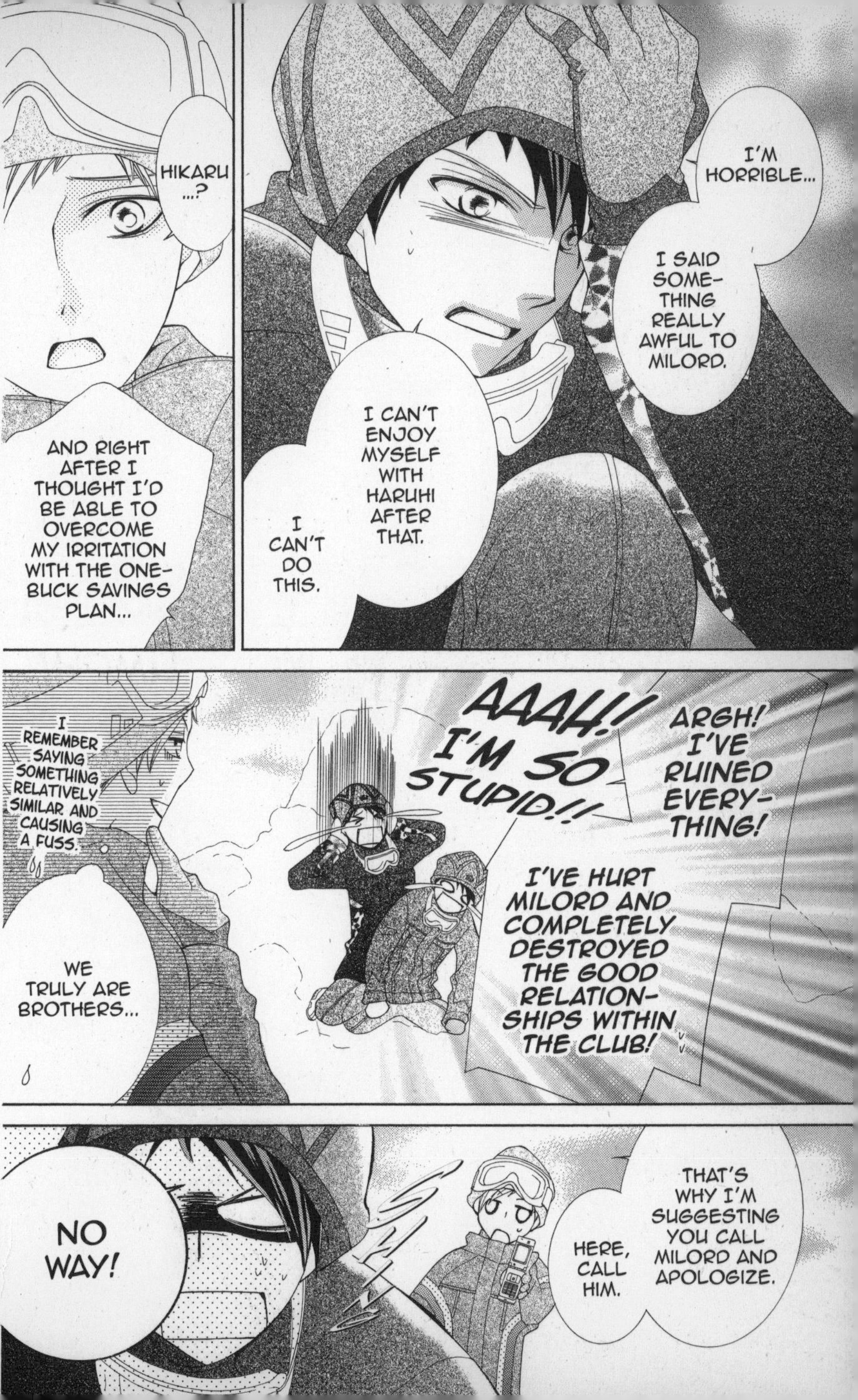
I'M HORRIBLE...
I SAID SOMETHING REALLY AWFUL TO MILORD.
I CAN'T ENJOY MYSELF WITH HARUHI AFTER THAT.
I CAN'T DO THIS.
HIKARU ...?
AND RIGHT AFTER I THOUGHT I'D BE ABLE TO OVERCOME MY IRRITATION WITH THE ONE-BUCK SAVINGS PLAN...
ARGH! I'VE RUINED EVERYTHING!
AAAH!! I'M SO STUPID!!
I'VE HURT MILORD AND COMPLETELY DESTROYED THE GOOD RELATIONSHIPS WITHIN THE CLUB!
I REMEMBER SAYING SOMETHING RELATIVELY SIMILAR AND CAUSING A FUSS.
WE TRULY ARE BROTHERS...
THAT'S WHY I'M SUGGESTING YOU CALL MILORD AND APOLOGIZE.
HERE, CALL HIM.
NO WAY!

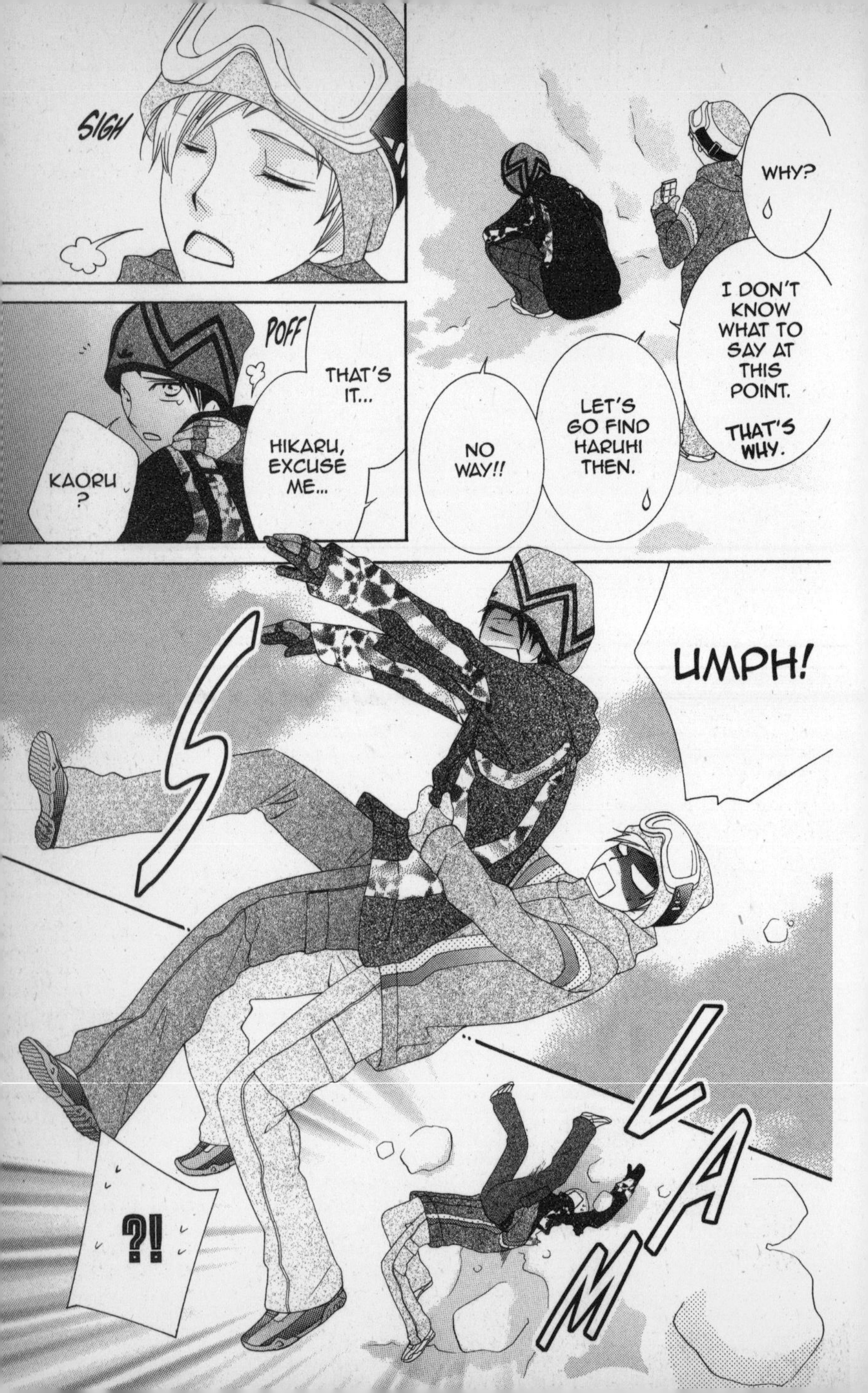
WHY?
I DON'T KNOW WHAT TO SAY AT THIS POINT.
THAT'S WHY.
LET'S GO FIND HARUHI THEN.
NO WAY!!
SIGH
POFF
THAT'S IT...
HIKARU, EXCUSE ME...
KAORU?
UMPH!
SLAM
?!

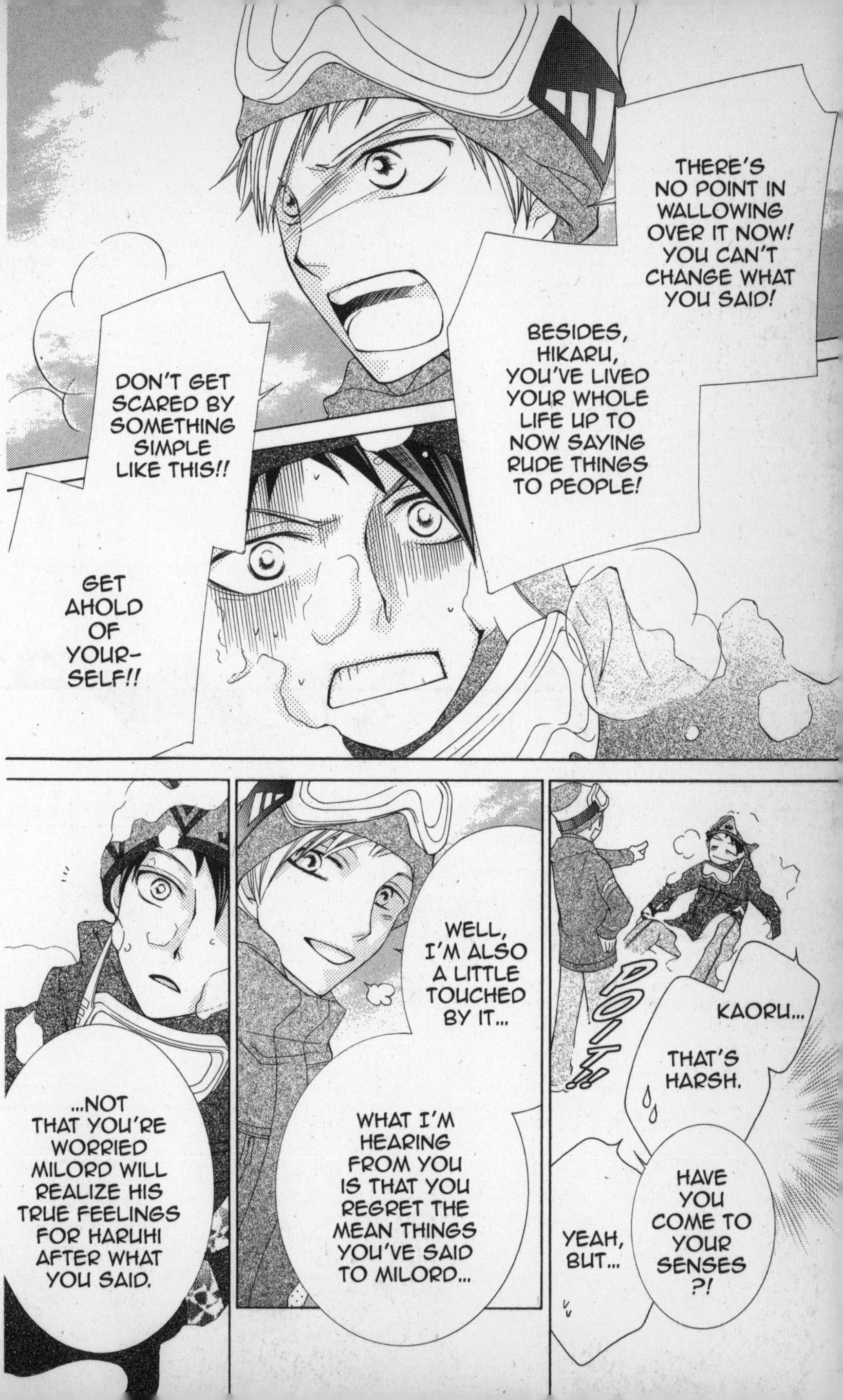
THERE'S NO POINT IN WALLOWING OVER IT NOW! YOU CAN'T CHANGE WHAT YOU SAID!
BESIDES, HIKARU, YOU'VE LIVED YOUR WHOLE LIFE UP TO NOW SAYING RUDE THINGS TO PEOPLE!
DON'T GET SCARED BY SOMETHING SIMPLE LIKE THIS!!
GET AHOLD OF YOURSELF!!
KAORU... THAT'S HARSH.
POIT!!
HAVE YOU COME TO YOUR SENSES?!
YEAH, BUT...
WELL, I'M ALSO A LITTLE TOUCHED BY IT...
WHAT I'M HEARING FROM YOU IS THAT YOU REGRET THE MEAN THINGS YOU'VE SAID TO MILORD...
...NOT THAT YOU'RE WORRIED MILORD WILL REALIZE HIS TRUE FEELINGS FOR HARUHI AFTER WHAT YOU SAID.

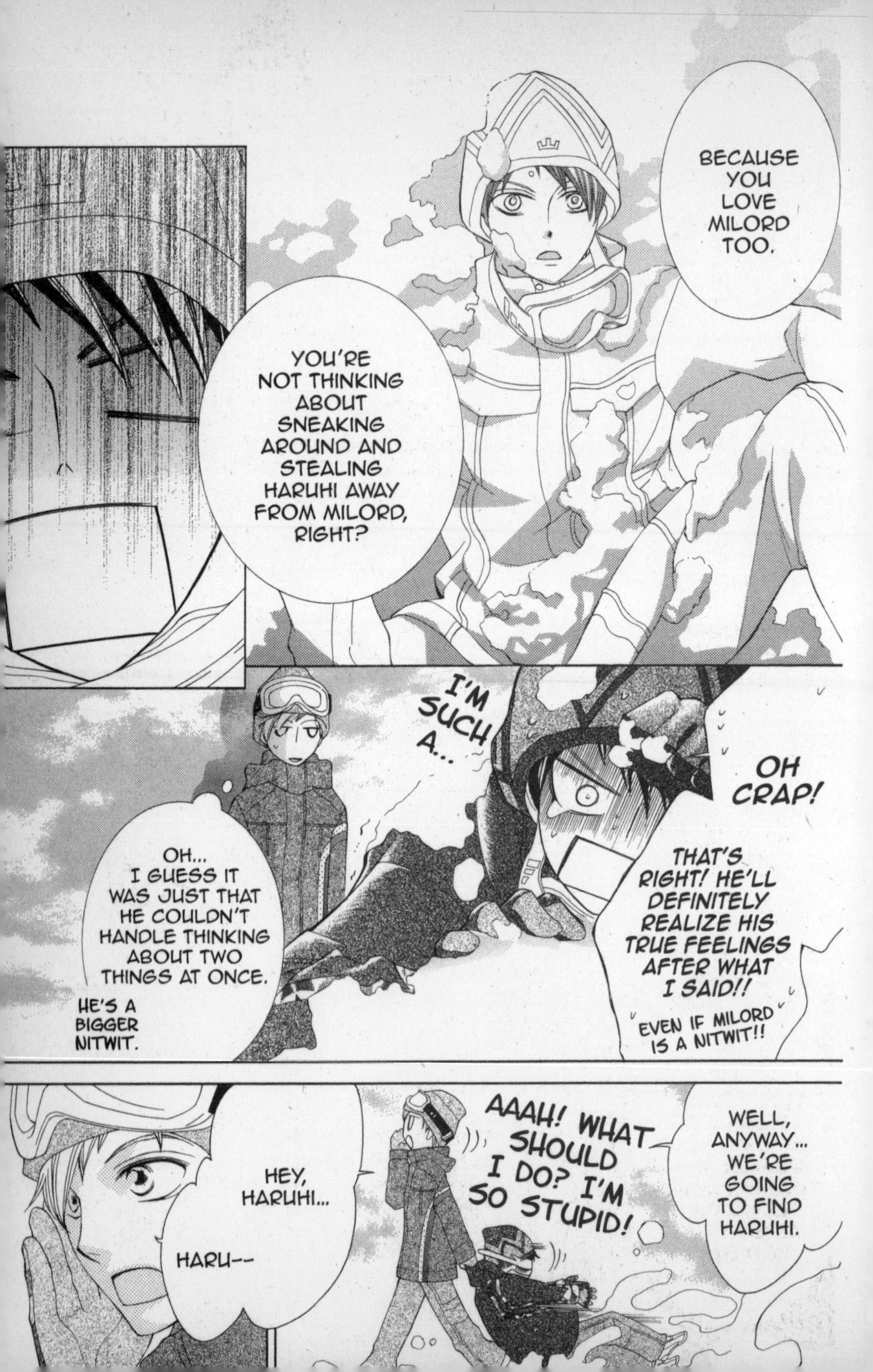
BECAUSE YOU LOVE MILORD TOO.
YOU'RE NOT THINKING ABOUT SNEAKING AROUND AND STEALING HARUHI AWAY FROM MILORD, RIGHT?
I'M SUCH A...
OH CRAP!
THAT'S RIGHT! HE'LL DEFINITELY REALIZE HIS TRUE FEELINGS AFTER WHAT I SAID!!
EVEN IF MILORD IS A NITWIT!!
OH... I GUESS IT WAS JUST THAT HE COULDN'T HANDLE THINKING ABOUT TWO THINGS AT ONCE.
HE'S A BIGGER NITWIT.
WELL, ANYWAY... WE'RE GOING TO FIND HARUHI.
AAAH! WHAT SHOULD I DO? I'M SO STUPID!
HEY, HARUHI...
HARU--

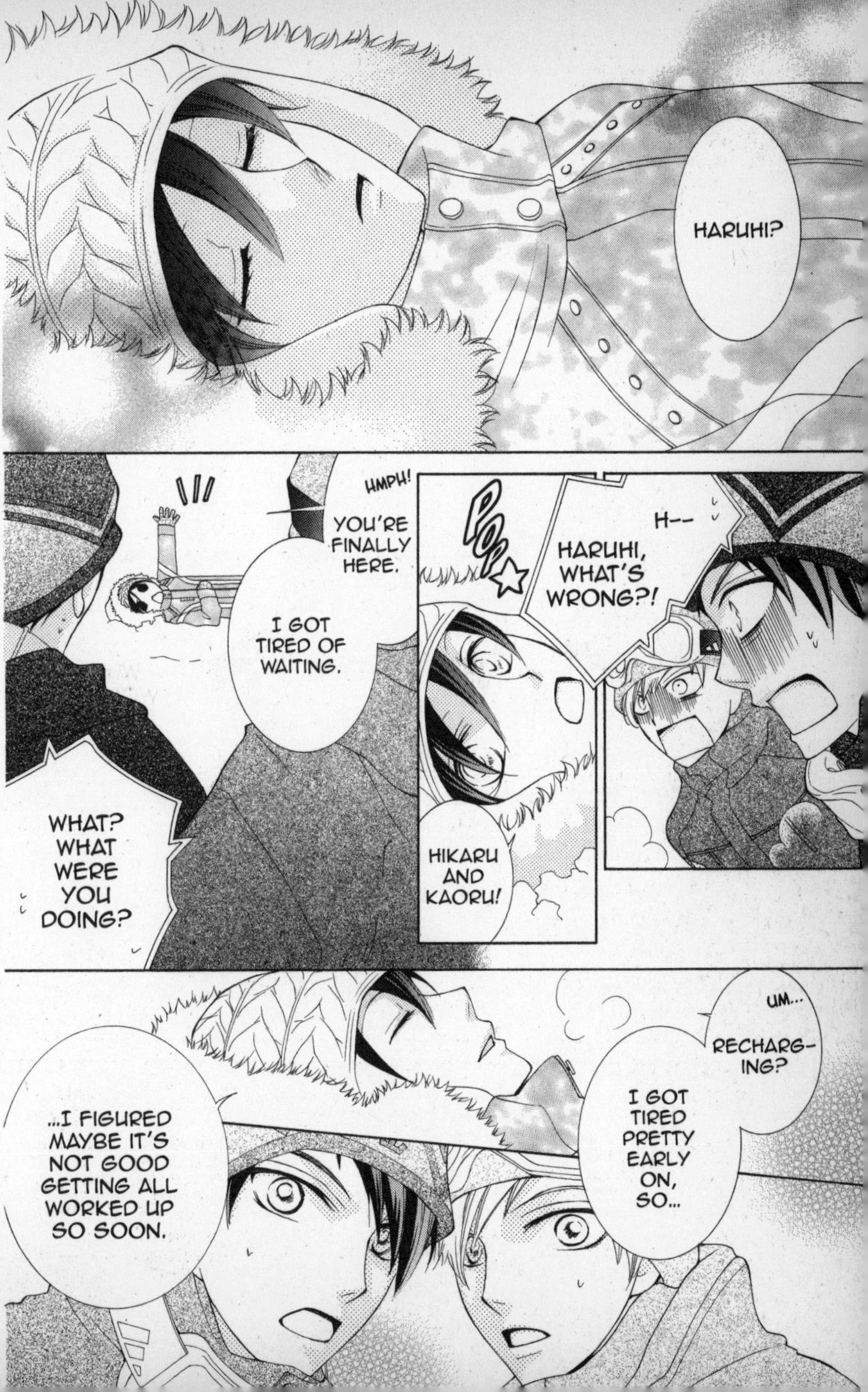
HARUHI?
H--
HARUHI, WHAT'S WRONG?!
POP☆
HIKARU AND KAORU!
HMPH!
YOU'RE FINALLY HERE.
I GOT TIRED OF WAITING.
WHAT? WHAT WERE YOU DOING?
UM... RECHARG-ING?
I GOT TIRED PRETTY EARLY ON, SO...
...I FIGURED MAYBE IT'S NOT GOOD GETTING ALL WORKED UP SO SOON.

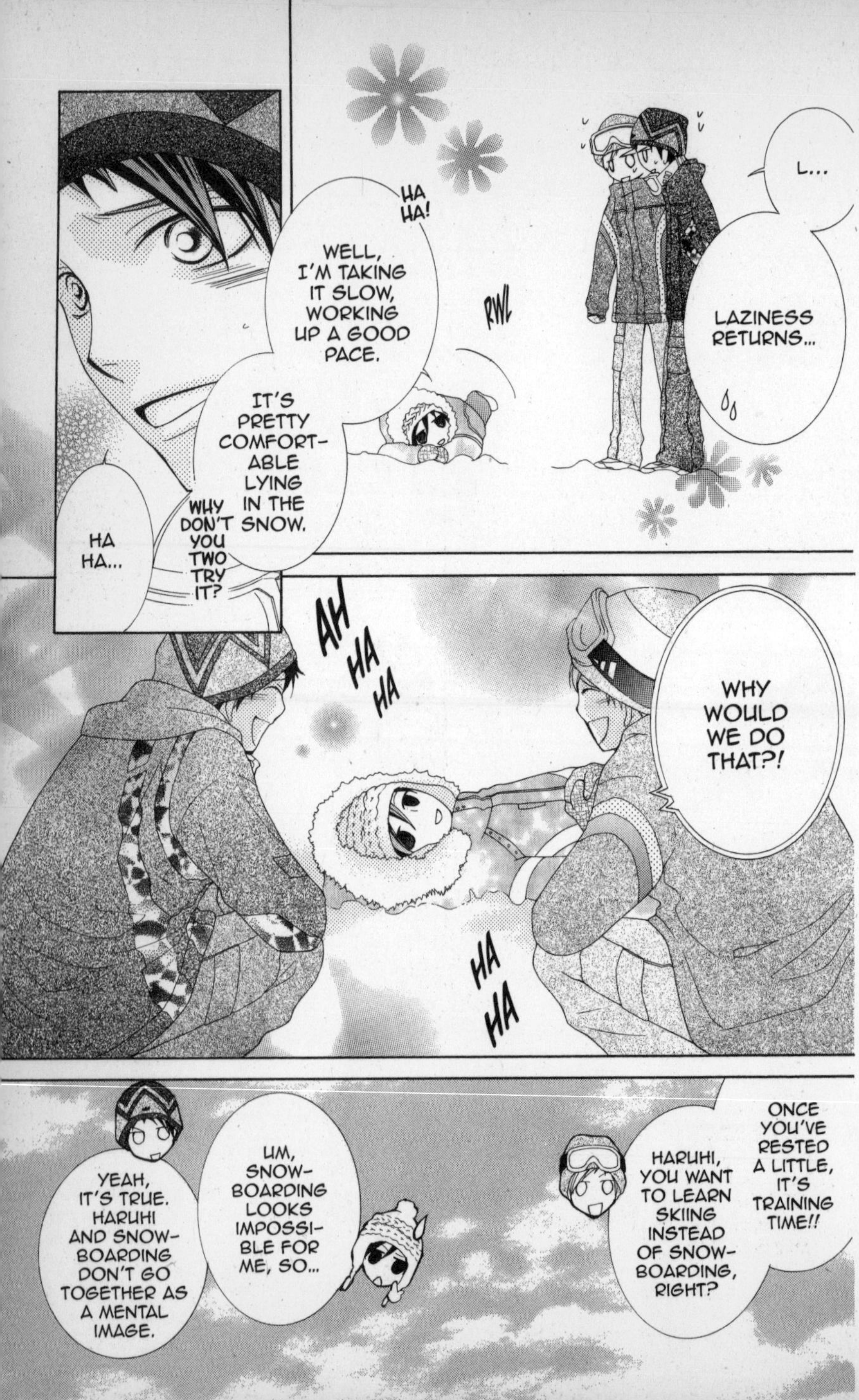
L...
LAZINESS RETURNS...
HA HA!
WELL, I'M TAKING IT SLOW, WORKING UP A GOOD PACE.
RWL
IT'S PRETTY COMFORT-ABLE LYING IN THE SNOW.
WHY DON'T YOU TWO TRY IT?
HA HA...
WHY WOULD WE DO THAT?!
AH HA HA
HA HA
ONCE YOU'VE RESTED A LITTLE, IT'S TRAINING TIME!!
HARUHI, YOU WANT TO LEARN SKIING INSTEAD OF SNOW-BOARDING, RIGHT?
UM, SNOW-BOARDING LOOKS IMPOSSI-BLE FOR ME, SO...
YEAH, IT'S TRUE. HARUHI AND SNOW-BOARDING DON'T GO TOGETHER AS A MENTAL IMAGE.

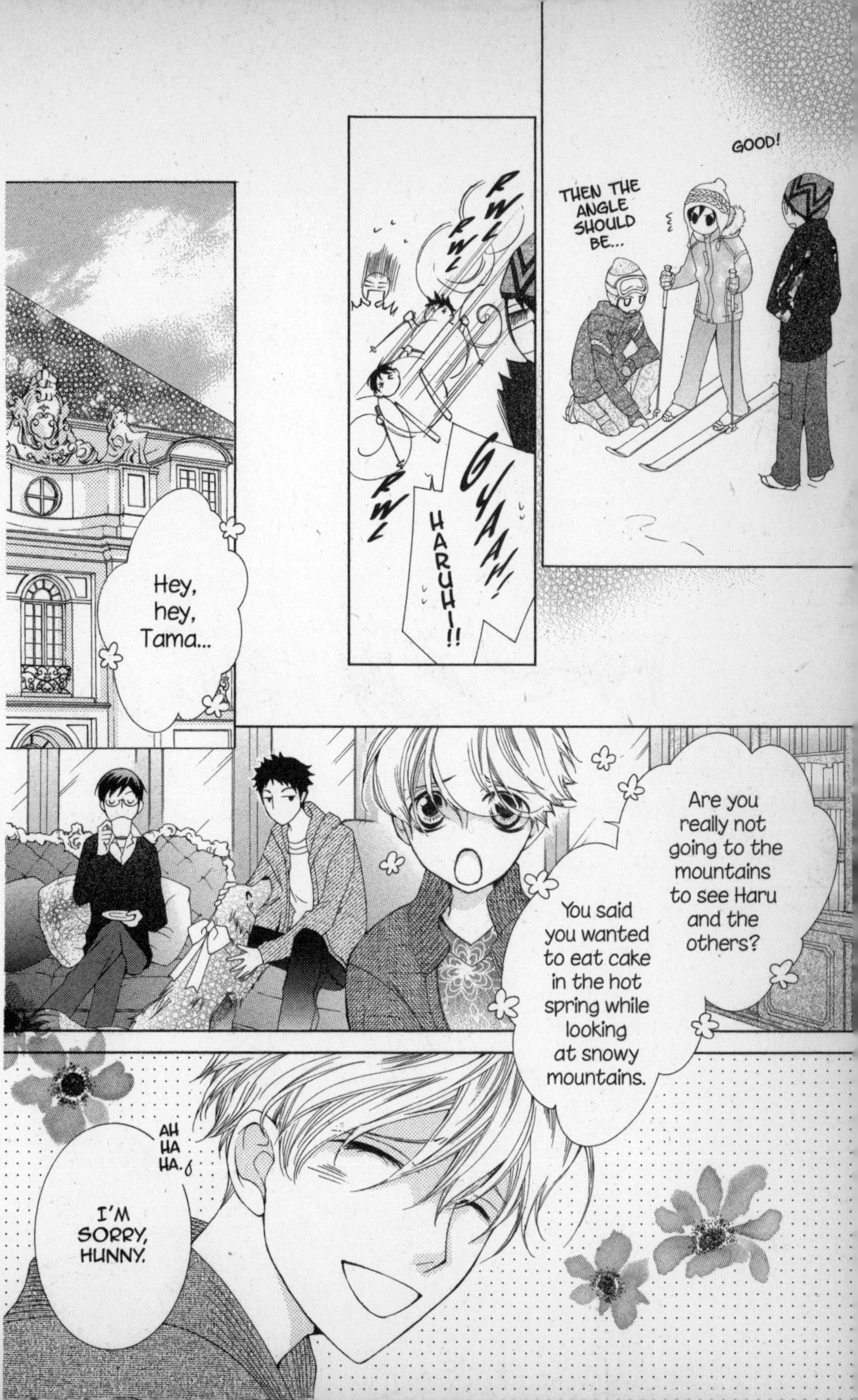
GOOD!
THEN THE ANGLE SHOULD BE...
RWL RWL
GYAAAH!
HARUHI!!
RWL
Hey, hey, Tama...
Are you really not going to the mountains to see Haru and the others?
You said you wanted to eat cake in the hot spring while looking at snowy mountains.
AH HA HA.
I'M SORRY, HUNNY.

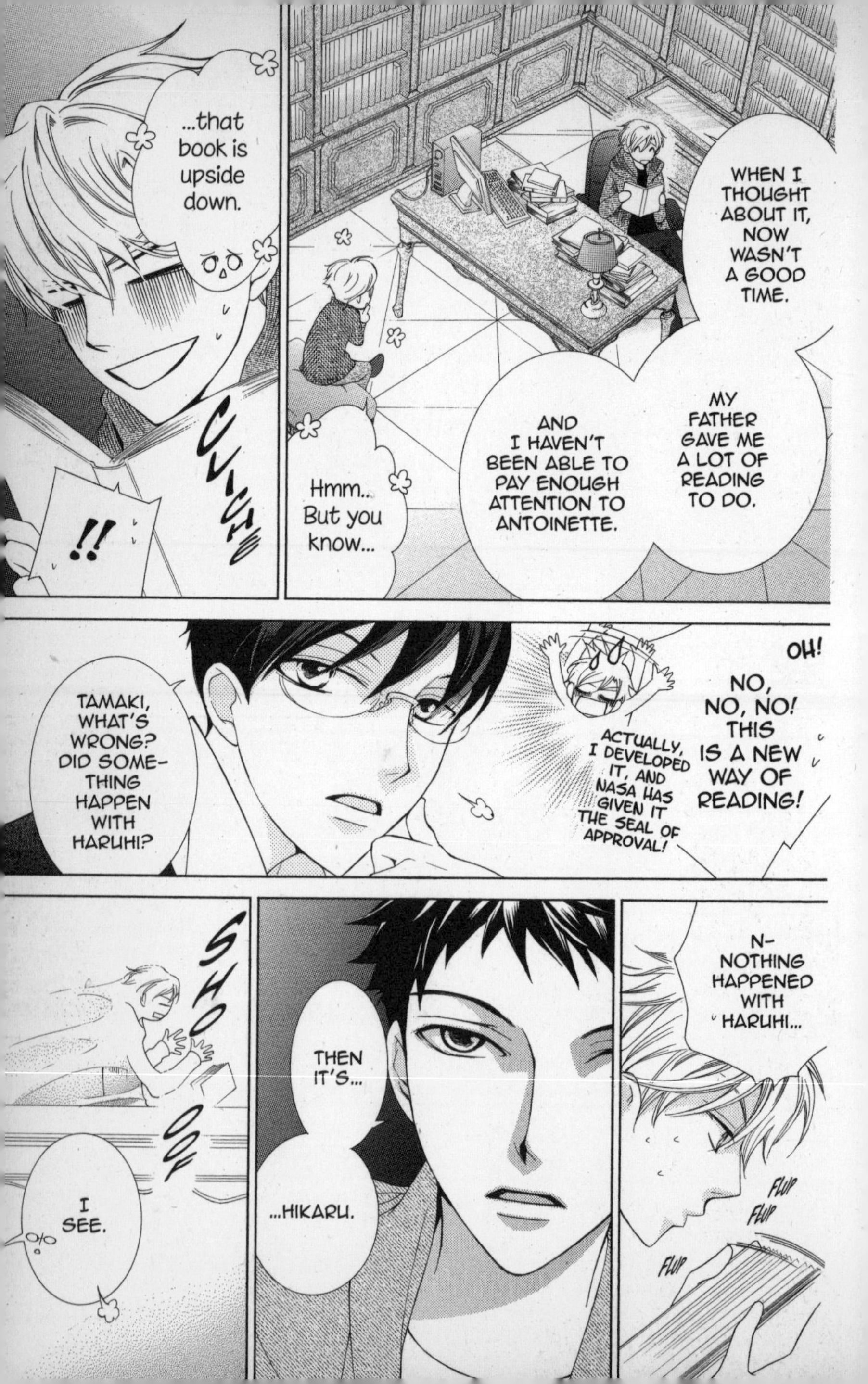
WHEN I THOUGHT ABOUT IT, NOW WASN'T A GOOD TIME.
MY FATHER GAVE ME A LOT OF READING TO DO.
AND I HAVEN'T BEEN ABLE TO PAY ENOUGH ATTENTION TO ANTOINETTE.
Hmm... But you know...
...that book is upside down.
!!
OH!
NO, NO, NO! THIS IS A NEW WAY OF READING!
ACTUALLY, I DEVELOPED IT, AND NASA HAS GIVEN IT THE SEAL OF APPROVAL!
TAMAKI, WHAT'S WRONG? DID SOMETHING HAPPEN WITH HARUHI?
N-NOTHING HAPPENED WITH HARUHI...
THEN IT'S...
...HIKARU.
I SEE.

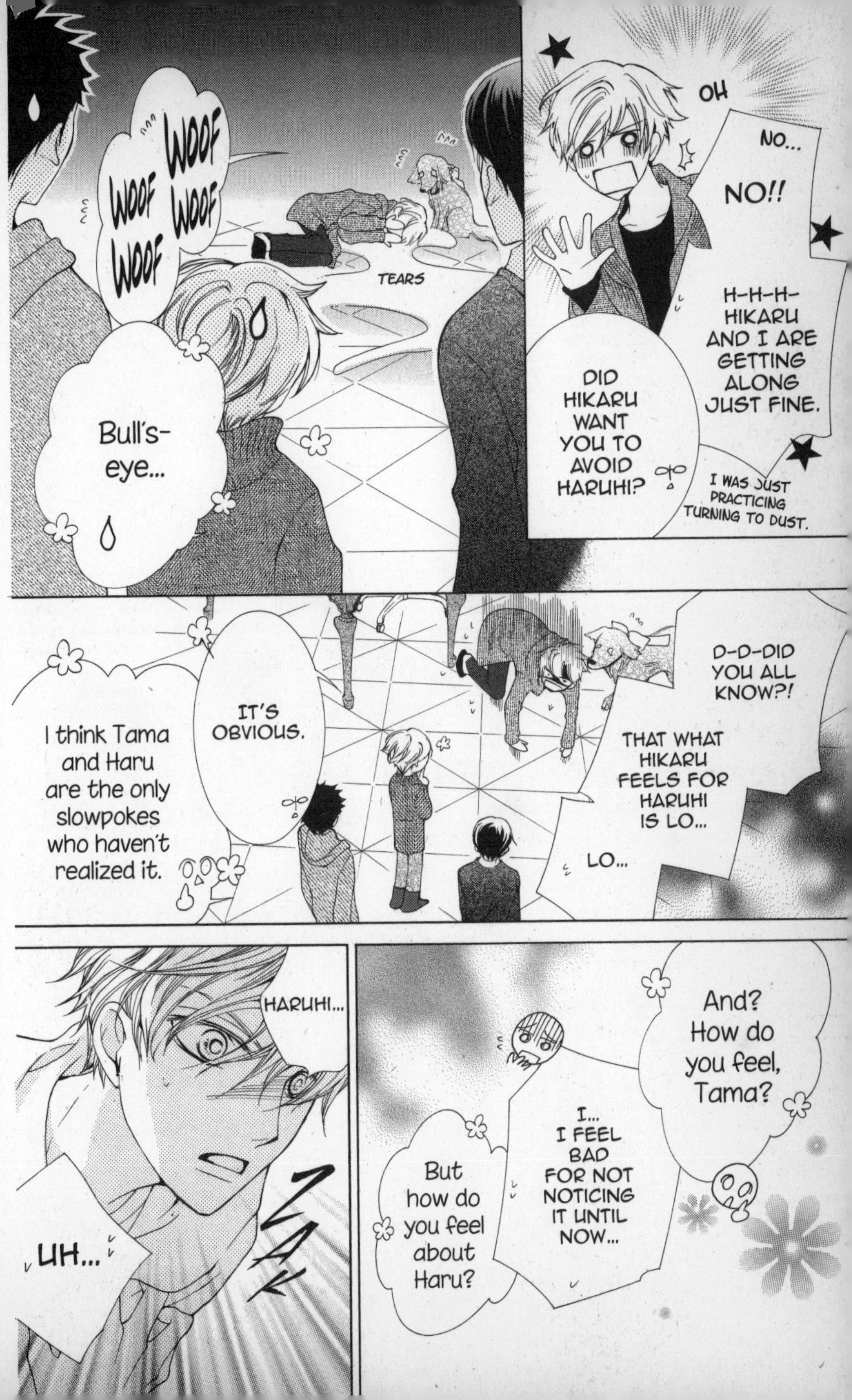
OH
NO...
NO!!
H-H-H-HIKARU AND I ARE GETTING ALONG JUST FINE.
I WAS JUST PRACTICING TURNING TO DUST.
DID HIKARU WANT YOU TO AVOID HARUHI?
TEARS
WOOF WOOF WOOF WOOF WOOF
Bull's-eye...
D-D-DID YOU ALL KNOW?!
THAT WHAT HIKARU FEELS FOR HARUHI IS LO...
LO...
IT'S OBVIOUS.
I think Tama and Haru are the only slowpokes who haven't realized it.
And? How do you feel, Tama?
I... I FEEL BAD FOR NOT NOTICING IT UNTIL NOW...
But how do you feel about Haru?
HARUHI...
UH...

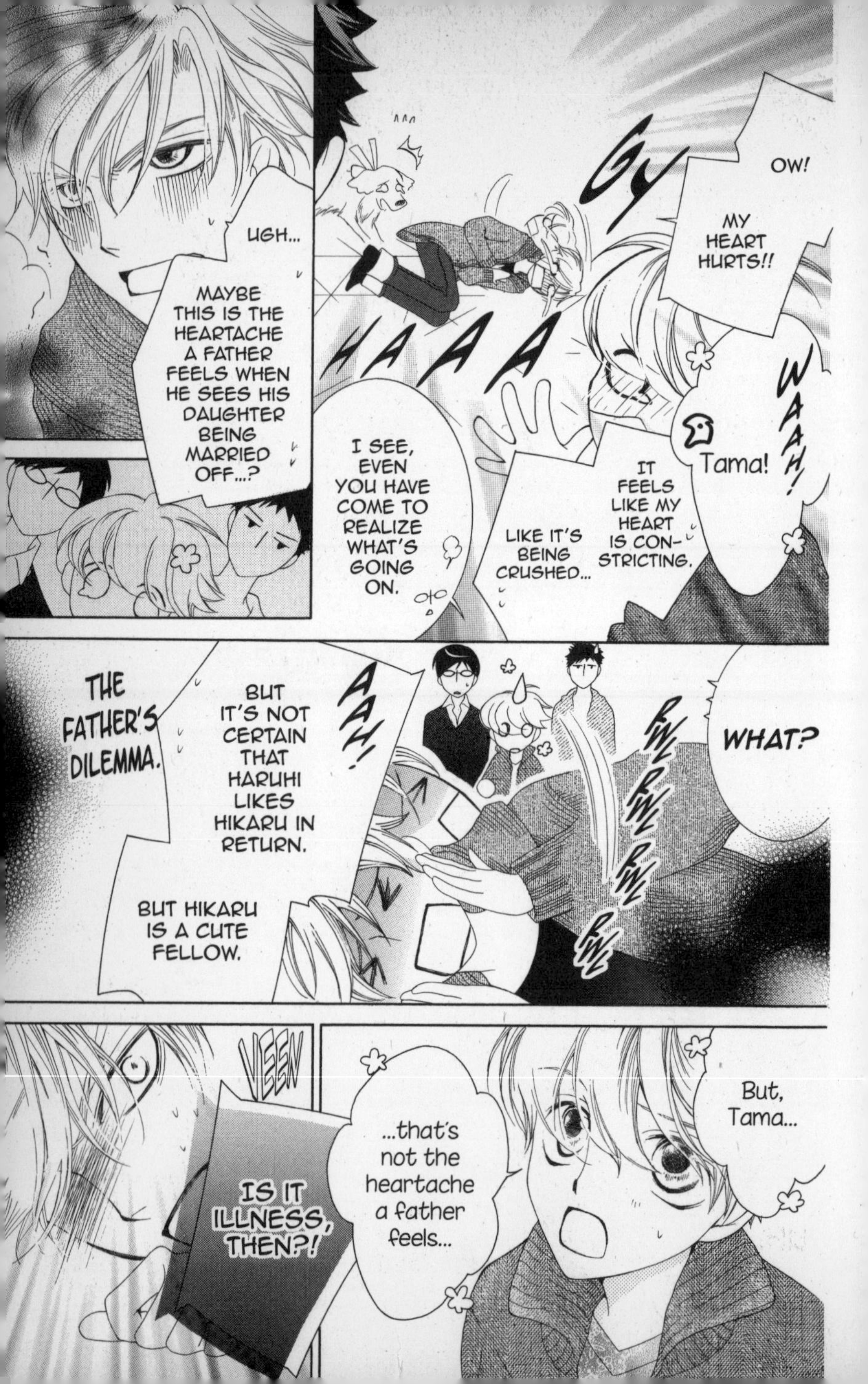
OW!
MY HEART HURTS!!
GY
HAAAA
Tama!
WAAAH!
IT FEELS LIKE MY HEART IS CONSTRICTING.
LIKE IT'S BEING CRUSHED...
I SEE, EVEN YOU HAVE COME TO REALIZE WHAT'S GOING ON.
UGH...
MAYBE THIS IS THE HEARTACHE A FATHER FEELS WHEN HE SEES HIS DAUGHTER BEING MARRIED OFF...?
WHAT?
RWLRWLRWLRWL
AAAH!
BUT IT'S NOT CERTAIN THAT HARUHI LIKES HIKARU IN RETURN.
BUT HIKARU IS A CUTE FELLOW.
THE FATHER'S DILEMMA.
But, Tama...
...that's not the heartache a father feels...
VEEN
IS IT ILLNESS, THEN?!

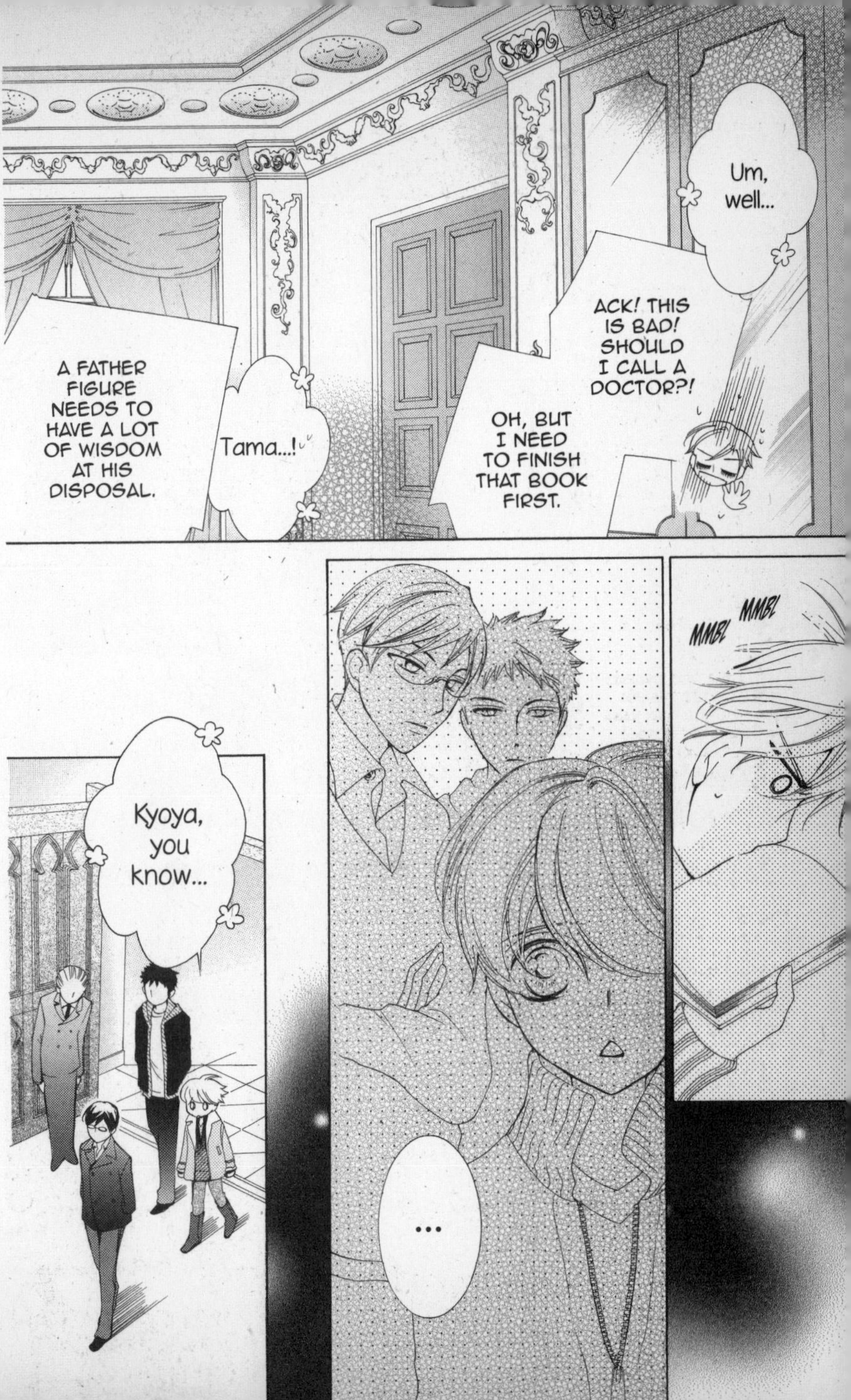
Um, well...
ACK! THIS IS BAD! SHOULD I CALL A DOCTOR?!
OH, BUT I NEED TO FINISH THAT BOOK FIRST.
Tama...!
A FATHER FIGURE NEEDS TO HAVE A LOT OF WISDOM AT HIS DISPOSAL.
MMBL
MMBL
...
Kyoya, you know...

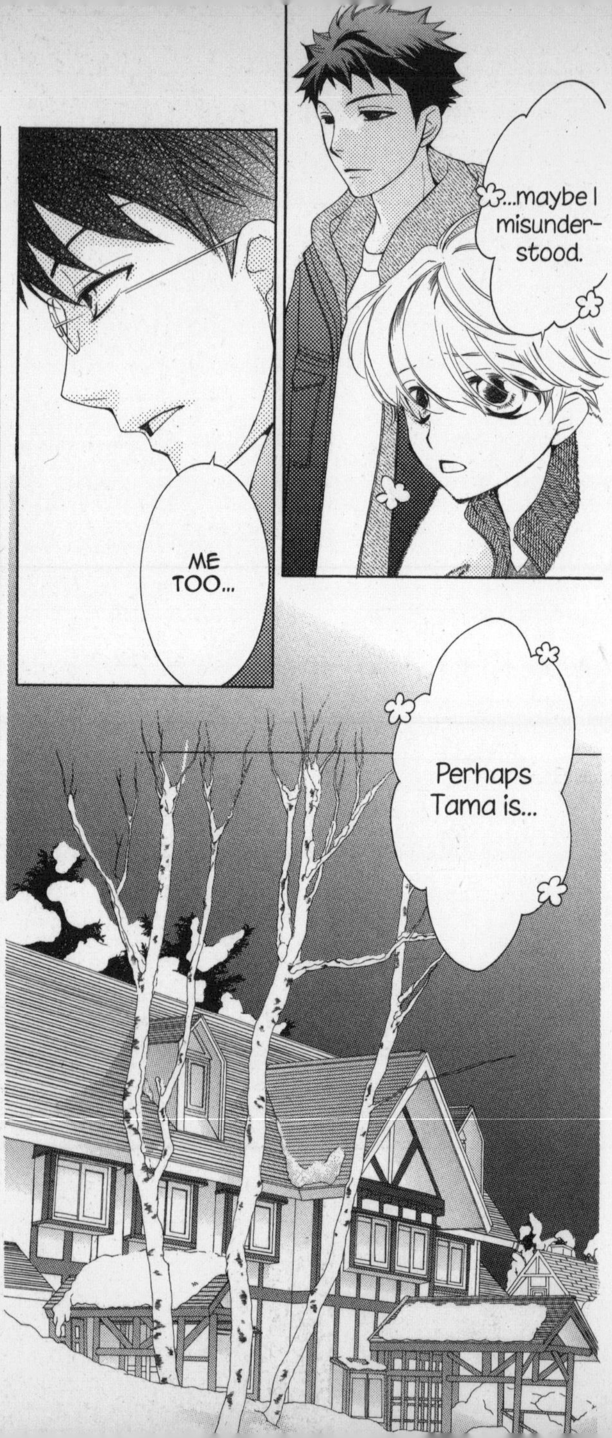
...maybe I misunderstood.
ME TOO...
Perhaps Tama is...

4

②WE HEADED TO A SECRET HOT SPRING RECOMMENDED BY KANA, BUT THE CAR WAS A TWO-WHEEL DRIVE, SO IT COULDN'T DRIVE UP THE STEEP, SNOWY MOUNTAIN. TO MAKE MATTERS WORSE, THE SNOW REDUCED VISIBILITY TO ZERO, AND WE RETREATED IN HORROR.
③BUT WE FOUND A BUS ROUTE THAT WOULD TAKE US UP THERE, SO WE PARKED THE CAR, TOOK THE BUS, AND WALKED THROUGH THE BLIZZARD TO REACH THE HOT SPRING.
④AFTER THAT ORDEAL, WE ENJOYED THE HOT SPRING, BUT THEN KANA REALIZED SHE FORGOT HER CELL PHONE THERE.
⑤WE TOOK A TAXI (!!) FROM THE FOOT OF THE MOUNTAIN ALL THE WAY UP TO MATSUKAWA HOT SPRING.
⑥WE WERE FINALLY SUPPOSED TO BE ON THE WAY BACK TO MORIOKA BY CAR, BUT WE WERE, FOR SOME REASON, HEADING THE WRONG WAY UP TO THE MOUNTAIN PEAK.
⑦WE EXPERIENCED THE HORROR OF ALMOST BEING STRANDED.
⑧THERE WERE A LOT OF AWFUL THINGS THAT HAPPENED, BUT I'D LIKE TO END THIS STORY BY MENTIONING THAT THE KOREAN NOODLES AT THE PYON PYON INN WERE DELICIOUS!!

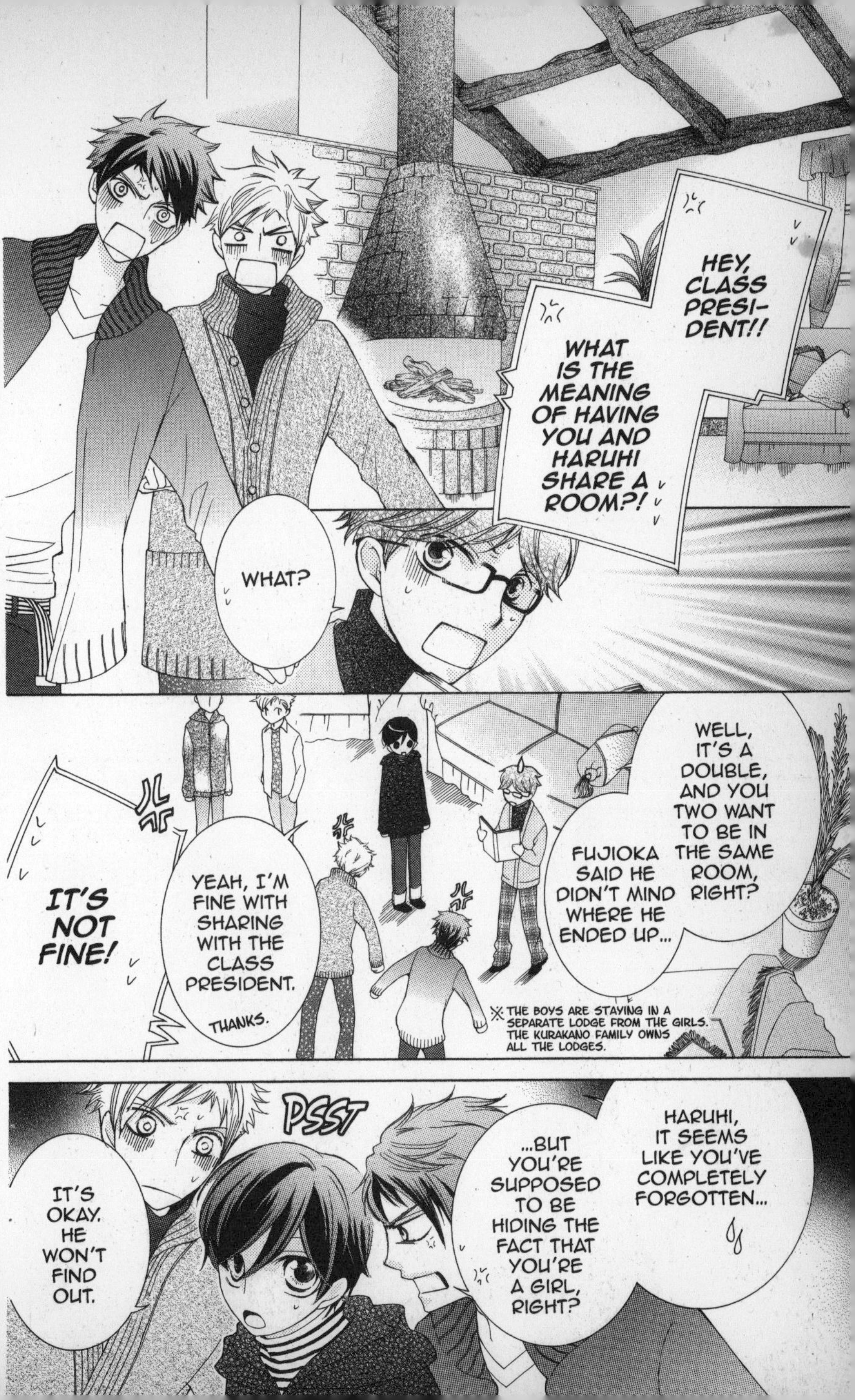
HEY, CLASS PRESI- DENT!!
WHAT IS THE MEANING OF HAVING YOU AND HARUHI SHARE A ROOM?!
WHAT?
WELL, IT'S A DOUBLE, AND YOU TWO WANT TO BE IN THE SAME ROOM, RIGHT?
FUJIOKA SAID HE DIDN'T MIND WHERE HE ENDED UP...
YEAH, I'M FINE WITH SHARING WITH THE CLASS PRESIDENT.
THANKS.
IT'S NOT FINE!
※ THE BOYS ARE STAYING IN A SEPARATE LODGE FROM THE GIRLS. THE KURAKANO FAMILY OWNS ALL THE LODGES.
PSST
HARUHI, IT SEEMS LIKE YOU'VE COMPLETELY FORGOTTEN...
...BUT YOU'RE SUPPOSED TO BE HIDING THE FACT THAT YOU'RE A GIRL, RIGHT?
IT'S OKAY. HE WON'T FIND OUT.

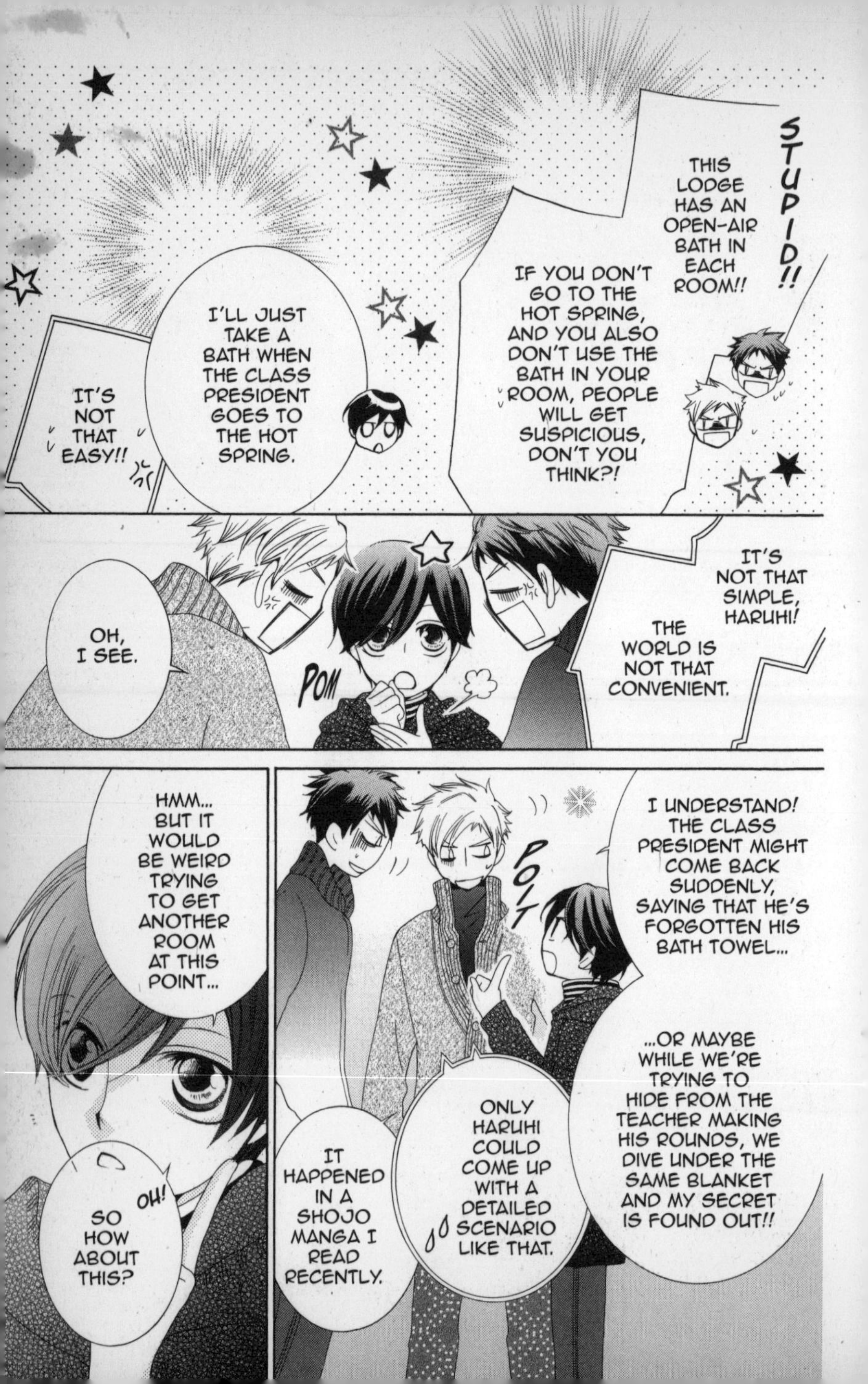
STUPID!!
THIS LODGE HAS AN OPEN-AIR BATH IN EACH ROOM!!
IF YOU DON'T GO TO THE HOT SPRING, AND YOU ALSO DON'T USE THE BATH IN YOUR ROOM, PEOPLE WILL GET SUSPICIOUS, DON'T YOU THINK?!
I'LL JUST TAKE A BATH WHEN THE CLASS PRESIDENT GOES TO THE HOT SPRING.
IT'S NOT THAT EASY!!
IT'S NOT THAT SIMPLE, HARUHI!
THE WORLD IS NOT THAT CONVENIENT.
POM
OH, I SEE.
I UNDERSTAND! THE CLASS PRESIDENT MIGHT COME BACK SUDDENLY, SAYING THAT HE'S FORGOTTEN HIS BATH TOWEL...
POIT
...OR MAYBE WHILE WE'RE TRYING TO HIDE FROM THE TEACHER MAKING HIS ROUNDS, WE DIVE UNDER THE SAME BLANKET AND MY SECRET IS FOUND OUT!!
ONLY HARUHI COULD COME UP WITH A DETAILED SCENARIO LIKE THAT.
IT HAPPENED IN A SHOJO MANGA I READ RECENTLY.
HMM... BUT IT WOULD BE WEIRD TRYING TO GET ANOTHER ROOM AT THIS POINT...
OH!
SO HOW ABOUT THIS?

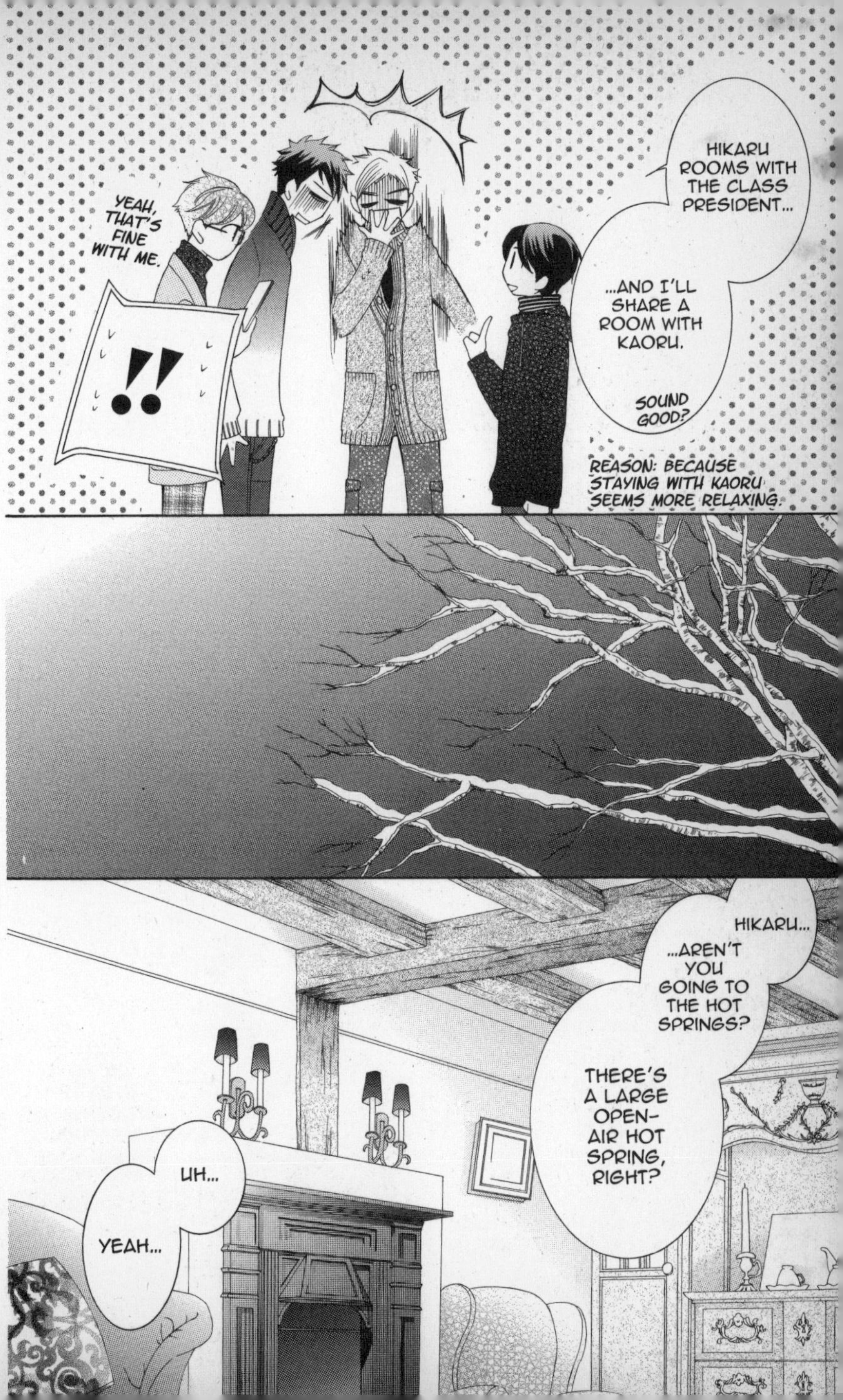
HIKARU ROOMS WITH THE CLASS PRESIDENT...
...AND I'LL SHARE A ROOM WITH KAORU.
SOUND GOOD?
REASON: BECAUSE STAYING WITH KAORU SEEMS MORE RELAXING.
YEAH, THAT'S FINE WITH ME.
!!
HIKARU...
...AREN'T YOU GOING TO THE HOT SPRINGS?
THERE'S A LARGE OPEN-AIR HOT SPRING, RIGHT?
UH...
YEAH...

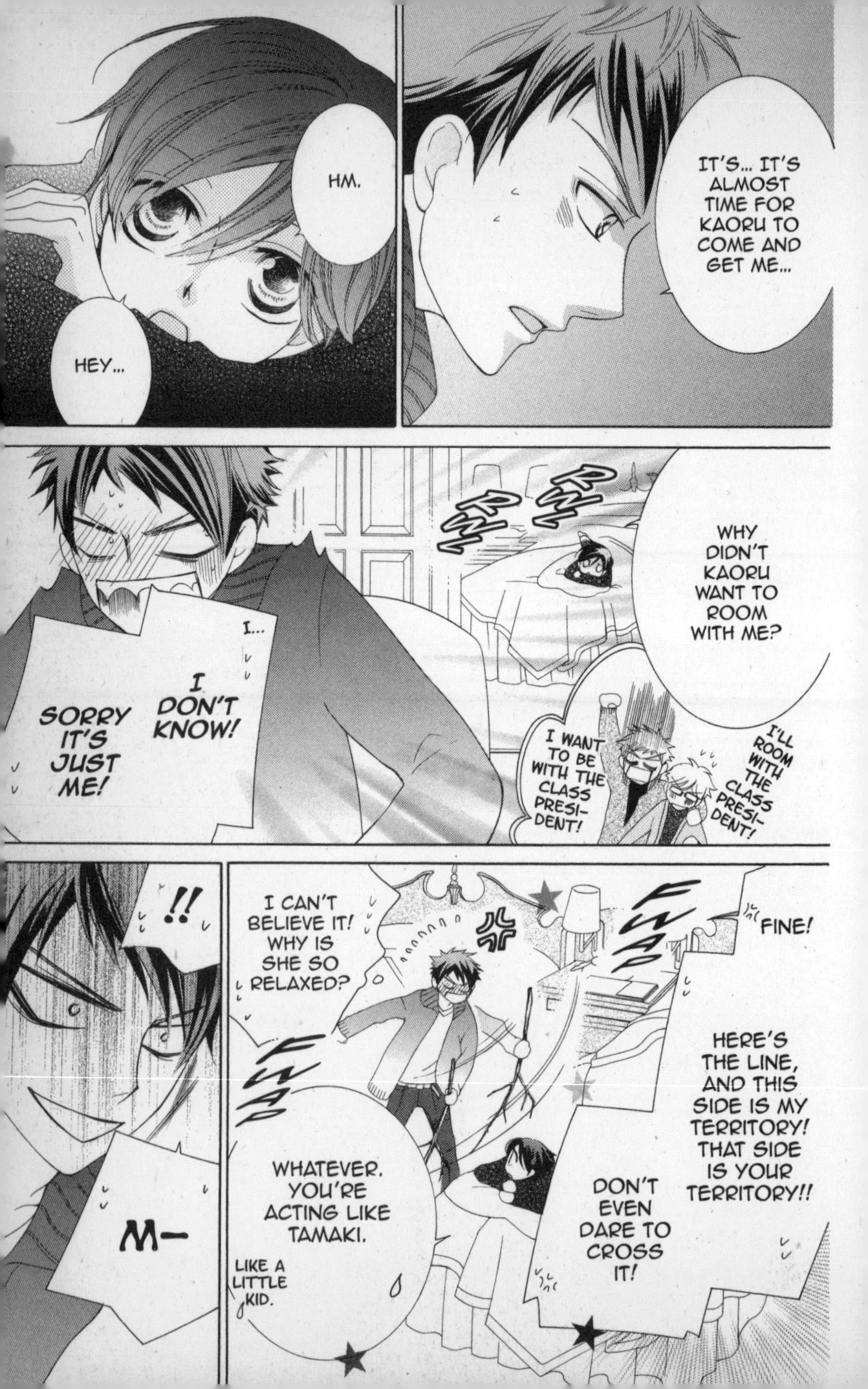
IT'S... IT'S ALMOST TIME FOR KAORU TO COME AND GET ME...
HM.
HEY...
WHY DIDN'T KAORU WANT TO ROOM WITH ME?
I'LL ROOM WITH THE CLASS PRESIDENT!
I WANT TO BE WITH THE CLASS PRESIDENT!
I...
I DON'T KNOW!
SORRY IT'S JUST ME!
FINE!
HERE'S THE LINE, AND THIS SIDE IS MY TERRITORY! THAT SIDE IS YOUR TERRITORY!!
FWAP
I CAN'T BELIEVE IT! WHY IS SHE SO RELAXED?
FWAP
DON'T EVEN DARE TO CROSS IT!
WHATEVER. YOU'RE ACTING LIKE TAMAKI.
LIKE A LITTLE KID.
!!
M—

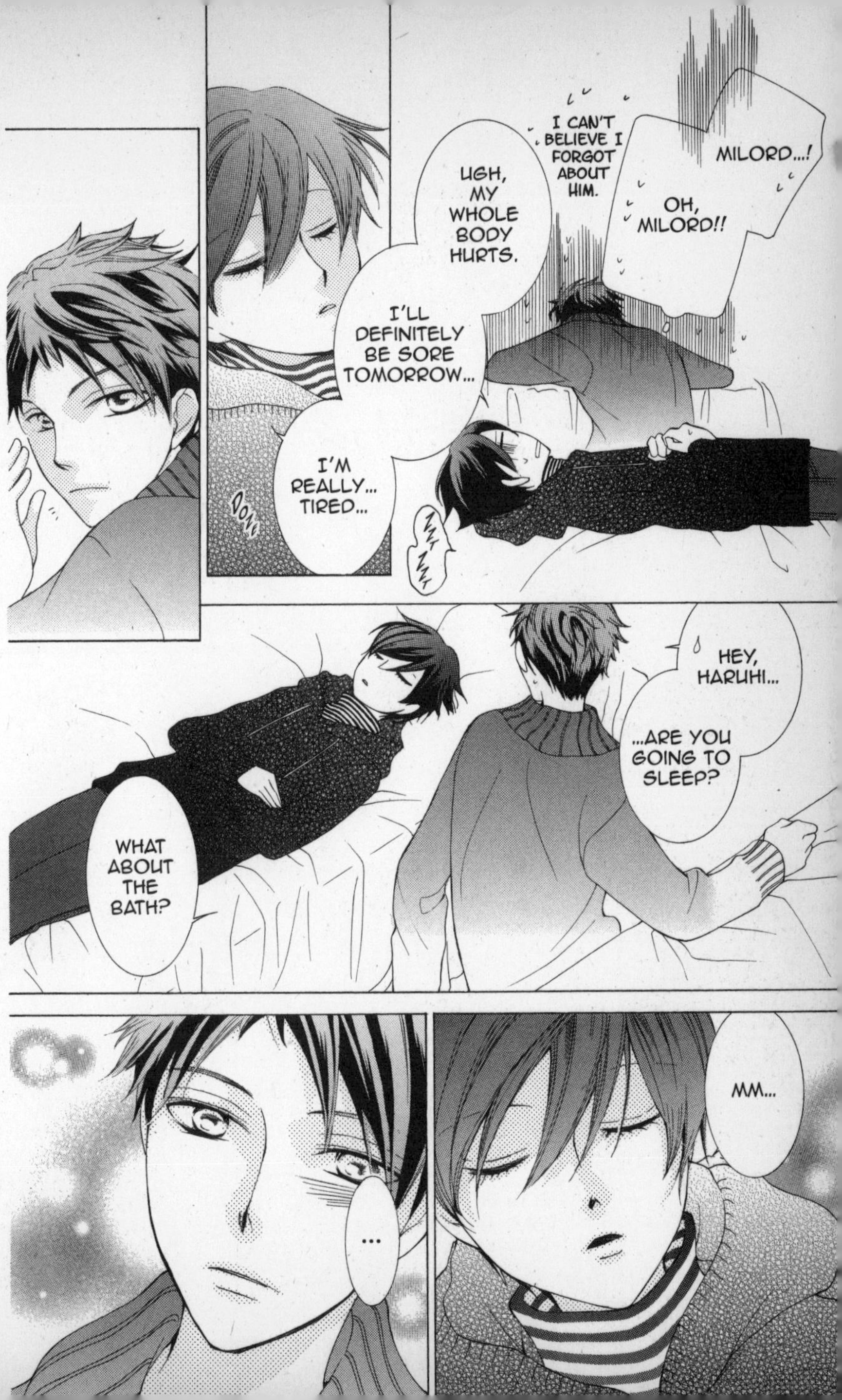
MILORD...!
OH, MILORD!!
I CAN'T BELIEVE I FORGOT ABOUT HIM.
UGH, MY WHOLE BODY HURTS.
I'LL DEFINITELY BE SORE TOMORROW...
I'M REALLY... TIRED...
HEY, HARUHI...
...ARE YOU GOING TO SLEEP?
WHAT ABOUT THE BATH?
MM...
...

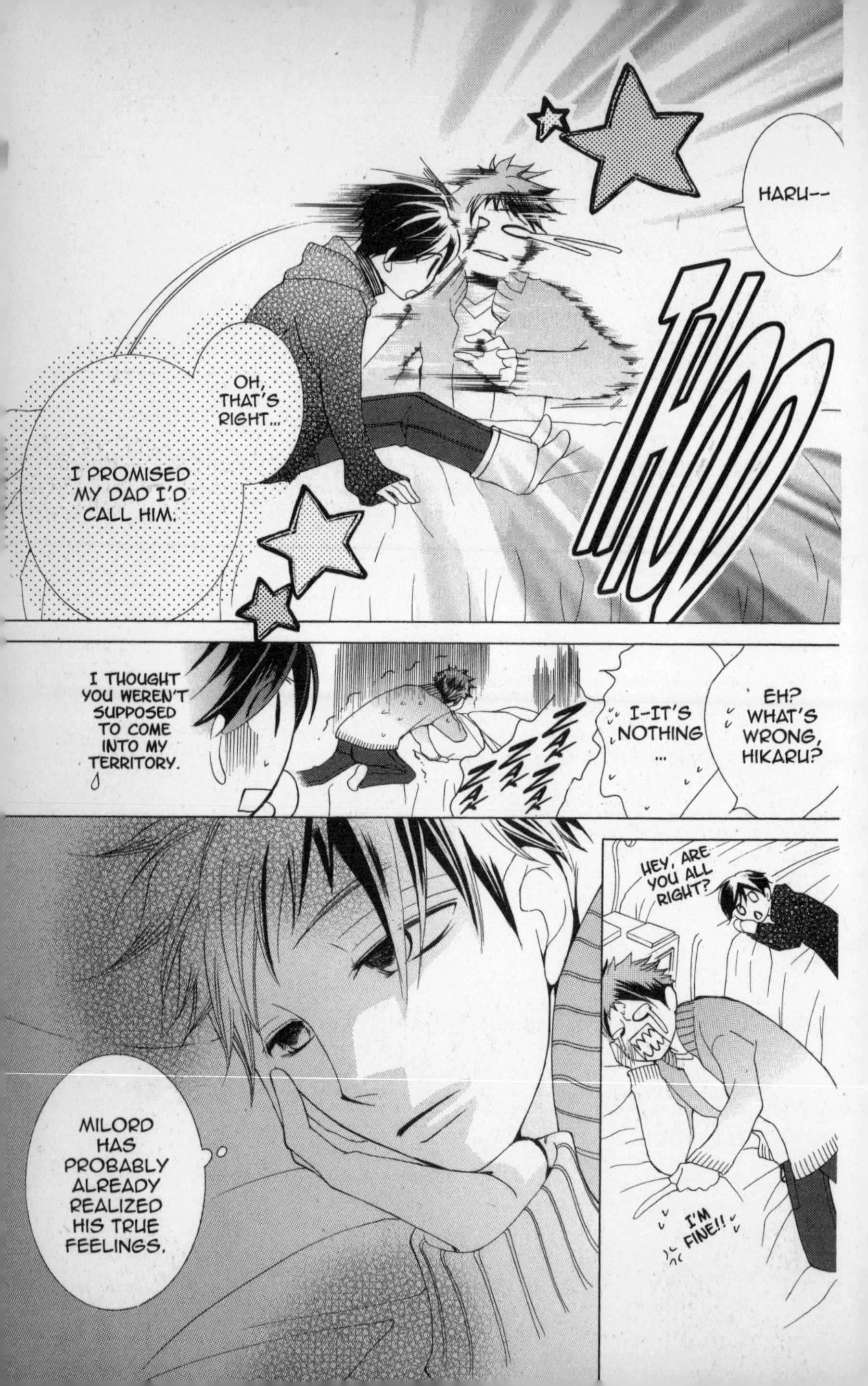
HARU--
OH, THAT'S RIGHT...
I PROMISED MY DAD I'D CALL HIM.
EH? WHAT'S WRONG, HIKARU?
I-IT'S NOTHING ...
I THOUGHT YOU WEREN'T SUPPOSED TO COME INTO MY TERRITORY.
HEY, ARE YOU ALL RIGHT?
I'M FINE!!
MILORD HAS PROBABLY ALREADY REALIZED HIS TRUE FEELINGS.

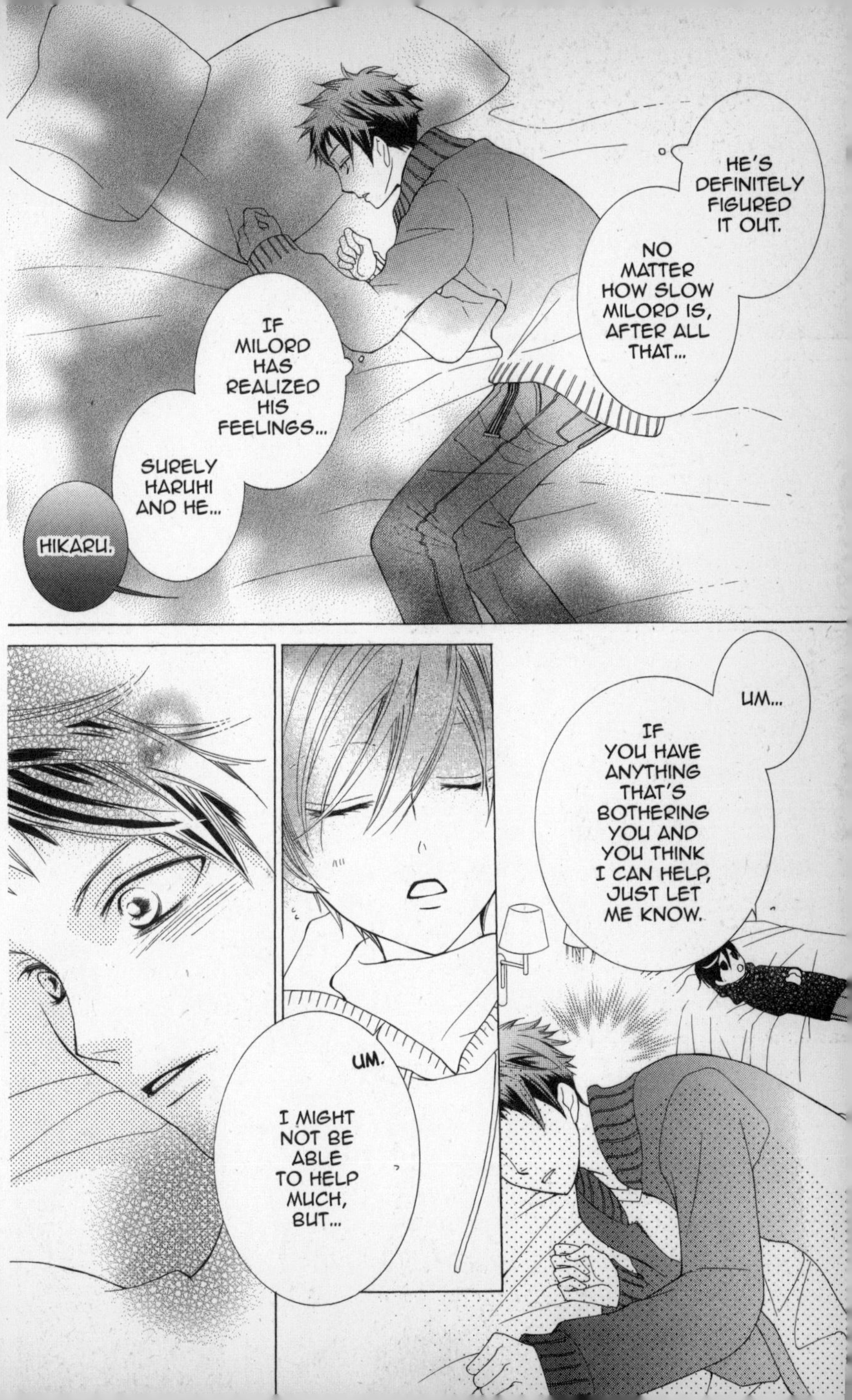
HE'S DEFINITELY FIGURED IT OUT.
NO MATTER HOW SLOW MILORD IS, AFTER ALL THAT...
IF MILORD HAS REALIZED HIS FEELINGS...
SURELY HARUHI AND HE...
HIKARU.
UM...
IF YOU HAVE ANYTHING THAT'S BOTHERING YOU AND YOU THINK I CAN HELP, JUST LET ME KNOW.
UM.
I MIGHT NOT BE ABLE TO HELP MUCH, BUT...

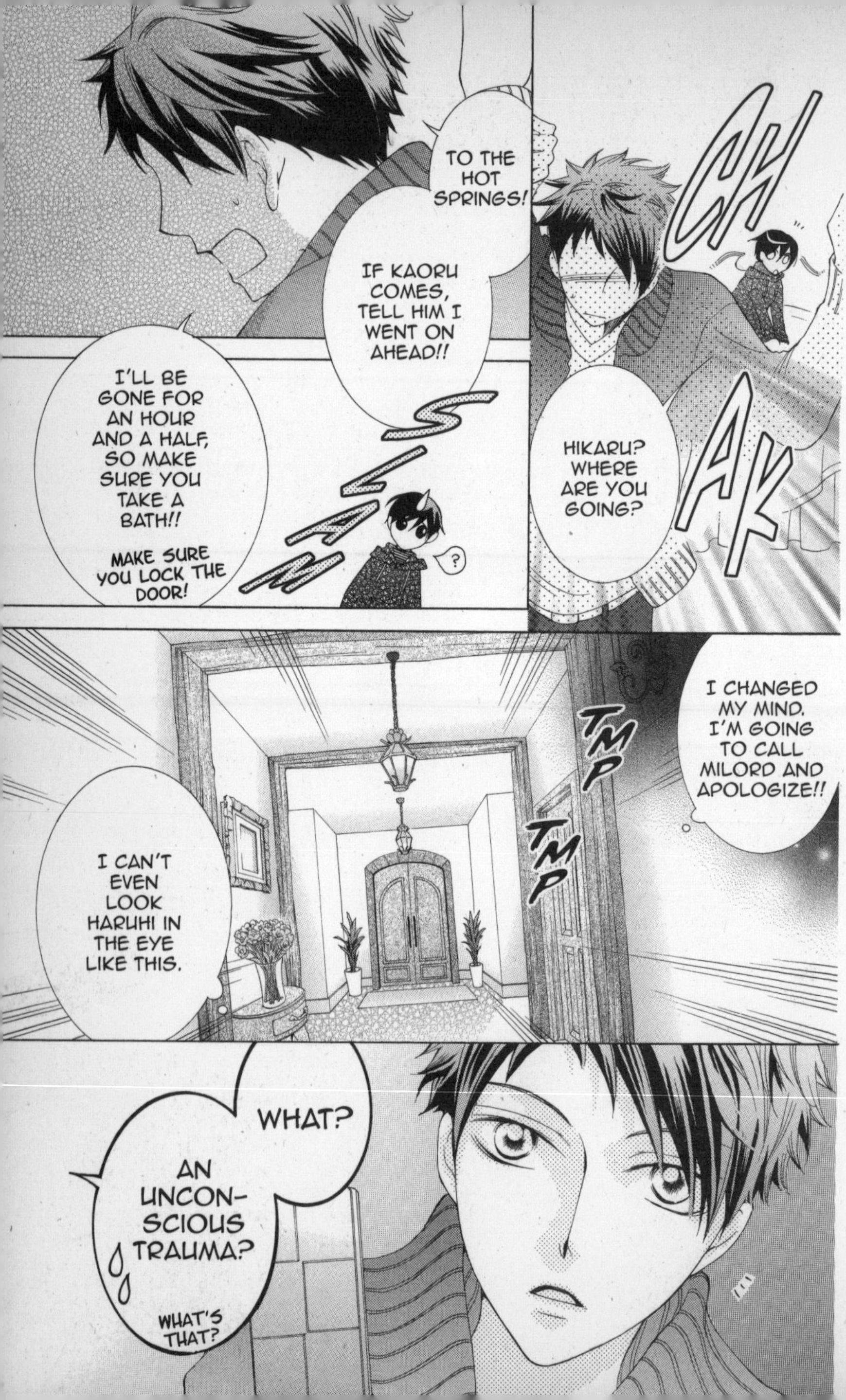
CH
AK
HIKARU? WHERE ARE YOU GOING?
TO THE HOT SPRINGS!
IF KAORU COMES, TELL HIM I WENT ON AHEAD!!
I'LL BE GONE FOR AN HOUR AND A HALF, SO MAKE SURE YOU TAKE A BATH!!
MAKE SURE YOU LOCK THE DOOR!
SLAM
?
I CHANGED MY MIND. I'M GOING TO CALL MILORD AND APOLOGIZE!!
TMP TMP
I CAN'T EVEN LOOK HARUHI IN THE EYE LIKE THIS.
WHAT?
AN UNCONSCIOUS TRAUMA?
WHAT'S THAT?

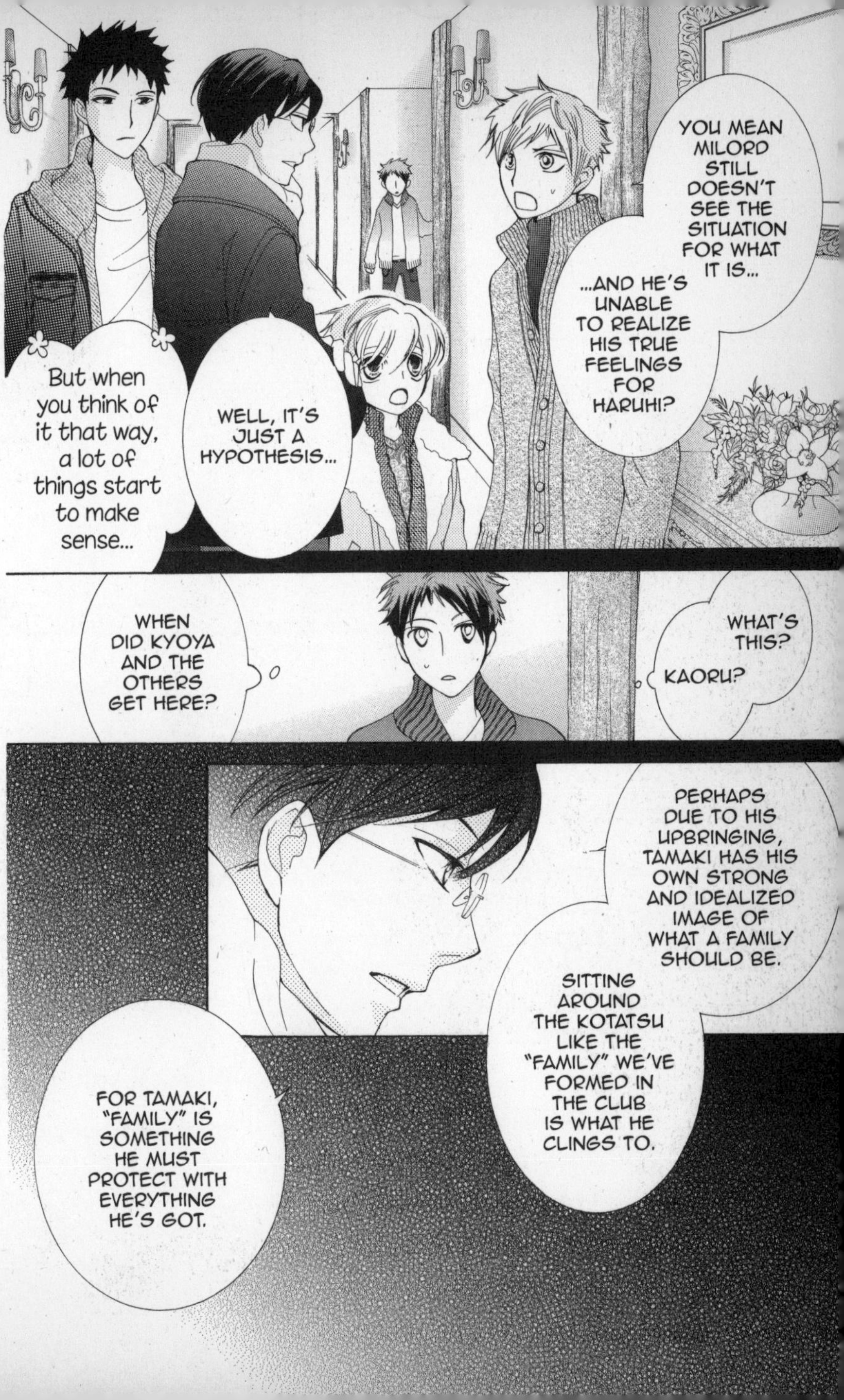
YOU MEAN MILORD STILL DOESN'T SEE THE SITUATION FOR WHAT IT IS...
...AND HE'S UNABLE TO REALIZE HIS TRUE FEELINGS FOR HARUHI?
WELL, IT'S JUST A HYPOTHESIS...
But when you think of it that way, a lot of things start to make sense...
WHAT'S THIS?
KAORU?
WHEN DID KYOYA AND THE OTHERS GET HERE?
PERHAPS DUE TO HIS UPBRINGING, TAMAKI HAS HIS OWN STRONG AND IDEALIZED IMAGE OF WHAT A FAMILY SHOULD BE.
SITTING AROUND THE KOTATSU LIKE THE "FAMILY" WE'VE FORMED IN THE CLUB IS WHAT HE CLINGS TO.
FOR TAMAKI, "FAMILY" IS SOMETHING HE MUST PROTECT WITH EVERYTHING HE'S GOT.

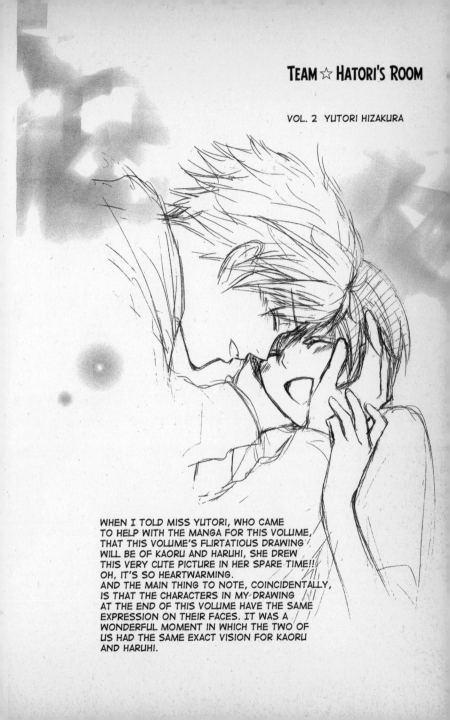

TEAM ☆ HATORI'S ROOM

VOL. 2 YUTORI HIZAKURA

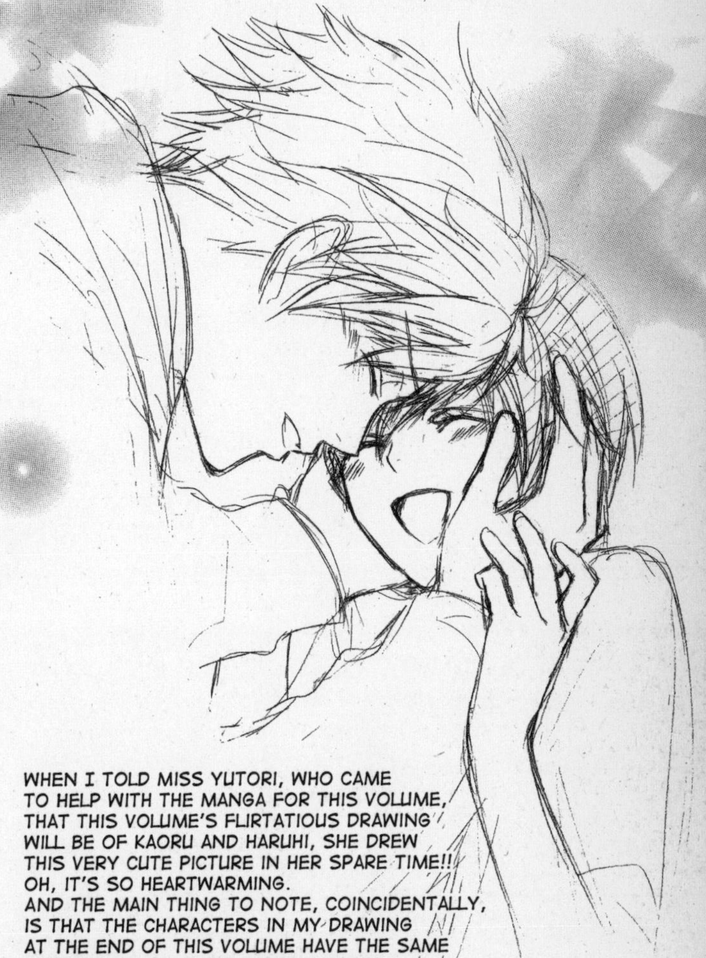

WHEN I TOLD MISS YUTORI, WHO CAME TO HELP WITH THE MANGA FOR THIS VOLUME, THAT THIS VOLUME'S FLIRTATIOUS DRAWING WILL BE OF KAORU AND HARUHI, SHE DREW THIS VERY CUTE PICTURE IN HER SPARE TIME!! OH, IT'S SO HEARTWARMING.
AND THE MAIN THING TO NOTE, COINCIDENTALLY, IS THAT THE CHARACTERS IN MY DRAWING AT THE END OF THIS VOLUME HAVE THE SAME EXPRESSION ON THEIR FACES. IT WAS A WONDERFUL MOMENT IN WHICH THE TWO OF US HAD THE SAME EXACT VISION FOR KAORU AND HARUHI.

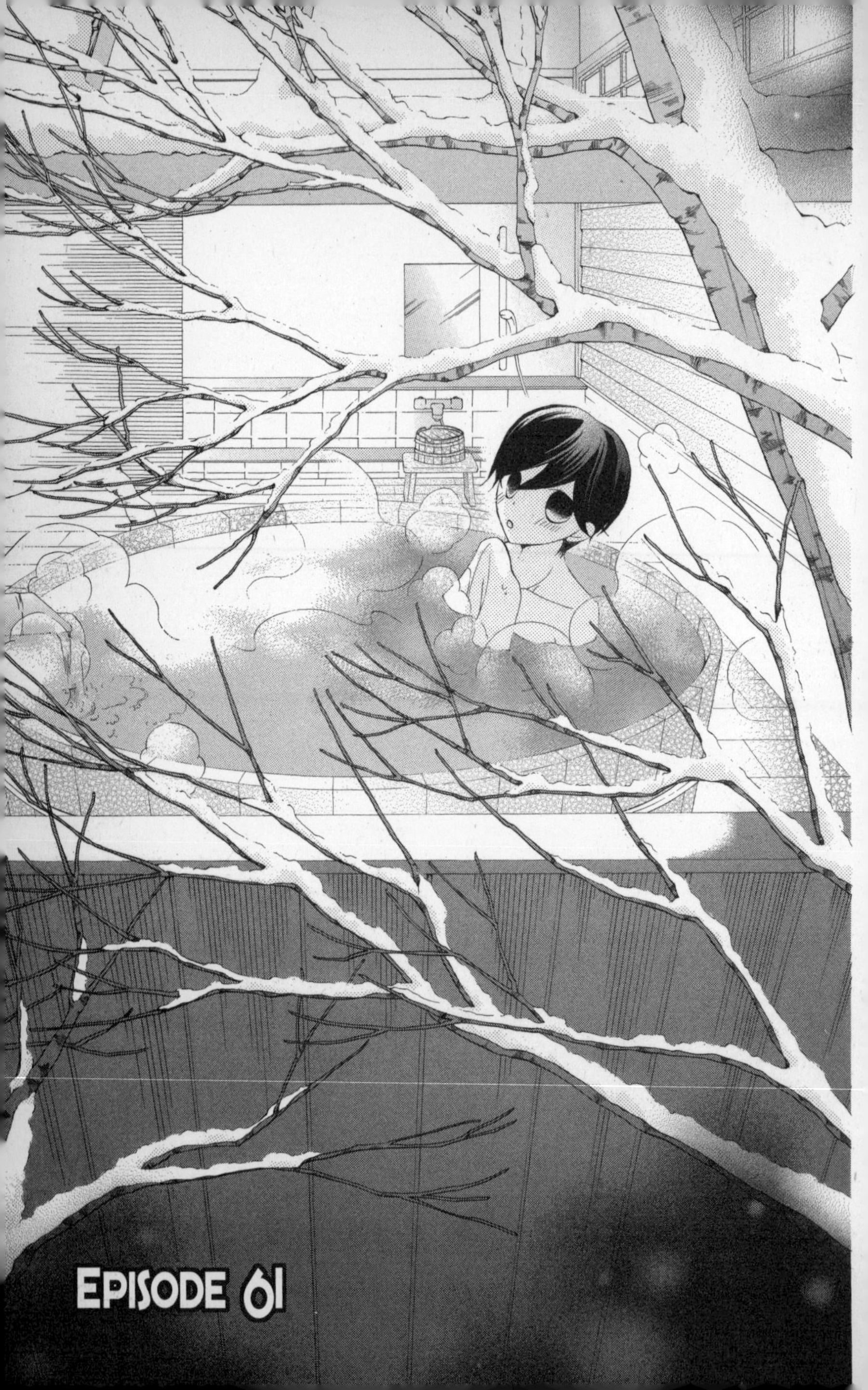
EPISODE 61

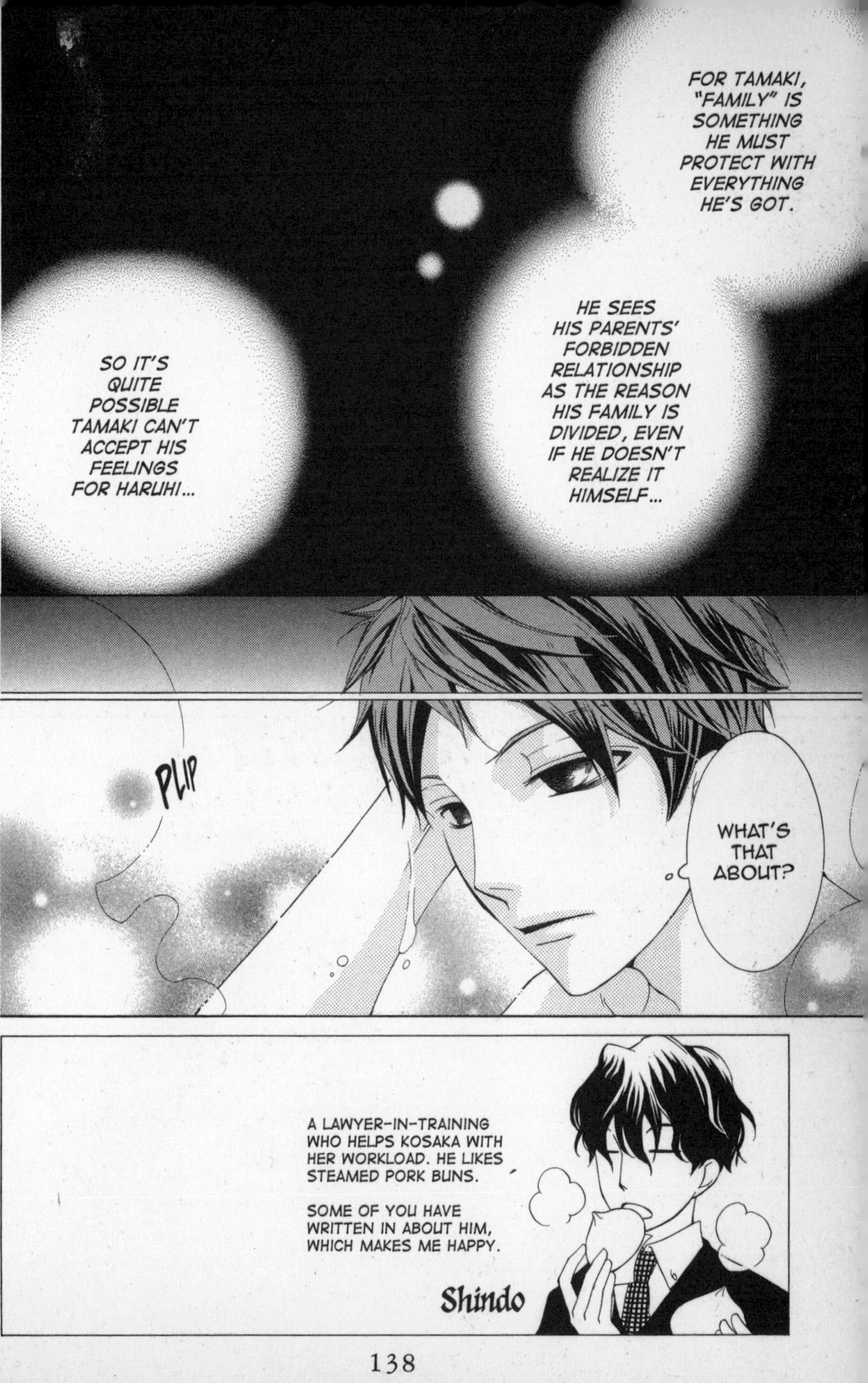
FOR TAMAKI, "FAMILY" IS SOMETHING HE MUST PROTECT WITH EVERYTHING HE'S GOT.
HE SEES HIS PARENTS' FORBIDDEN RELATIONSHIP AS THE REASON HIS FAMILY IS DIVIDED, EVEN IF HE DOESN'T REALIZE IT HIMSELF...
SO IT'S QUITE POSSIBLE TAMAKI CAN'T ACCEPT HIS FEELINGS FOR HARUHI...
WHAT'S THAT ABOUT?
PLIP
A LAWYER-IN-TRAINING WHO HELPS KOSAKA WITH HER WORKLOAD. HE LIKES STEAMED PORK BUNS.
SOME OF YOU HAVE WRITTEN IN ABOUT HIM, WHICH MAKES ME HAPPY.
Shindo

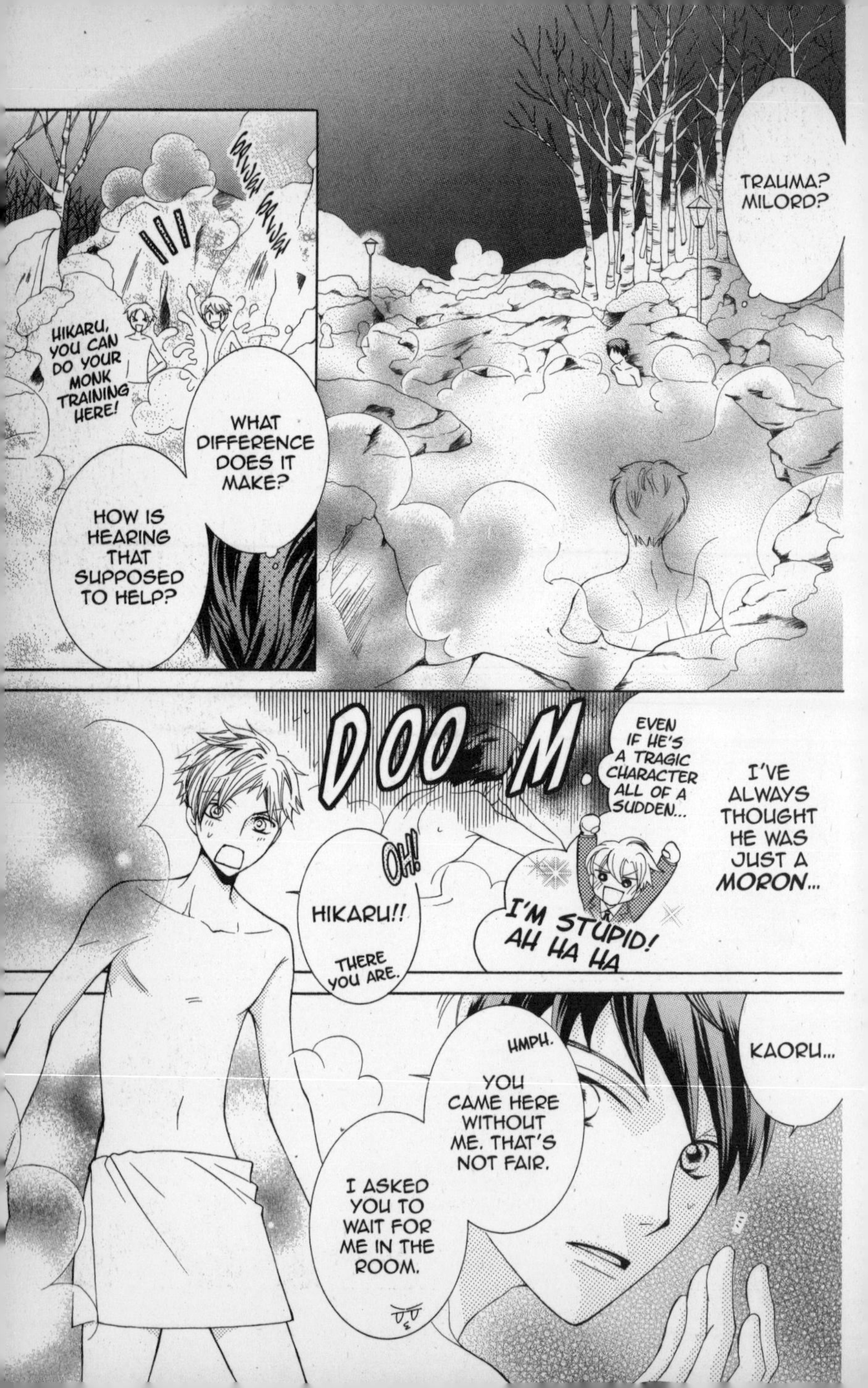
TRAUMA? MILORD?
HIKARU, YOU CAN DO YOUR MONK TRAINING HERE!
WHAT DIFFERENCE DOES IT MAKE?
HOW IS HEARING THAT SUPPOSED TO HELP?
I'VE ALWAYS THOUGHT HE WAS JUST A MORON...
EVEN IF HE'S A TRAGIC CHARACTER ALL OF A SUDDEN...
DOOM.
I'M STUPID! AH HA HA
OH!
HIKARU!!
THERE YOU ARE.
KAORU...
HMPH.
YOU CAME HERE WITHOUT ME. THAT'S NOT FAIR.
I ASKED YOU TO WAIT FOR ME IN THE ROOM.

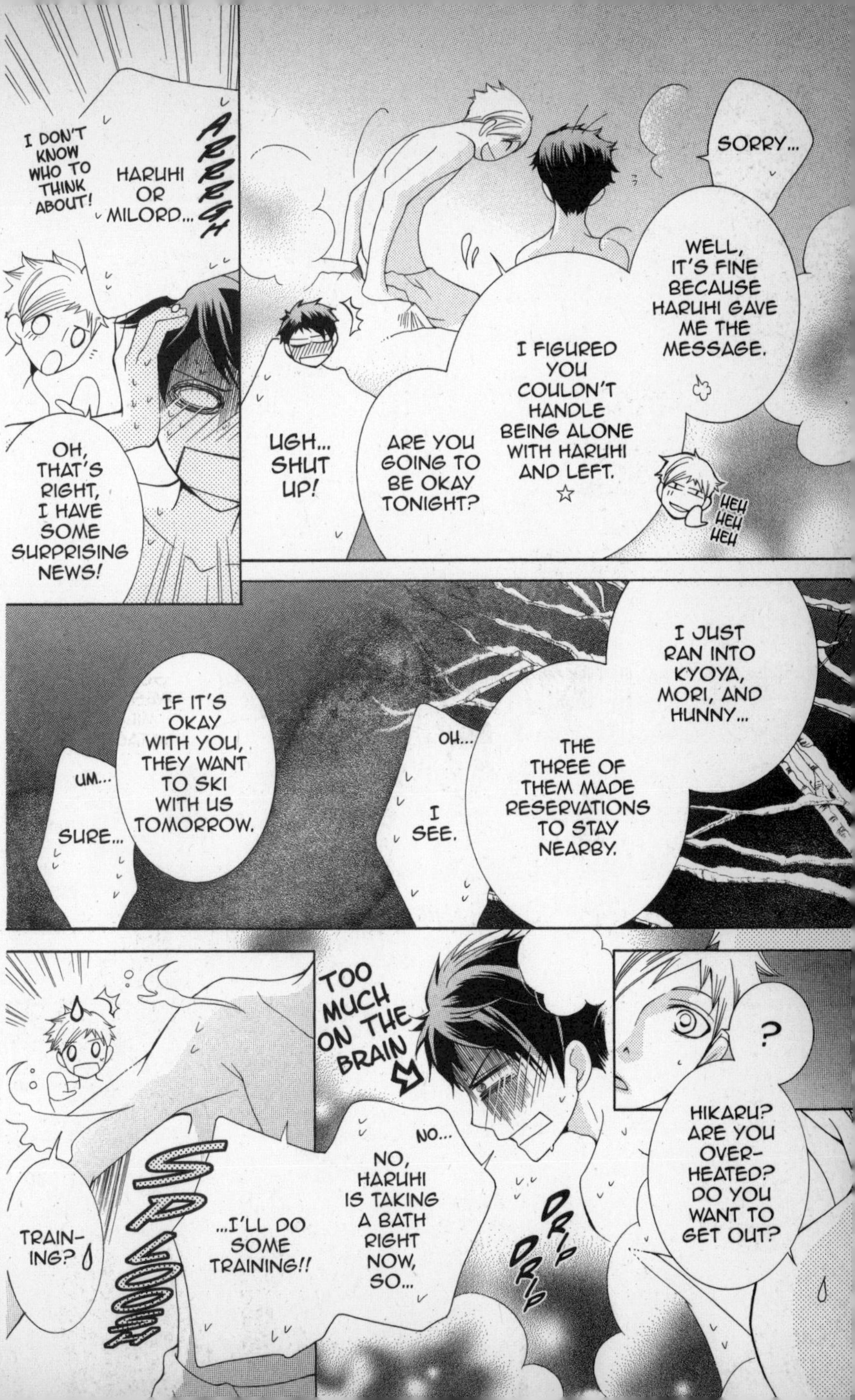
SORRY...
WELL, IT'S FINE BECAUSE HARUHI GAVE ME THE MESSAGE.
I FIGURED YOU COULDN'T HANDLE BEING ALONE WITH HARUHI AND LEFT. ☆
HEH HEH HEH
ARE YOU GOING TO BE OKAY TONIGHT?
UGH... SHUT UP!
ARRRGH
HARUHI OR MILORD...
I DON'T KNOW WHO TO THINK ABOUT!
OH, THAT'S RIGHT, I HAVE SOME SURPRISING NEWS!
I JUST RAN INTO KYOYA, MORI, AND HUNNY...
THE THREE OF THEM MADE RESERVATIONS TO STAY NEARBY.
OH... I SEE.
IF IT'S OKAY WITH YOU, THEY WANT TO SKI WITH US TOMORROW.
UM... SURE...
?
HIKARU? ARE YOU OVER-HEATED? DO YOU WANT TO GET OUT?
TOO MUCH ON THE BRAIN
DRIP DRIP
NO...
NO, HARUHI IS TAKING A BATH RIGHT NOW, SO...
...I'LL DO SOME TRAINING!!
SPLOOSH
TRAIN-ING?

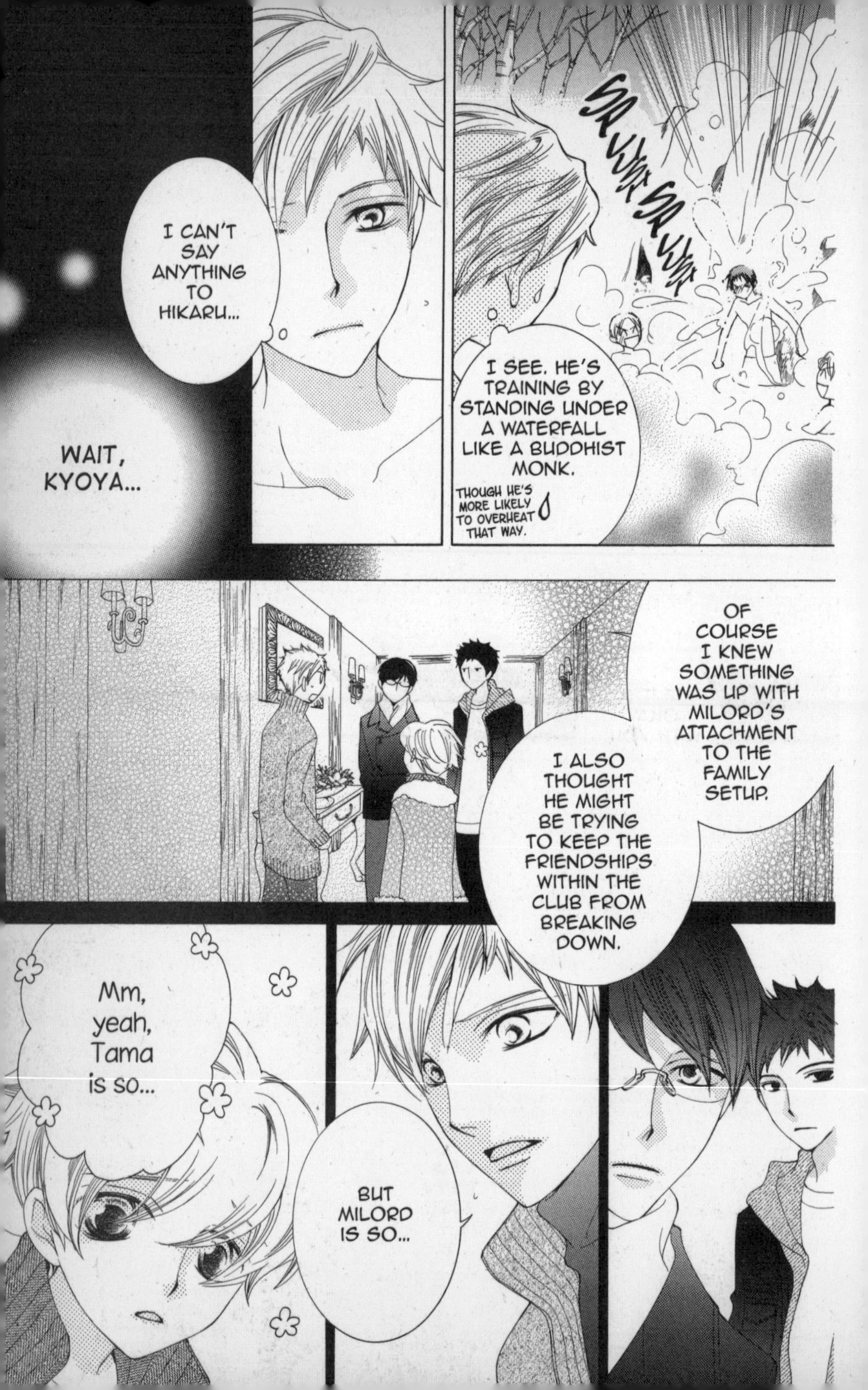

I SEE. HE'S TRAINING BY STANDING UNDER A WATERFALL LIKE A BUDDHIST MONK.
THOUGH HE'S MORE LIKELY TO OVERHEAT THAT WAY.
I CAN'T SAY ANYTHING TO HIKARU...
WAIT, KYOYA...
OF COURSE I KNEW SOMETHING WAS UP WITH MILORD'S ATTACHMENT TO THE FAMILY SETUP.
I ALSO THOUGHT HE MIGHT BE TRYING TO KEEP THE FRIENDSHIPS WITHIN THE CLUB FROM BREAKING DOWN.
BUT MILORD IS SO...
Mm, yeah, Tama is so...

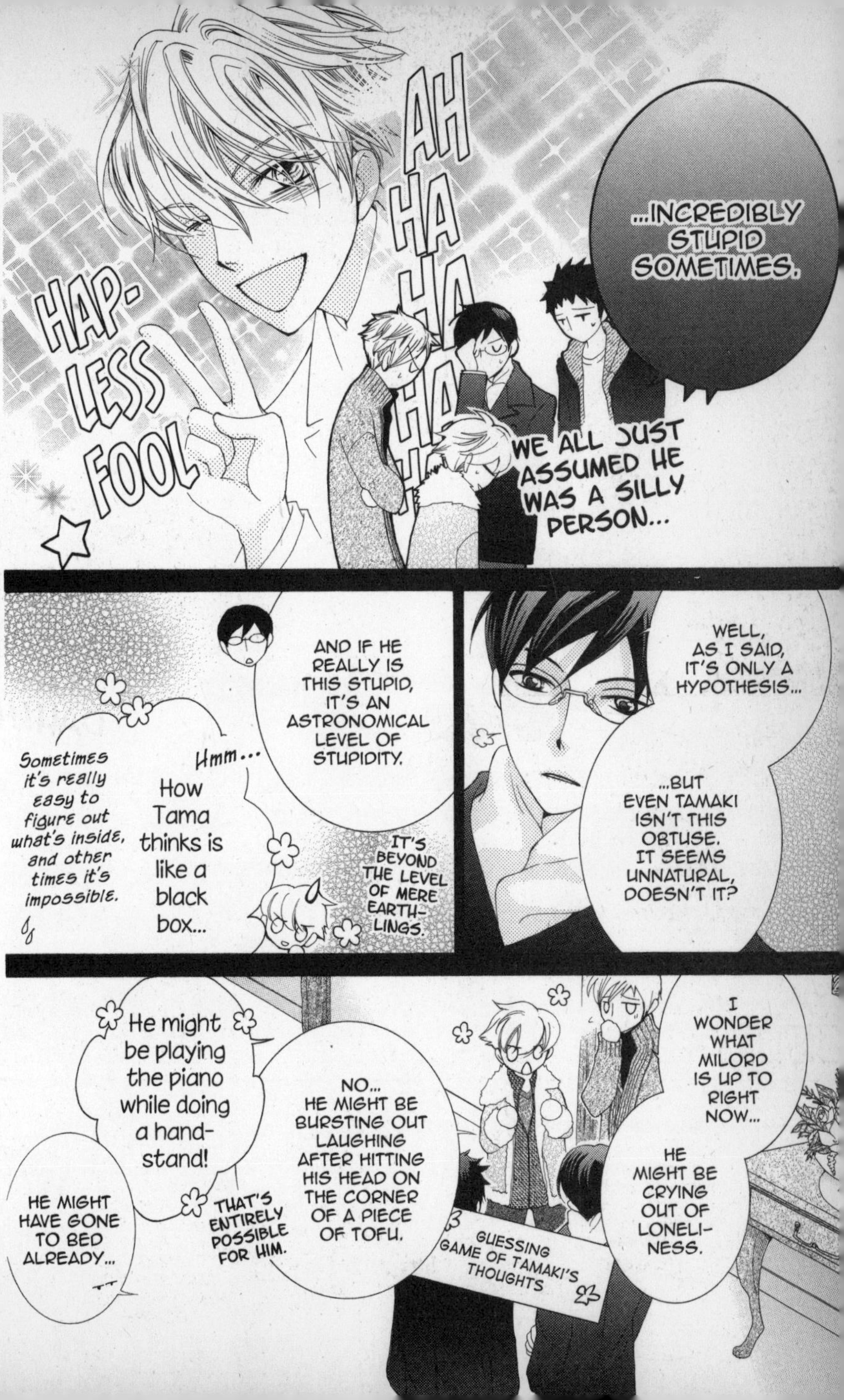
...INCREDIBLY STUPID SOMETIMES.
AH HA HA HA HA HA
WE ALL JUST ASSUMED HE WAS A SILLY PERSON...
HAP-LESS FOOL
WELL, AS I SAID, IT'S ONLY A HYPOTHESIS...
...BUT EVEN TAMAKI ISN'T THIS OBTUSE. IT SEEMS UNNATURAL, DOESN'T IT?
AND IF HE REALLY IS THIS STUPID, IT'S AN ASTRONOMICAL LEVEL OF STUPIDITY.
IT'S BEYOND THE LEVEL OF MERE EARTH-LINGS.
Hmm...
How Tama thinks is like a black box...
Sometimes it's really easy to figure out what's inside, and other times it's impossible.
I WONDER WHAT MILORD IS UP TO RIGHT NOW...
HE MIGHT BE CRYING OUT OF LONELI-NESS.
GUESSING GAME OF TAMAKI'S THOUGHTS
NO... HE MIGHT BE BURSTING OUT LAUGHING AFTER HITTING HIS HEAD ON THE CORNER OF A PIECE OF TOFU.
THAT'S ENTIRELY POSSIBLE FOR HIM.
He might be playing the piano while doing a hand-stand!
HE MIGHT HAVE GONE TO BED ALREADY...

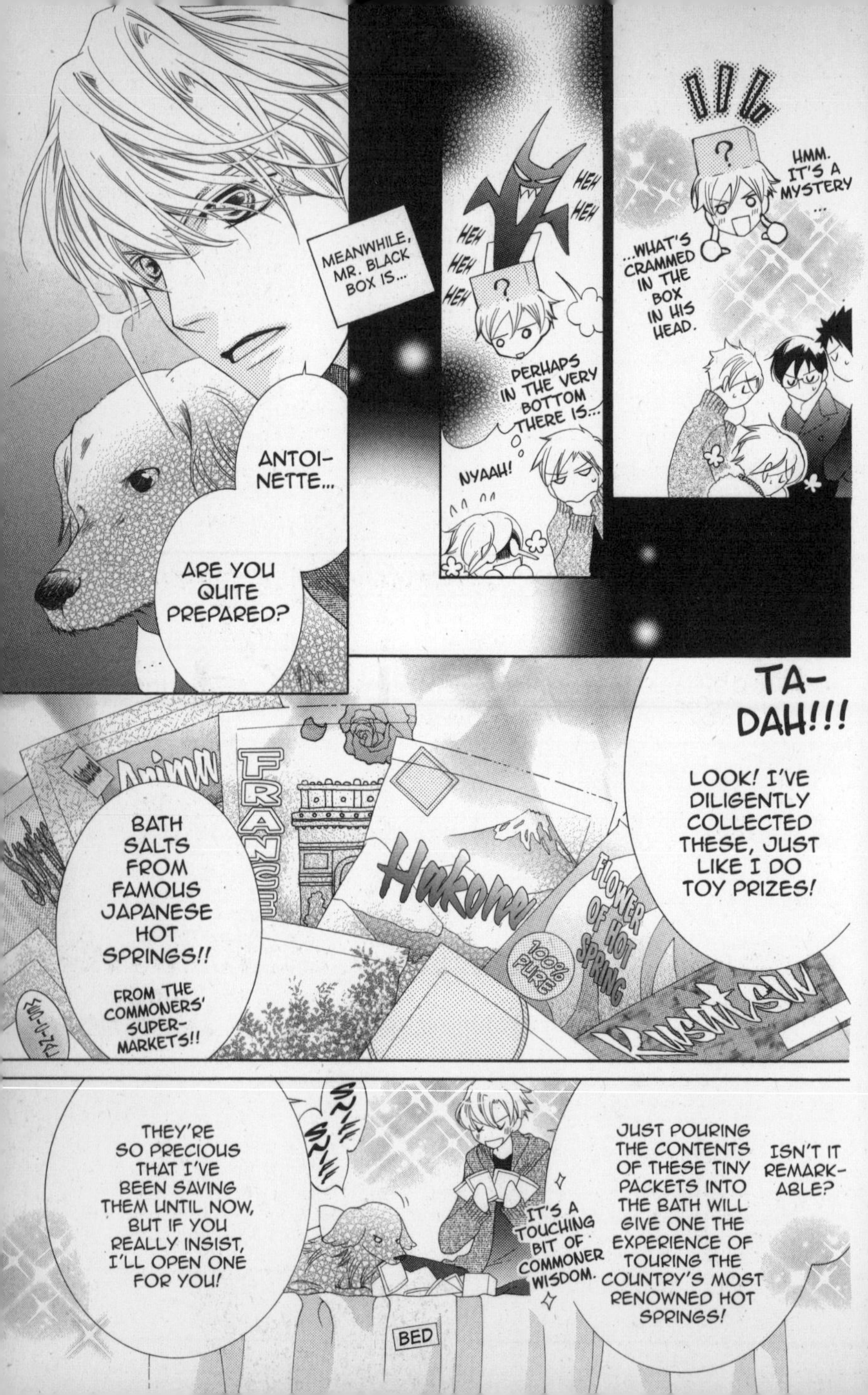
HMM. IT'S A MYSTERY ...
...WHAT'S CRAMMED IN THE BOX IN HIS HEAD.
HEH HEH
HEH HEH HEH
PERHAPS IN THE VERY BOTTOM THERE IS...
NYAAH!
MEANWHILE, MR. BLACK BOX IS...
ANTOI-NETTE...
ARE YOU QUITE PREPARED?
...
TA-DAH!!!
LOOK! I'VE DILIGENTLY COLLECTED THESE, JUST LIKE I DO TOY PRIZES!
BATH SALTS FROM FAMOUS JAPANESE HOT SPRINGS!!
FROM THE COMMONERS' SUPER-MARKETS!!
FRANCE
Hakone
FLOWER OF HOT SPRING
100% PURE
ISN'T IT REMARK-ABLE?
JUST POURING THE CONTENTS OF THESE TINY PACKETS INTO THE BATH WILL GIVE ONE THE EXPERIENCE OF TOURING THE COUNTRY'S MOST RENOWNED HOT SPRINGS!
IT'S A TOUCHING BIT OF COMMONER WISDOM.
SNIF SNIF
THEY'RE SO PRECIOUS THAT I'VE BEEN SAVING THEM UNTIL NOW, BUT IF YOU REALLY INSIST, I'LL OPEN ONE FOR YOU!
BED

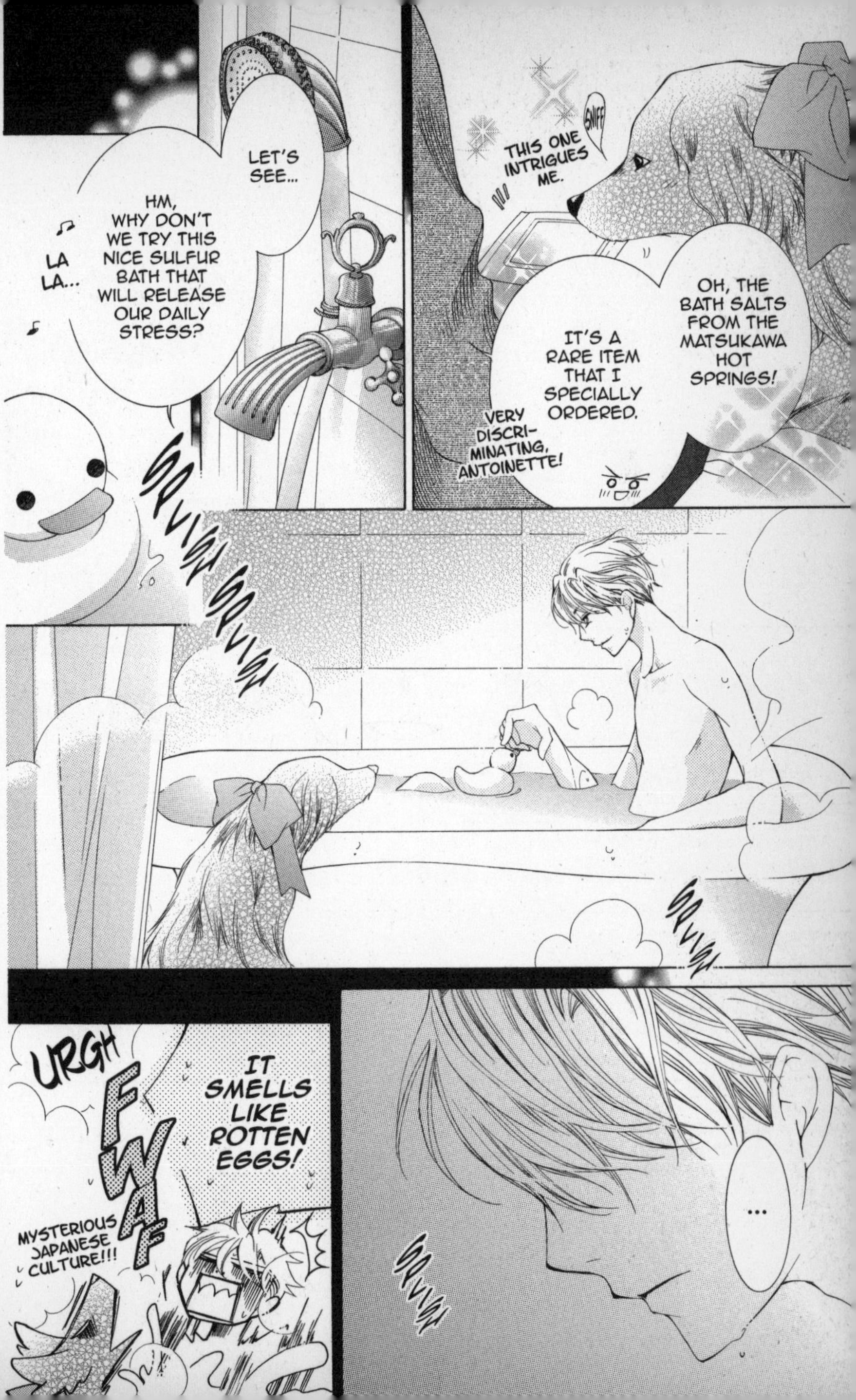
SNIFF
THIS ONE INTRIGUES ME.
OH, THE BATH SALTS FROM THE MATSUKAWA HOT SPRINGS!
IT'S A RARE ITEM THAT I SPECIALLY ORDERED.
VERY DISCRI-MINATING, ANTOINETTE!
LET'S SEE...
HM, WHY DON'T WE TRY THIS NICE SULFUR BATH THAT WILL RELEASE OUR DAILY STRESS?
LA LA...
...
URGH
FWAF
IT SMELLS LIKE ROTTEN EGGS!
MYSTERIOUS JAPANESE CULTURE!!!

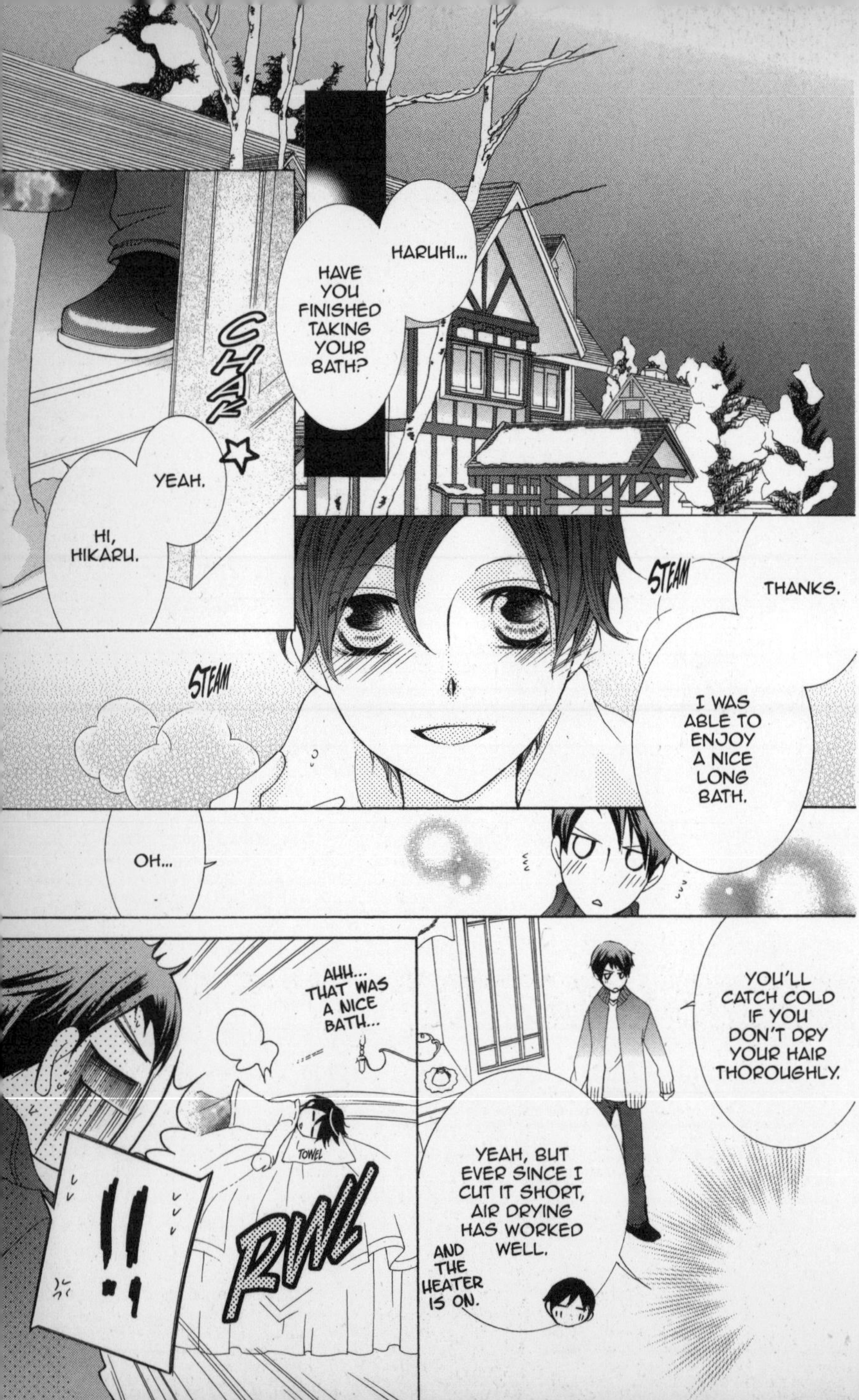
HARUHI...
HAVE YOU FINISHED TAKING YOUR BATH?
CHAK
YEAH.
HI, HIKARU.
STEAM
THANKS.
I WAS ABLE TO ENJOY A NICE LONG BATH.
STEAM
OH...
YOU'LL CATCH COLD IF YOU DON'T DRY YOUR HAIR THOROUGHLY.
YEAH, BUT EVER SINCE I CUT IT SHORT, AIR DRYING HAS WORKED WELL.
AND THE HEATER IS ON.
AHH... THAT WAS A NICE BATH...
TOWEL
RWL
!!

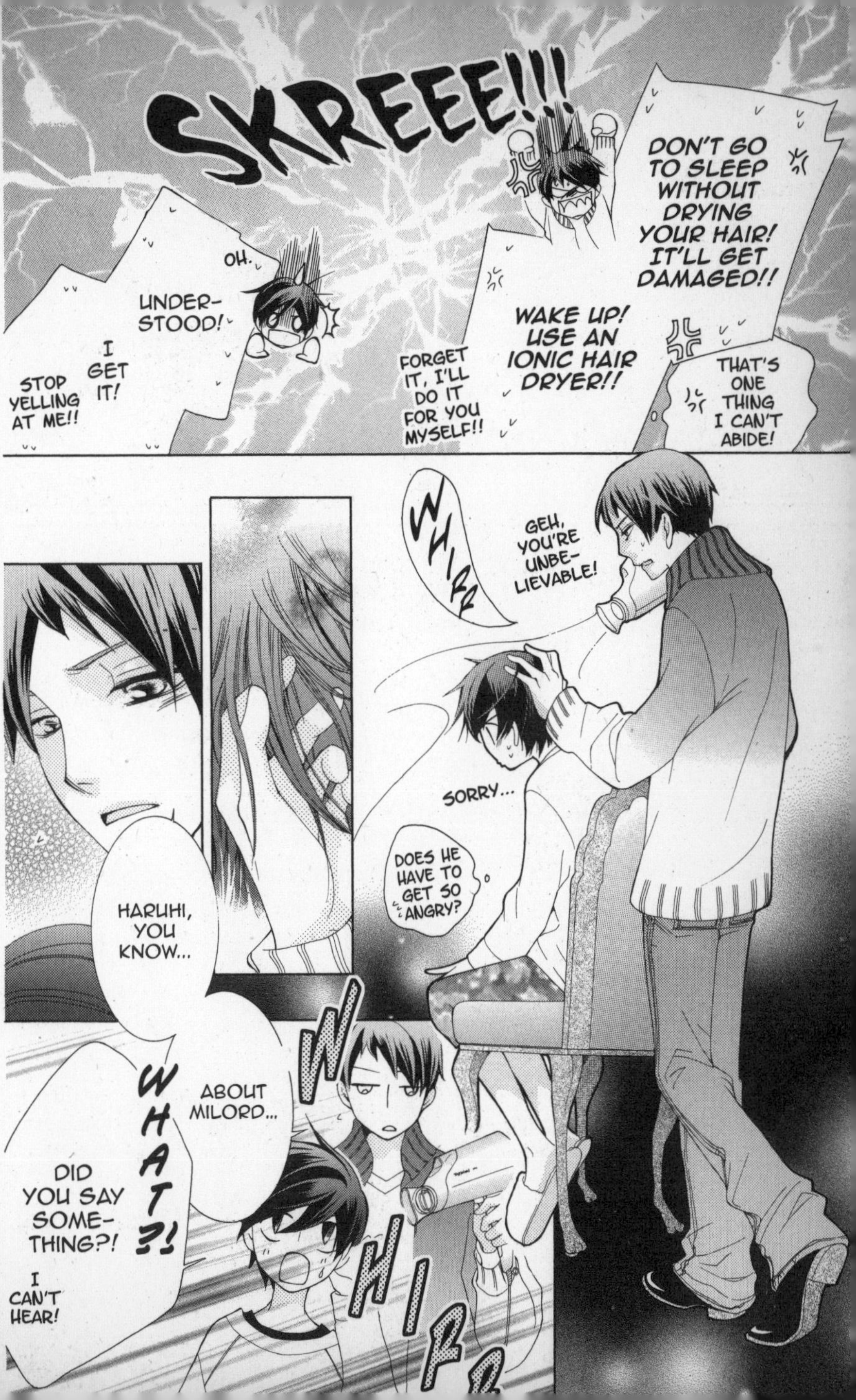
SKREEE!!!
DON'T GO TO SLEEP WITHOUT DRYING YOUR HAIR! IT'LL GET DAMAGED!!
THAT'S ONE THING I CAN'T ABIDE!
WAKE UP! USE AN IONIC HAIR DRYER!!
FORGET IT, I'LL DO IT FOR YOU MYSELF!!
OH.
UNDER-STOOD!
I GET IT!
STOP YELLING AT ME!!
WHIRR
GEH, YOU'RE UNBE-LIEVABLE!
SORRY...
DOES HE HAVE TO GET SO ANGRY?
HARUHI, YOU KNOW...
ABOUT MILORD...
WHAT?!
DID YOU SAY SOME-THING?!
I CAN'T HEAR!
WHIRR

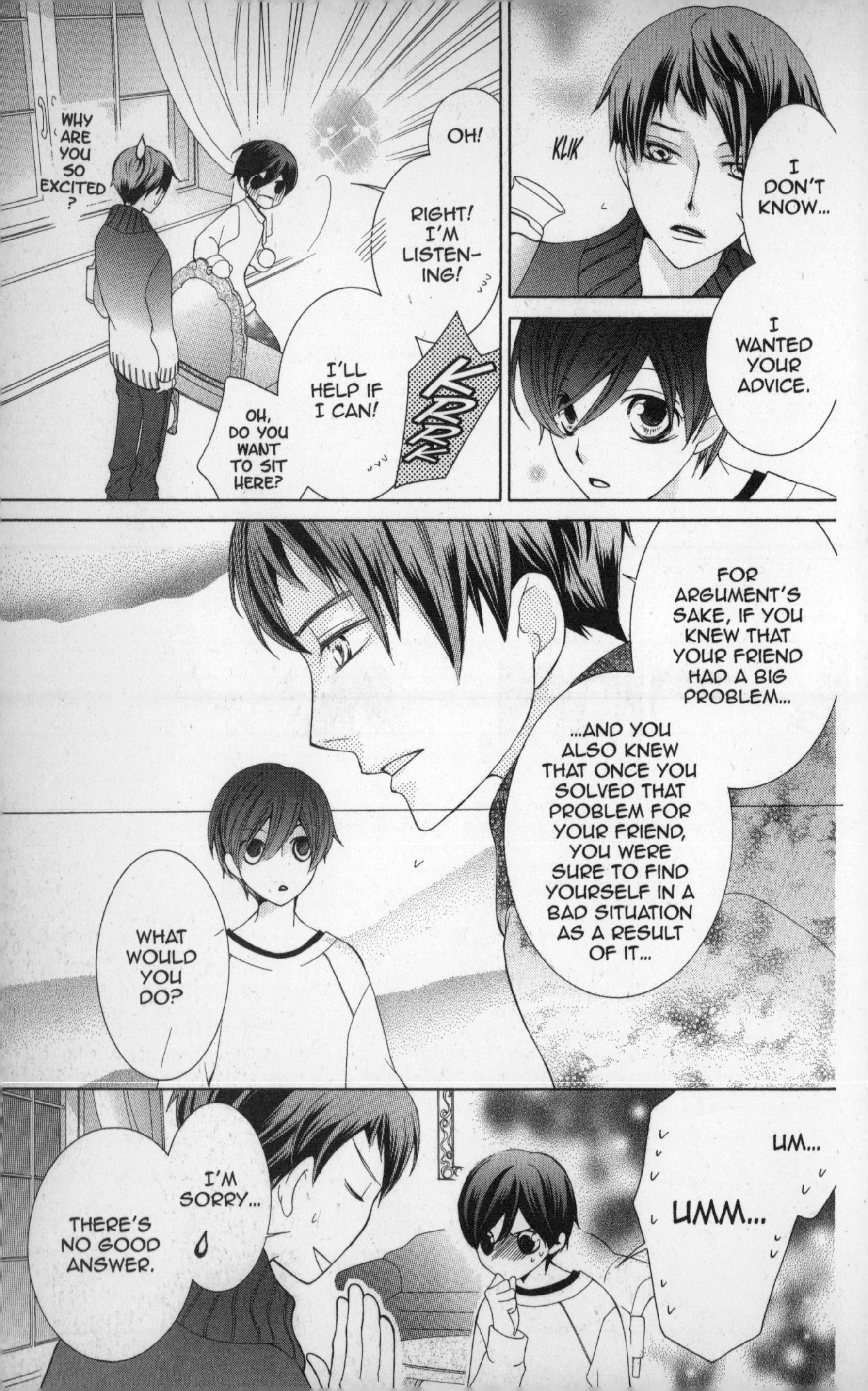
KLIK
I DON'T KNOW...
I WANTED YOUR ADVICE.
OH!
RIGHT! I'M LISTENING!
I'LL HELP IF I CAN!
KRRRK
OH, DO YOU WANT TO SIT HERE?
WHY ARE YOU SO EXCITED?
FOR ARGUMENT'S SAKE, IF YOU KNEW THAT YOUR FRIEND HAD A BIG PROBLEM...
...AND YOU ALSO KNEW THAT ONCE YOU SOLVED THAT PROBLEM FOR YOUR FRIEND, YOU WERE SURE TO FIND YOURSELF IN A BAD SITUATION AS A RESULT OF IT...
WHAT WOULD YOU DO?
UM...
UMM...
I'M SORRY...
THERE'S NO GOOD ANSWER.

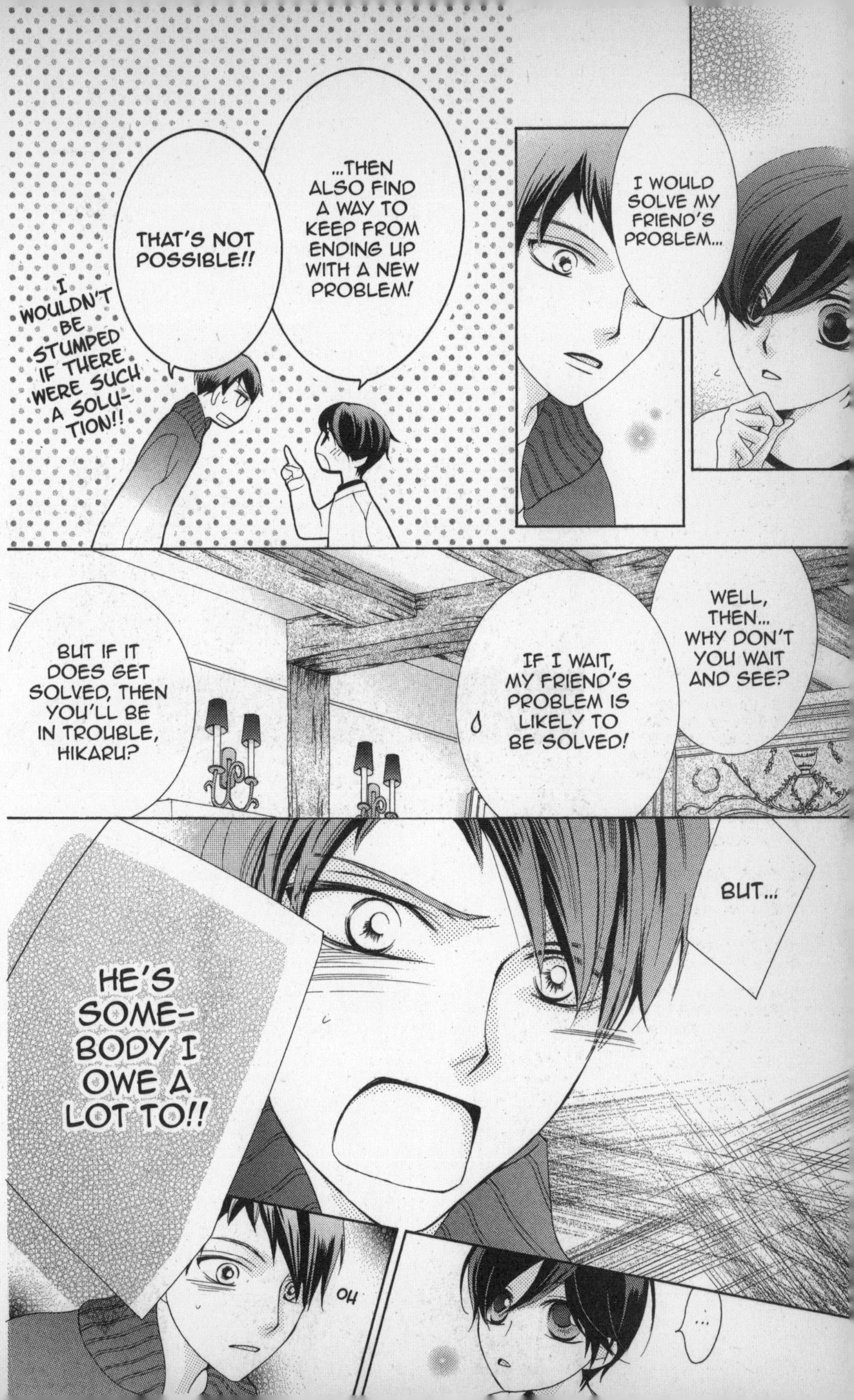
I WOULD SOLVE MY FRIEND'S PROBLEM...
...THEN ALSO FIND A WAY TO KEEP FROM ENDING UP WITH A NEW PROBLEM!
THAT'S NOT POSSIBLE!!
I WOULDN'T BE STUMPED IF THERE WERE SUCH A SOLU-TION!!
WELL, THEN... WHY DON'T YOU WAIT AND SEE?
IF I WAIT, MY FRIEND'S PROBLEM IS LIKELY TO BE SOLVED!
BUT IF IT DOES GET SOLVED, THEN YOU'LL BE IN TROUBLE, HIKARU?
BUT...
HE'S SOME-BODY I OWE A LOT TO!!
OH
...

5

✿THOSE OF YOU WHO HAVE READ THIS EPISODE ABOUT THE SNOWY MOUNTAINS MAY BE THINKING, "DOES THIS MANGA REALLY REFLECT THE ORDEAL THAT THE RESEARCH TRIP ENTAILED?" BUT BECAUSE I WAS ABLE TO EXPERIENCE IT, I AM ABLE TO DRAW THE MANGA WITH CONFIDENCE.

IT'S ALL RIGHT IF THE MOUNTAIN OF PHOTOS I TOOK FROM THE SKI LIFTS WERE HARDLY USED FOR THE MANGA.

I LEARNED THAT GOING SKIING CAN ACTUALLY LEAD TO GETTING STRANDED, AND WALKING OVER TO A FOREST ON THE EDGE OF THE MOUNTAIN IS REALLY DANGEROUS!!

THESE ARE THINGS I LEARNED FIRSTHAND. IT WAS A GREAT RESEARCH TRIP. KANA, THANK YOU SO MUCH!!

AND TO ALL THE READERS, PLEASE KEEP IN MIND THAT SNOWY MOUNTAINS ARE BEAUTIFUL YET HORRIFYING PLACES. PLEASE BE CAREFUL WHEN YOU GO HAVE FUN!! ESPECIALLY WHEN SKIING!! ALSO, MATSUKAWA HOT SPRINGS ARE THE BEST. ♥

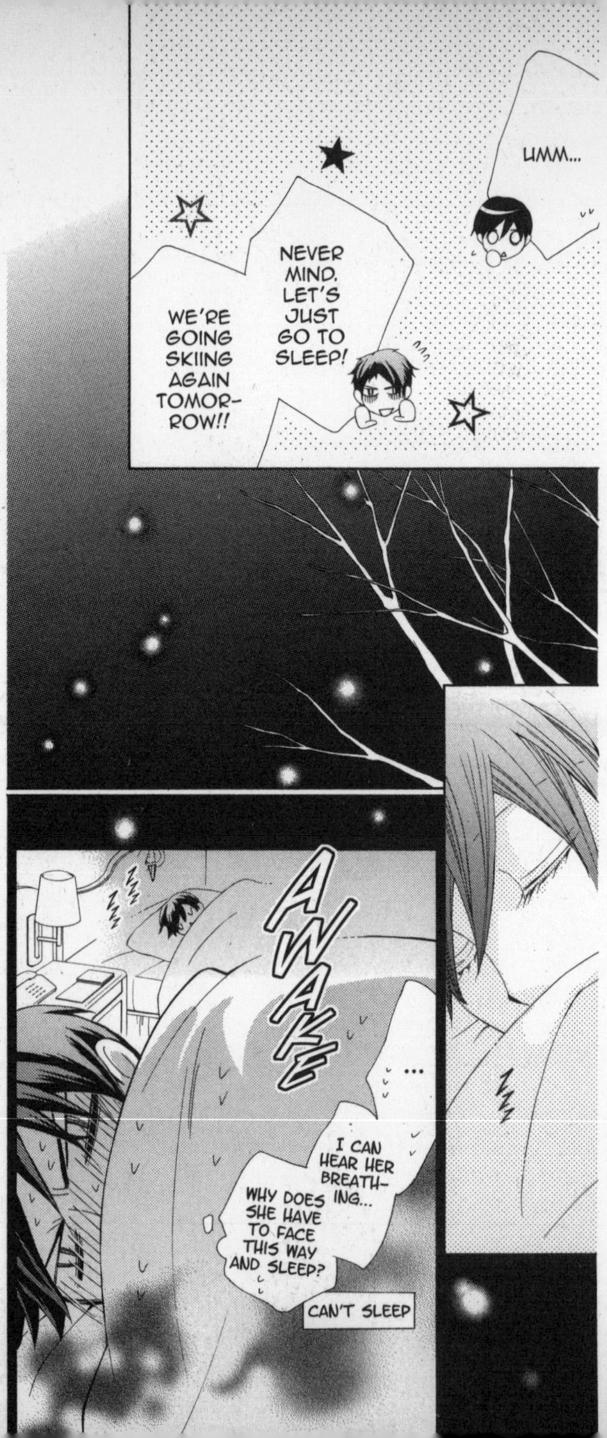
UMM...
NEVER MIND. LET'S JUST GO TO SLEEP!
WE'RE GOING SKIING AGAIN TOMORROW!!
AWAKE
...
I CAN HEAR HER BREATHING...
WHY DOES SHE HAVE TO FACE THIS WAY AND SLEEP?
CAN'T SLEEP

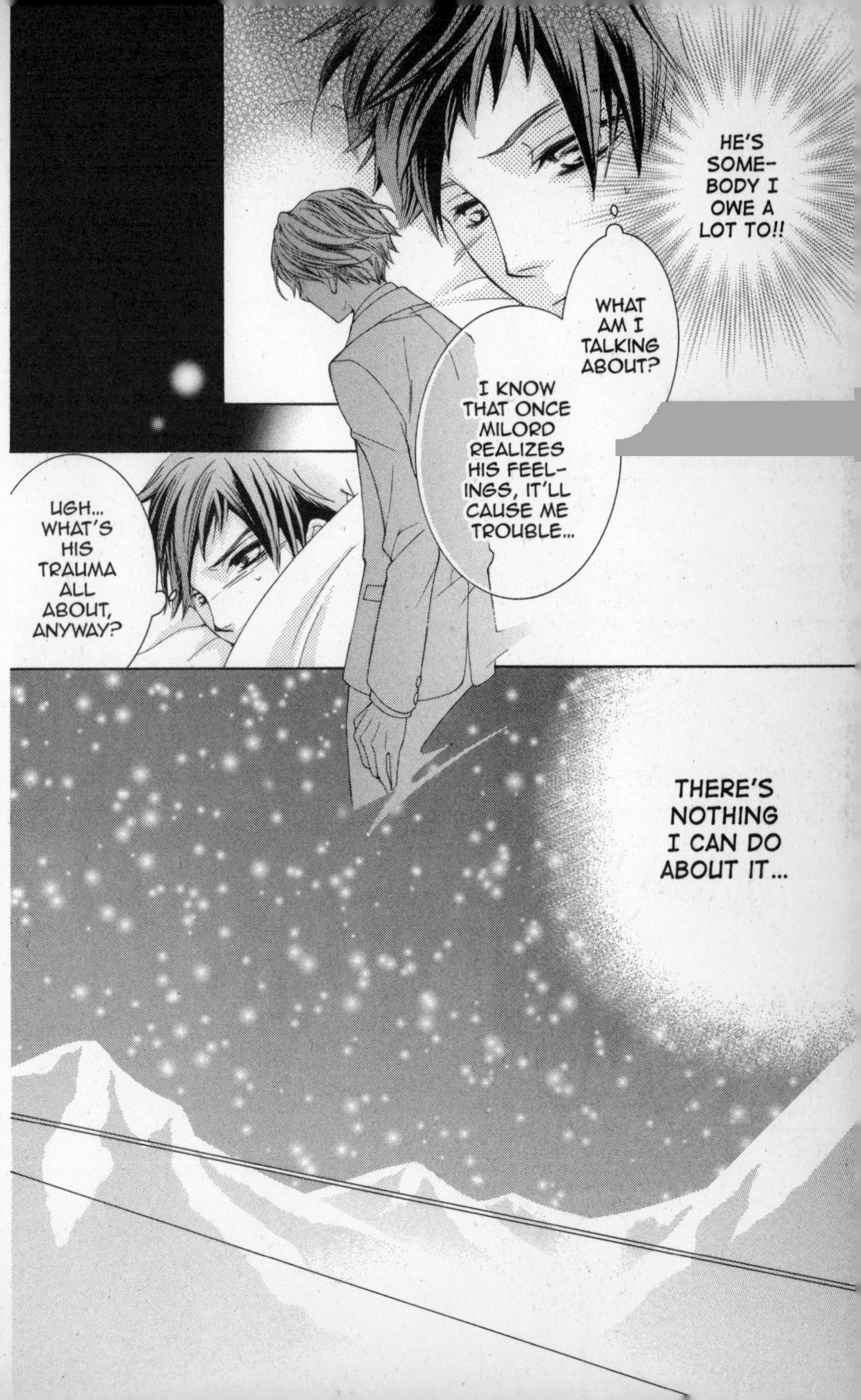
HE'S SOMEBODY I OWE A LOT TO!!
WHAT AM I TALKING ABOUT?
I KNOW THAT ONCE MILORD REALIZES HIS FEELINGS, IT'LL CAUSE ME TROUBLE...
UGH... WHAT'S HIS TRAUMA ALL ABOUT, ANYWAY?
THERE'S NOTHING I CAN DO ABOUT IT...

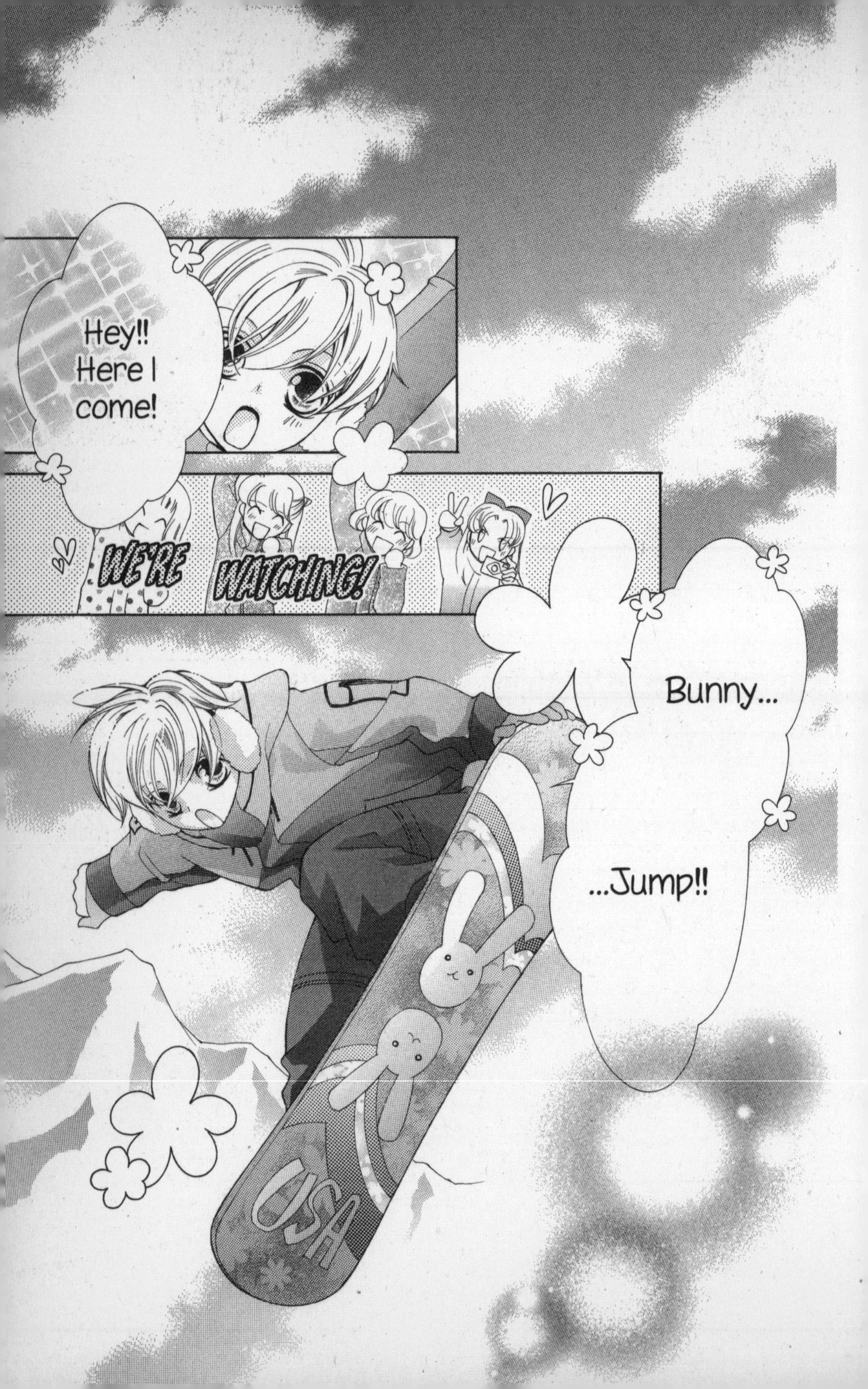
Hey!! Here I come!
WE'RE WATCHING!
Bunny...
...Jump!!
USA

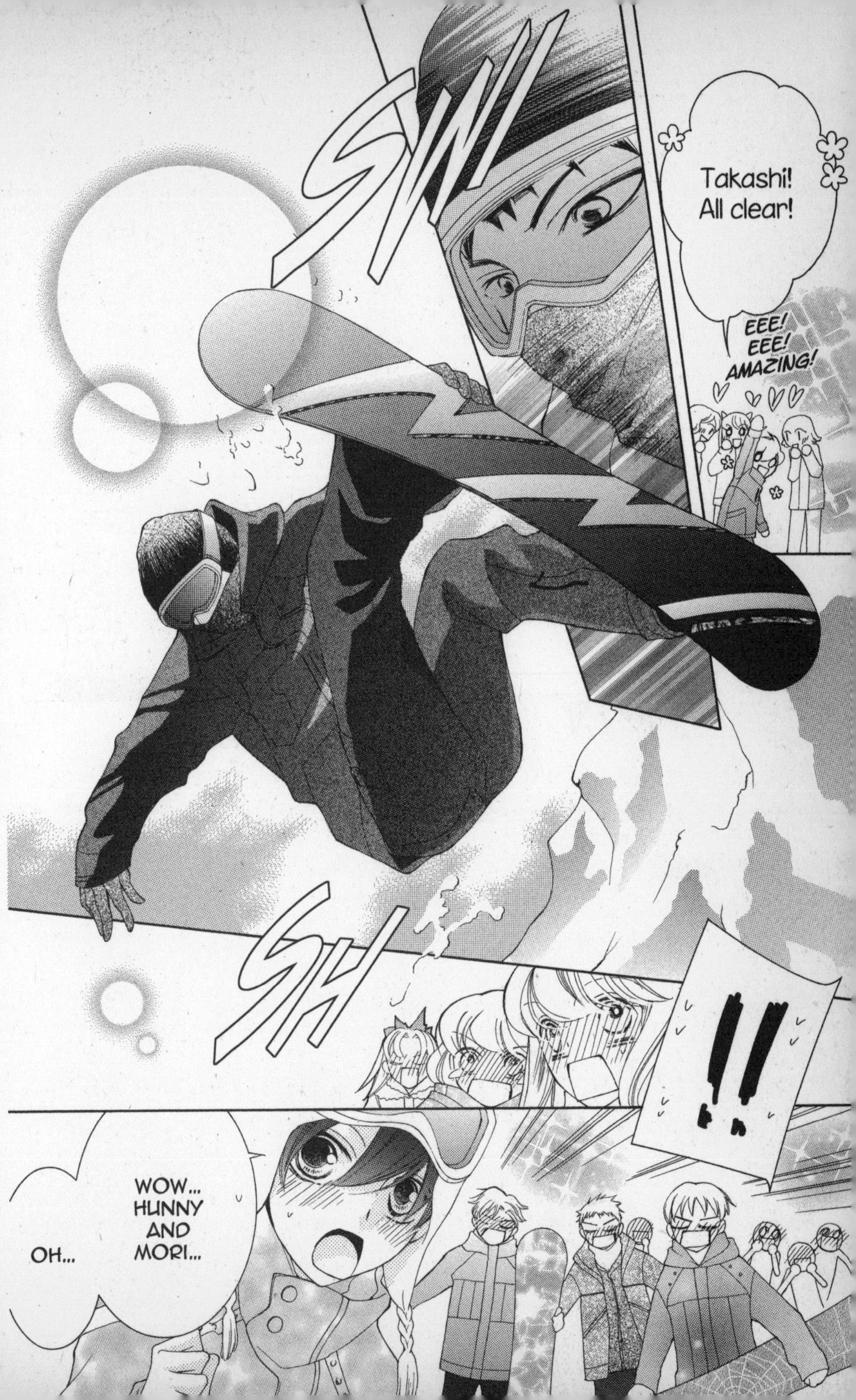
SWI
Takashi! All clear!
EEE! EEE! AMAZING!
SH
!!
WOW... HUNNY AND MORI...
OH...

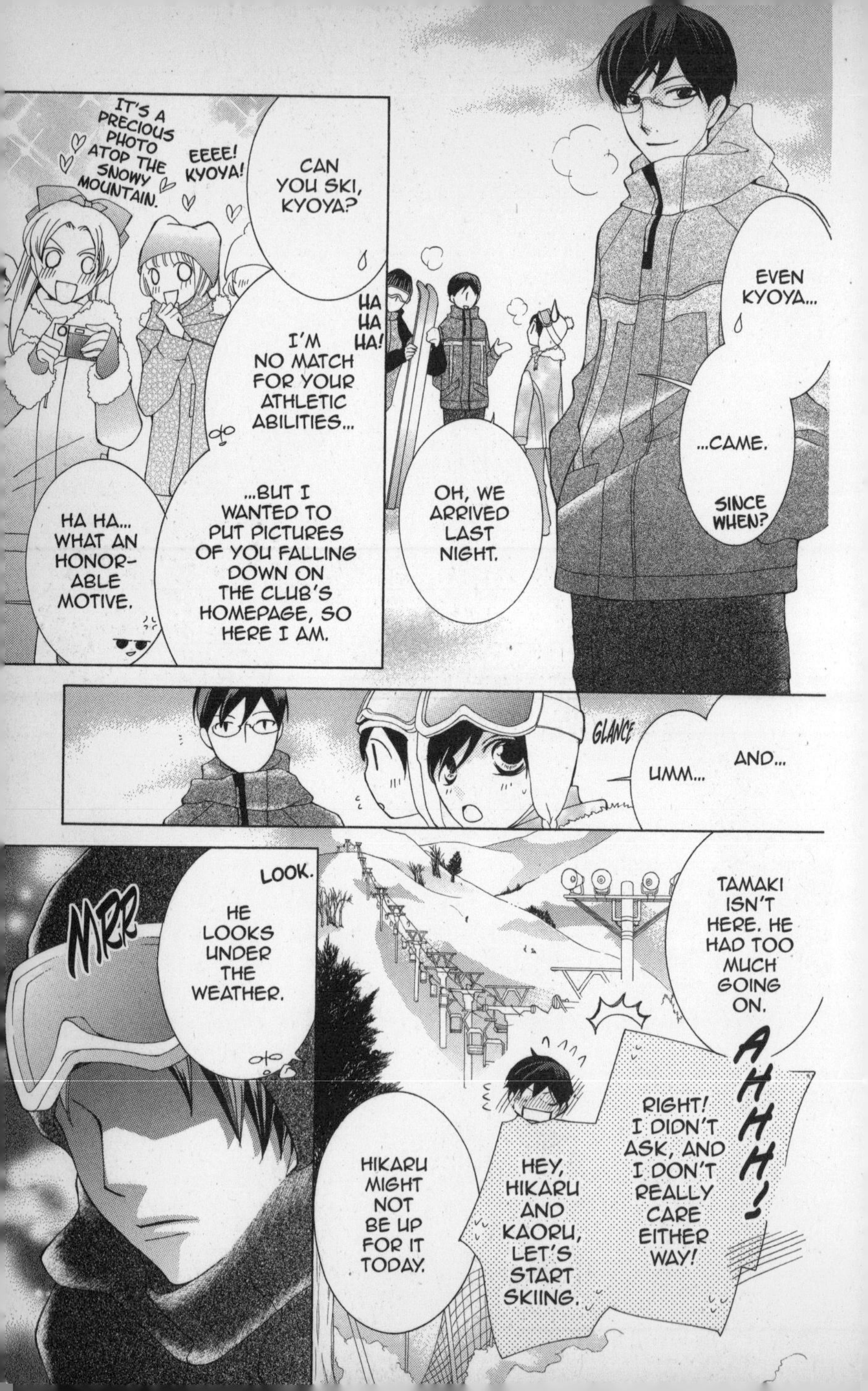
EVEN KYOYA...
...CAME.
SINCE WHEN?
OH, WE ARRIVED LAST NIGHT.
CAN YOU SKI, KYOYA?
HA HA HA!
I'M NO MATCH FOR YOUR ATHLETIC ABILITIES...
...BUT I WANTED TO PUT PICTURES OF YOU FALLING DOWN ON THE CLUB'S HOMEPAGE, SO HERE I AM.
EEEE! KYOYA!
IT'S A PRECIOUS PHOTO ATOP THE SNOWY MOUNTAIN.
HA HA... WHAT AN HONORABLE MOTIVE.
AND...
UMM...
GLANCE
TAMAKI ISN'T HERE. HE HAD TOO MUCH GOING ON.
AHHH!
RIGHT! I DIDN'T ASK, AND I DON'T REALLY CARE EITHER WAY!
HEY, HIKARU AND KAORU, LET'S START SKIING.
HIKARU MIGHT NOT BE UP FOR IT TODAY.
LOOK.
HE LOOKS UNDER THE WEATHER.
MRR

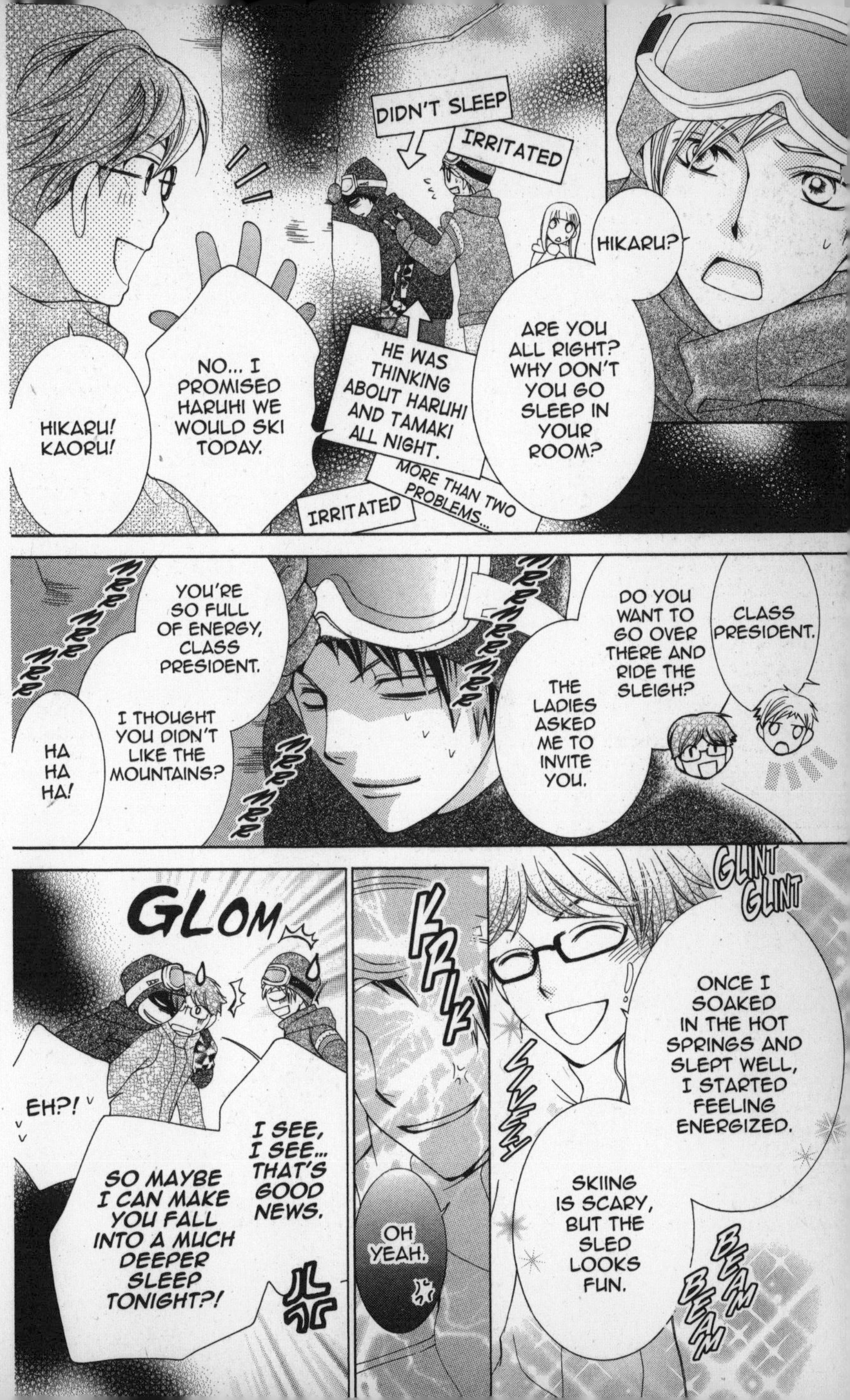
HIKARU?
ARE YOU ALL RIGHT? WHY DON'T YOU GO SLEEP IN YOUR ROOM?
DIDN'T SLEEP
IRRITATED
HE WAS THINKING ABOUT HARUHI AND TAMAKI ALL NIGHT.
MORE THAN TWO PROBLEMS...
IRRITATED
NO... I PROMISED HARUHI WE WOULD SKI TODAY.
HIKARU! KAORU!
CLASS PRESIDENT.
DO YOU WANT TO GO OVER THERE AND RIDE THE SLEIGH?
THE LADIES ASKED ME TO INVITE YOU.
YOU'RE SO FULL OF ENERGY, CLASS PRESIDENT.
I THOUGHT YOU DIDN'T LIKE THE MOUNTAINS?
HA HA HA!
GLINT GLINT
ONCE I SOAKED IN THE HOT SPRINGS AND SLEPT WELL, I STARTED FEELING ENERGIZED.
SKIING IS SCARY, BUT THE SLED LOOKS FUN.
BEAM BEAM
KRIK
OH YEAH.
GLOM
EH?!
I SEE, I SEE... THAT'S GOOD NEWS.
SO MAYBE I CAN MAKE YOU FALL INTO A MUCH DEEPER SLEEP TONIGHT?!

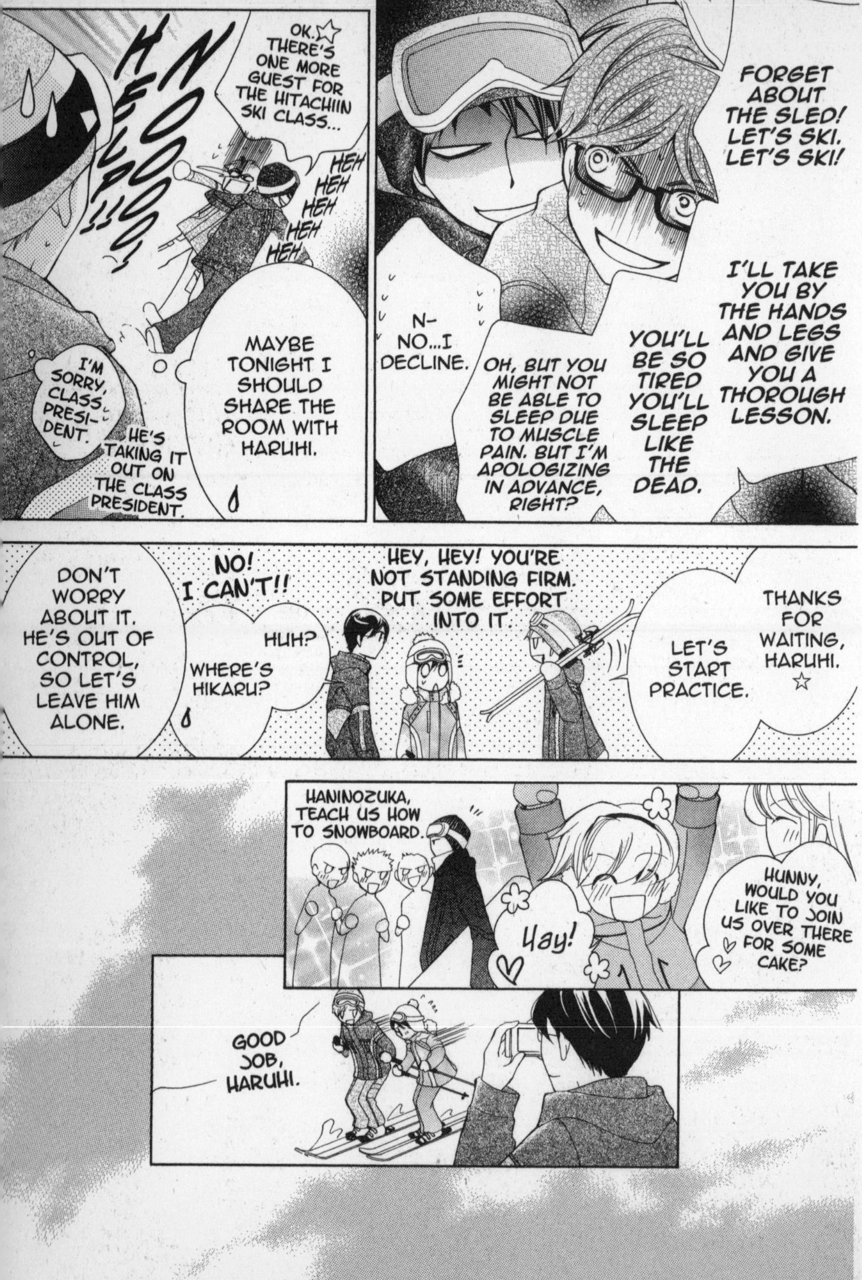
FORGET ABOUT THE SLED! LET'S SKI. LET'S SKI!
I'LL TAKE YOU BY THE HANDS AND LEGS AND GIVE YOU A THOROUGH LESSON.
YOU'LL BE SO TIRED YOU'LL SLEEP LIKE THE DEAD.
OH, BUT YOU MIGHT NOT BE ABLE TO SLEEP DUE TO MUSCLE PAIN. BUT I'M APOLOGIZING IN ADVANCE, RIGHT?
N-NO...I DECLINE.
OK.☆ THERE'S ONE MORE GUEST FOR THE HITACHIIN SKI CLASS...
HEH HEH HEH HEH HEH
NOOOOO!!
HELP!!
MAYBE TONIGHT I SHOULD SHARE THE ROOM WITH HARUHI.
I'M SORRY, CLASS PRESIDENT.
HE'S TAKING IT OUT ON THE CLASS PRESIDENT.
THANKS FOR WAITING, HARUHI. ☆
LET'S START PRACTICE.
HEY, HEY! YOU'RE NOT STANDING FIRM. PUT SOME EFFORT INTO IT.
NO! I CAN'T!!
HUH?
WHERE'S HIKARU?
DON'T WORRY ABOUT IT. HE'S OUT OF CONTROL, SO LET'S LEAVE HIM ALONE.
HUNNY, WOULD YOU LIKE TO JOIN US OVER THERE FOR SOME CAKE?
Yay!
HANINOZUKA, TEACH US HOW TO SNOWBOARD.
GOOD JOB, HARUHI.

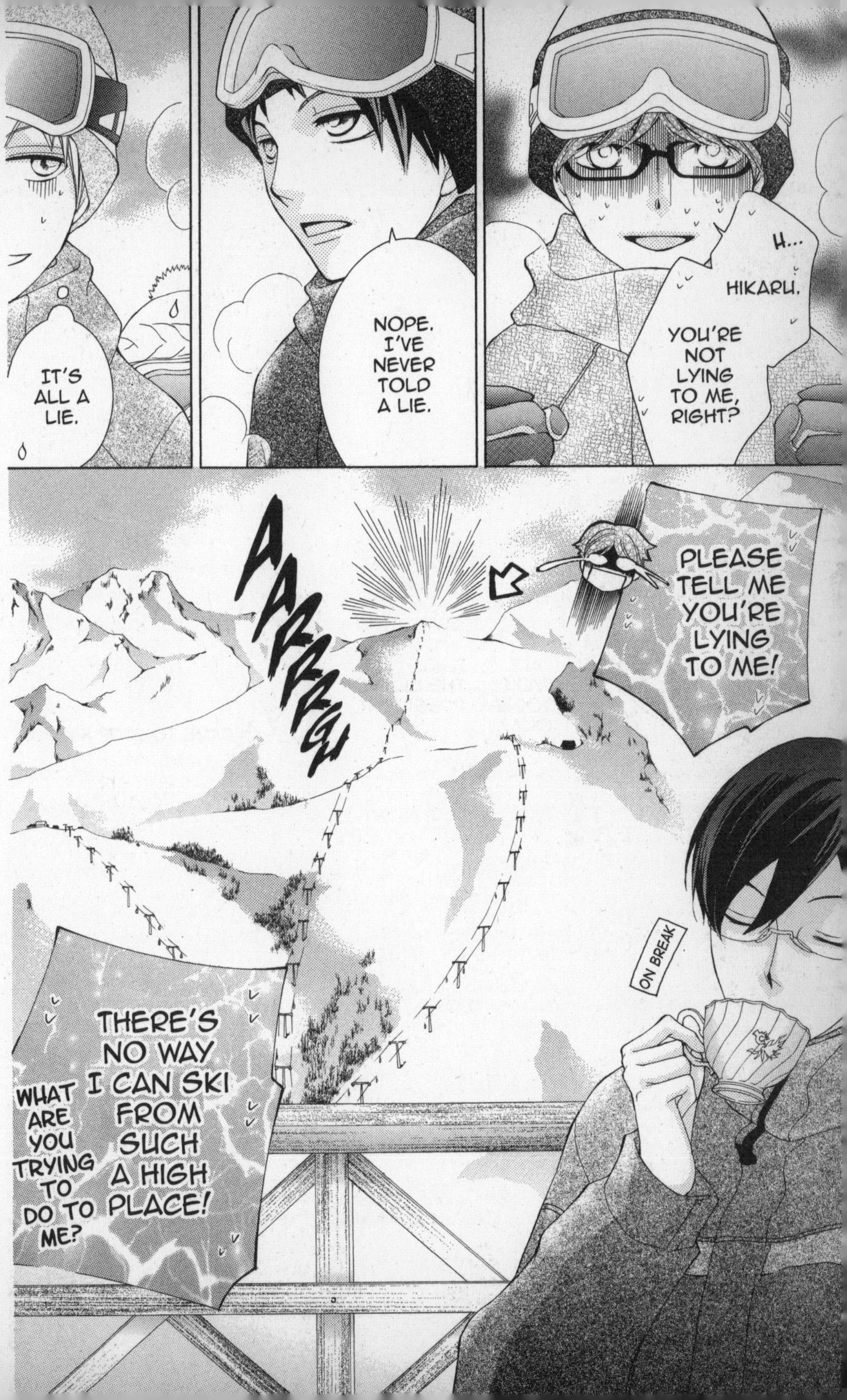
H...
HIKARU.
YOU'RE NOT LYING TO ME, RIGHT?
NOPE. I'VE NEVER TOLD A LIE.
IT'S ALL A LIE.
PLEASE TELL ME YOU'RE LYING TO ME!
AAAAAAGH
ON BREAK
THERE'S NO WAY I CAN SKI FROM SUCH A HIGH PLACE!
WHAT ARE YOU TRYING TO DO TO ME?

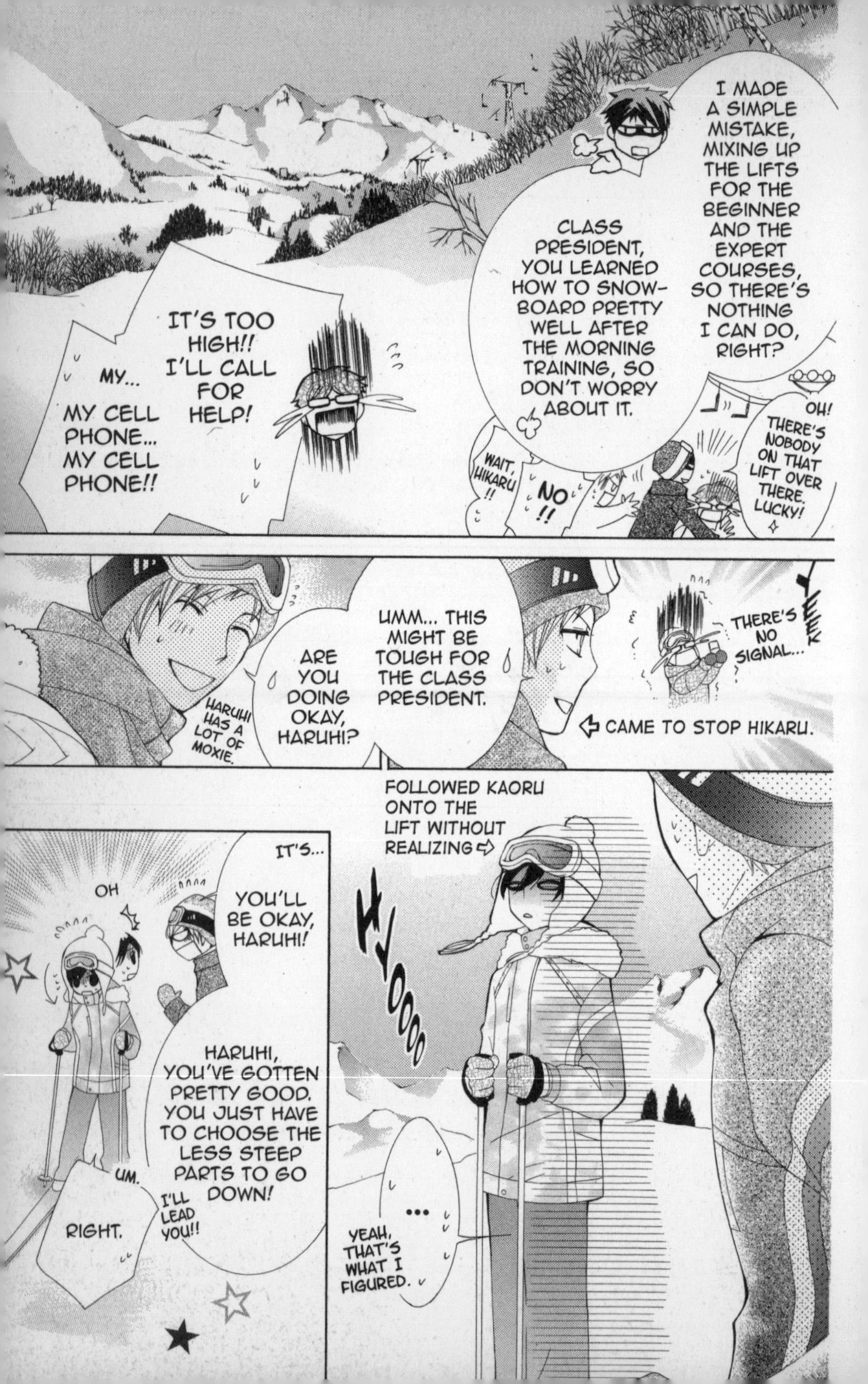
I MADE A SIMPLE MISTAKE, MIXING UP THE LIFTS FOR THE BEGINNER AND THE EXPERT COURSES, SO THERE'S NOTHING I CAN DO, RIGHT?
CLASS PRESIDENT, YOU LEARNED HOW TO SNOW-BOARD PRETTY WELL AFTER THE MORNING TRAINING, SO DON'T WORRY ABOUT IT.
OH! THERE'S NOBODY ON THAT LIFT OVER THERE. LUCKY!
NO!!
WAIT, HIKARU!!
IT'S TOO HIGH!! I'LL CALL FOR HELP!
MY... MY CELL PHONE... MY CELL PHONE!!
YEEK
THERE'S NO SIGNAL...
UMM... THIS MIGHT BE TOUGH FOR THE CLASS PRESIDENT.
CAME TO STOP HIKARU.
ARE YOU DOING OKAY, HARUHI?
HARUHI HAS A LOT OF MOXIE.
FOLLOWED KAORU ONTO THE LIFT WITHOUT REALIZING
HYOOOO
...
YEAH, THAT'S WHAT I FIGURED.
IT'S...
YOU'LL BE OKAY, HARUHI!
OH
HARUHI, YOU'VE GOTTEN PRETTY GOOD. YOU JUST HAVE TO CHOOSE THE LESS STEEP PARTS TO GO DOWN!
UM.
I'LL LEAD YOU!!
RIGHT.

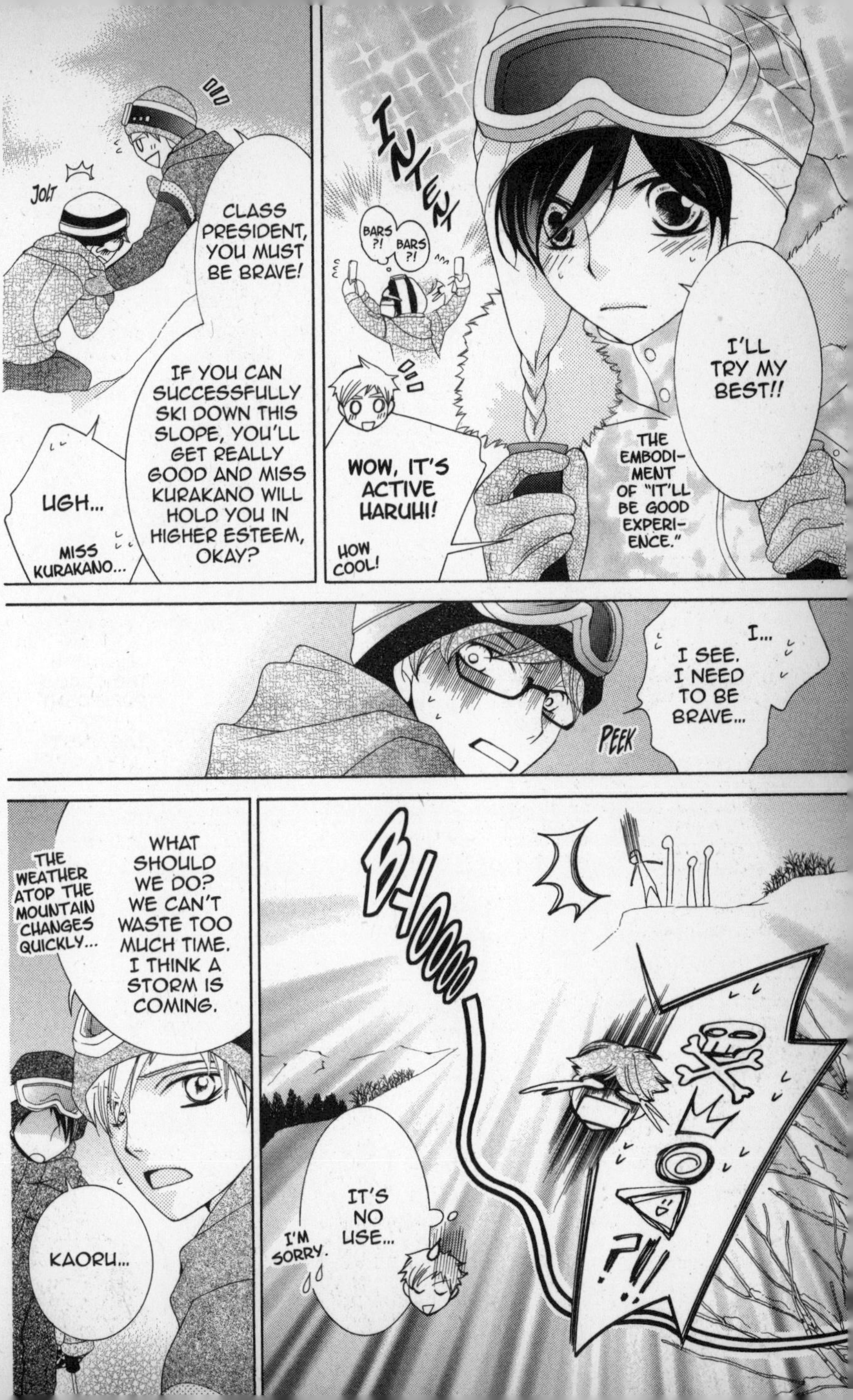
INTENT
BARS?!
BARS?!
I'LL TRY MY BEST!!
THE EMBODIMENT OF "IT'LL BE GOOD EXPERIENCE."
WOW, IT'S ACTIVE HARUHI!
HOW COOL!
CLASS PRESIDENT, YOU MUST BE BRAVE!
JOLT
IF YOU CAN SUCCESSFULLY SKI DOWN THIS SLOPE, YOU'LL GET REALLY GOOD AND MISS KURAKANO WILL HOLD YOU IN HIGHER ESTEEM, OKAY?
UGH...
MISS KURAKANO...
I... I SEE. I NEED TO BE BRAVE...
PEEK
?!!
IT'S NO USE...
I'M SORRY.
WHAT SHOULD WE DO? WE CAN'T WASTE TOO MUCH TIME. I THINK A STORM IS COMING.
THE WEATHER ATOP THE MOUNTAIN CHANGES QUICKLY...
KAORU...

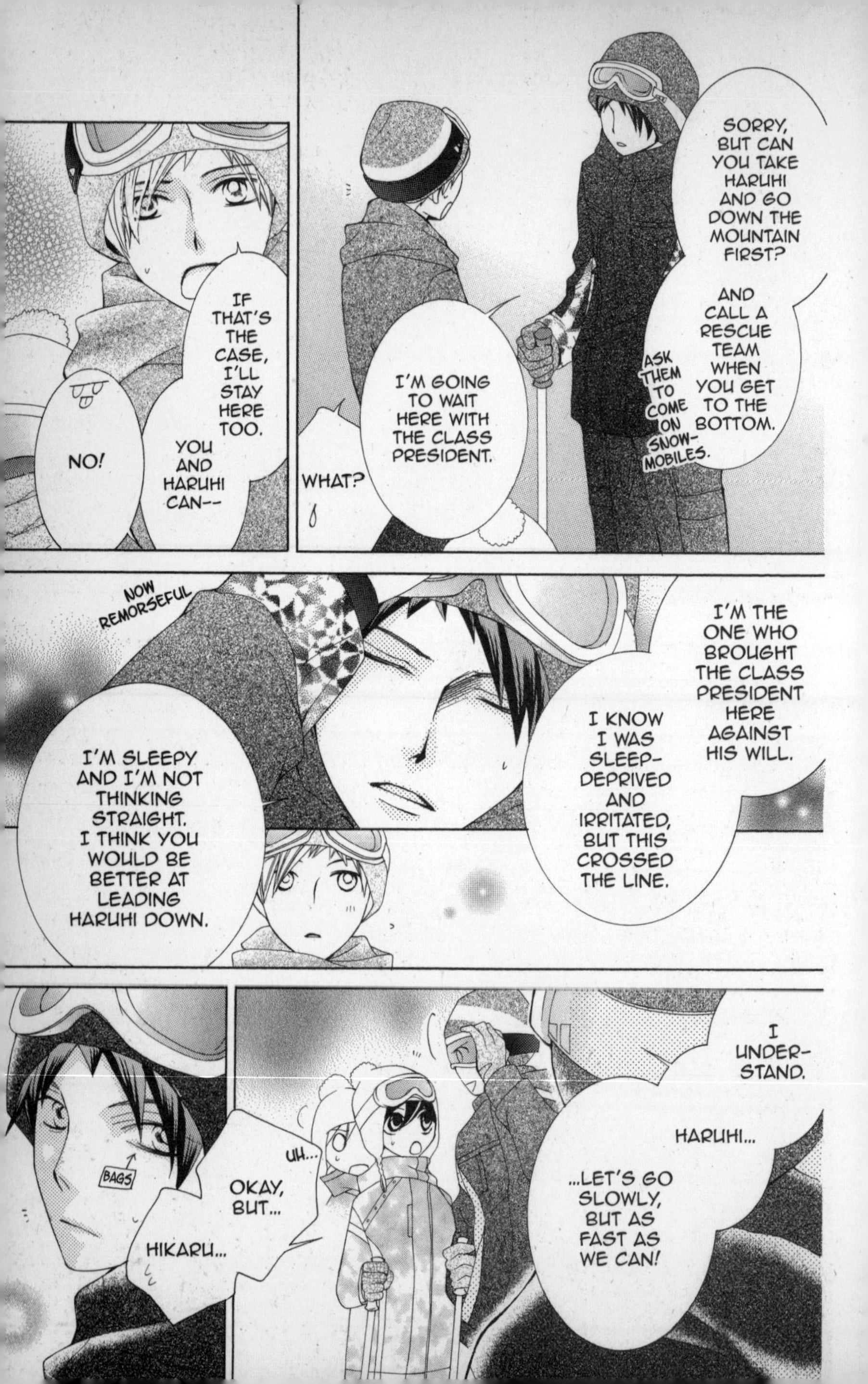
SORRY, BUT CAN YOU TAKE HARUHI AND GO DOWN THE MOUNTAIN FIRST?
AND CALL A RESCUE TEAM WHEN YOU GET TO THE BOTTOM.
ASK THEM TO COME ON SNOW-MOBILES.
I'M GOING TO WAIT HERE WITH THE CLASS PRESIDENT.
WHAT?
IF THAT'S THE CASE, I'LL STAY HERE TOO.
YOU AND HARUHI CAN--
NO!
I'M THE ONE WHO BROUGHT THE CLASS PRESIDENT HERE AGAINST HIS WILL.
I KNOW I WAS SLEEP-DEPRIVED AND IRRITATED, BUT THIS CROSSED THE LINE.
NOW REMORSEFUL
I'M SLEEPY AND I'M NOT THINKING STRAIGHT. I THINK YOU WOULD BE BETTER AT LEADING HARUHI DOWN.
I UNDER-STAND.
HARUHI...
...LET'S GO SLOWLY, BUT AS FAST AS WE CAN!
UH...
OKAY, BUT...
HIKARU...
BAGS

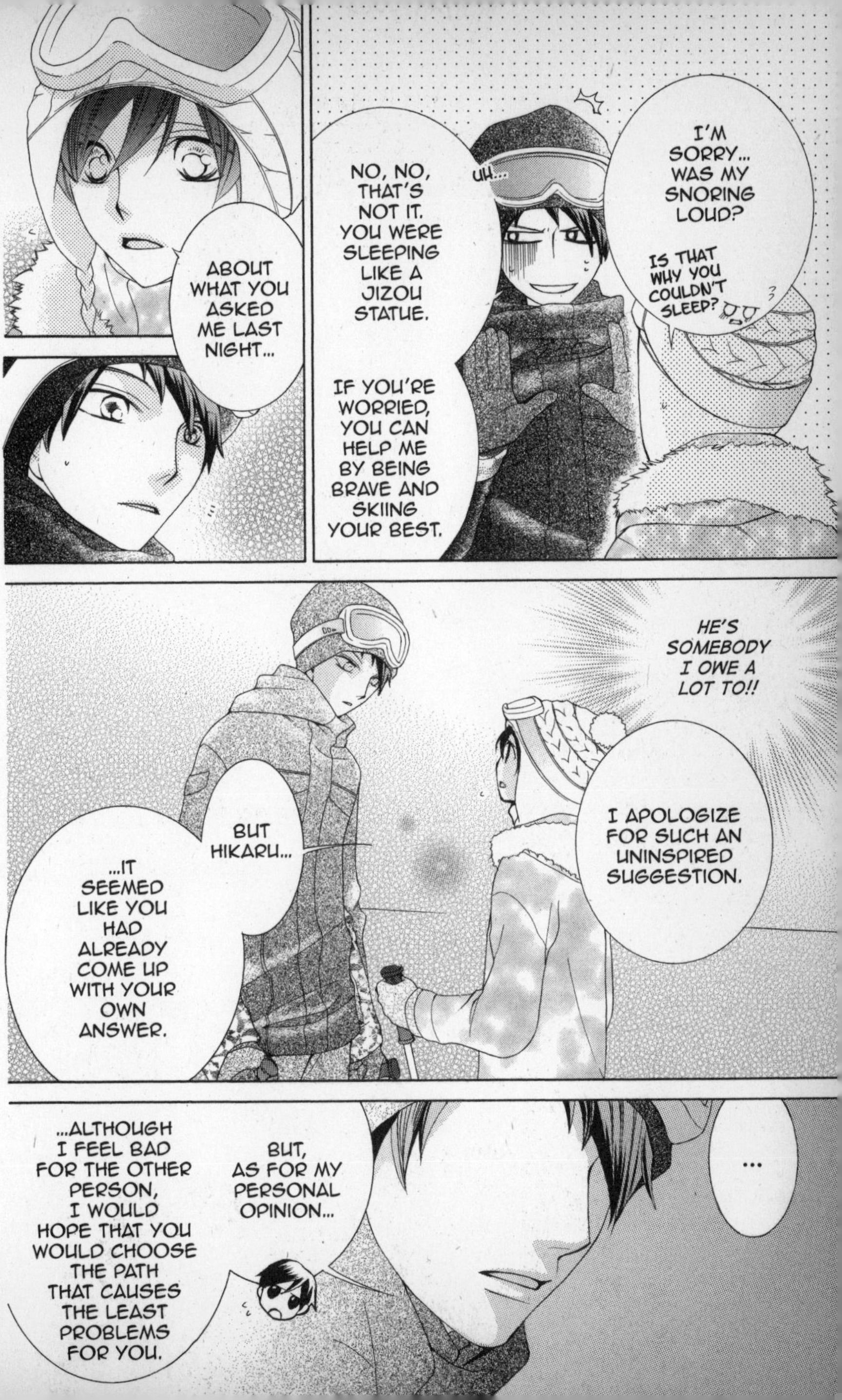
I'M SORRY... WAS MY SNORING LOUD?
IS THAT WHY YOU COULDN'T SLEEP?
UH...
NO, NO, THAT'S NOT IT. YOU WERE SLEEPING LIKE A JIZOU STATUE.
IF YOU'RE WORRIED, YOU CAN HELP ME BY BEING BRAVE AND SKIING YOUR BEST.
ABOUT WHAT YOU ASKED ME LAST NIGHT...
HE'S SOMEBODY I OWE A LOT TO!!
I APOLOGIZE FOR SUCH AN UNINSPIRED SUGGESTION.
BUT HIKARU...
...IT SEEMED LIKE YOU HAD ALREADY COME UP WITH YOUR OWN ANSWER.
...
BUT, AS FOR MY PERSONAL OPINION...
...ALTHOUGH I FEEL BAD FOR THE OTHER PERSON, I WOULD HOPE THAT YOU WOULD CHOOSE THE PATH THAT CAUSES THE LEAST PROBLEMS FOR YOU.

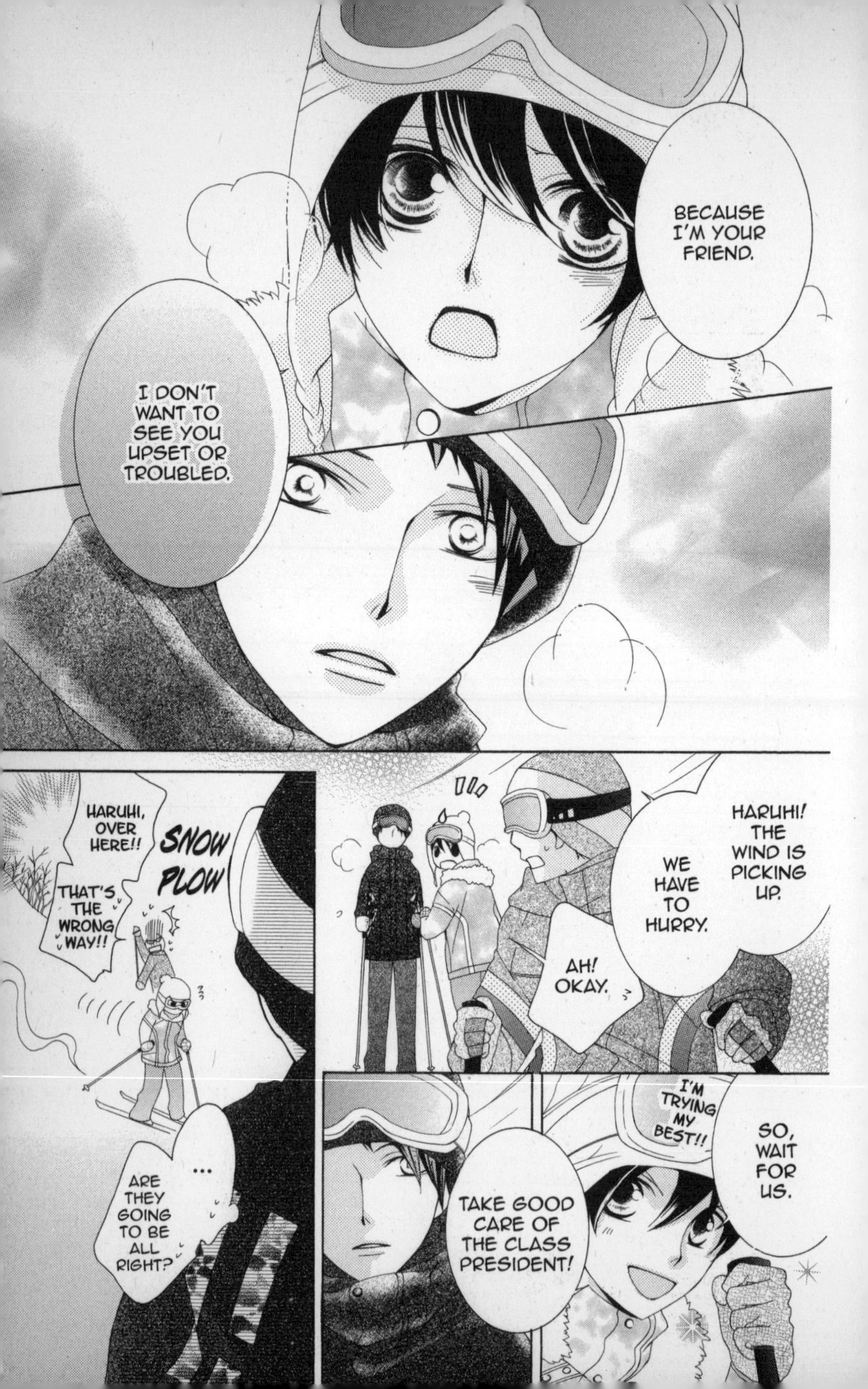
BECAUSE I'M YOUR FRIEND.
I DON'T WANT TO SEE YOU UPSET OR TROUBLED.
HARUHI! THE WIND IS PICKING UP.
WE HAVE TO HURRY.
AH! OKAY.
SO, WAIT FOR US.
I'M TRYING MY BEST!!
TAKE GOOD CARE OF THE CLASS PRESIDENT!
HARUHI, OVER HERE!!
SNOW PLOW
THAT'S THE WRONG WAY!!
...
ARE THEY GOING TO BE ALL RIGHT?

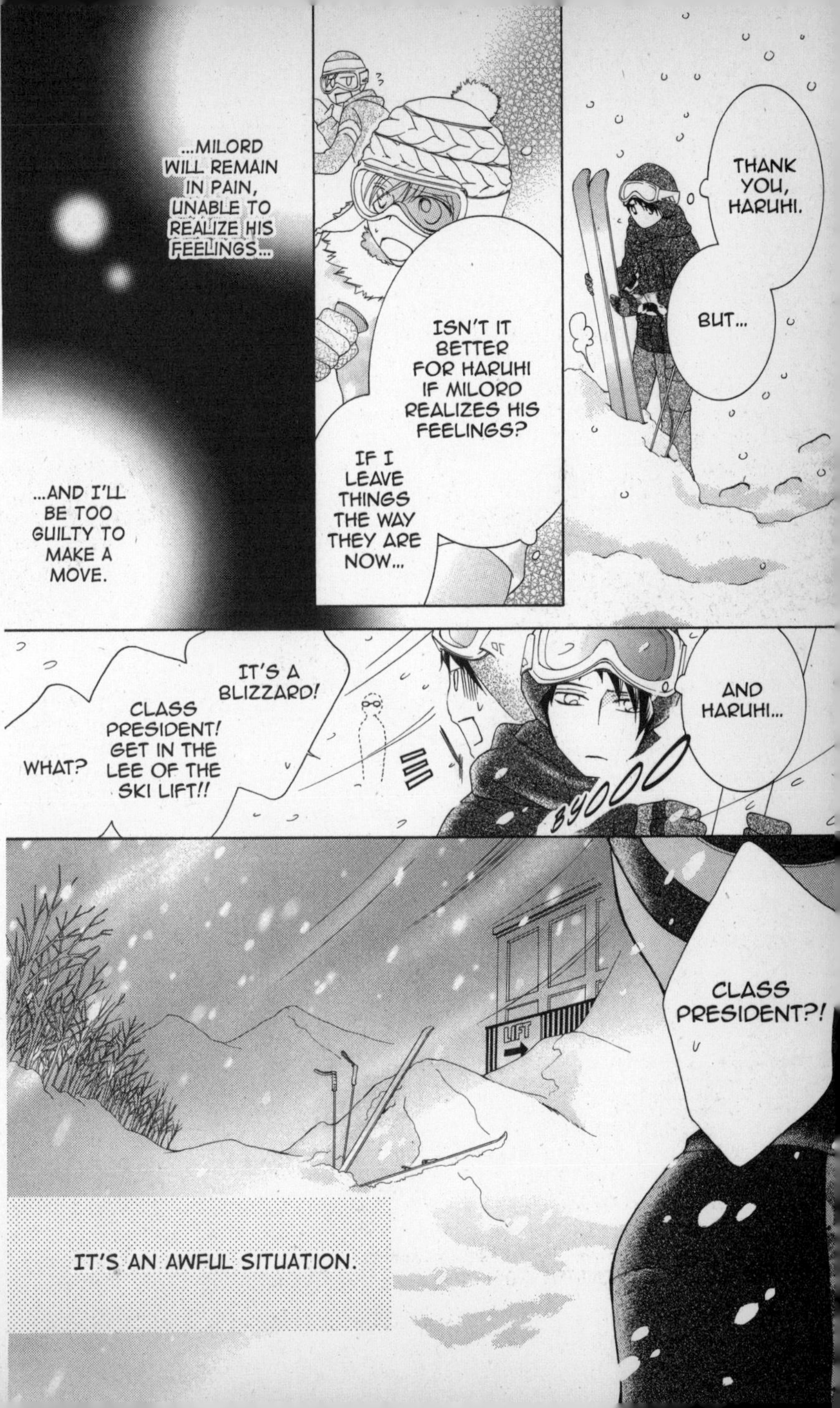
THANK YOU, HARUHI.
BUT...
ISN'T IT BETTER FOR HARUHI IF MILORD REALIZES HIS FEELINGS?
IF I LEAVE THINGS THE WAY THEY ARE NOW...
...MILORD WILL REMAIN IN PAIN, UNABLE TO REALIZE HIS FEELINGS...
...AND I'LL BE TOO GUILTY TO MAKE A MOVE.
AND HARUHI...
BYOOO
IT'S A BLIZZARD!
CLASS PRESIDENT! GET IN THE LEE OF THE SKI LIFT!!
WHAT?
CLASS PRESIDENT?!
LIFT
IT'S AN AWFUL SITUATION.

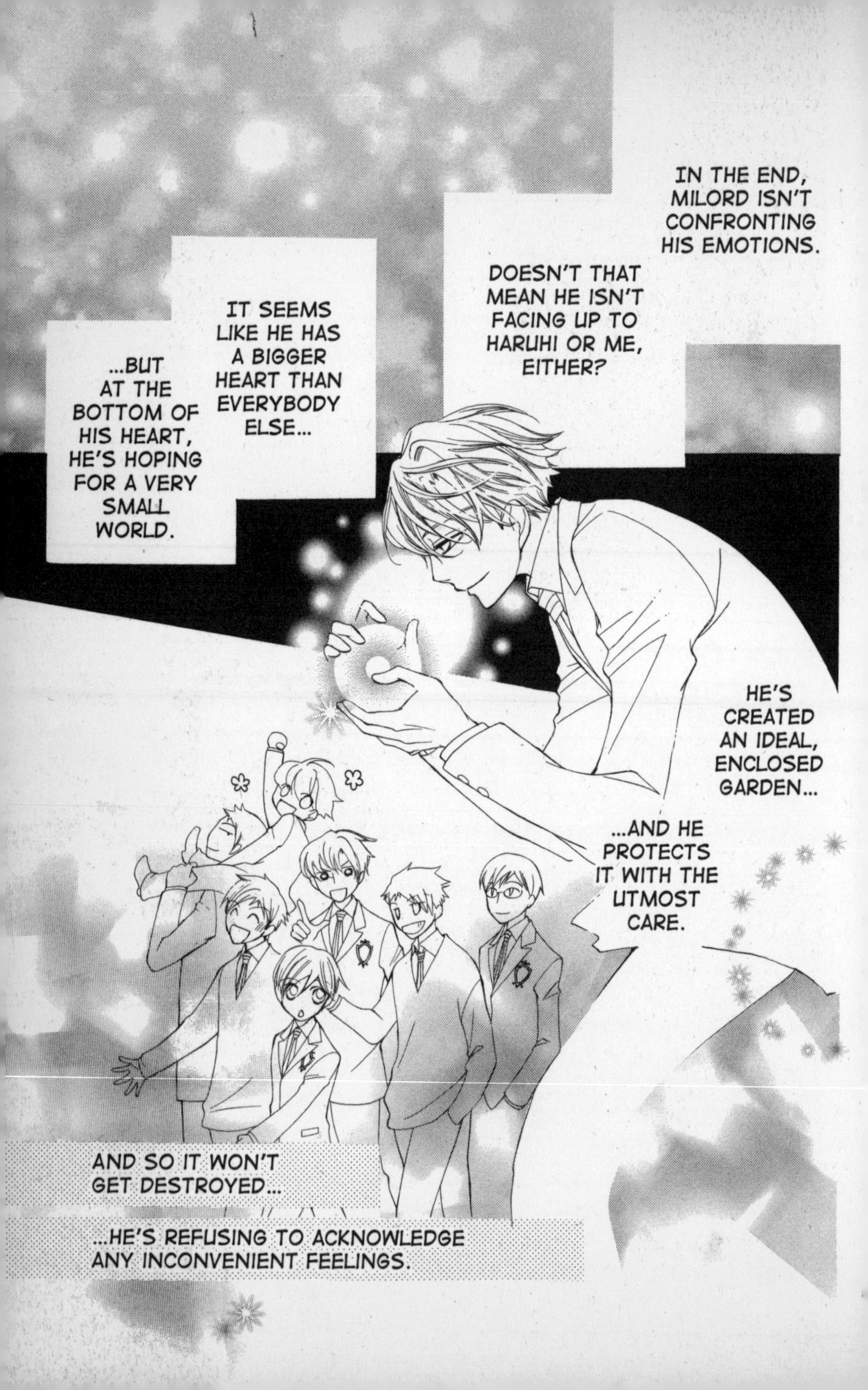
IN THE END, MILORD ISN'T CONFRONTING HIS EMOTIONS.
DOESN'T THAT MEAN HE ISN'T FACING UP TO HARUHI OR ME, EITHER?
IT SEEMS LIKE HE HAS A BIGGER HEART THAN EVERYBODY ELSE...
...BUT AT THE BOTTOM OF HIS HEART, HE'S HOPING FOR A VERY SMALL WORLD.
HE'S CREATED AN IDEAL, ENCLOSED GARDEN...
...AND HE PROTECTS IT WITH THE UTMOST CARE.
AND SO IT WON'T GET DESTROYED...
...HE'S REFUSING TO ACKNOWLEDGE ANY INCONVENIENT FEELINGS.

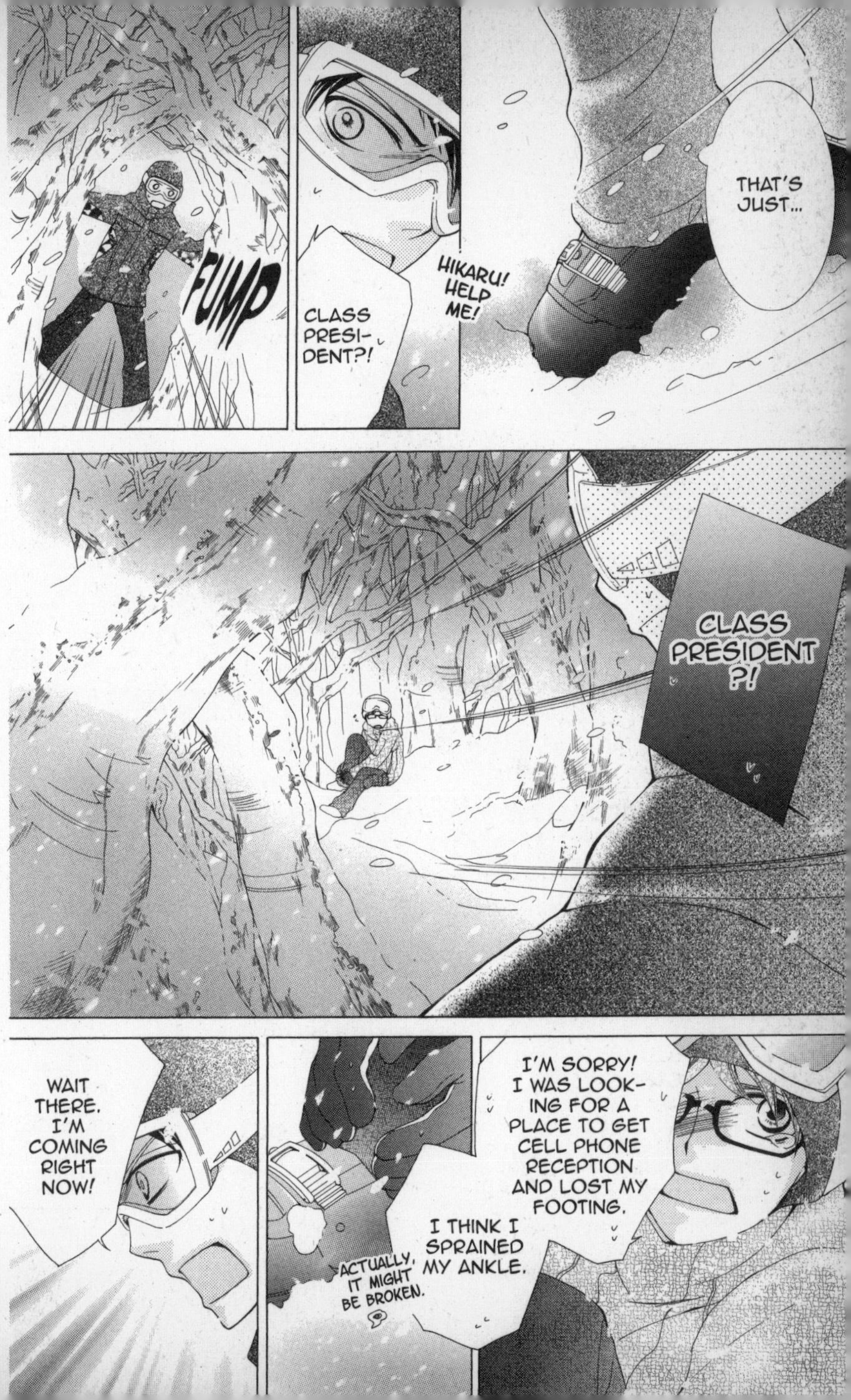
THAT'S JUST...
HIKARU! HELP ME!
CLASS PRESIDENT?!
FUMP
CLASS PRESIDENT ?!
I'M SORRY! I WAS LOOKING FOR A PLACE TO GET CELL PHONE RECEPTION AND LOST MY FOOTING.
I THINK I SPRAINED MY ANKLE.
ACTUALLY, IT MIGHT BE BROKEN.
WAIT THERE. I'M COMING RIGHT NOW!

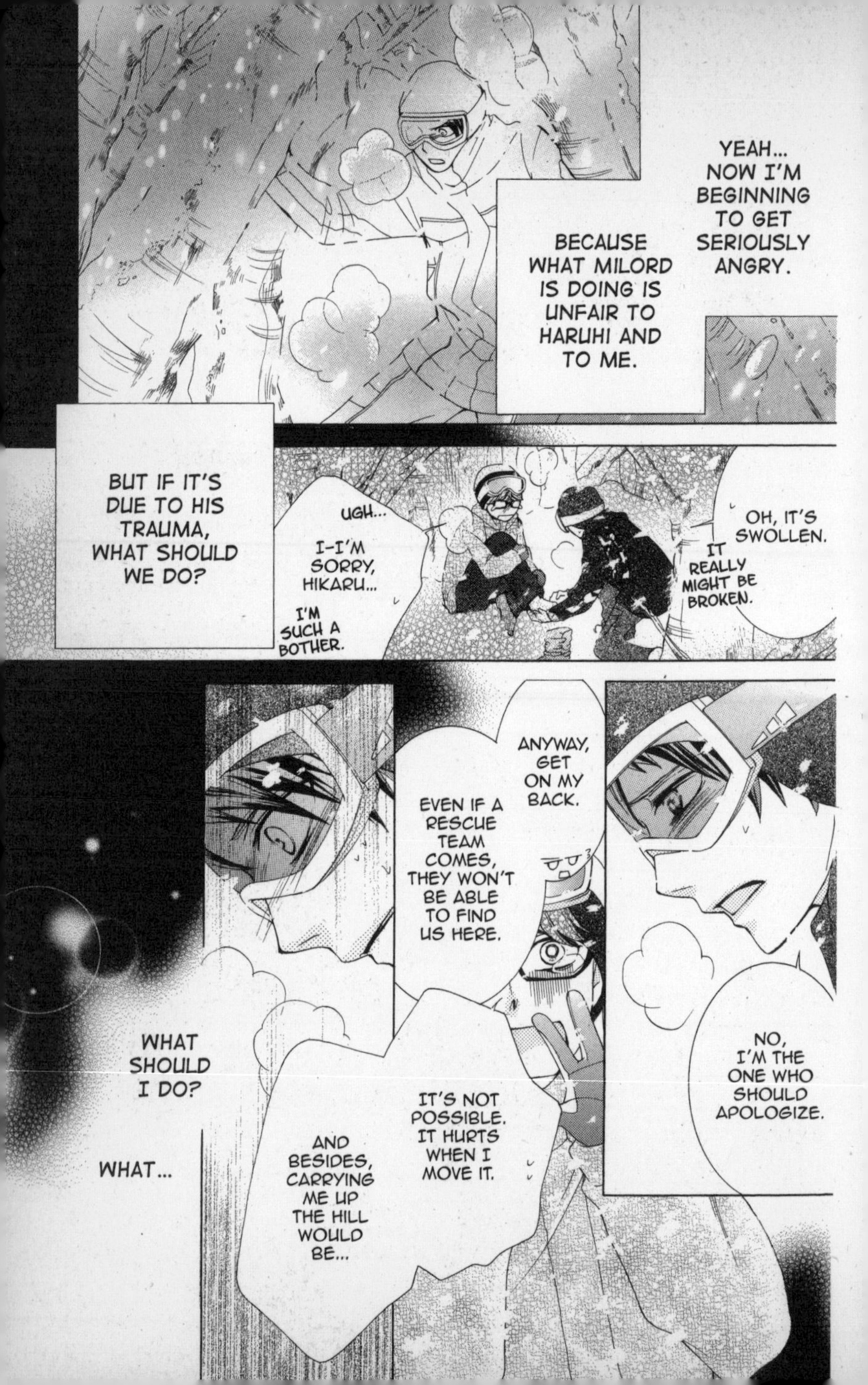
YEAH... NOW I'M BEGINNING TO GET SERIOUSLY ANGRY.
BECAUSE WHAT MILORD IS DOING IS UNFAIR TO HARUHI AND TO ME.
OH, IT'S SWOLLEN.
IT REALLY MIGHT BE BROKEN.
UGH...
I-I'M SORRY, HIKARU...
I'M SUCH A BOTHER.
BUT IF IT'S DUE TO HIS TRAUMA, WHAT SHOULD WE DO?
NO, I'M THE ONE WHO SHOULD APOLOGIZE.
ANYWAY, GET ON MY BACK.
EVEN IF A RESCUE TEAM COMES, THEY WON'T BE ABLE TO FIND US HERE.
IT'S NOT POSSIBLE. IT HURTS WHEN I MOVE IT.
AND BESIDES, CARRYING ME UP THE HILL WOULD BE...
WHAT SHOULD I DO?
WHAT...

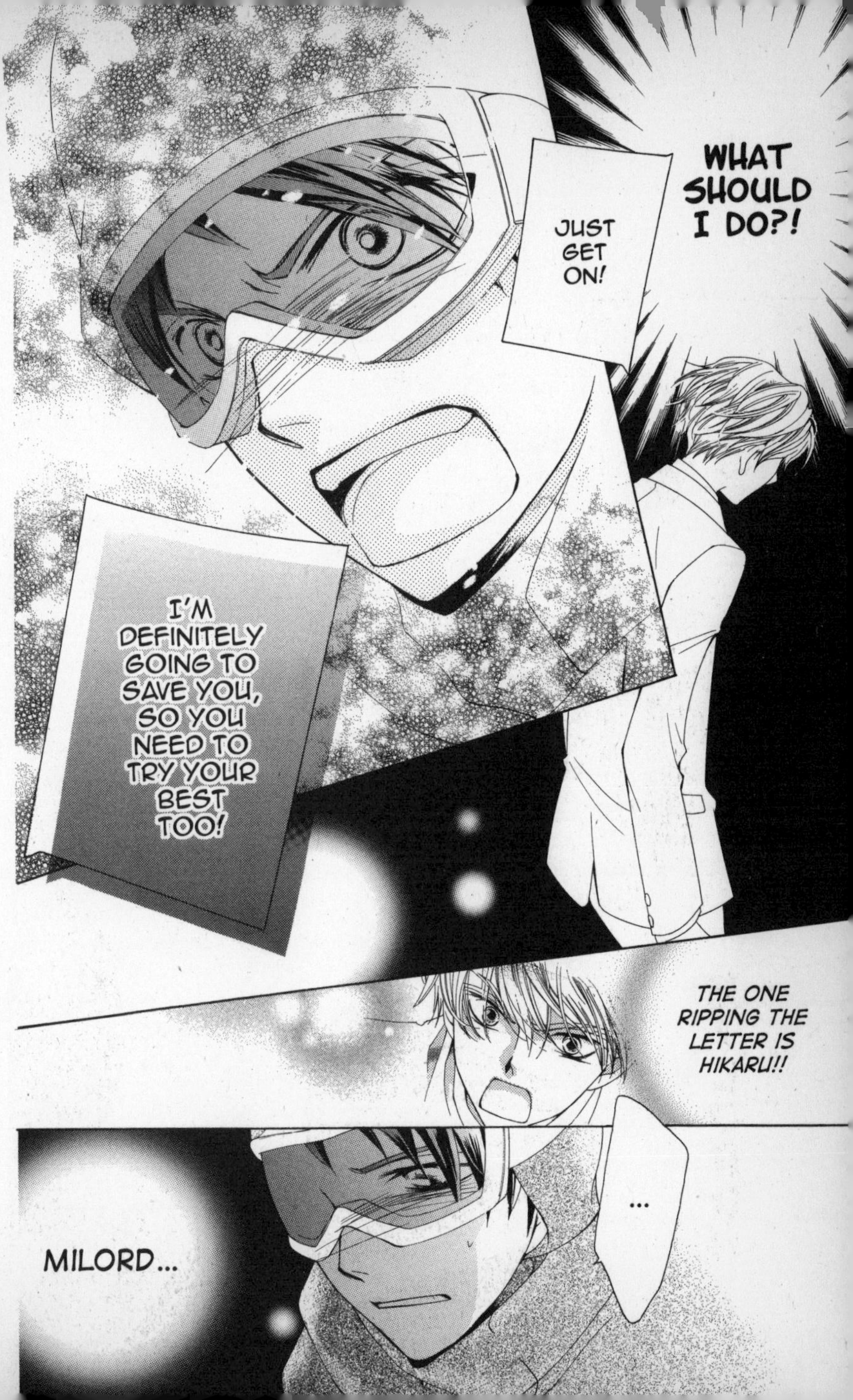
WHAT SHOULD I DO?!
JUST GET ON!
I'M DEFINITELY GOING TO SAVE YOU, SO YOU NEED TO TRY YOUR BEST TOO!
THE ONE RIPPING THE LETTER IS HIKARU!!
...
MILORD...

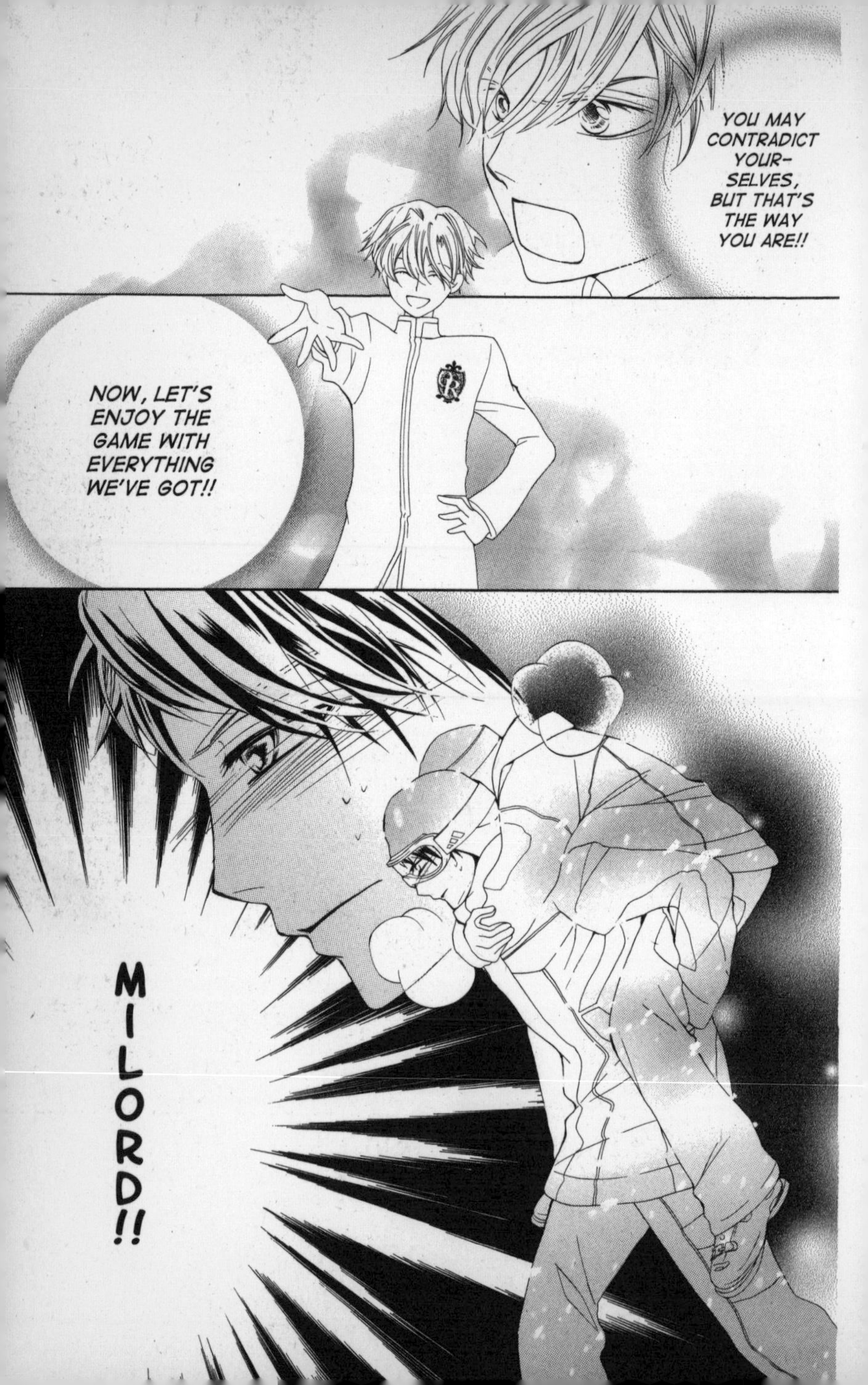
YOU MAY CONTRADICT YOUR-SELVES, BUT THAT'S THE WAY YOU ARE!!
NOW, LET'S ENJOY THE GAME WITH EVERYTHING WE'VE GOT!!
MILORD!!

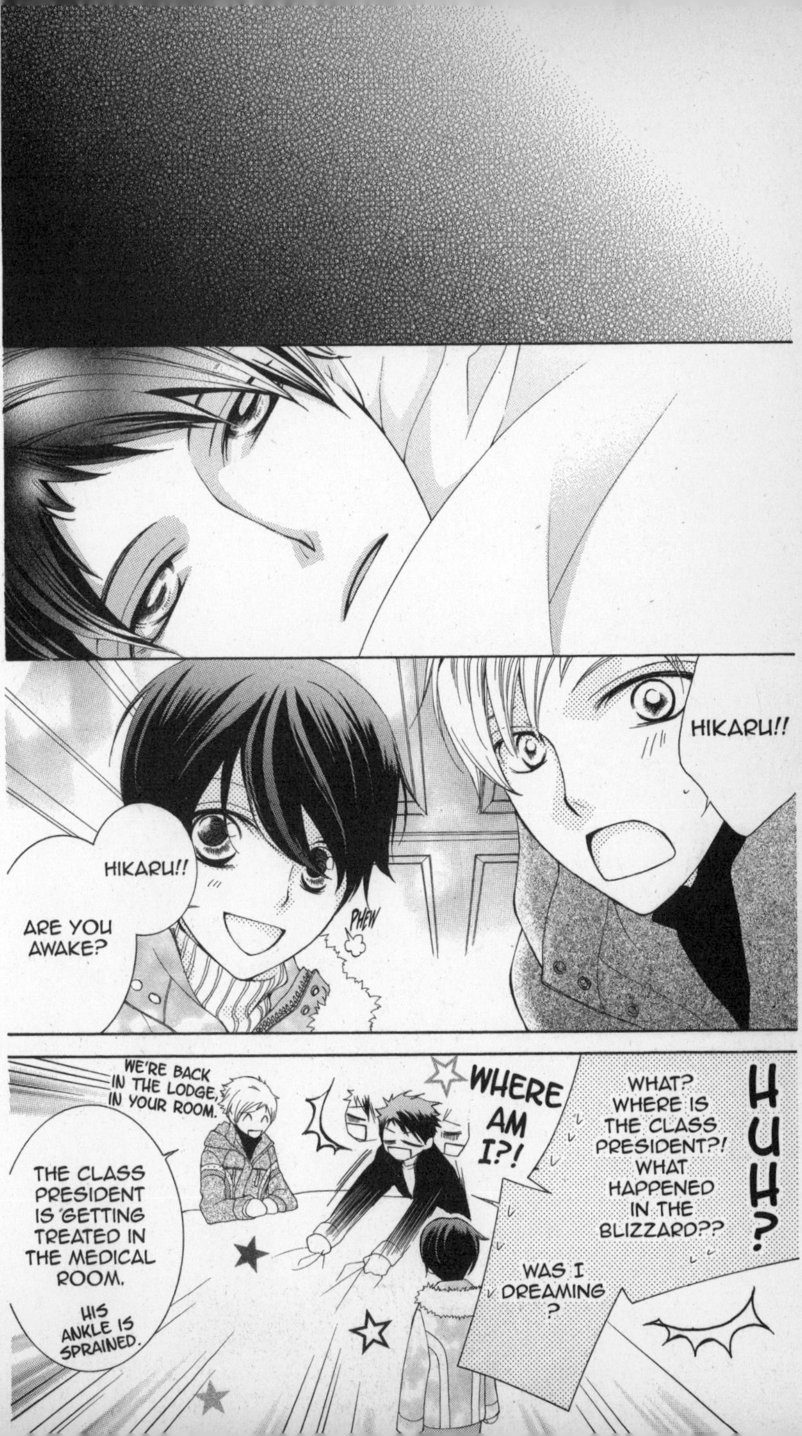
HIKARU!!
HIKARU!!
ARE YOU AWAKE?
PHEW
HUH?
WHAT? WHERE IS THE CLASS PRESIDENT?! WHAT HAPPENED IN THE BLIZZARD??
WHERE AM I?!
WAS I DREAMING?
WE'RE BACK IN THE LODGE, IN YOUR ROOM.
THE CLASS PRESIDENT IS GETTING TREATED IN THE MEDICAL ROOM.
HIS ANKLE IS SPRAINED.

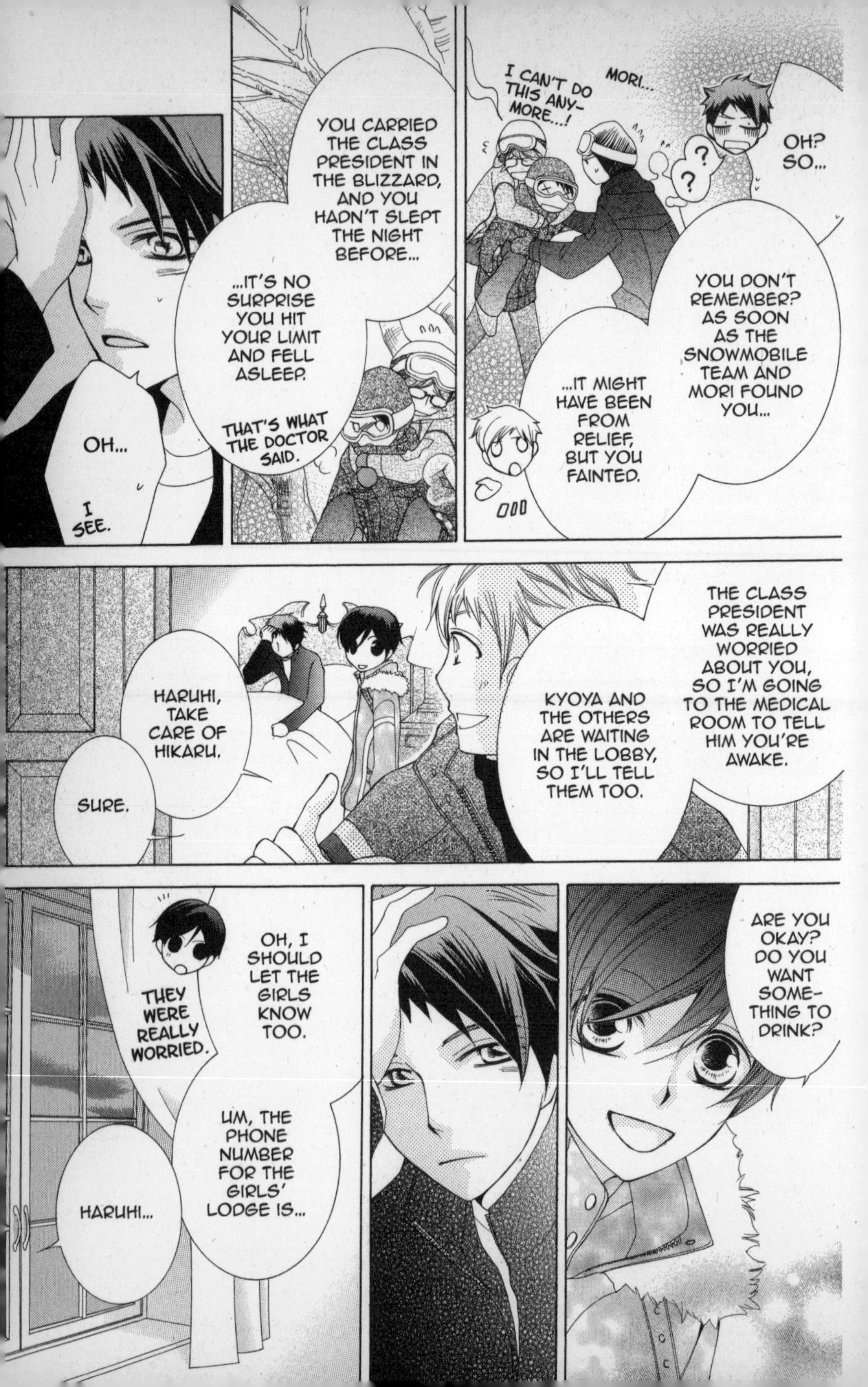

MORI...
I CAN'T DO THIS ANY-MORE...!
OH? SO...
YOU DON'T REMEMBER? AS SOON AS THE SNOWMOBILE TEAM AND MORI FOUND YOU...
...IT MIGHT HAVE BEEN FROM RELIEF, BUT YOU FAINTED.
YOU CARRIED THE CLASS PRESIDENT IN THE BLIZZARD, AND YOU HADN'T SLEPT THE NIGHT BEFORE...
...IT'S NO SURPRISE YOU HIT YOUR LIMIT AND FELL ASLEEP.
THAT'S WHAT THE DOCTOR SAID.
OH...
I SEE.
THE CLASS PRESIDENT WAS REALLY WORRIED ABOUT YOU, SO I'M GOING TO THE MEDICAL ROOM TO TELL HIM YOU'RE AWAKE.
KYOYA AND THE OTHERS ARE WAITING IN THE LOBBY, SO I'LL TELL THEM TOO.
HARUHI, TAKE CARE OF HIKARU.
SURE.
ARE YOU OKAY? DO YOU WANT SOME-THING TO DRINK?
OH, I SHOULD LET THE GIRLS KNOW TOO.
THEY WERE REALLY WORRIED.
UM, THE PHONE NUMBER FOR THE GIRLS' LODGE IS...
HARUHI...

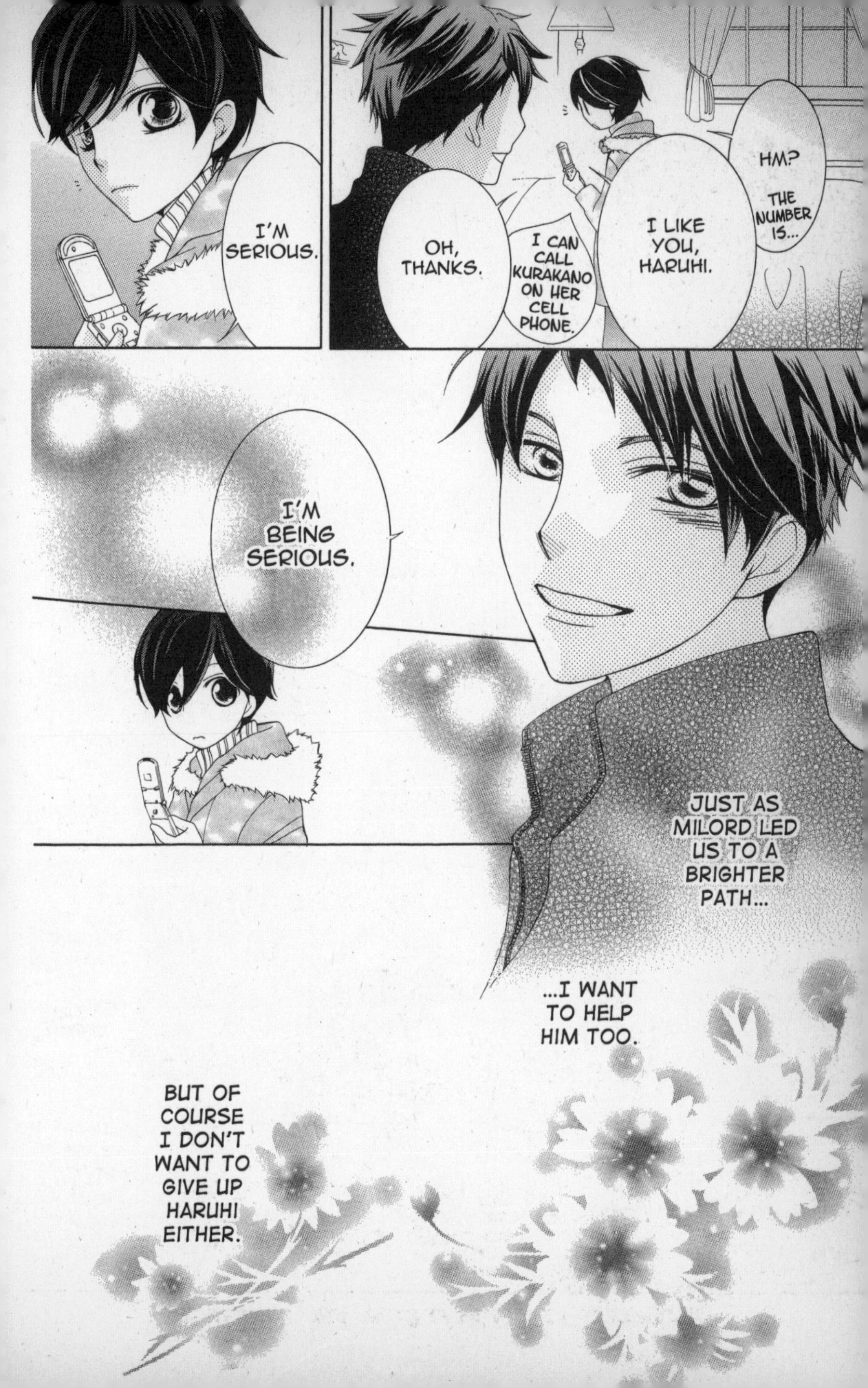
HM?
THE NUMBER IS...
I LIKE YOU, HARUHI.
I CAN CALL KURAKANO ON HER CELL PHONE.
OH, THANKS.
I'M SERIOUS.
I'M BEING SERIOUS.
JUST AS MILORD LED US TO A BRIGHTER PATH...
...I WANT TO HELP HIM TOO.
BUT OF COURSE I DON'T WANT TO GIVE UP HARUHI EITHER.

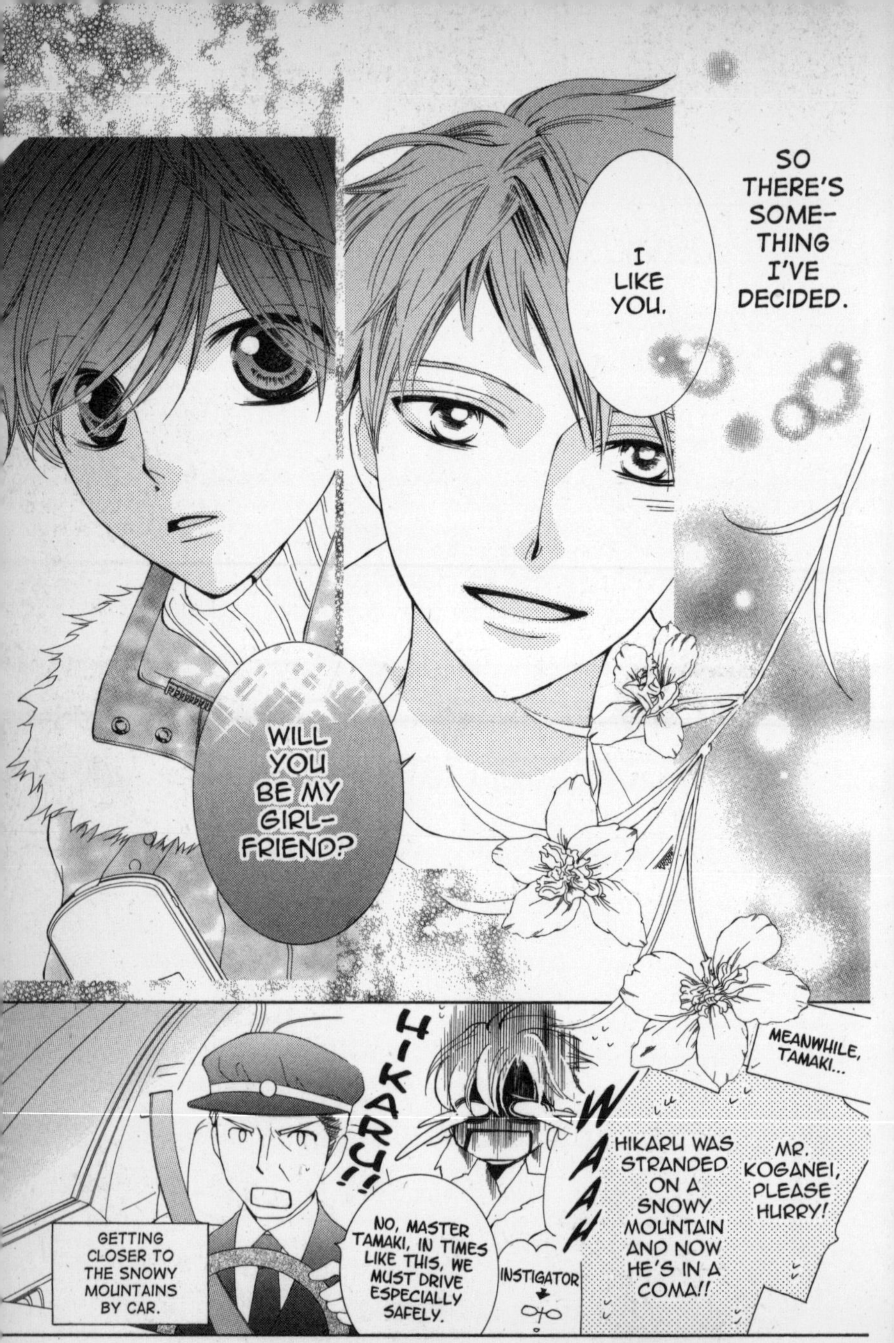
SO THERE'S SOME-THING I'VE DECIDED.
I LIKE YOU.
WILL YOU BE MY GIRL-FRIEND?
MEANWHILE, TAMAKI...
MR. KOGANEI, PLEASE HURRY!
HIKARU WAS STRANDED ON A SNOWY MOUNTAIN AND NOW HE'S IN A COMA!!
WAAAH
HIKARU!!
INSTIGATOR
NO, MASTER TAMAKI, IN TIMES LIKE THIS, WE MUST DRIVE ESPECIALLY SAFELY.
GETTING CLOSER TO THE SNOWY MOUNTAINS BY CAR.

OURAN HIGH SCHOOL HOST CLUB, VOL. 13/THE END

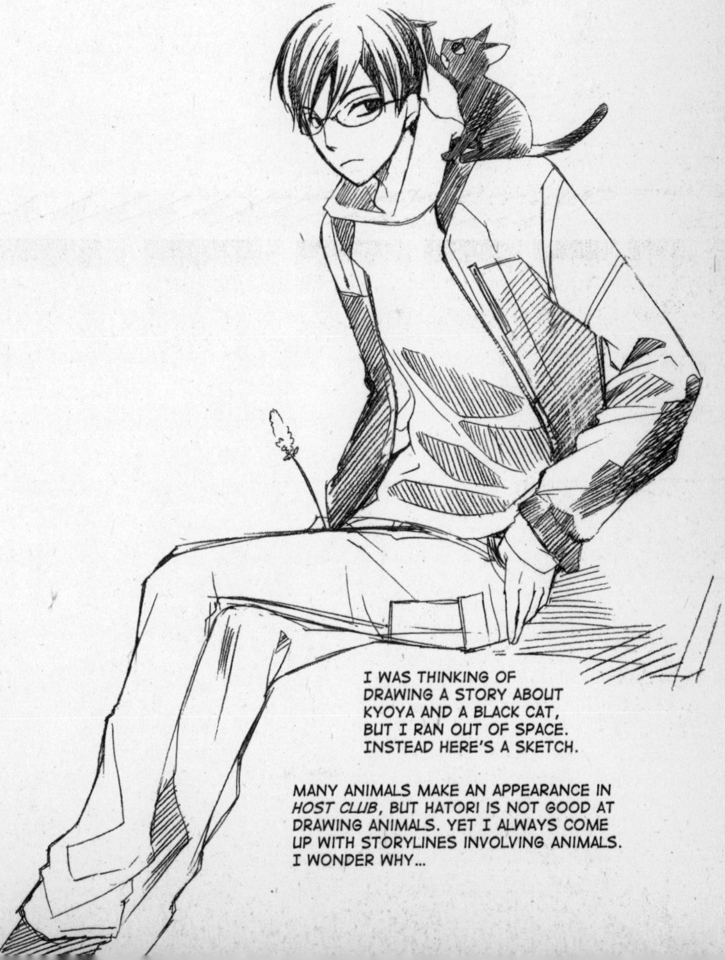

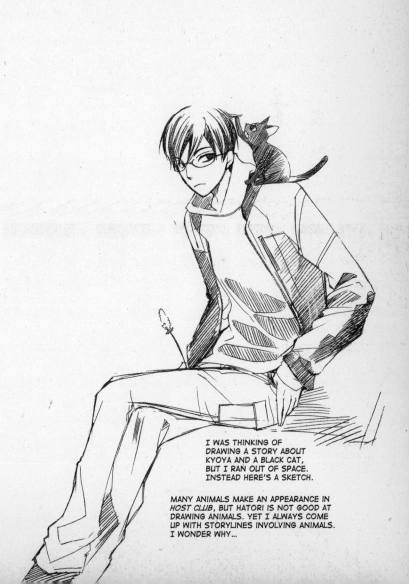

I WAS THINKING OF DRAWING A STORY ABOUT KYOYA AND A BLACK CAT, BUT I RAN OUT OF SPACE. INSTEAD HERE'S A SKETCH.

MANY ANIMALS MAKE AN APPEARANCE IN *HOST CLUB*, BUT HATORI IS NOT GOOD AT DRAWING ANIMALS. YET I ALWAYS COME UP WITH STORYLINES INVOLVING ANIMALS. I WONDER WHY...

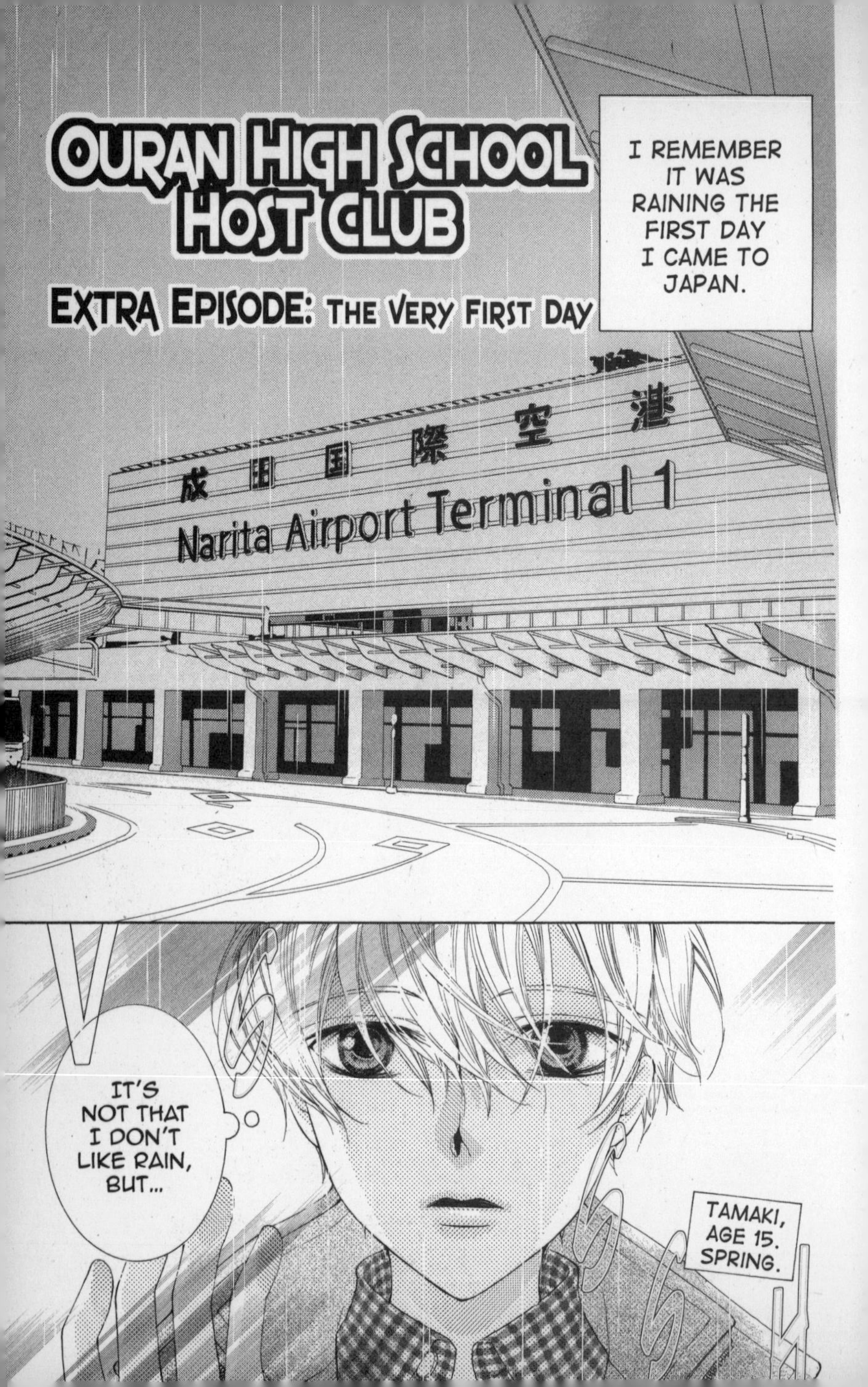
I REMEMBER IT WAS RAINING THE FIRST DAY I CAME TO JAPAN.
OURAN HIGH SCHOOL HOST CLUB
EXTRA EPISODE: THE VERY FIRST DAY
成田国際空港
Narita Airport Terminal 1
IT'S NOT THAT I DON'T LIKE RAIN, BUT...
TAMAKI, AGE 15. SPRING.

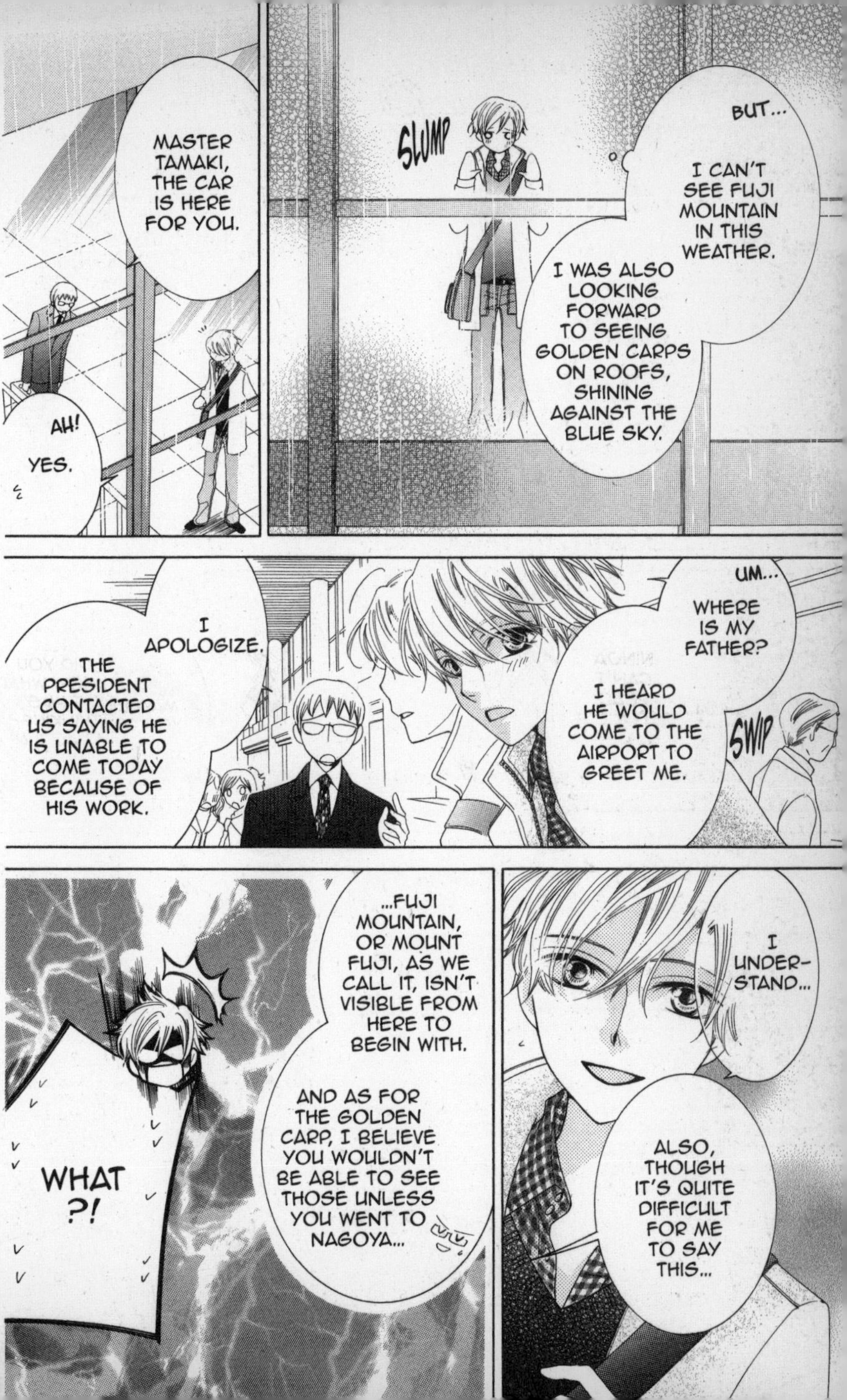
SLUMP
BUT...
I CAN'T SEE FUJI MOUNTAIN IN THIS WEATHER.
I WAS ALSO LOOKING FORWARD TO SEEING GOLDEN CARPS ON ROOFS, SHINING AGAINST THE BLUE SKY.
MASTER TAMAKI, THE CAR IS HERE FOR YOU.
AH!
YES.
UM...
WHERE IS MY FATHER?
I HEARD HE WOULD COME TO THE AIRPORT TO GREET ME.
SWIP
I APOLOGIZE.
THE PRESIDENT CONTACTED US SAYING HE IS UNABLE TO COME TODAY BECAUSE OF HIS WORK.
I UNDER-STAND...
ALSO, THOUGH IT'S QUITE DIFFICULT FOR ME TO SAY THIS...
...FUJI MOUNTAIN, OR MOUNT FUJI, AS WE CALL IT, ISN'T VISIBLE FROM HERE TO BEGIN WITH.
AND AS FOR THE GOLDEN CARP, I BELIEVE YOU WOULDN'T BE ABLE TO SEE THOSE UNLESS YOU WENT TO NAGOYA...
WHAT ?!

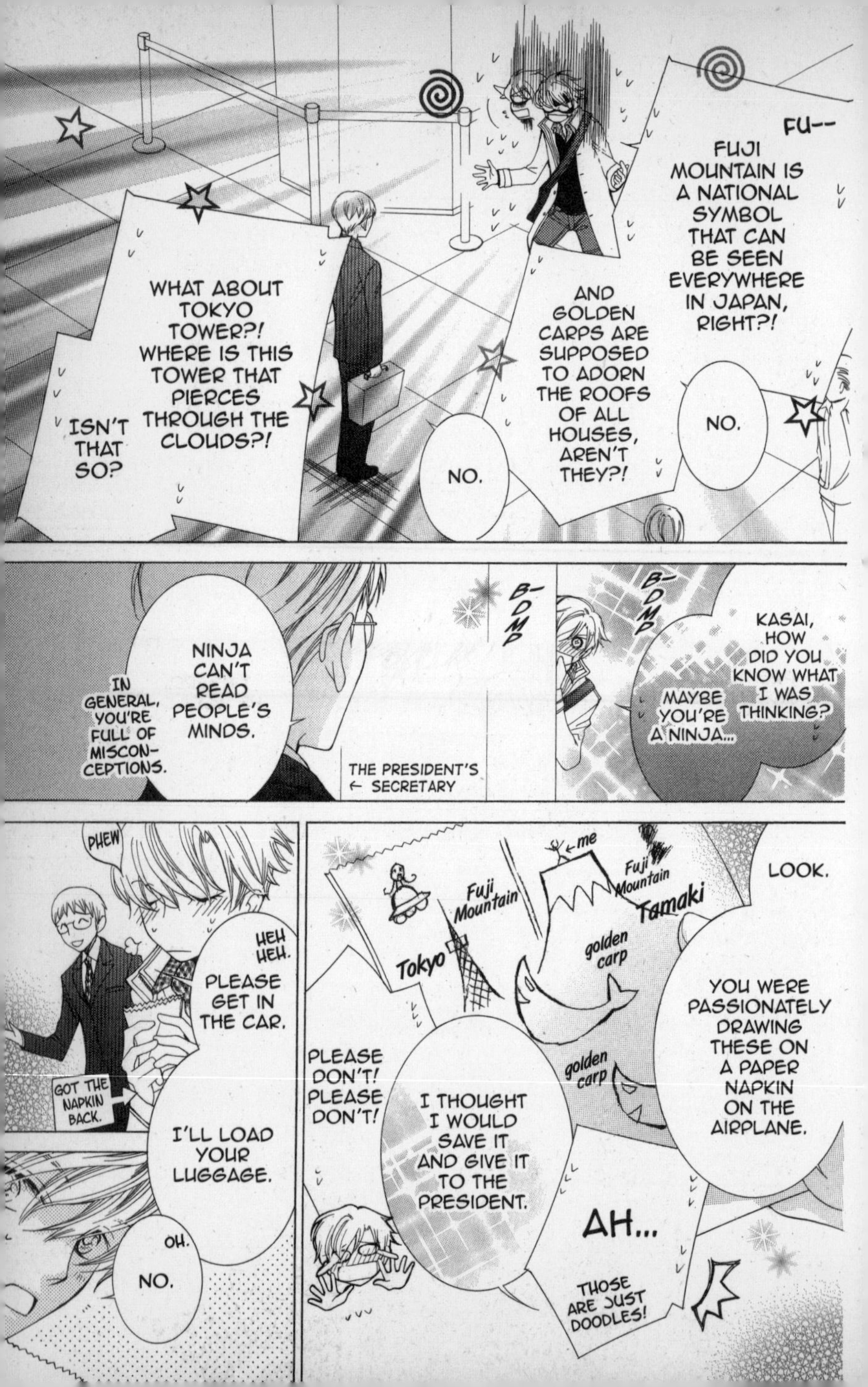
FU--
FUJI MOUNTAIN IS A NATIONAL SYMBOL THAT CAN BE SEEN EVERYWHERE IN JAPAN, RIGHT?!
NO.
AND GOLDEN CARPS ARE SUPPOSED TO ADORN THE ROOFS OF ALL HOUSES, AREN'T THEY?!
NO.
WHAT ABOUT TOKYO TOWER?! WHERE IS THIS TOWER THAT PIERCES THROUGH THE CLOUDS?!
ISN'T THAT SO?
B-DOMP
KASAI, HOW DID YOU KNOW WHAT I WAS THINKING?
MAYBE YOU'RE A NINJA...
B-DOMP
THE PRESIDENT'S ← SECRETARY
NINJA CAN'T READ PEOPLE'S MINDS.
IN GENERAL, YOU'RE FULL OF MISCONCEPTIONS.
LOOK.
YOU WERE PASSIONATELY DRAWING THESE ON A PAPER NAPKIN ON THE AIRPLANE.
←me
Fuji Mountain
Tamaki
Fuji Mountain
Tokyo
golden carp
golden carp
AH...
THOSE ARE JUST DOODLES!
I THOUGHT I WOULD SAVE IT AND GIVE IT TO THE PRESIDENT.
PLEASE DON'T! PLEASE DON'T!
PHEW
HEH HEH. PLEASE GET IN THE CAR.
GOT THE NAPKIN BACK.
I'LL LOAD YOUR LUGGAGE.
OH.
NO.

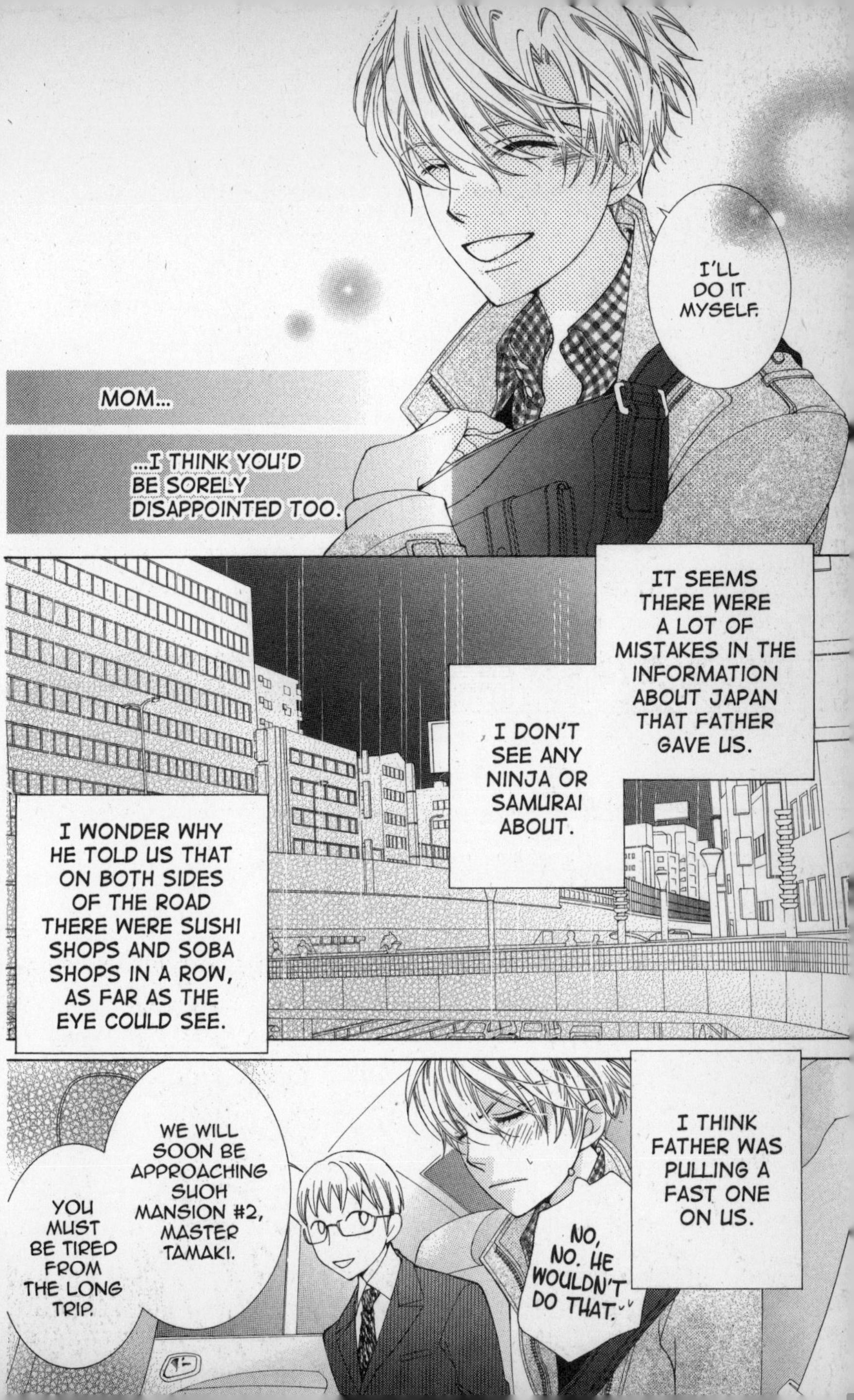
I'LL DO IT MYSELF.
MOM...
...I THINK YOU'D BE SORELY DISAPPOINTED TOO.
IT SEEMS THERE WERE A LOT OF MISTAKES IN THE INFORMATION ABOUT JAPAN THAT FATHER GAVE US.
I DON'T SEE ANY NINJA OR SAMURAI ABOUT.
I WONDER WHY HE TOLD US THAT ON BOTH SIDES OF THE ROAD THERE WERE SUSHI SHOPS AND SOBA SHOPS IN A ROW, AS FAR AS THE EYE COULD SEE.
I THINK FATHER WAS PULLING A FAST ONE ON US.
NO, NO. HE WOULDN'T DO THAT.
WE WILL SOON BE APPROACHING SUOH MANSION #2, MASTER TAMAKI.
YOU MUST BE TIRED FROM THE LONG TRIP.

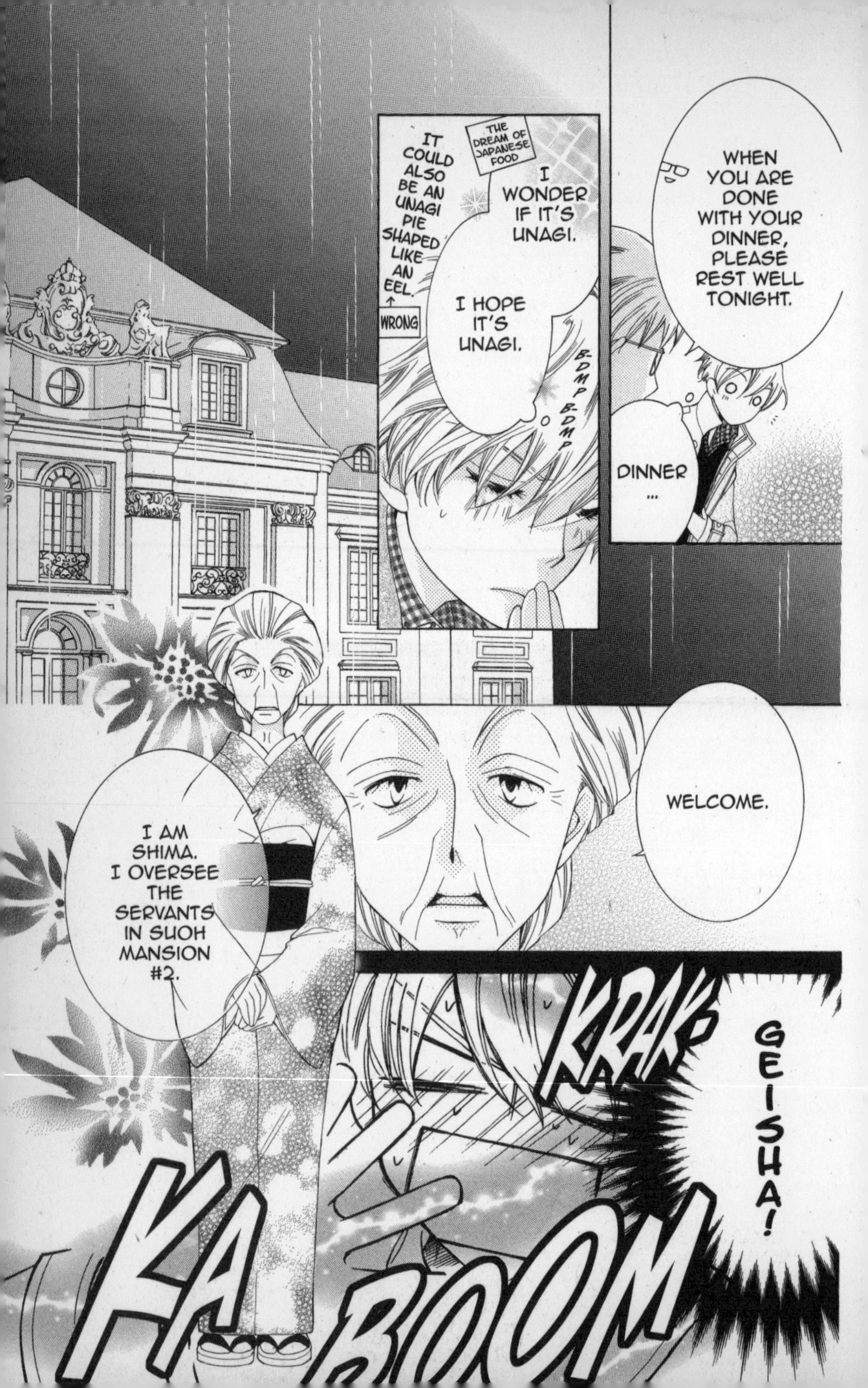
WHEN YOU ARE DONE WITH YOUR DINNER, PLEASE REST WELL TONIGHT.
DINNER...
I WONDER IF IT'S UNAGI.
THE DREAM OF JAPANESE FOOD
I HOPE IT'S UNAGI.
B-DMP B-DMP
IT COULD ALSO BE AN UNAGI PIE SHAPED LIKE AN EEL.
WRONG
WELCOME.
I AM SHIMA. I OVERSEE THE SERVANTS IN SUOH MANSION #2.
KRAK
GEISHA!
KA BOOM

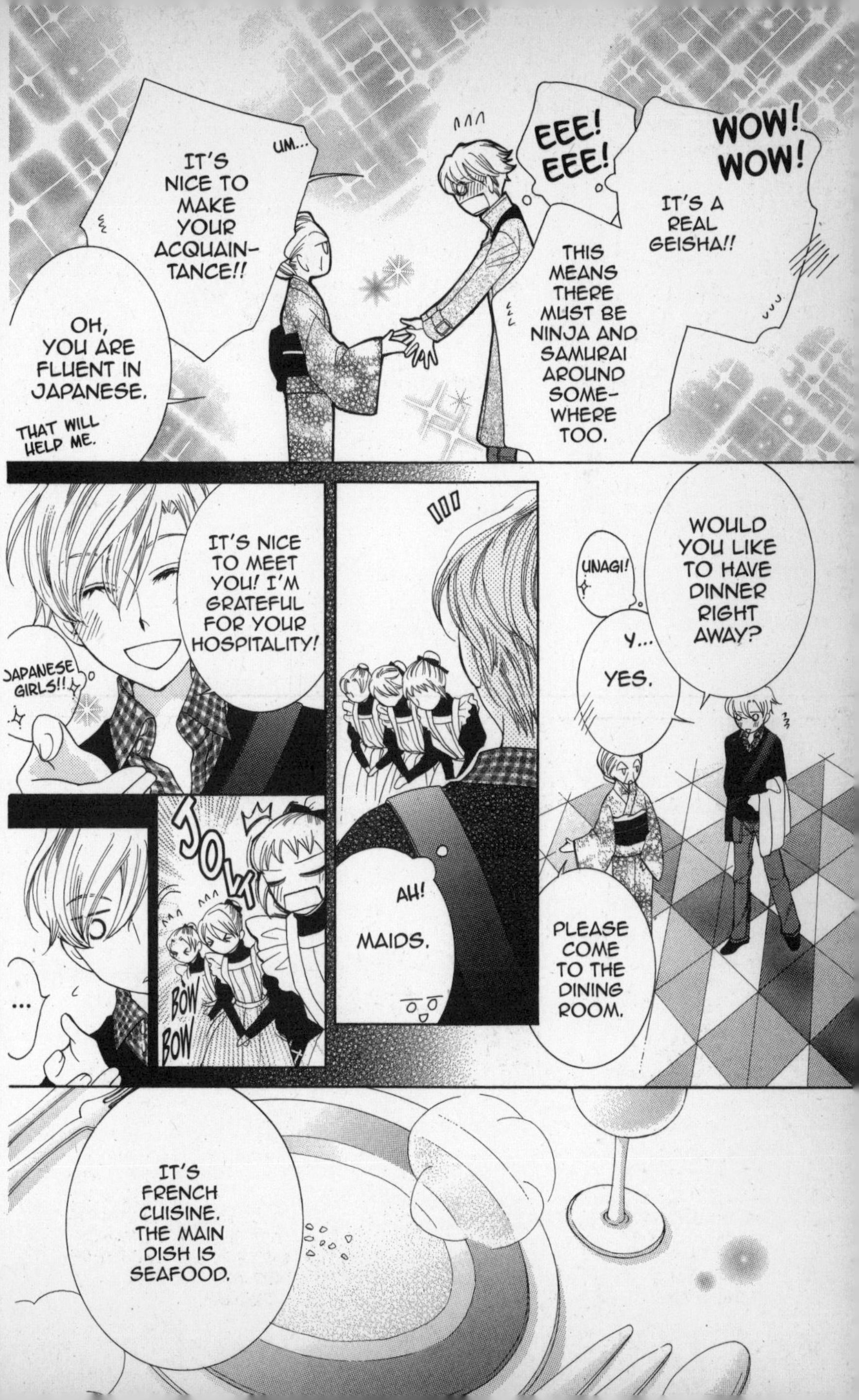

WOW! WOW!
IT'S A REAL GEISHA!!
EEE! EEE!
THIS MEANS THERE MUST BE NINJA AND SAMURAI AROUND SOMEWHERE TOO.
UM...
IT'S NICE TO MAKE YOUR ACQUAIN-TANCE!!
OH, YOU ARE FLUENT IN JAPANESE.
THAT WILL HELP ME.
WOULD YOU LIKE TO HAVE DINNER RIGHT AWAY?
UNAGI!
Y... YES.
PLEASE COME TO THE DINING ROOM.
AH! MAIDS.
IT'S NICE TO MEET YOU! I'M GRATEFUL FOR YOUR HOSPITALITY!
JAPANESE GIRLS!!
JOY
BOW BOW
...
IT'S FRENCH CUISINE. THE MAIN DISH IS SEAFOOD.

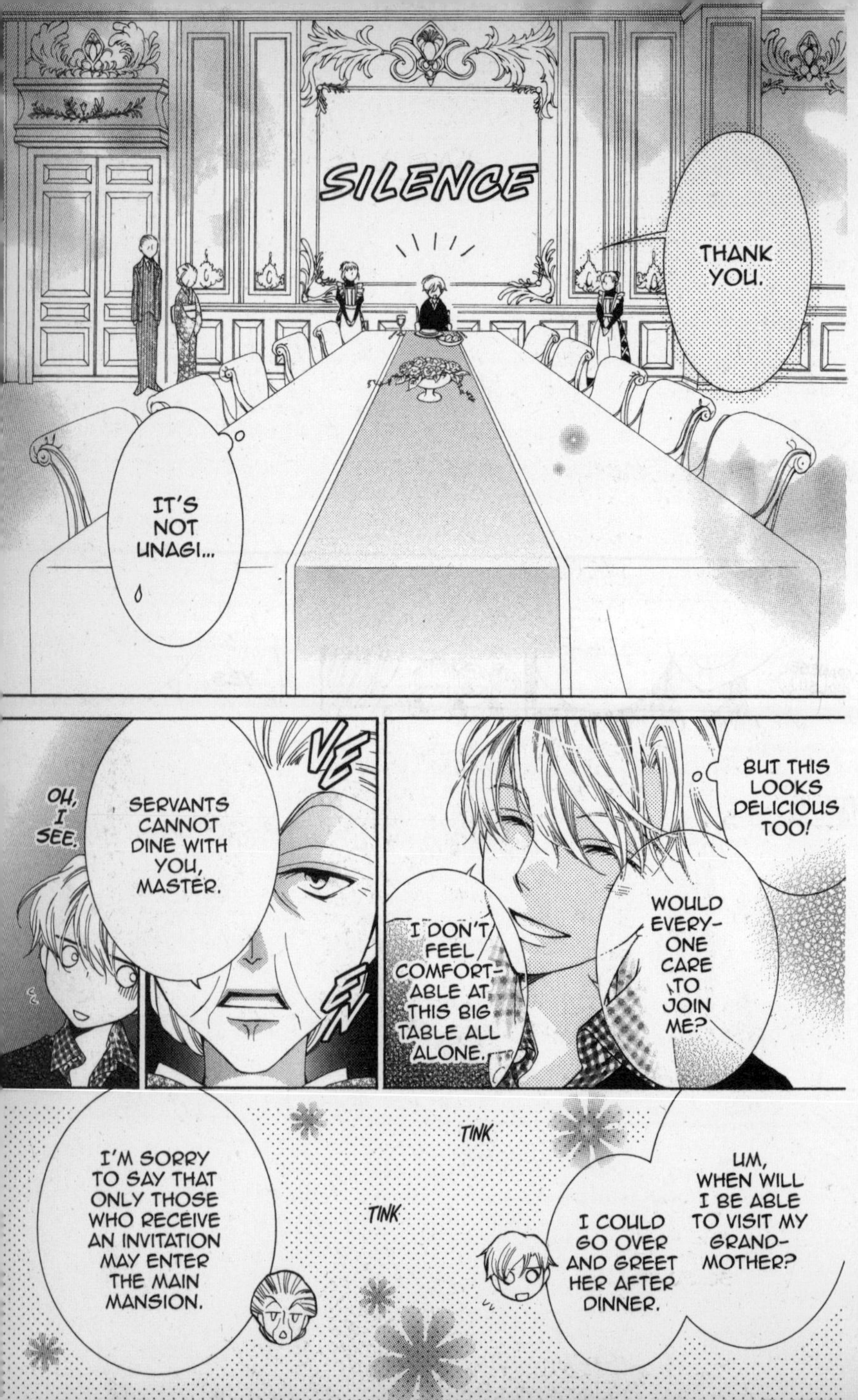
THANK YOU.
SILENCE
IT'S NOT UNAGI...
BUT THIS LOOKS DELICIOUS TOO!
WOULD EVERYONE CARE TO JOIN ME?
I DON'T FEEL COMFORTABLE AT THIS BIG TABLE ALL ALONE.
VE
EN
SERVANTS CANNOT DINE WITH YOU, MASTER.
OH, I SEE.
UM, WHEN WILL I BE ABLE TO VISIT MY GRANDMOTHER?
I COULD GO OVER AND GREET HER AFTER DINNER.
TINK
TINK
I'M SORRY TO SAY THAT ONLY THOSE WHO RECEIVE AN INVITATION MAY ENTER THE MAIN MANSION.

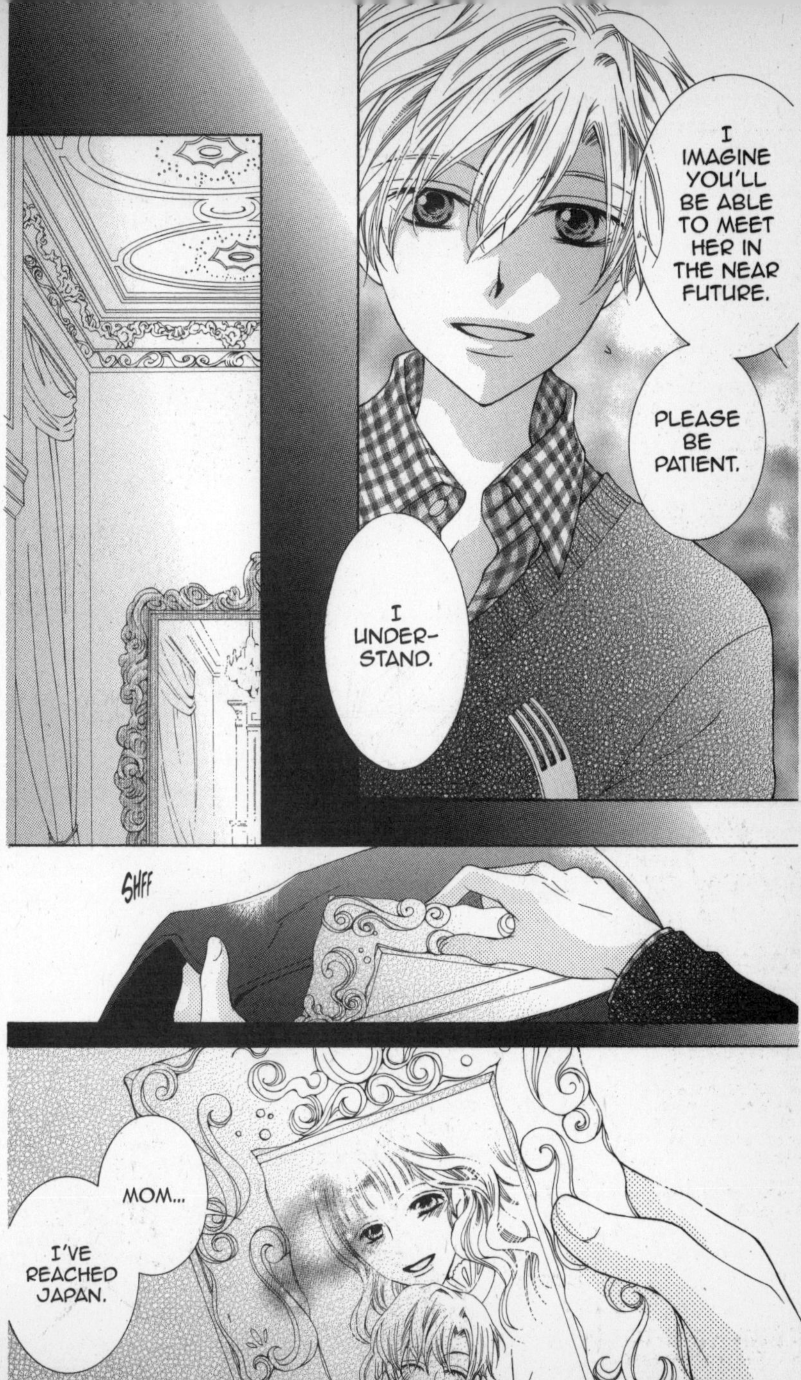
I IMAGINE YOU'LL BE ABLE TO MEET HER IN THE NEAR FUTURE.
PLEASE BE PATIENT.
I UNDER-STAND.
SHFF
MOM...
I'VE REACHED JAPAN.

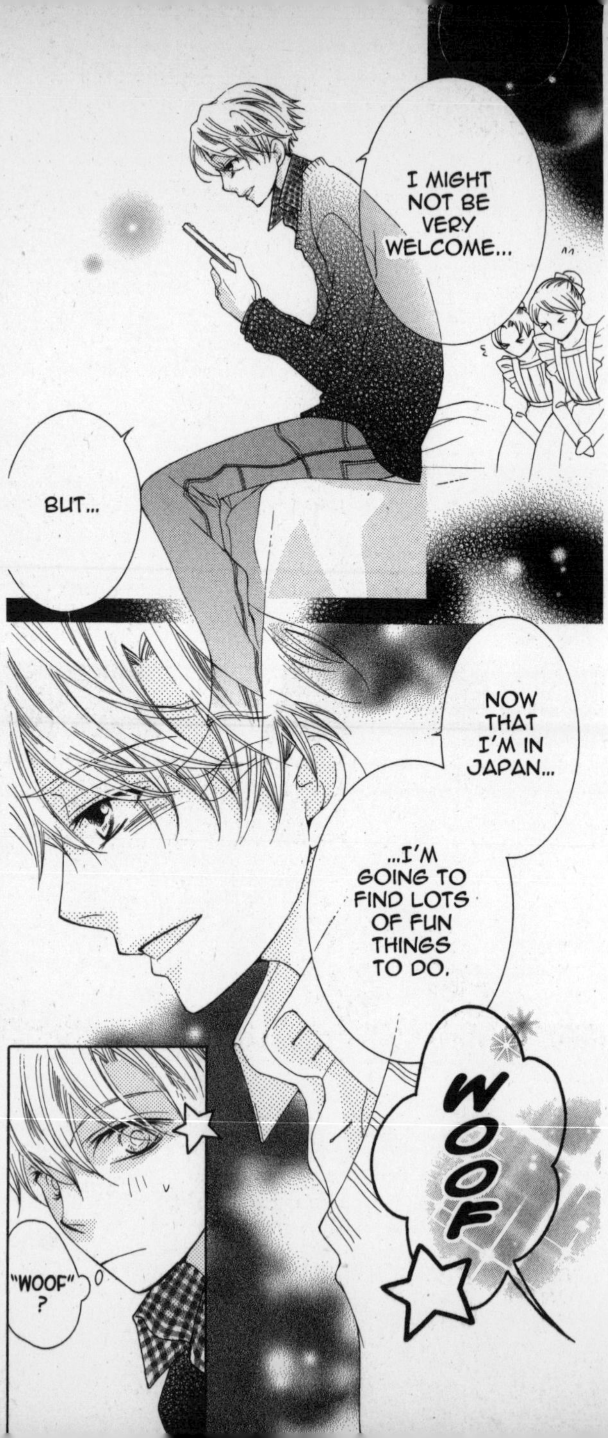
I MIGHT NOT BE VERY WELCOME...
BUT...
NOW THAT I'M IN JAPAN...
...I'M GOING TO FIND LOTS OF FUN THINGS TO DO.
WOOF
"WOOF"?

6

✿ FOR THIS VOLUME, VISITING A ✧ LAW FIRM ✧✧ FOR RESEARCH WAS VERY HELPFUL TOO. I ALWAYS THOUGHT, "I BET LAWYERS ARE REALLY BUSY," AND IT'S REALLY TRUE. I ENDED UP WONDERING, "WHEN DO THEY EVER SLEEP?"

IT'S A FRIGHTFULLY DIFFICULT JOB. THE PERSON WHO LET ME VISIT HER IN HER OFFICE WAS THE LAWYER WHO CONSULTS FOR MIKOTO ASOU'S LAWYER MANGA *SOKO O NANTOKA*.

✧KONAMI KATASE✧

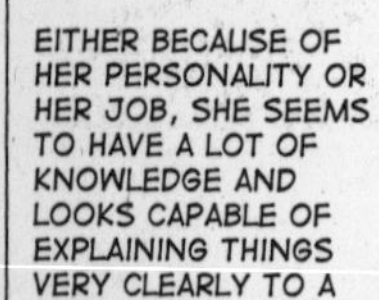
VERY AMIABLE
I LOVE MANGA.

SHE IS A VERY GOOD TALKER AND LISTENER.

EITHER BECAUSE OF HER PERSONALITY OR HER JOB, SHE SEEMS TO HAVE A LOT OF KNOWLEDGE AND LOOKS CAPABLE OF EXPLAINING THINGS VERY CLEARLY TO A WIDE VARIETY OF PEOPLE.

THANK YOU SO MUCH, KATASE!!

THE MANGA *SOKO O NANTOKA* IS VERY INTERESTING.

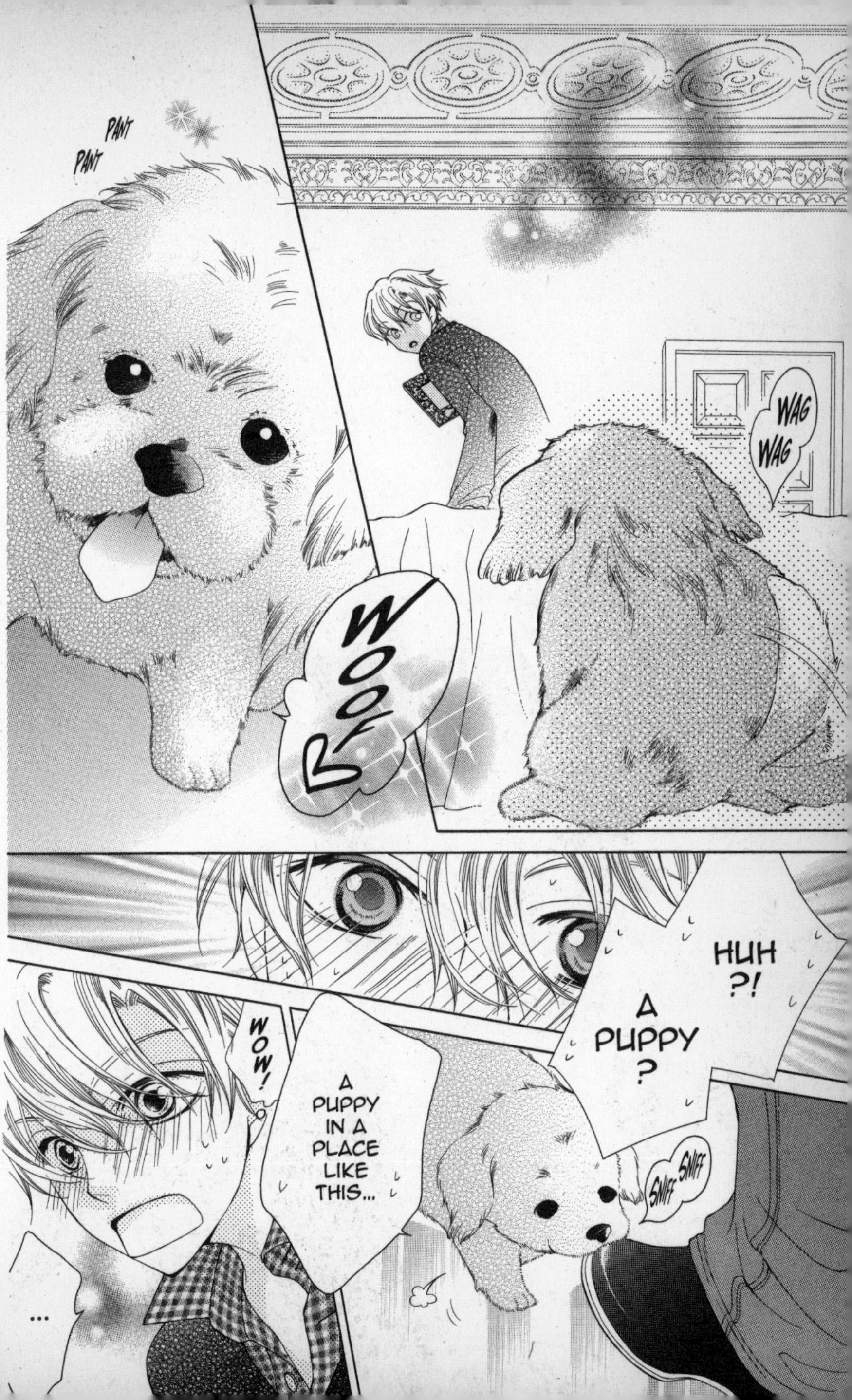
WAG WAG
WOOF ♥
PANT PANT
HUH ?!
A PUPPY ?
SNIFF SNIFF
WOW!
A PUPPY IN A PLACE LIKE THIS...
...

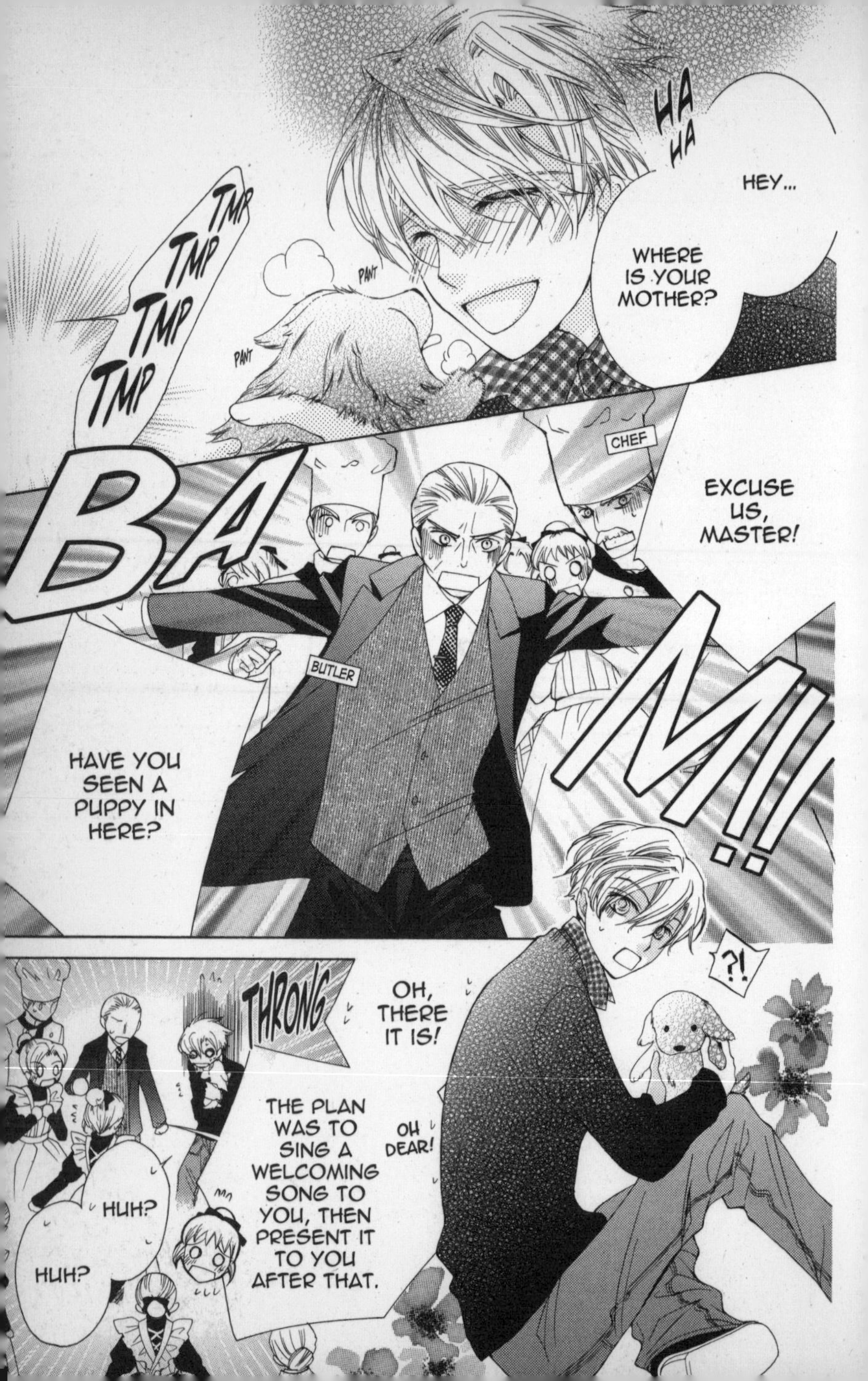
HA HA
HEY...
WHERE IS YOUR MOTHER?
PANT
PANT
TMP TMP TMP TMP
CHEF
EXCUSE US, MASTER!
BAMI!!
BUTLER
HAVE YOU SEEN A PUPPY IN HERE?
?!
OH, THERE IT IS!
THRONG
OH DEAR!
THE PLAN WAS TO SING A WELCOMING SONG TO YOU, THEN PRESENT IT TO YOU AFTER THAT.
HUH?
HUH?

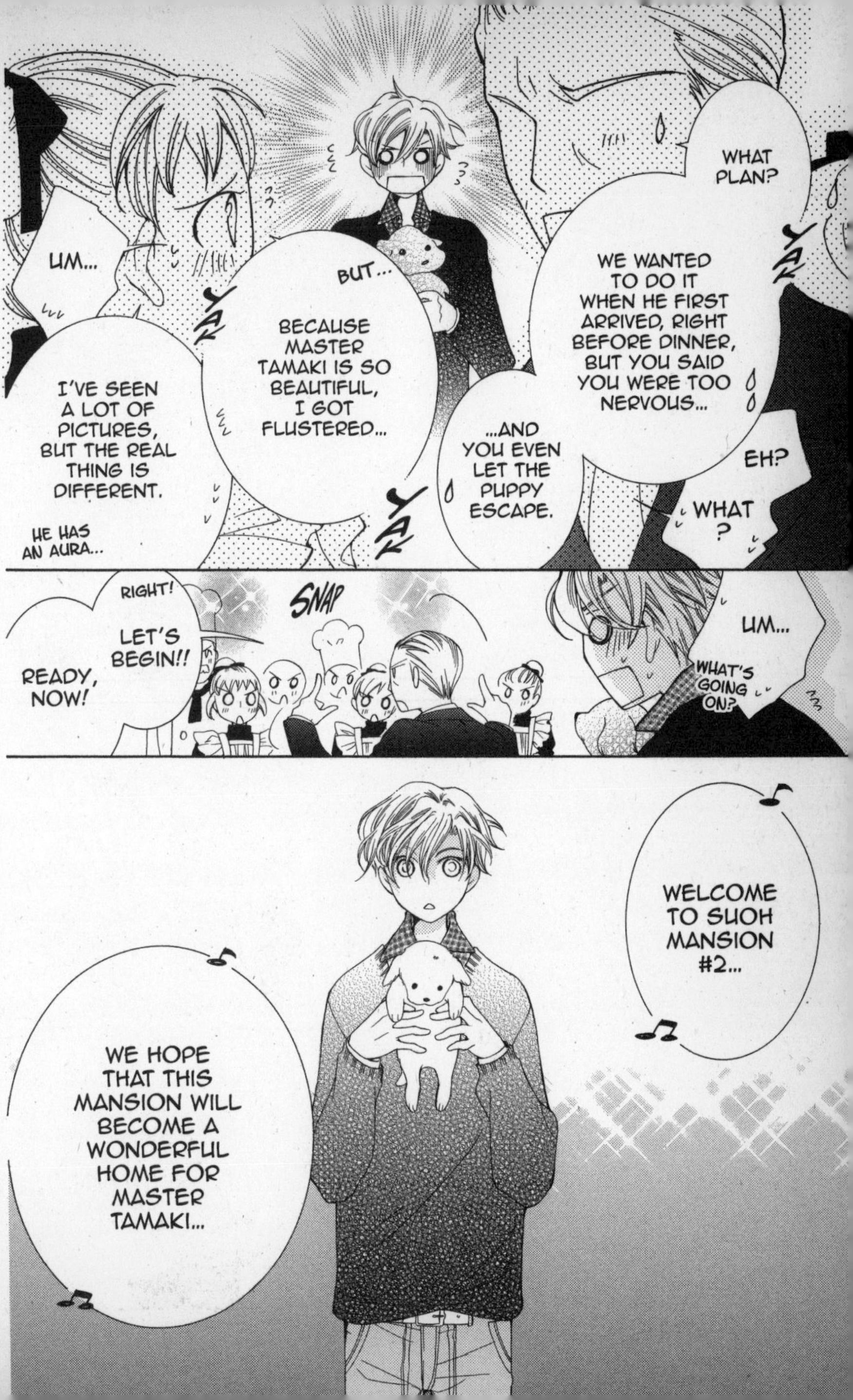
WHAT PLAN?
YAK
WE WANTED TO DO IT WHEN HE FIRST ARRIVED, RIGHT BEFORE DINNER, BUT YOU SAID YOU WERE TOO NERVOUS...
EH?
WHAT?
...AND YOU EVEN LET THE PUPPY ESCAPE.
YAK
BUT...
BECAUSE MASTER TAMAKI IS SO BEAUTIFUL, I GOT FLUSTERED...
YAK
UM...
I'VE SEEN A LOT OF PICTURES, BUT THE REAL THING IS DIFFERENT.
HE HAS AN AURA...
UM...
WHAT'S GOING ON?
SNAP
RIGHT!
LET'S BEGIN!!
READY, NOW!
WELCOME TO SUOH MANSION #2...
WE HOPE THAT THIS MANSION WILL BECOME A WONDERFUL HOME FOR MASTER TAMAKI...

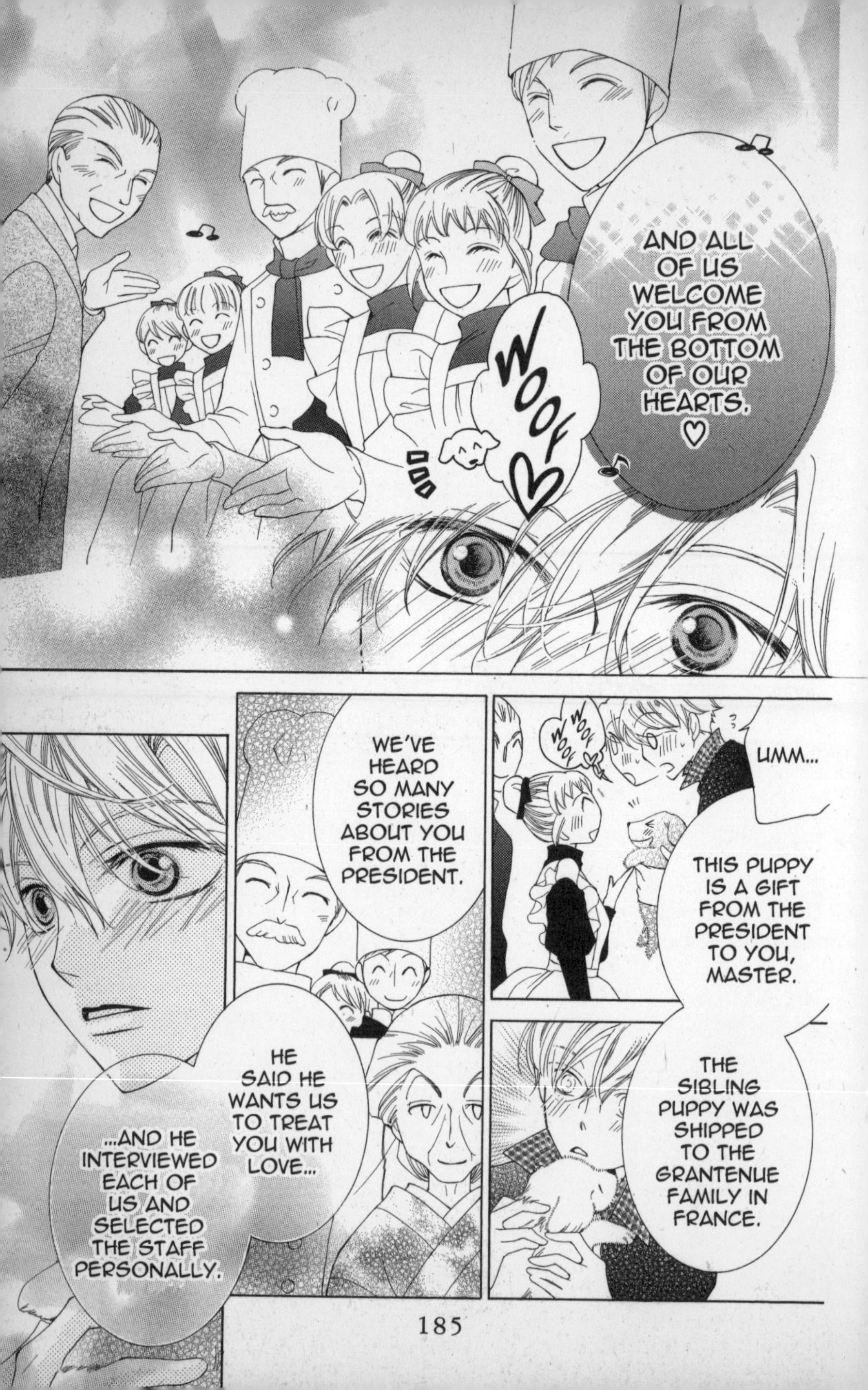
AND ALL OF US WELCOME YOU FROM THE BOTTOM OF OUR HEARTS. ♡
WOOF ♡
UMM...
WOOF WOOF
THIS PUPPY IS A GIFT FROM THE PRESIDENT TO YOU, MASTER.
THE SIBLING PUPPY WAS SHIPPED TO THE GRANTENUE FAMILY IN FRANCE.
WE'VE HEARD SO MANY STORIES ABOUT YOU FROM THE PRESIDENT.
HE SAID HE WANTS US TO TREAT YOU WITH LOVE...
...AND HE INTERVIEWED EACH OF US AND SELECTED THE STAFF PERSONALLY.

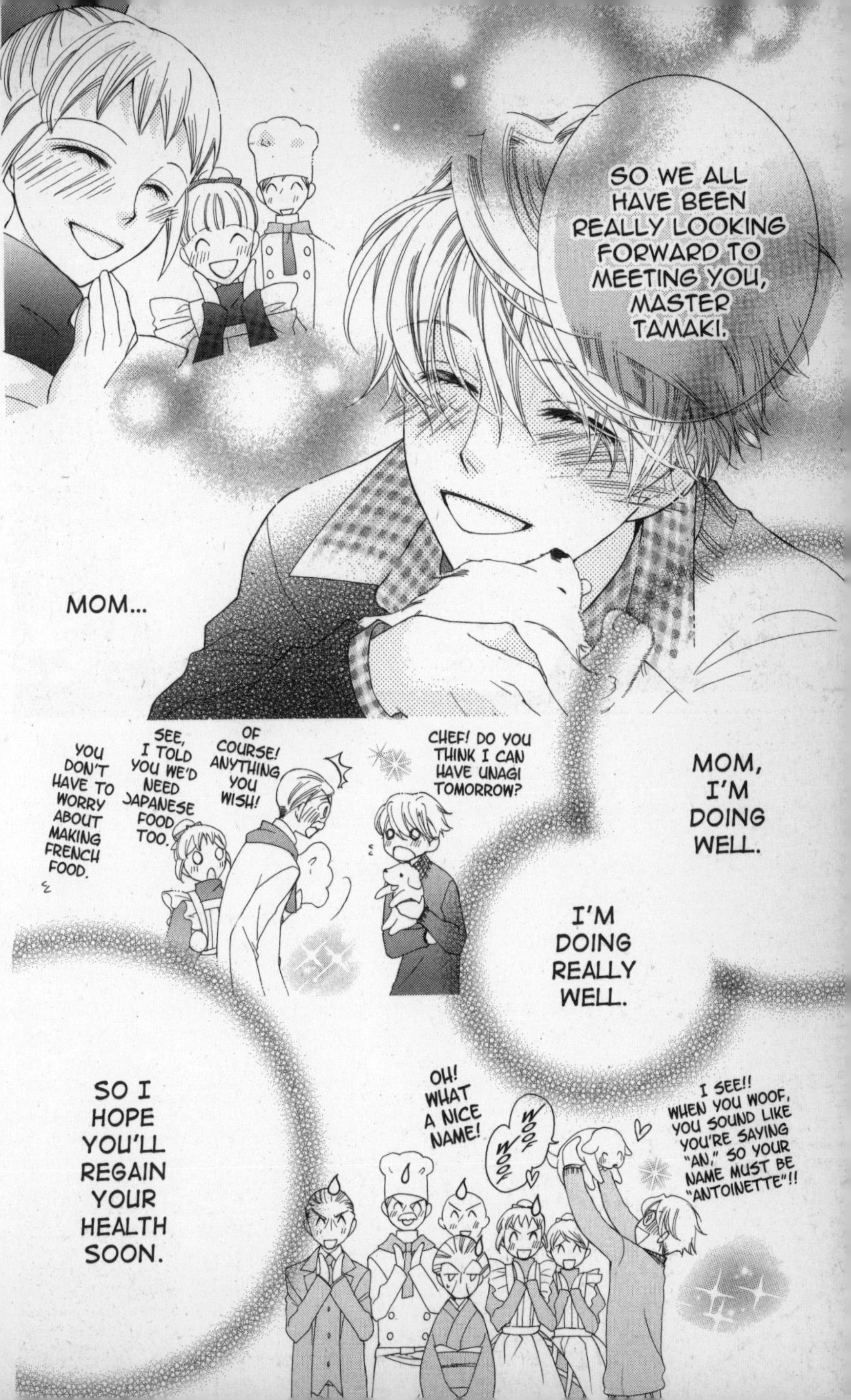
SO WE ALL HAVE BEEN REALLY LOOKING FORWARD TO MEETING YOU, MASTER TAMAKI.
MOM...
MOM, I'M DOING WELL.
CHEF! DO YOU THINK I CAN HAVE UNAGI TOMORROW?
OF COURSE! ANYTHING YOU WISH!
SEE, I TOLD YOU WE'D NEED JAPANESE FOOD TOO.
YOU DON'T HAVE TO WORRY ABOUT MAKING FRENCH FOOD.
I'M DOING REALLY WELL.
I SEE!! WHEN YOU WOOF, YOU SOUND LIKE YOU'RE SAYING "AN," SO YOUR NAME MUST BE "ANTOINETTE"!!
WOOF WOOF
OH! WHAT A NICE NAME!
SO I HOPE YOU'LL REGAIN YOUR HEALTH SOON.

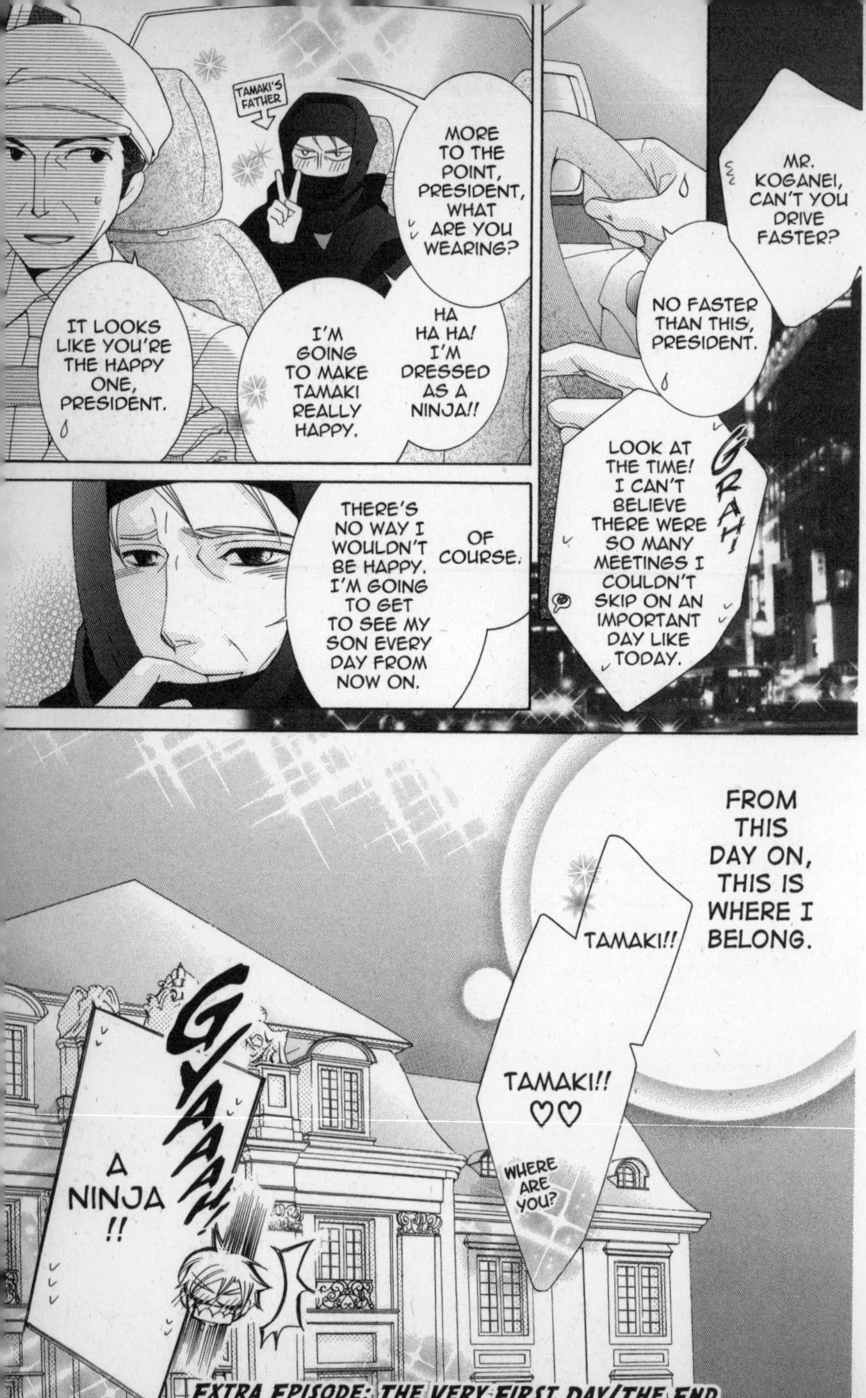
MR. KOGANEI, CAN'T YOU DRIVE FASTER?
NO FASTER THAN THIS, PRESIDENT.
LOOK AT THE TIME! I CAN'T BELIEVE THERE WERE SO MANY MEETINGS I COULDN'T SKIP ON AN IMPORTANT DAY LIKE TODAY.
GRAH!
TAMAKI'S FATHER
MORE TO THE POINT, PRESIDENT, WHAT ARE YOU WEARING?
HA HA HA! I'M DRESSED AS A NINJA!!
I'M GOING TO MAKE TAMAKI REALLY HAPPY.
IT LOOKS LIKE YOU'RE THE HAPPY ONE, PRESIDENT.
OF COURSE.
THERE'S NO WAY I WOULDN'T BE HAPPY. I'M GOING TO GET TO SEE MY SON EVERY DAY FROM NOW ON.
FROM THIS DAY ON, THIS IS WHERE I BELONG.
TAMAKI!!
TAMAKI!! ♡♡
WHERE ARE YOU?
GYAAAH!
A NINJA!!
EXTRA EPISODE: THE VERY FIRST DAY/THE END

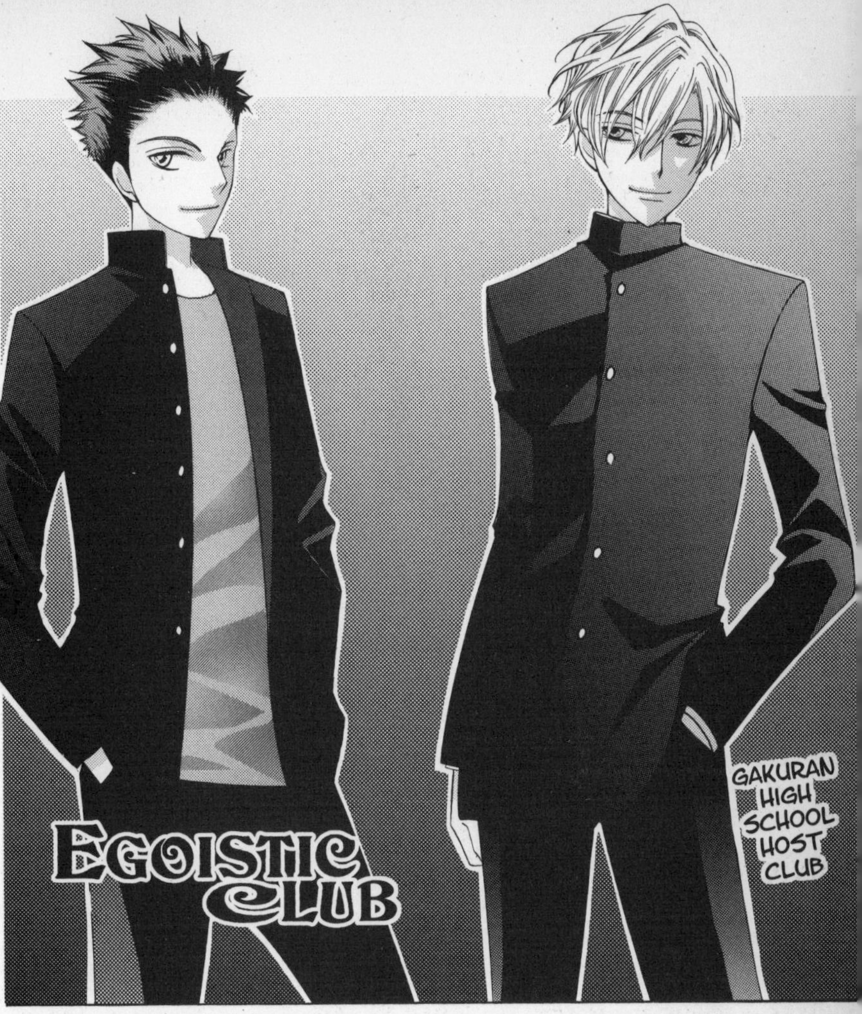
GAKURAN HIGH SCHOOL HOST CLUB
EGOISTIC CLUB

HELLO, EVERY-BODY! THIS IS HATORI, WHO MOVED JUST RECENTLY! I DON'T WANT TO MOVE AGAIN FOR A WHILE! (I USED UP ALL MY ENERGY.)

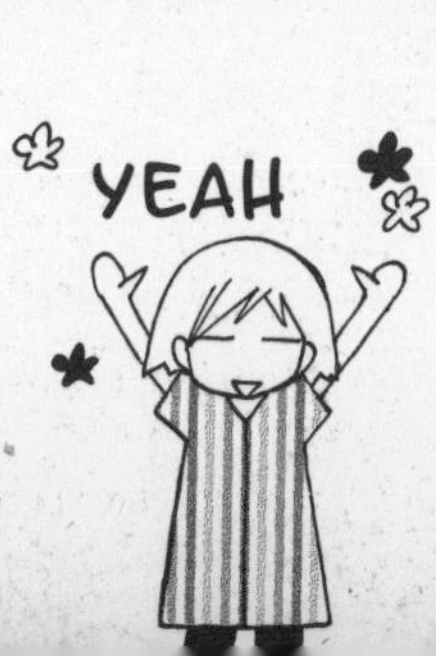
YEAH

SO THIS TIME, I'D LIKE TO INTRODUCE YOU TO THE NEW EDITOR WE'VE BEEN WAITING FOR... ☆

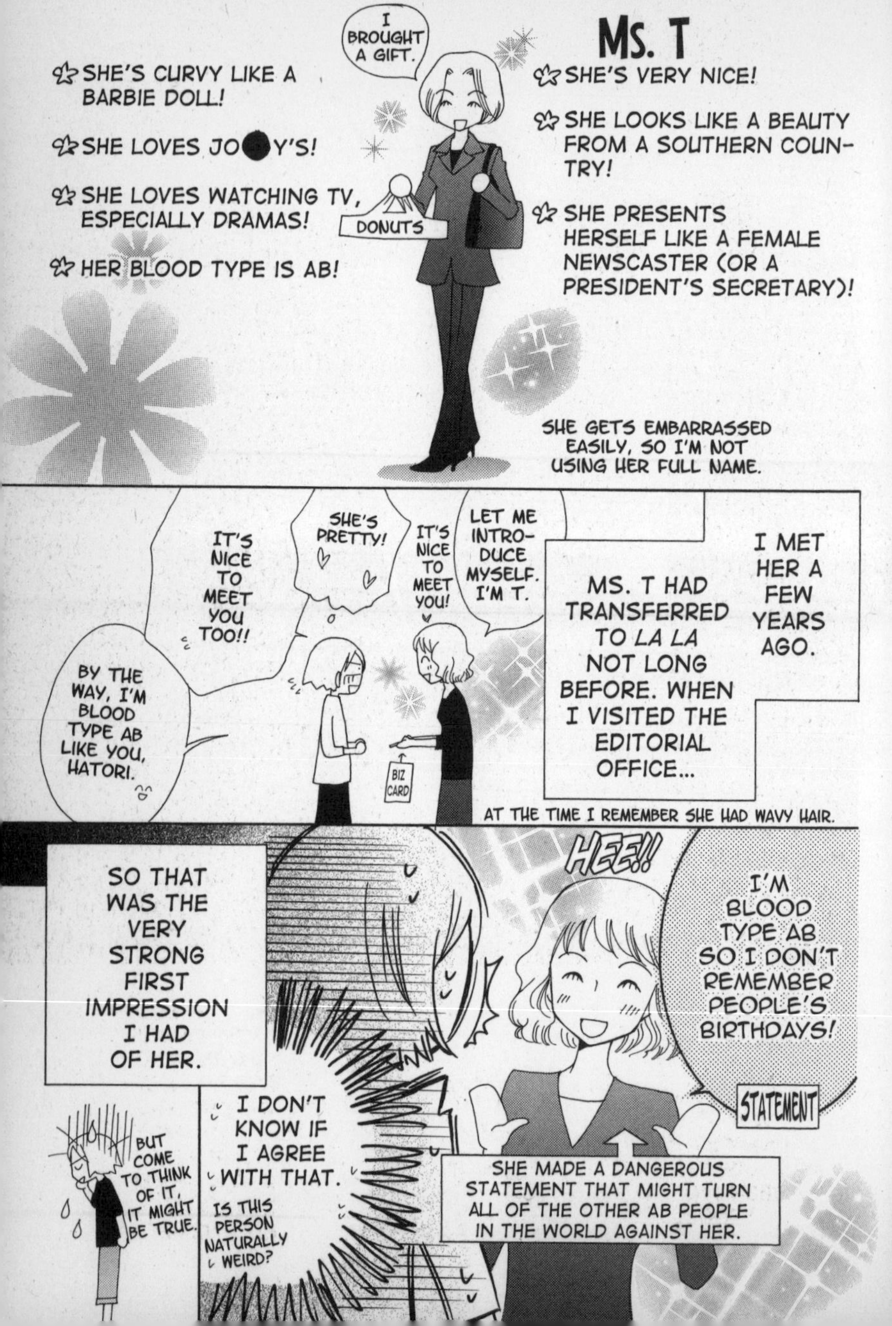

MS. T
I BROUGHT A GIFT.
SHE'S VERY NICE!
SHE LOOKS LIKE A BEAUTY FROM A SOUTHERN COUNTRY!
SHE PRESENTS HERSELF LIKE A FEMALE NEWSCASTER (OR A PRESIDENT'S SECRETARY)!
SHE'S CURVY LIKE A BARBIE DOLL!
SHE LOVES JO[redacted]Y'S!
SHE LOVES WATCHING TV, ESPECIALLY DRAMAS!
HER BLOOD TYPE IS AB!
DONUTS
SHE GETS EMBARRASSED EASILY, SO I'M NOT USING HER FULL NAME.
I MET HER A FEW YEARS AGO.
MS. T HAD TRANSFERRED TO *LA LA* NOT LONG BEFORE. WHEN I VISITED THE EDITORIAL OFFICE...
LET ME INTRODUCE MYSELF. I'M T.
IT'S NICE TO MEET YOU!
SHE'S PRETTY!
IT'S NICE TO MEET YOU TOO!!
BY THE WAY, I'M BLOOD TYPE AB LIKE YOU, HATORI.
BIZ CARD
AT THE TIME I REMEMBER SHE HAD WAVY HAIR.
HEE!!
I'M BLOOD TYPE AB SO I DON'T REMEMBER PEOPLE'S BIRTHDAYS!
STATEMENT
SHE MADE A DANGEROUS STATEMENT THAT MIGHT TURN ALL OF THE OTHER AB PEOPLE IN THE WORLD AGAINST HER.
I DON'T KNOW IF I AGREE WITH THAT.
IS THIS PERSON NATURALLY WEIRD?
SO THAT WAS THE VERY STRONG FIRST IMPRESSION I HAD OF HER.
BUT COME TO THINK OF IT, IT MIGHT BE TRUE.

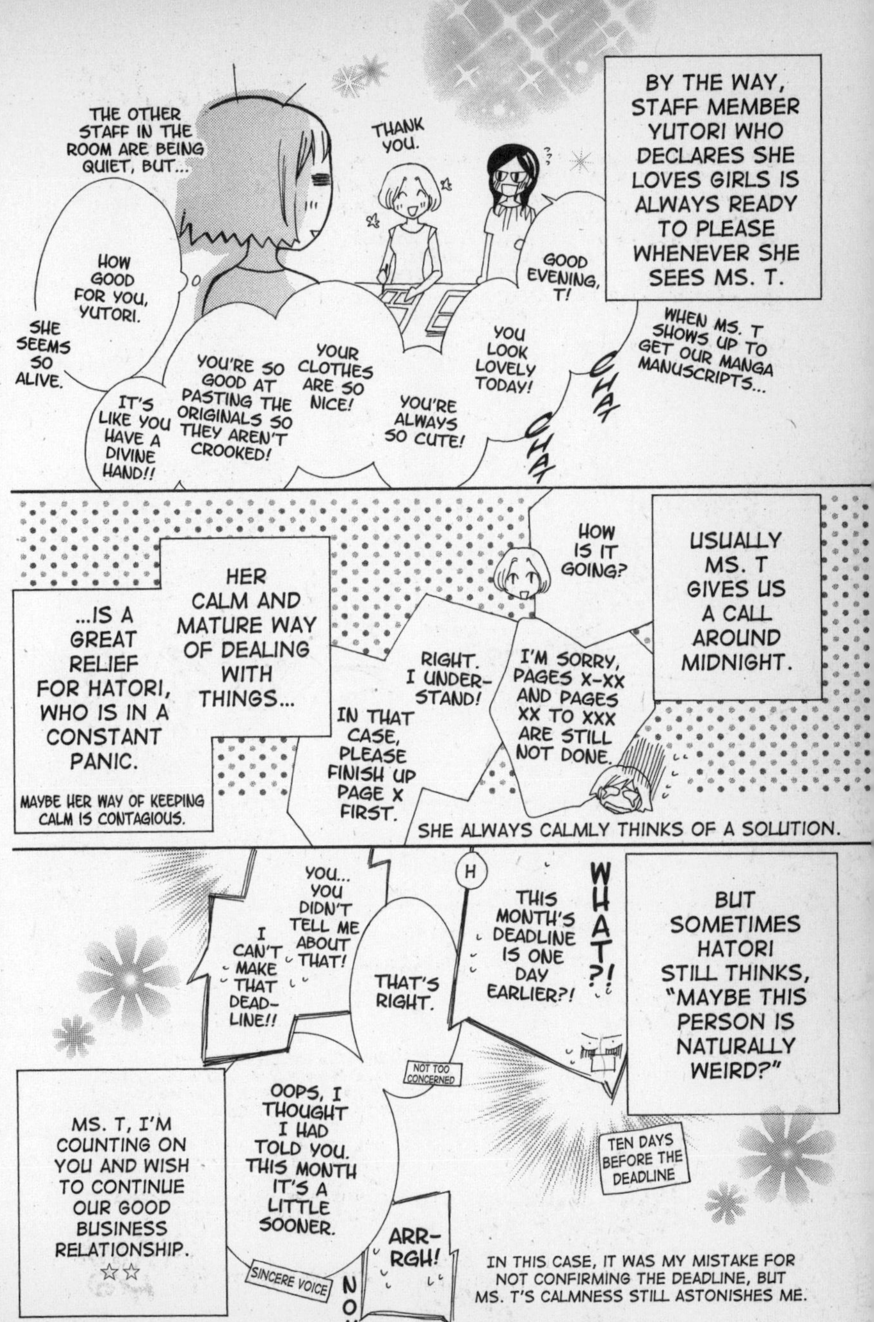
BY THE WAY, STAFF MEMBER YUTORI WHO DECLARES SHE LOVES GIRLS IS ALWAYS READY TO PLEASE WHENEVER SHE SEES MS. T.
GOOD EVENING, T!
WHEN MS. T SHOWS UP TO GET OUR MANGA MANUSCRIPTS...
CHAK CHAK
YOU LOOK LOVELY TODAY!
YOUR CLOTHES ARE SO NICE!
YOU'RE ALWAYS SO CUTE!
THANK YOU.
YOU'RE SO GOOD AT PASTING THE ORIGINALS SO THEY AREN'T CROOKED!
IT'S LIKE YOU HAVE A DIVINE HAND!!
THE OTHER STAFF IN THE ROOM ARE BEING QUIET, BUT...
HOW GOOD FOR YOU, YUTORI.
SHE SEEMS SO ALIVE.
USUALLY MS. T GIVES US A CALL AROUND MIDNIGHT.
HOW IS IT GOING?
I'M SORRY, PAGES X-XX AND PAGES XX TO XXX ARE STILL NOT DONE.
RIGHT. I UNDER-STAND!
IN THAT CASE, PLEASE FINISH UP PAGE X FIRST.
SHE ALWAYS CALMLY THINKS OF A SOLUTION.
HER CALM AND MATURE WAY OF DEALING WITH THINGS...
...IS A GREAT RELIEF FOR HATORI, WHO IS IN A CONSTANT PANIC.
MAYBE HER WAY OF KEEPING CALM IS CONTAGIOUS.
BUT SOMETIMES HATORI STILL THINKS, "MAYBE THIS PERSON IS NATURALLY WEIRD?"
H
THIS MONTH'S DEADLINE IS ONE DAY EARLIER?!
WHAT?!
TEN DAYS BEFORE THE DEADLINE
THAT'S RIGHT.
NOT TOO CONCERNED
YOU... YOU DIDN'T TELL ME ABOUT THAT!
I CAN'T MAKE THAT DEAD-LINE!!
OOPS, I THOUGHT I HAD TOLD YOU. THIS MONTH IT'S A LITTLE SOONER.
SINCERE VOICE
ARR-RGH!
NO!!
IN THIS CASE, IT WAS MY MISTAKE FOR NOT CONFIRMING THE DEADLINE, BUT MS. T'S CALMNESS STILL ASTONISHES ME.
MS. T, I'M COUNTING ON YOU AND WISH TO CONTINUE OUR GOOD BUSINESS RELATIONSHIP. ☆☆

Special Thanks!!

- TO YAMASHITA, MS. T, AND EVERYONE IN THE EDITORIAL DEPARTMENT.
- AND TO EVERYONE INVOLVED IN PUBLISHING THIS BOOK.
- ALL THE STAFF ➡ YUI NATSUKI, RIKU, AYA AOMURA, YUTORI HIZAKURA, SUBARU AMASAWA, AND BISCO HATORI'S MOTHER.
- EMERGENCY HELPERS ➡ NATSUMI SATO, MIDORI SHIINO, AND YOUKO SANO.

AND TO YOU, THE READERS OF THIS BOOK!!!

FLIRTATIOUS DRAWING: KAORU AND HARUHI IN THE SNOWY MOUNTAINS.

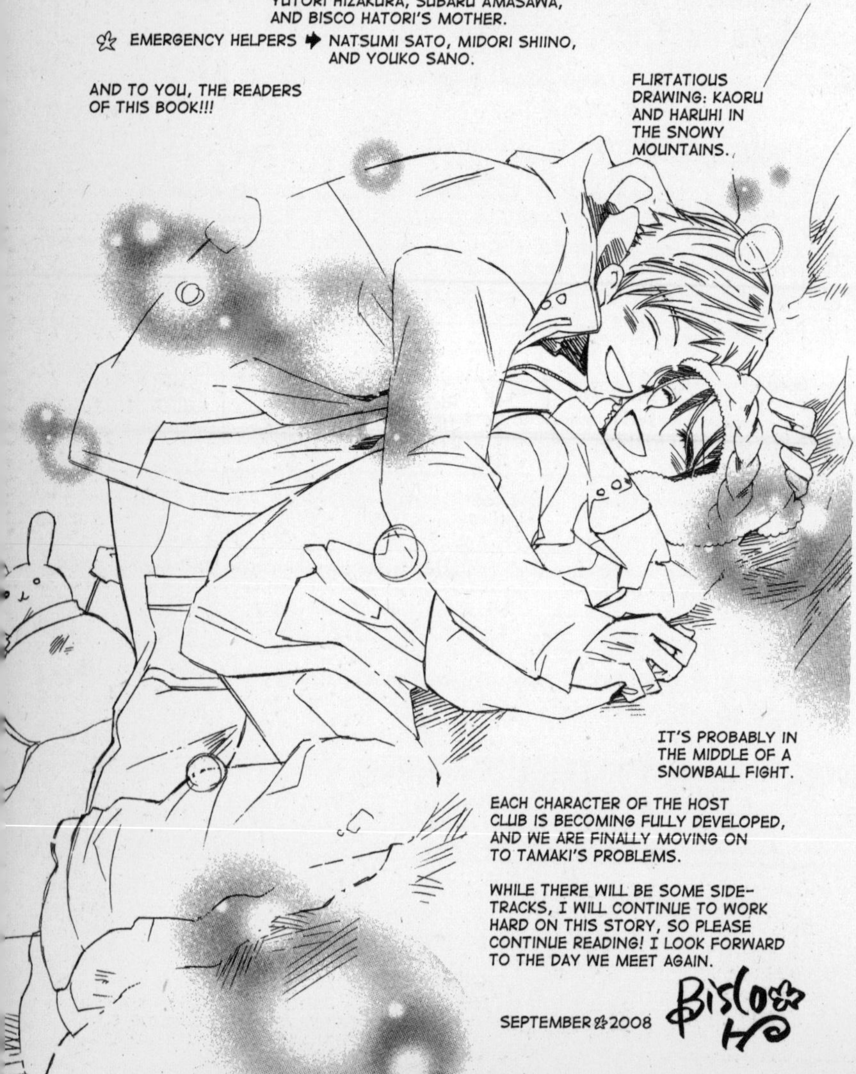

IT'S PROBABLY IN THE MIDDLE OF A SNOWBALL FIGHT.

EACH CHARACTER OF THE HOST CLUB IS BECOMING FULLY DEVELOPED, AND WE ARE FINALLY MOVING ON TO TAMAKI'S PROBLEMS.

WHILE THERE WILL BE SOME SIDE-TRACKS, I WILL CONTINUE TO WORK HARD ON THIS STORY, SO PLEASE CONTINUE READING! I LOOK FORWARD TO THE DAY WE MEET AGAIN.

SEPTEMBER 2008 Bisco H

EGOISTIC CLUB/THE END

EDITOR'S NOTES

EPISODE 57

Page 20: *Bihaku* means "beautiful white."

Page 26: *Motekyawa* means "desirable and cute."

EPISODE 58

Page 55: In Japan, backscratchers are called *mago no te*, or "grandchildren's hands."

EPISODE 59

Page 72: The host club members are cosplaying as characters from different Japanese folktales. Momotaro is a boy who is found inside a giant peach. "The Flower-Blossoming Old Man" is about an old man whose beloved dog dies, and when the dog's ashes are scattered beneath a cherry tree, the tree blooms.

Page 77: Urashima Taro is a fisherman who saves a turtle and is taken to an underwater palace as a reward.

Page 85: Issun Boushi is another character from a Japanese folktale. He's tiny and fights using a sewing needle as a sword.

EXTRA EPISODE

Page 186: The sound of the dog's bark is written in Japanese as *an*, hence Tamaki's comment.

EGOISTIC CLUB

Page 188: A *gakuran* is a type of boy's school uniform.

Author Bio

Bisco Hatori made her manga debut with *Isshun kan no Romance* (A Moment of Romance) in *LaLa DX* magazine. The comedy *Ouran High School Host Club* is her breakout hit. When she's stuck thinking up characters' names, she gets inspired by loud, upbeat music (her radio is set to NACK5 FM). She enjoys reading all kinds of manga, but she's especially fond of the sci-fi drama *Please Save My Earth* and *Slam Dunk*, a basketball classic.

OURAN HIGH SCHOOL HOST CLUB
Vol. 13
Shojo Beat Edition

STORY AND ART BY BISCO HATORI

Translation/Masumi Matsumoto
Touch-up Art & Lettering/Gia Cam Luc
Graphic Design/Amy Martin
Editor/Nancy Thistlethwaite

Ouran Koko Host Club by Bisco Hatori © Bisco Hatori 2008. All rights reserved.
First published in Japan in 2008 by HAKUSENSHA, Inc., Tokyo. English language
translation rights arranged with HAKUSENSHA, Inc., Tokyo.

Printed in Canada

Published by VIZ Media, LLC
P.O. Box 77010
San Francisco, CA 94107

10 9 8 7 6 5 4 3
First printing, November 2009
Third printing, July 2012

www.viz.com   www.shojobeat.com

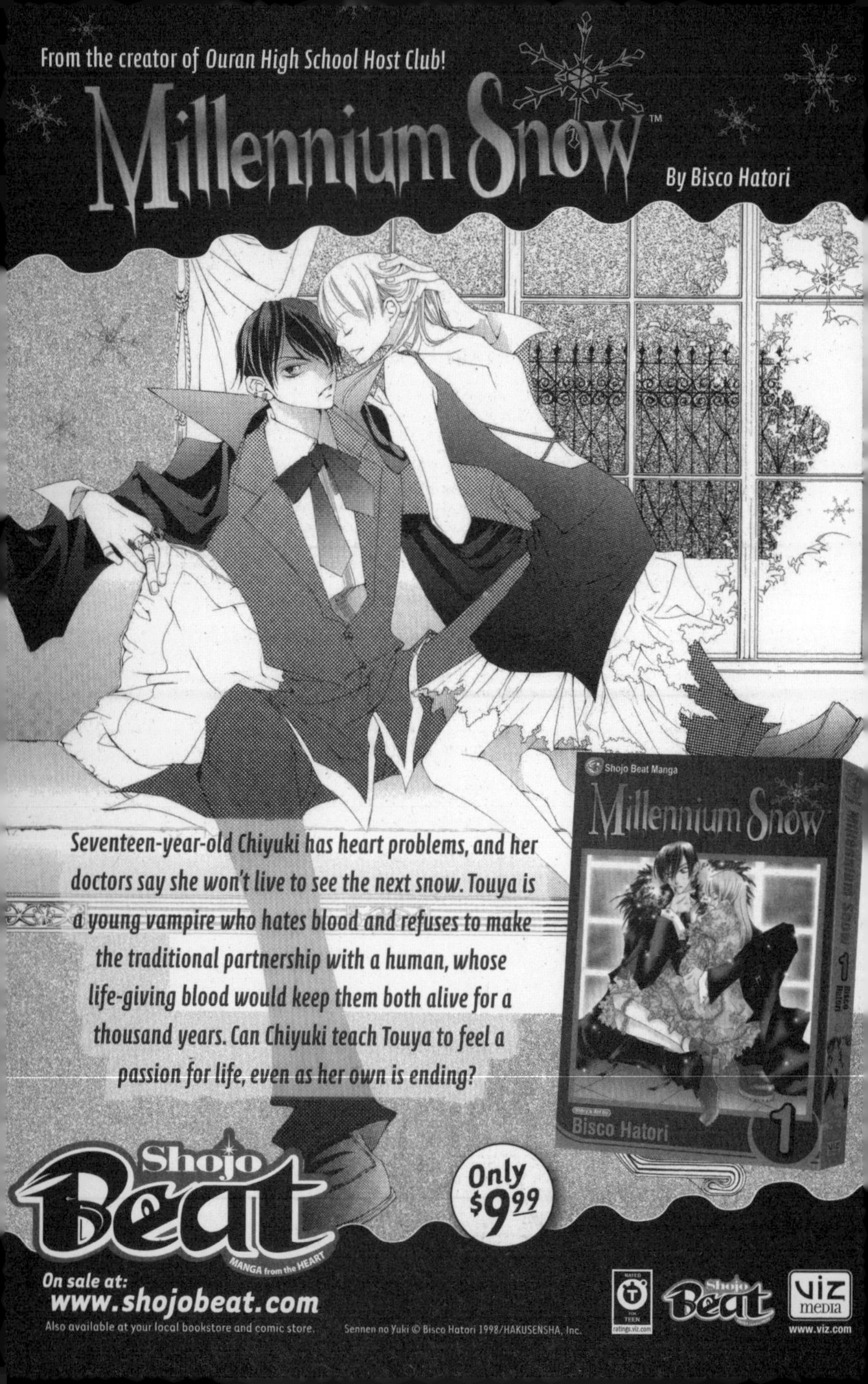
From the creator of Ouran High School Host Club!
Millennium Snow™
By Bisco Hatori
Shojo Beat Manga
Millennium Snow
Bisco Hatori
1
Seventeen-year-old Chiyuki has heart problems, and her doctors say she won't live to see the next snow. Touya is a young vampire who hates blood and refuses to make the traditional partnership with a human, whose life-giving blood would keep them both alive for a thousand years. Can Chiyuki teach Touya to feel a passion for life, even as her own is ending?
Shojo Beat
MANGA from the HEART
Only $9.99
On sale at:
www.shojobeat.com
Also available at your local bookstore and comic store.
Sennen no Yuki © Bisco Hatori 1998/HAKUSENSHA, Inc.
RATED T TEEN
ratings.viz.com
Shojo Beat
VIZ media
www.viz.com

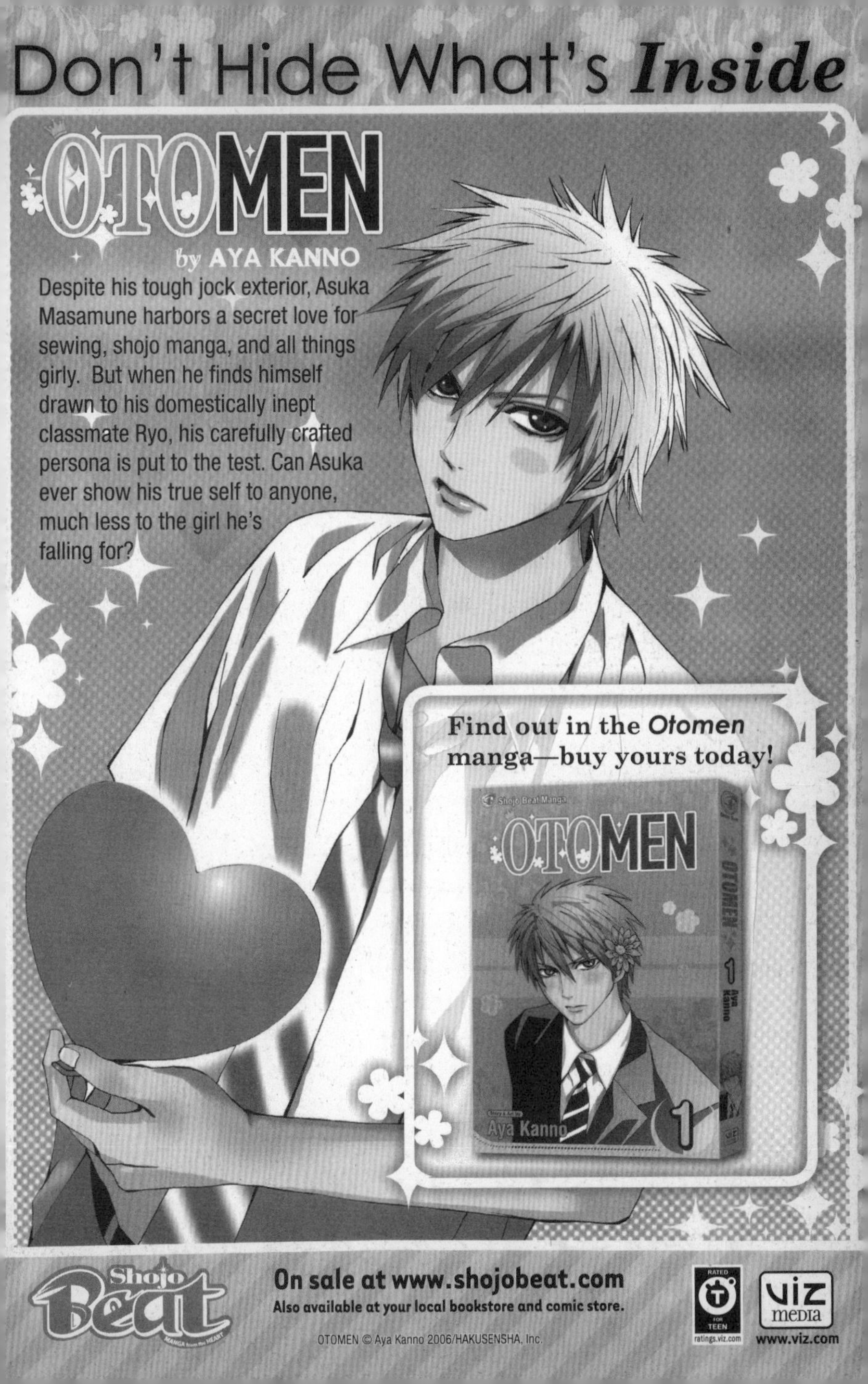
Don't Hide What's Inside
OTOMEN
by AYA KANNO
Despite his tough jock exterior, Asuka Masamune harbors a secret love for sewing, shojo manga, and all things girly. But when he finds himself drawn to his domestically inept classmate Ryo, his carefully crafted persona is put to the test. Can Asuka ever show his true self to anyone, much less to the girl he's falling for?
Find out in the Otomen manga—buy yours today!
Shojo Beat Manga
OTOMEN
Aya Kanno
1
Shojo Beat
On sale at www.shojobeat.com
Also available at your local bookstore and comic store.
OTOMEN © Aya Kanno 2006/HAKUSENSHA, Inc.
RATED T FOR TEEN
ratings.viz.com
VIZ media
www.viz.com